MUSIC IN THE ELEMENTARY SCHOOL

An Activities Approach to Music Methods and Materials

SECOND
EDITION

ROBERT EVANS NYE

SCHOOL OF MUSIC, UNIVERSITY OF OREGON

VERNICE TROUSDALE NYE

SCHOOL OF EDUCATION, UNIVERSITY OF OREGON

Prentice-Hall, Inc., Englewood Cliffs, New Jersey

PRENTICE-HALL INTERNATIONAL, INC., *London*
PRENTICE-HALL OF AUSTRALIA, PTY., LTD., *Sydney*
PRENTICE-HALL OF CANADA, LTD., *Toronto*
PRENTICE-HALL FRANCE, S.A.R.L., *Paris*
PRENTICE-HALL OF INDIA (PRIVATE) LTD., *New Delhi*
PRENTICE-HALL OF JAPAN, INC., *Tokyo*
PRENTICE-HALL DE MEXICO, S.A., *Mexico City*

Library of Congress Catalog Card Number 63–12365

Printed in the United States of America
C–60816

"A skillful teacher may, and often does, give a clever and useful lesson on something with which yesterday he was comparatively unaquainted. . . . But the most elementary singing lesson involves, on the part of him who gives it, a sympathy of eye and ear that can be attained only when it has become a part of his being, and when thus attained and made available, can no more be lost or forgotten, like the knowledge of mere facts, than the power of speaking or understanding his native tongue."

John Hullah, 1874

PREFACE

The preparation of the teacher of music should include a clear concept of the place occupied by music activities in the elementary school. In college classes, a workshop-type organization helps to develop this concept, for it provides the student the opportunity to plan, execute, and evaluate the various activities with his instructor and his classmates. Chapters One, Two, and Three present a background for this approach, and subsequent chapters offer suggestions for its development in music education classes. The authors urge observation and participation in elementary classrooms as much as possible in order to better relate theory and practice.

Many college classes begin with an emphasis on singing. Others stress listening or instrument playing. Whatever his preference, the instructor will find the organization of this book sufficiently flexible to serve his program. The authors find the sequence of activities given here most suitable for them, particularly when working with elementary-education majors who have a limited musical background. Concentrating first upon rhythmic responses and the playing of instruments in the order of the chapters of this book, the instructor can review music fundamentals, emphasize physical responses, and thus prepare the way for a later special concentration on singing.

The *Things To Do* sections assist in planning class activities. Extensive *reference lists* help locate materials. The *Music Series Guides* help the student become familiar with the specific titles he will find in his student and professional teaching. Access to sets of these books is a necessity for the music major. The songs (page numbers) listed in the Guides should be regarded as music to be evaluated, not as material listed selectively. In this edition of *Music in the Elementary School* the Guides often contain page numbers that refer the reader to classified indexes, reflecting the improvement in indexing which is characteristic of the later series books.

Basic equipment for an activities class includes recordings, record player, piano, autoharps, keyboard instruments of the bell and xylophone type, and a variety of percussion instruments. The student should be familiar with recorder-type and flute-type instruments. Movable furniture is necessary, and a reference shelf containing all current methods books in elementary music is recommended.

Basic Music for Classroom Teachers, Second Edition, by Nye and Bergethon (Prentice-Hall, Inc., 1962) has as its purpose the learning of music fundamentals in a manner that introduces some methodology, and *Singing With Children,* by Nye, Nye, Aubin, and Kyme (Wadsworth Publishing Company, 1962) has as its purpose the providing of selected songs with specific instructions for their use in methods classes, in student teaching, and in professional teaching. However, *Music in the Elementary School* emphasizes the learning of methods and materials and endeavors to reveal clearly music's position as a vital part of the general education of every American child.

The education and teaching experience of one of the authors has been predominantly within the field of music; that of the other has been predominantly within the field of education. They hope that their collaboration will reinforce the position of music as an essential part of elementary education.

ROBERT EVANS NYE
VERNICE TROUSDALE NYE

CONTENTS

Chapter One

AN INTRODUCTION TO MUSIC EDUCATION

A CHALLENGE TO EDUCATION

Music education in the United States is in many ways more advanced than in the school systems of other nations. Our democratic heritage insists that every child shall have education in music as a part of his rightful general education. The acceptance of the concept that all children shall have opportunity for musical growth is evidence of the recognition by the people of the United States of the power of good music instruction to raise the aesthetic, cultural, and spiritual level of a mass society. This is a highly significant step forward. The excellence of musical performance demonstrated by select groups of students comprising many of our secondary-school bands, orchestras, and choruses is without parallel in the world, and the growth of the community symphony orchestra is impressive. In contrast, far too many children have had little or no guidance in the development of any musical competence. Also, the quality of the music pouring from the mass media of radio and television does not reveal suitable standards of taste. It implies that the cultural level of the nation in music is in urgent need of improvement.

Education's challenge today is to assure that music in our society plays a genuinely cultural-educational role rather than one with an overemphasis on commercialized entertainment that has been described by some as sordid and cheap.

At the time this edition of *Music in the Elementary School* is being written, there is a lack of unanimity concerning the well-being of elementary music education. While some believe that the quality of music teaching has improved, and that teachers of music are better prepared for their work than in earlier years, others are convinced that the opposite is true, and claim that the situation in most elementary school classrooms

1

today is reminiscent of that of from forty to fifty years ago.   Research reveals evidence that music programs are seriously deficient—or even absent—in many schools.   This fact, among others, has led United States Commissioner of Education Sterling M. McMurrin to make numerous comments about the inadequacies in the education of American youth in the arts.   In March 1962, Commissioner McMurrin stated in an address:

> One of the major deficiencies in our national effort to meet the challenges before us is the almost complete failure of the American people to recognize that the strength of a nation lies in its art and music and literature, and in its philosophical sophistication and the quality of its social sciences, just as much as in its physics and chemistry or its electrical engineering. When we raise the question of the survival of our nation it is a question in proximate range of statesmanship and machinery.   But when we speak of the decline or rise of our culture and the strength of the nation for the long haul ahead, it is a question of the full cultivation of our spiritual, artistic, moral, and intellectual resources.   Those who suppose that great music or great poetry or a knowledge of classical literature are not essential to either the quality or even the survival of a nation and its culture are quite unaware of the lessons of the past.[1]

There are those who believe that the condition of the arts today constitutes a warning to society that should be heeded.

The challenge to improve music instruction in the elementary schools is obvious.   Therefore it is essential that teachers understand the function of music in society, its purposes in general education, and its place in the elementary school curriculum.   It is also essential that music specialists and classroom teachers are prepared to work together to meet this challenge.

MUSIC IN PRESENT-DAY SOCIETY

Music has been essential to man throughout history.   It is equally essential today.   Music has the power to unite and solidify social groups from the family to the world community.   The family that can "make music together" is a happier and more closely-knit social group.   The most successful efforts to improve international relations are said to be through cultural exchanges of the arts, particularly music, which communicates feelings and emotions despite language barriers.   Music enriches and dignifies man's social activities, ceremonies, and worship.   That music is closely related to man's spiritual resources is illustrated by a statement attributed to Sibelius: "All great art is basically religious in that

---

[1] "Report on Special U.S. Conference," *Washington Music Educator*, Vol. 7, No. 4. (Spring, 1962), p. 30.

it is concerned with the eternal mystery of life and death." Music enhances spiritual meanings.

When new art forms appear, the old are not discarded, because humanity remains essentially the same through the ages. Thus, music gives evidence of permanence, stability, and order in our changing world. For example, Mozart communicates to us clearly today through the art form of music, while old forms of communication in other areas (such as smoke signals, the Pony Express, and the crystal radio receiver) will no longer suffice.

It has been repeatedly demonstrated that any tyrant must control the arts in order to control his people. The arts are allies of freedom and democracy in that they represent freedom of the human spirit to communicate with society.

Every normal human being, regardless of age, needs to explore, to experiment, and to create. Music is a warmly human creative and performing art and offers many opportunities to satisfy these innate desires. It therefore can compensate for the artificiality and boredom found in industrial work processes from which creativity, imagination, and individual expression have been removed. The beauty of music adds *quality* to living, and helps people learn *how* to live on a higher plane; it offers one of the best means to relieve the tensions, stresses, and strains of contemporary life. With the increased amount of leisure time resulting from mechanization and automation, it has become necessary for society to provide opportunities for worthy cultural and recreational uses of this leisure time. Since music has something of value to offer everyone, regardless of age, ability, and economic or social status, it provides one of the most promising solutions for this problem.

PURPOSES OF MUSIC INSTRUCTION

Major Purposes:
    to understand and appreciate aesthetic qualities of music
    to transmit the cultural heritage
    to foster creativity
Other Important Purposes:
    to teach social education
    to provide worthy recreation
    to improve physical and mental health
    to develop intellectual capacities

The underlying factor upon which success in the foregoing purposes depends is *the acquisition and utilization of music skills.*

TO UNDERSTAND AND APPRECIATE
THE AESTHETIC QUALITIES OF MUSIC

The primary function of music in the elementary school is to develop in children the ability to respond to beautiful sound with pleasure and understanding. Beauty is an essential element in the health and happiness of mankind. All normal human beings need to symbolize their experiences through art media, and music satisfies this need through its unique organization of pitches, tone qualities, and rhythms that comprise *aural* beauty, or beauty that we hear. When all children receive the education in music to which they are entitled, their perception and discrimination of aural beauty will be reflected in a higher quality of the music utilized in their daily living.

TO TRANSMIT THE CULTURAL HERITAGE

A basic purpose of general education is to transmit our cultural heritage. Music is a significant part of that heritage, and as such it occupies a unique position in general education. Throughout history, man has conceptualized his every activity by making music about it. To overcome weariness and boredom he created work songs and humorous songs. To survive hardships and to sustain hope, he created the American spiritual. He expressed all his other reactions and emotions normally and naturally through the medium of music. Music, man, and living are one. A simple illustration is the music in a series book for the fifth grade in which the history of the United States is presented chronologically in song.[2] Music has important relationships to literature, dance, and science also. It is a superior means for children to learn about human experiences; it assists understanding of man from primitive times to the present day. Because music is an accurate reflection of humanity through the ages, no program of general education can omit it without failing to meet acceptable standards.

TO FOSTER CREATIVITY

Survival of cultures and nations depends upon man's ability to make changes, to meet changes, and to adjust or control them. This requires creative minds. Research has disclosed that creativity is a way of thinking and of confronting problems that is *transferable* from one type

---

[2] William R. Sur, et al., *This Is Music: Book Five.* (Boston: Allyn and Bacon, Inc., 1962), pp. 18–161.

of experience to another.[3] For example, once a child has learned to be creative, he is inclined to be creative in meeting most or all of his problems, whatever they may be. Music, with its varied activities, offers unique possibilities for children to learn to be creative on their own levels of development. Aspects of song interpretation, vocal or instrumental composition, the addition of sound effects, and the addition of instrumental or vocal parts are illustrations of this. Creativity takes place whenever the child discovers new relationships and whenever he projects himself into an activity and makes it something that at the time belongs uniquely to him. When one school administrator remarked to a music supervisor that in his opinion the study of music was not at all helpful in solving the scientific problems involved in "getting man to the moon," the supervisor explained why the development of creativity through experiences in music may be one of the very practical ways to lead to the ultimate solution of such problems. Aside from the considerations of national and cultural survival, the healthy personality needs the opportunities to create that good music instruction can provide.

TO TEACH SOCIAL EDUCATION

Man is a social being and music is a social art; thus man and music are naturally linked together. The varied activities of the music program are superior vehicles for assisting children to obtain those socio-psychological needs of every human being: acceptance, belonging, and success. Because of this, good music instruction is of marked importance in building healthy social relationships, group discipline, and wholesome personalities. Through music activities, children can learn to understand that individual differences are characteristic of humanity, to know and to understand themselves, and to be sensitive to the feelings and problems of others.

TO PROVIDE WORTHY RECREATION

Every human being needs the pleasures that come from pure enjoyment and worth-while recreational pursuits. Music includes strong elements of play that teachers can guide into channels of musical learning in the classroom. As mentioned earlier, our society is endeavoring to adjust to the increasing amount of leisure time that automation in industry and commerce has brought. Music is a significant cultural and recreational experience. If the elementary schools of the United States provide the basic musical education that all children are entitled to receive, the future

3 Viktor Lowenfeld, "Recent Research in Creative Arts," *National Education Association Journal,* (November, 1958), pp. 538–40.

adolescent and adult population will be able to use its leisure time to better advantage, and in a manner that promotes cultural and social growth.

TO IMPROVE PHYSICAL AND MENTAL HEALTH

For physical and mental health, as well as for better learning, release from physical tension and rest from mental weariness are necessary. To stand up and sing or to perform an action song following quiet and confining desk work, or to rest and relax to appropriate recorded music following physical exertion, are examples of using music to provide a balance in the school day for purposes of physical and mental health. The body and the mind need carefully selected and contrasting activities to be healthy in the school environment. Musical rhythmic activities help develop bodily co-ordination and pleasurable responses to rhythm, while proper singing and playing of wind instruments develop breath control and lung capacity.

Wholesome emotional development is essential to mental health. Children and adults need to express their emotions, and music is a superior means for doing this, since it is a way to communicate the feelings and emotions of individuals and of social and cultural groups. The creative activities mentioned earlier contribute in an important way to emotional, social, and personal development, all of which contribute to mental health. The enjoyment and understanding of the beauty of musical sound contribute to emotional growth, since music can speak to both the well adjusted and to the emotionally-disturbed child in ways that convey no threat or fear. It provides means through which children can develop their capacity to respond sensitively and emotionally in wholesome ways, provided they have the skilled guidance of good music teachers that makes this possible.

TO DEVELOP INTELLECTUAL CAPACITIES

From teacher-guided analyses of music come knowledge, understanding, and appreciation. *Knowledge* of music comes primarily from the study of *the music itself*. The learning of facts about music, such as those concerned with music theory and composers, is best derived from this study. Children need to discover what music communicates, and by what technical means this communication takes place. Such communication is based upon the feelings and responses of the listener or participant, and may be a mood, a description, a story, or it may have non-programmatic characteristics such as beauty for its own sake, contrast, tension and release, form, or other intellectual design. The vehicles of this communication include melody, dynamics, style, harmony, rhythm, repetition, contrast, variation, instrumentation, and tone quality.

The ability to use musical skills and knowledge in the solution of musical problems indicates the degree of *understanding* possessed by an individual. Problems are confronted and solved that concern listening, composing, performing, reading notation, improvising, or interpreting music. Music has as much intellectual content as any other area of education; thus it can serve intellectual development very well. A balance should be maintained between feelings (emotional responses) and the intellectual factors of knowledge and understanding. The proportions of this balance are determined by the characteristics of the age group in question and by the musical background of the group.

TO ACQUIRE AND UTILIZE MUSIC SKILLS

Growth in music skills is essential, because without it, the preceding purposes of music education cannot be realized. For example, if listening skills have not been developed, children can comprehend little of what they hear. Persistent singing with faulty pitch and with poor tone quality will fail to develop understanding either of aesthetic concepts or of our cultural heritage, and it will discourage creativity. Failure to understand music notation constitutes a barrier to learning to sing or play music literature. Unless music is performed in a way that is appealing and satisfying, the purposes of social education, recreation, and physical and mental health cannot be served. Therefore, the development of music skills has a logical and essential purpose in the education of children. All teachers of music must be prepared to teach these skills if the purposes of music in the curriculum are to be realized.

MUSIC TEACHERS AND PLANS OF ORGANIZATION

TEACHERS OF MUSIC

Currently there exist in the elementary schools of the United States three general groups of music teachers. One is composed of classroom teachers who are expected to know how to teach every aspect of the total educational program. It is assumed that these teachers can know the individual child very well, can include music at whatever point it is needed during the school day, and can achieve an interrelation of music and other subjects. A second group is composed of specialized music teachers who are responsible solely for the teaching of music. The teachers in this group are considered capable of creditable work in teaching music subject matter and skills, and of being able to organize a logical sequence of music activities throughout a school. The third group is composed of both classroom teachers and special music teachers. Those in this group usually work together on a co-operative basis. It is assumed that the teachers in this group should be able to combine the advantages of the first two groups, thus making possible a superior learning situation for children.

PLANS OF ORGANIZATION

There are many plans of organization of general music programs in elementary schools. Most of them are found in the six plans listed below, although variations are possible in all of them, such as in plan four, where the departmentalization of music instruction by a specialist in the subject frequently begins at grade levels other than the fourth grade.

1. Music instruction in grades one through six is assigned to classroom teachers.
2. Music instruction in grades one through six is assigned to classroom teachers, who are assisted by a music specialist (consultant), who is on call.
3. Music instruction in grades one through six is assigned to classroom teachers, who are supervised by a music specialist (supervisor).
4. Music instruction in grades one through three is assigned to classroom teachers with consultant help; music instruction in grades four through six is assigned to music specialists.
5. Music instruction in grades one through six is assigned to music specialists, who are assisted by classroom teachers who teach music the days the specialist is not present.
6. Music instruction is assigned to music specialists in grades one through six.

The instruction of instrumental music (band and orchestra) ordinarily begins in grade four or five, and is assigned to specialists in instrumental music.

The supervision of these music programs is sometimes the responsibility of elementary school principals and sometimes the responsibility of music specialists. This is a matter of controversy in education, some believing that all supervisory authority should be vested in the principal and others believing that only teachers educated specifically in a specialized area such as music should have this authority. Research indicates that supervision is apt to be ineffective when persons not musically qualified are assigned this work, and that most principals lack the time to be able to supervise efficiently.

TITLES OF MUSIC SPECIALISTS

Music specialists are given a variety of titles. A *director of music* is a person who has administrative authority for the total music program, and who is responsible directly to the superintendent of schools, who has delegated this authority to him. A *music supervisor* has primary responsibility for the quality of instruction in music, including the improvement of teaching and the evaluation of the program. He may be responsible either to the director of music or to the elementary principals. A *music co-ordinator* is a supervisor who co-ordinates music with other curricular areas and with community music work. A *music consultant* is a resource person who assists the classroom teachers in the teaching of music. A *music teacher* is a specialist who teaches children music. A *music specialist* is a person qualified by special education in music and education to assume the responsibilities indicated by any of the above titles. However, it is very difficult for boards of education to assign a specific title to many music specialists, since some of them may be acting in several or even all of the capacities indicated by these title descriptions. Further complications result when some directors of music are named consultants because the word "consultant" is believed by many to be more "democratic" than the word "director." Thus it is possible to find "consultants" who are really directors of music with considerable authority, and at the same time to find "directors" of music who possess little authority and therefore must operate largely as consultants. For these reasons, it is often necessary to analyze the duties of the positions held by many music specialists to determine whether these positions are, or are not, adequately or accurately described by their titles.

THE EXPANDING MUSIC CURRICULUM

It is well known that knowledge has expanded at a growing rate in this century. The elementary school general music program has grown in comparable fashion. Whereas this curriculum was once concerned exclusively with singing and note reading largely for the purpose of assisting congregational singing in the churches as well as for the purpose of the efficient learning of more music, the purposes of instruction stated earlier in this chapter imply that today's curriculum is more complex than it once was because of stated emphases on aesthetics, cultural education, creativity, social education, recreation, physical and mental health, intellectual development, and the acquisition and utilization of music skills.

The phonograph was invented by Thomas A. Edison in 1887. Subsequent refinements in this means of communication resulted in its acceptance in the early part of the twentieth century by teachers of school music as a means of expanding knowledge of music literature. Certain outstanding teachers such as Mrs. Satis Coleman[4] of Lincoln School, Teachers College, Columbia University, who taught there in the 1920's, contributed to an expanding concept of the content of music in elementary education. Mrs. Coleman constructed a curriculum upon the historical evolution of music and upon the study of music of primitive cultures. She believed that children should re-create the musical history of the race as a part of their natural development. In this curriculum, singing merged with the making and playing of simple instruments, dancing, and the composition of both poetry and music. She believed that there was a musical instrument to match the capacity of every child and that experience with simple instruments should precede experience with complex instruments such as the piano. These ideas have contributed strongly to today's music curriculum.

The music program, or curriculum, must adjust to the general pattern of organization of the school. Most elementary schools have a grade level plan that has been basic to education in the United States since about 1850. This has promoted definite expectancies of pupil achievement at each of the grade levels. Series books in most of the subject areas are written with this in mind, and teachers need to know the expected grade levels of accomplishment whether they teach in schools having this plan of organization or not.

There are some other types of school organization plans with which the reader may wish to become familiar. They can be studied in books listed in References at the end of this chapter. It is important to keep in mind that music can be taught successfully in any of them.

RECENT INNOVATIONS

The *nongraded plan* of organization is used in relatively few schools, largely, but not exclusively, at the primary level. Currently in an experimental stage of development, it is an attempt to acknowledge the great individual differences that commonly exist among children by permitting them to make continuous progress, each at his own rate, usually in a "primary school" that rejects definite grade level standards. It is believed that in order for this plan to find wide acceptance, it will be necessary to prepare teachers who are able to analyze the needs, interests and abili-

---

4 Satis N. Coleman, *Creative Music for Children.* (New York: G. P. Putnam's Sons, 1922).

ties of each child and who are capable of organizing individualized instruction for all children in every area of learning. It will also be necessary to have a great variety and amount of instructional materials and to have a smaller pupil-teacher ratio than is now prevalent. The nongraded plan is an educational theory being tested.

The *teaching machine* is an aspect of "programmed instruction." Programmed instruction by means of textbooks and workbooks is well known and is not new, although its organization may be improved. The teaching machine, however, has caught the imagination of the American public. It is a device that presents a question or other stimulus, provides a way to respond to it, and includes a means of informing the student whether or not his response is correct. The subject matter dealt with by the machine is assumed to be carefully prepared, item by item (thus *programmed*). The psychological advantages of the machine are said to be that its operation requires active participation, it provides for individual differences of certain types, it yields immediate knowledge of the correctness of the answers, it has planned continuity, it spaces review and repetition, and it reduces anxiety. Each "program" must be examined in light of the purposes of music instruction, to determine how it coincides with the concepts of learning, and how logical the organization of the subject matter is. Experimentation and evaluation should be undertaken prior to any large-scale adoption of the machine. The teaching machine is assumed to relieve the teacher of some routine teaching and thus permits him to do more with the *art* of teaching. It by no means replaces teachers. Machines dealing with facts about music are not intended to teach music itself, which is primarily listening, singing, playing, and moving to music.

Team teaching of many types is under current experimentation. The "team" may be of professional teachers, or of professional teachers and noncertified persons who do routine and clerical work to relieve the teachers so that they may use more of their time for teaching. When the team consists of professional teachers, those with complementary strengths and weaknesses can be combined to make a more effective learning situation for the children. Sometimes student teachers are used as members of teams. There are currently so many types of team teaching under trial that only a description of any specific instance will give the inquirer an accurate idea of how the term is being employed. The principal effect upon music to date is that the member of the team most competent to teach music does so. In some instances this appears to be a step toward departmentalization.

Televised instruction in elementary schools has made substantial gains in recent years. Normally, television is in no way a substitute for teachers, although it is being used in this capacity to teach foreign languages in schools unable to find qualified language teachers. However, this is an emergency situation. Normally, television provides assistance and enrichment. The most widely used programs are those concerned with languages, science, and mathematics, and they are ordinarily employed to help teachers whose skills have not kept pace with the increase of knowledge in those areas.

Successfully televised music programs have dealt with rhythm in the primary grades and music appreciation in the intermediate grades. Because children learn from examples of good models, television obviously possesses great potential in the teaching of music. Some schools have regular weekly television programs as a part of general music. In this way, the music specialist is able to be seen and heard in many classrooms simultaneously. The classroom teachers are expected to prepare for, and to follow up each presentation, and to continue teaching each day what is begun in the lesson presented by the specialist. It should be remembered that these television programs are designed to provide helpful enrichment. They are *not* meant to be substitutes for the regular music program.

A particularly appropriate use of television within a school system is to prepare the children for special events such as a concert to be performed by a visiting group. By this means the specialist can help the children learn much more from the concert experience than they otherwise could. Another use is very significant to college teacher education classes: by closed circuit television, the college class comes directly into the elementary classroom. Such observation by television is assuming increasing importance as larger college enrollments and the shortage of nearby elementary classrooms for observation purposes compound the difficulty of bringing the teacher-in-training in contact with children.

Individualized use of the tape recorder, in which a student enters a booth or alcove and works with a recorder or recorders by himself, is widely used. It is possible that tone matching, voice quality, and part singing are among the aspects of music that can be improved through planned uses of tape recorders by individual children. The tape recorder has long been used in teaching groups of students, and this use is constantly increasing.

THINGS TO DO

1. Compare the elementary school curriculum of your experience with that described in this chapter. What were its purposes and its plan of organization? How was it supervised?

2. What evidence can you present that music is functioning positively as

a cultural force in American society today? What evidence can you present that it is not functioning as well as it should?

3. Know Satis N. Coleman's contributions to the elementary music curriculum.

4. Discuss the commercial uses and misuses of music, and their significance in terms of cultural standards.

5. Listen to educational radio or television programs designed to enrich elementary school music and evaluate them in terms of the purposes of music education.

6. Investigate and observe if possible music teaching in (1) an elementary school that has a nongraded plan of organization, and (2) in a school that has team teaching.

7. Investigate programs of music learning by means of teaching machines. Build a program for the teaching of a selected aspect of music learning that would be suitable for use on a teaching machine.

REFERENCES AND MATERIALS

GENERAL BACKGROUND

Britton, Allen P., "Music Education: An American Specialty," *Music Educators Journal,* June–July, 1962, pp. 27–9, 55–60. A short history and discussion of American music education, grades 1–12. Reprinted from *One Hundred Years of Music in America,* ed. Paul Henry Lang. New York: G. Schirmer, Inc., 1961.

PURPOSES OF MUSIC INSTRUCTION

Wilson, A. Verne, "Why Music Education?" *National Elementary Principal,* December, 1959, pp. 4–8. Reprinted in *Music Education for Elementary School Children,* Washington, D.C.: Music Educators National Conference, 1960.

SCHOOL ORGANIZATION PLANS

American Educational Research Association, "Curriculum Planning and Development," *Review of Educational Research,* 1960, 30:184–279.

Beck, Robert, Walter Cook and Nolan Kearney, *Curriculum in the Modern Elementary School,* 2nd ed. Englewood Cliffs, N.J.: Prentice-Hall, Inc., 1960.

Goodlad, John I., and Robert H. Anderson, *The Non-Graded Elementary School.* New York: Harcourt, Brace & World, Inc., 1959.

Klausmeier, Herbert J., and Kathrine Dresden, *Teaching in the Elementary School.* New York: Harper and Row, 1962, Chapter 4.

MUSIC TEACHERS

Andrews, Frances M., and Clara E. Cockerille, *Your School Music Program.* Englewood Cliffs, N.J.: Prentice-Hall, Inc., 1958. Pages 75–85 are concerned with the music specialist as teacher and supervisor.

Kilpatrick, Lula, "Classroom Teachers *Can* Teach Music!" *National Elementary Principal,* December, 1959, pp. 9–13. Reprinted in *Music Education for Elementary School Children,* Washington, D.C.: Music Educators National Conference, 1960.

Marvel, Lorene, *The Music Consultant at Work.* New York: Teachers College, Columbia University, 1960.

Chapter Two

MUSIC AND CHILD DEVELOPMENT

Elementary music education is concerned, first, with children's development through music and, second, with the development of music skills, realizing, however, that children cannot develop through music without these skills. There is no problem concerning the value of skills; if there is a problem it is concerned with how and in what context the skills are to be attained. Research in music education as it relates to child development has not given teachers of music entirely clear answers to questions in pedagogy as they apply to levels of musical maturity. However, teachers of music need to incorporate what knowledge is currently available in their efforts to help children become musically responsive people. There are similarities in patterns of physical, mental, social and emotional growth at certain stages or ages of development, and teachers must be able to utilize this knowledge. It is important that teachers understand that music should be part of a balanced daily program of education, and not merely the mastery of a body of skills. How much a music program contributes to the development of children depends upon the quality and logic of its organization, its content, and the methods used to teach music.

MUSIC CONTRIBUTES TO CHILD DEVELOPMENT

Every child has needs that the elementary school attempts to satisfy. They include those of security with adults and with his peers; acceptance by his own age group and by adults; a feeling of belonging; success in meeting some problems, including mastery of significant skills; achieving happiness; creating; aesthetic experiences; expanding his knowledge of the environment; and in increasing understanding and appreciation of his role in a democratic society. Therefore, the organization, content, and methods of the music program are concerned with these needs.

The organization of the music program refers to the music teaching staff, procurement of equipment and supplies, making facilities available, scheduling, and other aspects of making an educational program possible. A successful program is based upon a musically and educationally competent staff. Reorganization and co-ordination of all these factors should constantly be taking place in order to improve the program. Satisfactory organization should assist in meeting children's needs by providing for a variety of instructional materials and equipment, meeting individual differences among children, making opportunities to explore and to create music, and creating consistent and sequential procedures that lead to the attainment of necessary skills and of favorable habits and attitudes. Each child is unique. He has his own rate of learning, his own interests, needs, and abilities, thus necessitating an organization that makes possible a general music program of varied activities. These activities should assist the child's wholesome development by helping him to find enjoyment, emotional expression, release of tensions, understanding of himself and others, appreciation of the beautiful, and creative self-expression.

The content of the music program should be of such quality and scope that it may contribute to the child's happiness and feeling of wellbeing; it should expand the understanding of the present-day life of others in the school, in the community, in the United States, and in the world; it should increase the understanding of life in the past; it should further worthy citizenship, and spiritual and aesthetic development. The content should stimulate experimentation, creativity, and the development of skills, knowledge, and understanding in music.

The methods of teaching music determine how effectively the needs of children are met. Important emphases in method include being certain that children have a part in the planning, that they see purpose and meaning in what they are doing, that they actively participate, that they have a part in evaluating the learning activities, and that they have opportunities to create and to solve problems that are meaningful to them. Effective methods are based upon the teacher's knowledge of how boys and girls grow and learn, his command of performing skills in music, his ability to organize, his employment of a variety of instructional materials, and his mastery of the content of the music curriculum. He incorporates all these aspects in his music teaching.

ASPECTS OF GROWTH

There are five major aspects of growth. These aspects are physical, social-emotional, intellectual, aesthetic, and spiritual. Each aspect influences all of the others. Growth is a continuous process from birth to death. However, it rarely proceeds in an orderly and uniform manner. The degree and quality of growth in each aspect of development is dependent upon heredity, the environment of the home, school, and community, the type of teacher, and the physical condition of the individual. Children vary in their growth patterns. In some areas of music growth is slow while in others it occurs rapidly. For instance, a certain child may be advanced in vocal skills but retarded in rhythmic responsiveness. It is not unusual for a pupil to progress in music for a given period of time, then reach a plateau and show little obvious advancement. He may even regress temporarily. However, normal growth follows a sequential pattern, and is continuous despite temporary pauses. It results from environmental and hereditary influences.

Society makes certain demands known as *development tasks*[1] of every person at specific age levels. When these demands are in conflict with a child's normal growth pattern, a situation can develop that retards all aspects of his growth. This could occur when a child finds that he cannot sing in tune when the other children can, or that he cannot respond rhythmically as the others do. The teacher's responsibility is to identify the variance and to work sympathetically with the child on his level to correct it.

The relationship of music to the five major aspects of growth is given below:

PHYSICAL GROWTH

Music activities can assist physical growth by improving muscular co-ordination, by relating good posture to voice quality and control, by increasing understanding of breathing, singing, enunciation, diction and the changing voice, and by fostering muscular precision and control. The ability to respond skillfully to rhythmic stimuli is highly important in developing poise, bodily grace, and a feeling of well-being: the schools should place more emphasis on this than most of them do. Throughout history music has been important to the physical laborer, who has created work songs to unite with others in rhythmic acts of physical co-ordination, and to relieve him of tedium and frustration. The kindergarten child who expresses his feelings about the music he hears through bodily movements finds that he can control his physical actions in a meaningful way. The first-grade child who pounds a large drum with a beater feels the power that comes from muscular co-ordination and rhythmic pulse.

---

[1] Robert J. Havighurst. *Developmental Tasks and Education.* (New York: Longmans, Green and Company, 1954), pp. 33–62.

Upper elementary grade children who work out patterned movements to a recording can develop co-ordination that permits them to control their bodies with confidence. When some sixth-grade boys whose voices are in the first stage of change select or create vocal parts in their new range, they can identify the changing voice as a natural, expected event that carries with it no difficulty or embarrassment. The importance of posture and breathing in various physical activities can be demonstrated by their effect upon tone quality and pitch accuracy in singing and in playing instruments.

SOCIAL AND EMOTIONAL GROWTH

Music can reflect in dramatic ways man's need for belonging—to the family, the clan, the city, state, and nation. It has the power to unify social groups. Man uses it constantly in social functions and ceremonies from the cradle to the grave. It can assist children in finding emotional security and social competence, and in understanding and taking part in aspects of democratic group living. The emotional communication of spirituals, other folk songs, and recorded instrumental music assists children in expressing their own emotions and feelings. Through group musical performance in the classroom, in the chorus, band, and orchestra, children can feel pride and security in belonging to a group and contributing their best efforts to it. By becoming competent in accompanying, playing an instrument, or solo singing, children can win prestige with their peers because of successful achievement. A higher level of social accomplishment evolves when children can evaluate and appreciate the performances of individuals and of groups of which they are not participating members. Teachers can help children become sensitive to the feelings of others through music activities. Children should have opportunities to develop their creative capacities in music, for they can thereby express their innermost thoughts and feelings. Many a sensitive teacher has realized that music activities offer unique opportunities to gain understanding of children's personal and social problems. Through observing children in music, teachers gain insight into their thinking, abilities, problems, social background and experience. This knowledge can be used as a guide in preparing appropriate musical materials and opportunities. Skilled teachers utilize music to change and to improve the emotional climate of a classroom or school.

INTELLECTUAL GROWTH

Music is an abstract art through which man conceptualizes his experiences, from simple everyday affairs to the loftiest. Opportunities for intellectual growth abound in music activities in which children are encouraged to find out *what, how and why.* For example, deciding what a certain musical composition communicates, and how it does this, is an intellectual exercise of vast proportions.   Less complex examples include finding out why one percussion instrument is more suitable than another for use with a song or a recording, and what types of music are best suited for background music to use with a play; deciding how to determine the precise interpretation of a song or instrumental perform- ance, and learning some simple composition techniques and how they should be used.   The content of music stimulates the intellect through the study of notation, form, style, history, acoustics, instrumentation, melody, rhythm and harmony.   Such study is primarily the study of music itself; facts about music should be learned in this context.   Good music teaching is marked by a proper balance between intellectual and emo- tional elements, recognizing that the emotional is basic at this age, and the intellectual an outgrowth of it.

AESTHETIC AND SPIRITUAL GROWTH

Aesthetic growth results from value judgments concerned with the good, the true, and the beautiful.   To learn to recognize, identify and analyze aural beauty is a major purpose of music teaching.   Contact with and evaluation of the good and the less good, the beautiful and the less beautiful in many different kinds of music fosters the development of aesthetic standards.   When the seven-year-old makes thoughtful decisions concerning the appropriateness of different percussion instru- ments to play with a recording; when eleven-year-olds determine which recorded version of an excerpt of symphonic music is best—and state the reasons why; when a class determines carefully which performances are and are not suitable to be presented in an assembly; and when children are continually evaluating their progress in singing and in blending voices, opportunities for aesthetic growth are present.

Through the ages music has been a means through which man has attempted to understand the unknown and to satisfy his spiritual desires. Aesthetic and spiritual values seem closely related, both being present in music of quality.   The class that engages in group music activities, as well as the child who composes music by himself, finds that discipline and order are essential to produce beauty.   Since discipline and order are closely related to problems of right and wrong, music activities of quality may assist the growth of aesthetic responses, ethical conduct, and spiritual acuity.

PROVIDING FOR INDIVIDUAL DIFFERENCES

There is considerable variance of ability in music. The teacher can observe marked individual differences in degrees of interest, creativity, sensitivity, and acquisition of skills. Gifted children have special needs to be met in order that they may continue to grow in musical responsiveness in accordance with their capacities. However, the children who react to music at lower levels of responsiveness need worthy and challenging experiences that are on *their* level. If children of average and below-average levels find that the music activities the teacher organizes are too complicated for them to do satisfactorily, and if children who are above-average in musical ability find these activities too simple for them, they tend to lose interest. Thus, to meet varying needs, a variety of materials, media, and methods is necessary. The music program, both for the daily lesson and for the term, must somehow be designed to provide for the interests, needs, and abilities of each child. The child who excels in rhythmic responses may be below-average in singing, and one who plays classroom instruments well may not have developed adequate listening skills of the type needed to hear recorded music.

The existence within each grade level, of children with marked differences in terms of musical competence, vocal control, and aural understanding further emphasizes the need for developing teaching procedures and activities which will take account of these differences and result in more effective learning on the part of all children. One is forced to question the continued acceptance of scheduling music classes and categorizing music activities in terms of grade level, per se.[2]

In order for a teacher to guide learners in accordance with their unique differences, he must analyze information from many sources concerning each child. While some of this comes from casual observation and can be remembered easily, other information comes from keeping records and studying previous records containing data on each pupil. A teacher can use the results of such an analysis to attempt to provide for the maximum musical growth of each child. Sources of information and techniques to acquire information include the following:

1. **Pupil-teacher conferences** — to learn about pupil interests, performing experiences, and family musical background.

2 Robert G. Petzold, "The Development of Auditory Perception of Musical Sounds by Children in the First Six Grades" (mimeographed report). (Madison, Wisconsin: School of Music, University of Wisconsin, n.d.), p. 32.

2. Observations — of attitude, facial expression revealing enjoyment, emotional involvement and ease of voice production, ability to stay on pitch, facility on instruments, ability in part singing, muscular coordination, rhythmic skill, creative responses.

3. Anecdotal records — are dated records of significant observed behavior, not interpreted at the time.

4. Health records — reveal any deviation from the norm affecting music activities, including eyesight and hearing.

5. Cumulative records — are a compiled record that begins when a child enters school; it may indicate the scope and sequence of musical experiences experienced by the child.

6. Check-lists — are lists indicating types of musical experiences and levels of musical performance.

7. Class discussions — reveal likes, dislikes, prejudices, problems, appreciations.

8. Tape recordings of musical performances — reproduce range, tone quality, enunciation, expression, skill, accuracy.

9. Interviews with previous teachers — reveal prior musical problems, performances, experiences that relate to the present.

10. Parent-teacher conferences — reveal family musical interests and conditions affecting present musical responsiveness.

11. Conferences with private music teachers — reveal abilities, attitudes, interests.

12. Tests of voice range — reveal vocal problems and comfortable singing range. (Use piano or bells.)

Time spent collecting information by any of the above means is wasted unless the assembled information is *analyzed, interpreted,* and *used* as a basis for planning and providing appropriate experiences and for selecting instructional materials that aid in assisting the child to overcome his weaknesses, to build upon his strengths, and to increase his understanding, skill, and appreciation of music, and to improve his attitude toward music.

A good instructional program tends to increase differences rather than to decrease them. While there are many likenesses in mankind that must be effectively utilized in teaching, differences are to be expected; they add interest and challenge to teaching. Since most advances in civilization have resulted from creativity and individuality, teachers should encourage children to develop these traits. It is good to be constructively different.

THE CHARACTERISTICS OF CHILDREN AND IMPLICATIONS FOR THE TEACHING OF MUSIC

To be able to teach children skillfully, it is vital that the teacher know each one of them and perceive how he interacts with people. In order to understand a child, the teacher needs to know the general characteristics of his age group. It should be recognized, however, that no one list of general characteristics will apply to all children at any age. Because certain characteristics are typical of an age group, it does not follow that they will appear in every child. Also, it cannot be assumed that a specified characteristic will always be found at a particular age level; for some children, it may appear earlier or later than is indicated on the following. However, knowledge of normal expectations for any age group is of great value in organizing music curricula because it points out the deviations from the norm which identify the unique abilities and differing problems of children.

A characteristic of children is that they are sensitive to musical tones that communicate beauty, feelings, and emotions. This implies that at every grade level the teacher, through his own sensitivity to these aspects, stimulates children's ability to respond to tonal beauty. Recordings and record players must be of superior quality to communicate aural beauty properly; the teacher's singing and speaking voice should be aesthetically acceptable. The teacher appreciates and nurtures the human need for beauty which contributes a quality factor to living; he provides a classroom environment that inspires aesthetic growth and appreciation through all the senses; he develops understanding of human feelings and their expression through the medium of music.

Developmental Characteristics	*Suggested Implications for the Teacher of Music*
KINDERGARTEN: AGE FIVE	
Large muscles better developed than small muscles; constantly physically active.	Physical activities involving large muscles are stressed; fundamental

movements such as walking, running, and hopping are related to music; movements of animals are imitated; activities include free rhythmic responses to recordings and piano selections that "tell what to do"; the accompaniment follows the movement at first, then later the child learns to follow the music; *simple* directed singing games and dances; creative and spontaneous movement.

Language development is limited; speech skills are little developed but both language and speech are improving rapidly.

Chants and calls, finger plays, singing games and songs with words that are colorful, rhythmic, repetitious and sometimes nonsensical; provision for much spontaneous and creative response to the sound of words and to music; singing and chanting of Mother Goose rhymes and neutral syllables.

Attention span is very short; most children are very active and aggressive.

Provide music through the day for short periods of time; utilize music in other areas and to change the tempo of the day to provide for activity and rest; use a variety of types of songs to relieve tension and fatigue and to provide relaxation; include songs involving names, touching objects, and repeating phrases; provide opportunity for each child to learn perseverance on his level.

Some children are shy and are limited in ways of expressing ideas and feelings.

Help children listen to music and respond to it in creative ways; encourage dramatizations and imitations of people, animals, and things.

Very self-centered; wants to be involved and motivated; cares little what his peers think; is very individualistic.

The child is given individual help and the opportunity to sing individually and in small groups before singing in larger groups; he sings co-operatively in large groups when he is socially and intellectually mature enough to co-operate in a group; provision is made for enjoyment of music and help in gradually and sequentially increasing his understanding of it; the teacher must establish limits in group response activities; the child needs help in learning to co-operate in singing, taking turns, listening to others; songs in which the child is clearly identified are utilized; the teacher substitutes the child's name for the name in the song; the teacher leads in creating calls, chants, and conversational singing which include the child's name; short, repetitious songs for fun and singing and acting out are used.

The harmonic sense is undeveloped.

The teacher emphasizes the melodic line and the rhythm, not harmony; songs that require no chord changes in their accompaniment are included; complex harmonic accompaniments are avoided or kept to a minimum.

Enjoys the security of repetitious activity.

Repetitive songs, motions, or ideas and repetitive manipulative experiences with percussion instruments and bells are employed.

Desires to be accepted by adults; needs warmth and security from them; enjoys individual attention.

The teacher sings to the child often, and provides a simple, pleasant and secure environment; he gives security and respect, and avoids unpleasant experiences and situations; he involves every child by providing activities in which each child can succeed; children should feel success with music that is interesting and appealing; provision should be made for spontaneous and creative responses to music; the teacher should give encouragement and recognition for children's efforts in music; music should be provided to suit the moods of the children.

Beginning to develop independence; tries to help himself; gradually depends less upr adults.

The teacher should be certain that each child is helped in singing, interpreting or playing music to increase music skills in order to develop self-confidence and independence; song content can aid children in adjusting to new or frightening experiences; encourage children to make up new words, chants, motions or rhythms, to play different percussion instruments, and to experiment with sound; discussions and evaluations assist social development; opportunities are provided for children to help plan music activities, to select songs, recordings, appropriate percussion instruments, and to decide how to interpret music.

Teeth and bony structures are growing and changing; vigorous action results in fatigue.

A variety of music activities from very active to restful is employed; a *minimum* of twenty minutes of music is distributed throughout the day; action songs and finger plays are used; children listen to many kinds of music, from types that stimulate vigorous action to types that encourage rest and relaxation; creative bodily movements and use of percussion instruments are encouraged.

The beginning of co-operative play in relatively small groups.

Music activities should help children grow in understanding and appreciation of others and of the quality of work done; discussion and evaluation aid children in developing their powers of communication and in their ability to relate to and respect others; social consciousness should be helped to grow.

Very inquisitive about his surroundings; he is eager to learn and to respond; is very alert; learns through manipulating concrete objects and re-enacting real situations.

Provide opportunity to use and experiment with a variety of musical materials; plan music experiences that build sensitivity to beauty of melody, rhythm, and form, and recognition of happy, sad, slow, fast, high, and low; experiment with types of sound obtainable from wood, metal, glass, stone and various percussion instruments introduced one at a time; simple imitations and dramatizations are employed.

Interested in the "here and now," "what and what for," and in realizing immediate goals.

Songs about everyday experiences such as mother and family, playthings, people they know, pets and animals; children need simple directions, given clearly and explicitly, and musical activities that can be completed in short periods of time; the teacher gives each child opportunities to succeed; music is used as a "core" for learning content in other areas.

Lives in a world of make-believe and imagination; the child is imitative.

Provide opportunity to make creative responses in singing, listening, and rhythm; children should imitate the movement of animals and dramatize songs in a simple manner; songs about inanimate objects and talking animals and the creative activities related to them should aid in children's enjoyment, encourage initiative, develop self-confidence, help children recognize their own possibilities, limitations, and capabilities in learning co-operation with the group, stimulating imagination, overcoming shyness, relieving aggressive feelings, and expressing their ideas and personal feelings; songs are taught by rote; the teacher's voice and recordings should be good models; the teacher's attitudes, skills, appreciations and enthusiasm are imitated by the children; musical models in the home are very important.

Voices are small; the pitch sense is often underdeveloped.

Many children need help in finding their singing voices; the teacher uses tone-matching games, calls, chants, and singing conversations to build pitch concepts; the teacher establishes the pitch of songs by means of the piano, pitch pipe, or bells; he gives individual and small-group assistance in finding the singing voice and its range; children are helped to learn to listen to pitches and to recorded music; the teacher has the children imitate vocally such sounds of their environment as train and factory whistles, church bells, chimes, and the sounds of animals and machines; oral, aural, and visual aids are necessary in building pitch concepts; the teacher makes certain that children enjoy music and want to take part in singing; children have opportunities to play very simple songs or parts of songs on the bells; the teacher emphasizes first listening to his or children's singing, then having children imitate this good example.

Creative, spontaneous, and uninhibited.

The teacher encourages creating chants, interesting word-rhythms, rhythmic movement, and dramatizations; spontaneous singing is encouraged as children play with toys or play on the playground; children dramatize roles of people and animals well known to them; space is provided for the children to move freely; percussion instruments, scarves, and balloons can assist creative responses to rhythm.

EARLY ELEMENTARY: AGES SIX AND SEVEN

Extend and refine the experiences indicated for five-year-olds. Children in many school systems do not have kindergarten experience and many six-year-olds perform on the level of five-year-olds.

Many children are still unable to sing in tune; most voices are light and high in quality, but some are low, and there will be many different ranges present. The overlapping of the different ranges at beginning of the school year will permit about five or six consecutive pitches to be sung by the large majority of the class, usually from middle C to the G or A above.

The teacher assists each child in learning to sing in tune; children are guided to do much individual singing, singing in pairs, and in small groups; the teacher helps children to experiment with their voices to determine the difference between speaking and singing; children need good models to imitate both in school and at home; the teacher begins the school year with songs of limited range to assure the largest degree of success; this range is gradually extended; individual singing independent of the teacher's voice or the recording is encouraged.

Slow growth; children like warm, personal attention.

The teacher employs a small repertory of simple songs well learned and frequently repeated; music repetition is necessary in learning to hear pitch differences and to match tones; nursery rhymes are reviewed; children are seated near the teacher when they sing; children's names are often substituted for those in songs and are used in question-answer games and in singing conversations.

Large muscles are more developed than small muscles; children tend to move with the entire body as a unit; a lengthening of the limbs.

Free rhythmic movements and fundamental movements such as walking, running, skipping, hopping, and galloping are stressed; finger plays develop small muscles; emphasis is given to impersonation of animals, people, and things; keeping perfect time in various tempos is not expected of most children because they need to experiment in their own ways to develop muscular control; all children are encouraged to improvise rhythmic responses of their own and to take part in activities that lead to improvement in poise, balance, and bodily control in response to rhythmical stimuli; at first the accompaniment follows the response, then later the children become able to respond to accompaniments of various tempos; suitable furniture and seating arrangements are provided.

At age six eye-hand co-ordination is poorly developed.

Rote singing and rote playing are emphasized; incidental use is made of large-sized notation on charts.

At age seven the heart grows rapidly; muscular development is uneven; motor skills are steadily developing; eye-hand co-ordination improves; attention span increases.

Time allotted to strenuous physical activity should be brief; active musical activities should be interspersed with quiet responses; singing games and dances can be more complex; there can be greater variety and skill in fundamental movements; percussion instruments are played with more skill and control; some children will play piano, bells, and autoharp; more songs and longer songs with more verses can be learned.

Eyes of six-year-olds not ready for close work; eyes of seven-year-olds better developed but still not ready for sustained close work.

The teacher uses simple notation on large charts, flannel board and chalk board for simple chants, phrases and parts for singing and playing; children observe the teacher as he notates songs they have created; rote songs are sung from charts; music textbooks with large, clear print are introduced in the second grade; the teacher sings short songs already familiar to the children while the class does guided observation of aspects of notation in the books.

Missing front teeth of seven-year-olds make perfect pronunciation and diction difficult.

The teacher emphasizes vowel sounds rather than consonant sounds in simple chants and singing activities; Latin syllables and neutral syllables such as *loo* and *la* can be sung; pronunciation and enunciation should not be overstressed.

Six-year-olds are extremely active and constantly on the move; they have a relatively short attention span; they are easily fatigued; at age seven children alternate between very active and quiet behavior.

Use music to provide necessary activity and rest and to relieve tensions and fatigue; children need short, frequent, and varied periods of music; listening experiences should be of brief duration; purposes for listening should be few and explicitly stated; listening skills should be developed gradually as the nervous system becomes more mature.

Eager and anxious to learn.

Involve the child in planning and evaluating a variety of musical experiences; gradually and consistently introduce music vocabulary; expand the types and number of musical experiences.

The harmonic sense is largely undeveloped.

The teacher includes songs and chants that need no chord changes in accompaniments; complex harmonic accompaniments are avoided.

Children are highly competitive; they fight

The teacher gives children oppor-

with words rather than with fists; six-year-olds are aggressive, egotistical, and often un-co-operative.

tunity to perform and to succeed individually; he develops social consciousness and social skills by guiding the children to appreciate each other's accomplishments, to help each other, and to appreciate the rewards of co-operative effort.

Children are highly imaginative and enjoy imitating; they are interested in and curious about their surrounding environment; they enjoy sounds and sound effects.

Opportunity is provided for creative reproduction of rhythms from the environment; the teacher should stimulate interest in aesthetic aspects of the environment through the use of the senses—hearing, seeing, feeling, and smelling; in spontaneous and guided dramatizations children imitate sounds and movements of airplanes, missiles, jets, trains, and other machines, the sound of wind and evidence of its action, water, thunder, people's speech, sounds and movements of animals, and the movements and moods of people; to implement the above, the teacher employs a variety of materials that may include recordings, piano, percussion instruments, bells, pictures, music charts, bulletin boards, chalk board, recorder, opaque projector, slides, film strips and movies; there is experimenting with various materials to discover different sounds resulting from them and the way they are struck; children help decide suitable sound effects to enhance their songs; sounds heard in the environment are reproduced.

Rudimentary understanding of time, space, and money values.

The teacher uses line notation to show relative length of note values that have been felt through physical responses; this is later compared with music notation; the teacher begins to teach the understanding of simple music design such as the phrase, contrasting sections, tonal and rhythm patterns, concepts of fast and slow, high and low, and related moods; children learn to comprehend simple note values through identification with simple rhythmic responses involving the entire body.

Learn through use of concrete materials, in terms of experience background, and through participation under wise supervision; little utilization of the abstract.

Provide opportunity to experiment, to listen, and to participate in learning tone production on wood, metal, skin and other media; explore uses of simple instruments, introducing them gradually, one at a time, and teach the use of each thoroughly after stimulating interest in what each can do; listen to and watch various types of musical performance; create and explore uses of voice, instruments, words, tunes, and accompaniments; guide listening with a few *specific* purposes; do creative development of music through interpretation, dramatization, bodily movement, and the addition of codas, introductions, and instrumental parts; teach songs and music of quality that deal with the here and now, including those that reflect the expanding technological age in which these children live, but still on their maturity level (remember that some of today's six-year-olds have been all over the world by means of both television and travel); children can learn music best by means of direct and simple physical responses, feelings and moods; they are able to do only very simple analysis of music design.

Children need encouragement, acceptance, and praise from adults.

Provide opportunity for each child to develop his special talents and interests in music to the maximum degree; provide opportunity to perform acceptably both individually and in groups in order to feel success and acceptance from the teacher, and to grow in assuming responsibility, co-operation, and in social competency; provide a warm, interesting, challenging environment that includes a teacher who knows when and how to give encouragement and praise; because of the children's great need for acceptance by adults, they try to imitate, and thus are susceptible to the teacher's example of enthusiasm, interest, skill, and love for music; teachers should not underestimate this age, but should provide a music program of quality that sets the stage for greater skill in performance, listening, and appreciation of music; it is here that the teacher can utilize this characteristic of seeking the approval of adults, not to dictate learning, but to develop the skills that will progressively be used as a basis for children's future growth in musical competencies, and in their self-reliance and their independence from adults.

At age seven group activities are increasing in popularity; there is some evidence that interests of boys and girls are diverging.

Provide group singing games, action songs, and mass percussion instrument experiences; boys and girls should be given some opportunity to select songs and activities in accordance with possible different interests.

At age seven the concept of the right and wrong ways of doing things is beginning to emerge.

Provide opportunities for children to evaluate the quality of singing and playing; work with children on ways to improve the sound of their singing and playing, and on the proper care of instruments and other materials.

MIDDLE ELEMENTARY: AGES EIGHT AND NINE

The attention span is increasing; capable of prolonged interest.

The music period is extended to as long as thirty minutes, depending on the nature and variety of the activities; children can do guided listening to music for a longer period of time; a greater number of longer songs with greater variety of content and skills can be taught.

Slow steady growth; girls are more mature than boys; this age group has better co-ordi-

The teacher provides opportunities to make substantial use of music nota-

nation, is conscious of detail, and is able to devote attention to activities that require control of small muscles of body, hands, feet, and eyes; children are more interested in detailed and intricate work.

tion in singing, playing, and creating music; more detailed work is planned in the reading of music; use of music text books is emphasized; more complex folk dances can be learned; children can conduct all common meters, with some able to direct music activities of the class with skill; the teacher guides the children in consistent progress in standards of musical performance; children play percussion instruments more effectively; recorder-type instruments can be played; the teacher provides each child opportunity to develop his musical and dramatic skills; individual and group lessons in band and orchestra instruments often begin in fourth grade for the physically mature; lessons on half-sized string instruments are sometimes begun in third grade, and for the less mature nine-year-olds; there is increasing utilization of the piano and other keyboard instruments by children in the music class and at home; songs of wider range can be sung.

Posture needs attention.

Moving to music and proper singing can aid posture; a variety of music activities can relieve tension and fatigue that cause poor posture.

Vocal cords and lungs are developing rapidly; more control of voice and of breathing; the singing voice of the nine-year-old is better in quality, range and dependability.

More complex song material of wider ranges can be used; part singing is a goal; the children can study the problem of finding the best places in songs to take breaths.

The harmonic sense is not well developed for the eight-year-olds, but a growing number of nine-year-olds possess it.

The teacher plans special added parts for children who possess ability to sing harmony; rounds and easy descants are used in working for the harmonic readiness of the group; the autoharp is employed in listening activities to help children to be aware of the necessity of chord changes; simple two-part singing is achieved during the fourth grade year.

Communication skills are more highly developed, including reading skills and a larger vocabulary.

Music text books are used more analytically; music is read from books, charts, flannel boards, magnetic boards, and from projections on a screen; the repertoire of songs increases; music vocabulary grows.

Need for encouragement, acceptance, and praise from adults; sensitive to criticism.

Provide opportunity and encouragement for each child to develop his special talents and interests in music to a maximum degree; provide opportunity to perform acceptably both individually and in groups in order to feel success and acceptance from the teacher and to grow in responsibility, co-operation, and social competence; provide a warm, interesting, challenging environment with an understanding teacher who knows when and how to give encouragement and praise; because of children's great need for acceptance from adults they try to imitate the teacher's example in enthusiasm, interest, and skill in music; this sets the stage for greater skill in performance and appreciation of music.

Peers become important; children are better able to co-operate and work in groups; interest in gangs of the same sex and secret codes is strong, particularly at age nine; this is a time of joining groups; eight-year-olds are usually interested in cowboys, rough and ready play, and they are prone to accidents.

Opportunity is provided for group exploration, discussion, experimentation, sharing, creating and evaluating; music clubs and choruses can be organized; use "mystery tunes," notation treated as a code, and songs about Scouts and other groups; there is opportunity for singing, dancing, creating, dramatizing, and playing instruments in and for groups. These activities are planned by the teacher to improve mutual acceptance of children and the individual child's relationship to and status with his peers; songs that involve group endeavor and songs of action are emphasized; easy folk dances, play-party games, fun and stunt songs, call and response songs are enjoyed; dialogue songs are used in which boys sing one part and girls another; there is improved group activity in music.

The age of hero worship begins to emerge at about age nine; children need good adult models; children are interested in patriotism.

Provision is made for reading books written for this age level about composers, musicians, instruments, and the history of music; song material and recordings can relate to musical or historical heroes; dramatizations of the lives of composers, musicians, or heroes are employed in musical ways; patriotic songs and songs concerned with great men are stressed.

Interest in other cultures and in the expanding world environment.

The teacher utilizes songs about the problems of the peoples of the world community, with words that mention mechanical progress in production, travel, and communication throughout history.

Children enjoy ridiculous humor and the humor in everyday situations; a growing appreciation of imaginary adventure.

The teacher uses songs of humor and nonsense, and plans listening experiences involving adventure and humor; dramatizations and interpretations include comedy.

They are rather indiscriminately interested in anything new to them, particularly the eight-year-olds; they are eager to expand their knowledge.

The teacher introduces new and more complex aspects of music notation and vocabulary; a system of note reading can be employed; information about band and orchestra instruments begins to be emphasized.

An increasing number of individual differences and abilities appear; a wide range of reading abilities is evident.

The teacher uses a variety of techniques to learn the background and level of musical performance of each child, such as: parent-teacher conferences, teacher-pupil conferences, observations, anecdotal records of children's performance and attitude, the study of cumulative records and reports, interviews with former teachers, simple and appropriate tests—both standard and teacher-prepared; the teacher plans for the development of each child's musical abilities and needs; attention is given to special individual problems as well as to developing group skills; a music program possessing a variety of activities for the advanced, slow, and average child is a necessity; emphasize reading and pronouncing the words of songs.

Rapid development in independence and in work-study habits.

The teacher provides opportunity for the development of creative ideas; special class instruction in piano and strings begins in third grade, and in woodwinds, brasses and "chorus" in fourth grade; the teacher uses pupil leaders in singing and directing; guidance is necessary to establish progressive and consistently high standards of work and performance; provision for independent work is made, such as individual reading of books, playing instruments, composing, and the bringing of selected favorite recordings from home with the stipulation that the child is able to explain to the class the reason for the recording's special worth.

These children need guidance and experience in evaluation of their individual performances and of the performances of others; greater skill in self-evaluation.

The teacher plans successful music activities to build self-confidence; there should be freedom for musical experimentation and invention; guidance is provided in choices and evaluation of related motion pictures, radio and television programs, and of recordings; emphasis is given to improving tone quality in singing, more critical listening, and in developing more musical discrimination and taste; good standards of musical quality should be provided by the teacher, some of the children, and recordings.

Nine-year-olds are very conscious of what is right and what is wrong; they desire to do things correctly; they seek help on specific skills and on mastering information.

The teacher gives guidance in evaluating and using music skills and materials; help is provided for the uncertain singer; special individual and group work is planned for those who need them and for the specially talented; teachers should not "sell this age short"—they should provide a music program of high quality and appeal for it.

Continue to learn best through use of varied and concrete materials and through active participation under wise supervision.

Provide varied music activities and materials, and opportunity to explore the potentialities of voices and instruments; create words, tunes, instrumental accompaniments, introductions, codas, and interludes; plan guided listening with specific purposes; provide for creative interpretations of music, including dramatization and bodily movement; use music that deals with the present and the known.

Understand concepts of simple fractions, time, and money.

Meter signatures are taught.

LATER ELEMENTARY: AGES TEN AND ELEVEN

A pause in physical growth to be followed by a period of rapid growth; girls mature more rapidly than boys; rapid growth implies an awkward stage.

Rhythmic activities that develop muscular co-ordination, grace, and poise are employed; plan activities that reduce awkwardness and self-consciousness to a minimum; the teacher does not expect as much from most boys as he does from most girls in work dependent upon physical maturity; the teacher discusses the effects of physical change on the voice and the ability to play certain band and orchestra instruments.

The harmonic sense develops rapidly; the voice range extends; the diaphragm is developing and expanding; some sixth-grade boys will develop voices in the first stage of the change.

Part singing is stressed; more complex songs can be sung; the first stage of the changing voice lowers the range of some boys' voices by about the interval of a fourth, which makes part singing a necessity in some songs; the teacher uses the tape recorder to assist in the evaluation of voice qualities and general vocal performance of individuals and groups; the teacher plans activities to expand the vocal range and to improve enunciation and diction.

Children have increased energy; they are interested in active activities.

Teach various dance steps related to music, social studies or physical education.

A wide range of individual ability.

The teacher analyzes every child in terms of his abilities, capabilities, level of performance, and needs; the teacher needs to possess the knowledge of the various levels of musical accomplishment present in kindergarten through grade seven in singing, playing, rhythmic responses, listening, creating, and comprehension of notation, and to apply this knowledge in organizing a music program that meets these individual differences; provide opportunity for every child, including the specially talented, to progress at his own rate; when necessary the teacher seeks assistance from guidance personnel, parents, other school music teachers, and private music teachers in the community; the school provides a wide variety of types and levels of instructional materials.

Interests of boys and girls are usually divergent.

The teacher includes activities in which boys and girls sing in turn or have separate parts, and in which dance partners change frequently; he selects songs and rhythmic responses that appeal to both boys and girls; he encourages children to create in terms of their varying interests.

Teasing and hostility between boys and girls.

The teacher attempts to offset this through carefully planned coeducational activities that involve both sexes in participation and evaluation; feelings and relationships are discussed.

Listless at times, but highly active generally.

The teacher plans both quiet and active types of music including listening to recordings, listening to performances of others, quiet songs, action songs, singing games, rhythmic responses, dramatizations, and playing instruments; music is interspersed throughout the day as it is needed to relieve emotional tensions and fatigue and to supply variety.

Seeks the approval of the peer group; needs to "belong"; is inclined to be overcritical of self and others; is often prejudiced.

The teacher provides opportunity to work and play together and to learn and share music experiences in group situations; he plans for the success of each child in some aspect of music; band, orchestra, and chorus groups are offered; the teacher guides the children in development of appreciation of each child's contributions and skills; he emphasizes the unique contributions of all peoples through study of the music of the world; performers from various racial and socio-economic groups are invited to demonstrate music skills and their characteristic music to the class.

The ability to work both independently and with others is more highly developed; the ability to follow the leadership of others is present.

The teacher helps children formulate standards that encourage the best efforts of individuals and groups; he aids the child in consistent, sequential, and thoroughly learned activities and provides opportunity for children to analyze, evaluate and improve their musical learning; there is opportunity for the children to suggest, organize, plan, create, initiate and evaluate a variety of types of music activities; time and assistance are provided for individuals to improve and perfect needed musical skills, attitudes, and appreciations.

Pre-adolescents often become extremely critical, unpredictable, and defiant.

To avoid or eliminate this implied problem, a music lesson should include activities that are made meaningful and purposeful through co-operative selecting, planning, developing, and evaluating by the teacher and the children; ask children to assume leadership roles; provide encouragement and praise as it is deserved and needed; the music activities should be selected in terms of interests, needs, and abilities of each child.

Resentment of any kind of attention or activity that appears to cause an individual to lose status with his group; seeks to conform to standards exemplified by child leaders in the group and by the majority of his peers.

The teacher refrains from types of criticism and overpraise that would cause an individual to lose status with the group; encouragement and praise is often given privately; the teacher utilizes the child "leaders" to establish standards of performance and behavior.

There is desire for the approval and understanding of adults even though there is effort to become more independent of them.

Provide increased opportunities for children to assume responsibility for their actions and ideas, to pursue their own interests, to explore, to experiment, and to create.

They are often silly; they giggle unnecessarily; they are loud, rough, and like to joke.

Provide songs, rhythmic responses, and instrumental activities that help self-understanding and provide opportunities for release of energy and relief from emotional tension.

Attracted to adults who possess humor, understanding and warmth, and who are constructive, mature, and positive in their approach.

The teacher participates with the children in music activities with interest, confidence, and enthusiasm; he reveals appreciation of appropriate humor; he is considerate and appreciative of each child's musical efforts; he respects each child's personality and utilizes constructive, positive criticism.

Interested in music concerned with adventure, mystery, humor, work, transportation, inventions, outer space; girls are more interested than boys in music concerned with home and family life.

The teacher includes the content mentioned in the music selected; a balance and variety of music content should be sought.

Wants to know *why* as well as *how*; is inquisitive about scientific reasons that support facts, situations and theories.

The study of acoustics is introduced; the scientific foundations of voice and instrumental tone production and their characteristic types and qualities are explored; harmonic principles as related to chord structure are studied; the causes of the future voice change, particularly in the boys, are made known; the general design of music structure in songs and in larger forms is analyzed.

Interest in and increased understanding of an expanding environment including time and

Emphasis is given to understanding various cultures of the world through

number concepts. More complete understanding of the contributions of past achievements to present-day culture.

music that reflects history, customs, religious and social problems; the children create, notate, and invent appropriate instrumental accompaniments as an outgrowth of their knowledge of history, customs, and cultures, and of time and number concepts related to notation. Include the opportunity to understand and appreciate the history of music and the musical contributions of all peoples.

Possess the background for understanding and enjoying fantasy.

The teacher provides opportunity for creative composition and dramatization inspired by fantasy; music that has fantasy content is utilized in listening activities; the ways in which musical tones communicate stories are explored and analyzed.

Sustained and intense interest in activities that hold meaning and purpose.

The music period can be lengthened; opportunity is provided to participate in band, orchestra, chorus, musical composition, reading books about music and musicians, the planning of special programs; the teacher involves the children in activities in which time is provided for them to attempt to perfect the activity.

HOW CHILDREN LEARN MUSIC

Teaching methods of years ago were basically simple. It was assumed that the teacher should present a body of subject matter to be memorized, recited back, and tested. This plan often had little meaning or purpose for the learner. Today's teaching methods are based upon concepts of learning. It is assumed that in order to teach effectively, the teacher must consistently enlarge his understanding of how children grow and learn. The conclusions of research point strongly toward basing methods of teaching music upon concepts such as the following:

CONCEPTS OF LEARNING MUSIC

Understanding concepts of learning stimulates teachers to seek better ways in which to help children grow and develop in their musical responsiveness. Children learn best:

1. when they are in a rich and stimulating musical environment
2. when they see meaning and purpose in what they are doing, can make functional application of what they are doing, and have a part in establishing their purposes
3. when they actively participate in a variety of musical activities
4. when their music activities relate to past experiences
5. when their music activities are on their own physical, intellectual, and social maturity level
6. when they have satisfying experiences in music
7. when their daily living needs are adequately met, and when they are in good health
8. when they have good models with which to identify, and which they can imitate
9. when they experience wholesome social and emotional relationships with their peers and with their teachers
10. when their interest is motivated, and when they are ready to learn
11. when their learning is reinforced by positive conditioning such as encouragement and recognition of progress
12. when they have a part in evaluating their progress in music
13. when they conceive of what they are doing as part of a larger pattern (or *Gestalt*)
14. when the activity involves frequent and brief periods of meaningful drill and repetition
15. when practice is characterized by continued change for the better, not by mere repetition of the same thing
16. when there is a problem to be solved

Effective teachers of music utilize techniques that help boys and girls *retain* what they have learned and *transfer* these learnings to other situations in music. They do this by planning carefully each music lesson, utilizing the concepts of learning listed above, and by relating each lesson to the previous lesson, each week's work in music to the previous week's, and relating the present year's work to the past year's work, thus developing sequence and continuity, and providing for transfer and generalizations of learning.

TRENDS IN TEACHING MUSIC

The greater need for music in a mechanized age as a wholesome relief from monotony and as a wholesome way to spend the increasing amount of leisure time resulting from automation, combined with recent research on how children grow and learn, has revolutionized the music program since the beginning of the twentieth century. Some of the trends that influence the teaching of music today are given below:

1. Music is not an isolated subject; it is a functional skill that relates to the part music plays in the lives of people.
2. Music is part of the entire school curriculum, to be engaged in whenever it is needed by the children, besides being a subject in its own right with a special period devoted to it.
3. Instrumental, vocal, and general music are taught from the same basic premises; the three areas have become more logically and closely related.
4. The characteristics of child development—the physical, social and emotional, intellectual, aesthetic, and spiritual—help determine content and sequence in music programs.
5. Music knowledge and understanding are taught through study and analysis of music itself rather than from memorizing facts about music.
6. Insistence on rigid standards of achievement in music has tended to lessen owing to increased recognition of the wide variations of ability present at any grade level.
7. Teachers of music plan for individuals and small groups as well as for an entire class; there is a trend toward increased concern for *each* child in music instruction.
8. The classroom teacher plans for a balance of activities during the school day that includes music; both classroom teacher and music specialist are also concerned with a balance of activities within the music program itself.
9. Specific musical activities are presented when children have sufficient maturity to profit from them. However, television, radio, recordings in the home, domestic and foreign travel, and increased contact with musical events in the community have prepared some children for certain musical experiences somewhat earlier than in former years.
10. Drill is employed in teaching music when children understand the purpose of what they are doing; it is employed for short periods at frequent intervals.
11. An increase in type and variety of music activities has been found necessary in order to provide for differences in children's abilities and interests.
12. More and varied instructional materials have been found necessary to meet the needs of today's music instruction. A single music text no longer suffices; it is supplemented by other texts and by other materials.
13. Music specialists are expected to have an understanding of the

elementary school curriculum; classroom teachers are expected to be musically competent.

14. Music skills and note reading are taught in relation to their immediate functional use by children or to children's genuine interest in them.

15. There is increased emphasis on music as a thinking, problem-solving process, with recognition of the importance of design in this art form and its connotations with regard to logic, order, and ethical and spiritual values.

16. There is more interest in the evaluation of entire music programs.

17. Teachers are more aware of the value of evaluating their teaching techniques and procedures and of the use of the results as a basis for improving the quality of teaching.

18. Music is more often related to home and community music activities than formerly.

19. Music specialists are being employed in larger numbers in situations where classroom teachers are not musically competent.

20. The quality of music instruction is under increasing scrutiny because of the knowledge that the purposes of music education can be achieved only through music experiences of quality.

THINGS TO DO

ASPECTS OF LEARNING: SOCIAL AND EMOTIONAL GROWTH

1. Discuss how a child's lack of success in relating himself to his peer group could affect his learning of music.

DEVELOPMENTAL CHARACTERISTICS AND TASKS

2. Review the developmental characteristics and their implications for teaching music on pages 21–40. Select a music activity and determine how it should be approached at a specific age level.

3. Observe children in an elementary school music class. Identify the developmental characteristics of the age level observed. Relate how the teacher incorporates his knowledge of these characteristics in his teaching.

4. Read and analyze the developmental tasks as defined by Robert J. Havighurst in *Developmental Tasks and Education,* Longmans, Green & Co., Inc., 1954, pp. 33–62, to determine their relation to music teaching.

CONCEPTS OF LEARNING

5. Select a music activity such as learning to sing a melody, play an instrument, or to respond with accuracy to rhythmic pulse, and discuss readiness factors for it.

6. Suggest two or three ways in which a teacher could motivate the learning of a music activity such as singing a song, listening to a recording, or responding to a rhythm.

7. According to the concepts of learning, what would underlie the successful teaching of music notation?

8. Observe children in an elementary school music class, and relate how the teacher uses concepts of learning in the lesson.

REFERENCES AND MATERIALS

GENERAL

Elliott, Raymond, *Teaching Music, Methods and Materials for Elementary Schools.* Columbus, Ohio: Charles E. Merrill Books, Inc., 1960, pp. 3–6.

CHILDREN'S GROWTH

Havighurst, Robert J., *Developmental Tasks and Education.* New York: Longmans, Green & Co., Inc., 1954, pp. 33–62.
Jenkins, Gladys, et al., *These Are Your Children,* rev. ed. Chicago: Scott, Foresman & Company, 1953.
Jersild, Arthur T., *Child Psychology,* 5th ed. Englewood Cliffs, N.J.: Prentice-Hall, 1960.
Olson, Willard C., *Child Development,* 2nd ed. Boston: D. C. Heath & Company, 1959.

LEARNING

Association for Supervision and Curriculum Development, *Learning and the Teacher.* Washington, D.C.: National Education Association, 1959.
————, *Learning More About Learning.* Washington, D.C.: National Education Association, 1959.
Klausmeier, Herbert J., *Learning and Human Abilities: Educational Psychology.* New York: Harper and Row, 1961.

Chapter Three

CLASSROOM MANAGEMENT AND PLANNING

A teacher's knowledge and skill in music are of value in the classroom only in terms of his ability to organize and manage the music activities in that classroom so that they strike a balance between the routine and the creative, between stability and change. Efficient routine is necessary to care for detail; the main reason for taking care of detail is to provide more pupil-teacher time and energy for creative and problem-solving types of learning and teaching. A teacher needs to know procedures that should be routinized and those that should not. The most effective and efficient routine procedures should be selected, then they should be used consistently so that they become habitual. They should be such that they have value in similar situations elsewhere in life. The children should have a part in planning classroom routines and carrying them out; children should understand fully the value of these procedures, exactly how they are to be done, and they should evaluate the degree of efficiency resulting from them. It is important that a new teacher not change routines already established in a school unless there is good and sufficient reason for change, and unless the children are guided into new and more efficient routines in a gradual way.

PHYSICAL CONDITIONS OF THE ROOM ENVIRONMENT

VENTILATION, TEMPERATURE, AND LIGHTING

It is obvious that learning is difficult when attempted in impure air, uncomfortable temperatures and improper lighting. The busy teacher who is in the same classroom all day will sometimes fail to notice insufficient ventilation, unhealthy temperatures, and improper lighting because of the gradual changes in the room as the day progresses. While teachers should always be alert to these factors, children should assume part of this responsibility. Classroom committees can be established to give children experience in assuming responsibility and to relieve the teacher of part of this routine task.

CLEANLINESS, BEAUTY, AND INTEREST

A room that is conducive to good learning is clean and has aesthetic appeal; it should be a healthful and beautiful place in which to live. Such things as cleanliness, furniture arrangement, and color schemes have subtle effects upon physical and emotional health. The learning of music should emphasize aural beauty, but this should be reinforced by visual beauty, for sensitivity to the beautiful should extend to all the senses. Children should become consciously involved in making their classroom a beautiful, interesting, and healthful place in which to learn, and they should reach a point where they will not tolerate uneven window shades or Venetian blinds, the leaving of litter on the floor after an activity has ended, unwatered and drooping plants, and dirty chalkboards. Bulletin boards can assist musical learning, and on them can be mounted information about community musical events, composers, recommended radio and television programs, musical achievements of pupils, charts, musical symbols, cartoons, jackets from books about music and from recordings, newspaper and magazine clippings, notation of unnamed familiar songs which are to be identified by studying this notation, favorite songs, rhythm patterns, and pictures relating to musical subjects. However, the bulletin board must be arranged attractively and changed frequently if it is to accomplish its mission of attracting maximum interest.

Centers of interest are features of the modern classroom, and the classroom teacher uses them to stimulate interest in many areas of study, including music. The music center has been called the "music corner." It is located out of the traffic lines, in a place in the room both secluded and accessible. It may consist of a table upon which various musical materials are placed, and could include a bulletin board. On the table could be books, bells and other small instruments, music to play on the instruments, recordings, record player, and, in lower primary grades, various sound-producing materials for experimentation. Children should be free to use the music center during the part of the school day set aside for special interests or at other times, such as before and after school and after satisfactorily completing other work. Soft mallets for the bells and earphones with the record player can eliminate interference with other activities in the room. By teacher-pupil planning, standards for the use of the music center must be established. These standards should indicate when and how children are to work in the music center.

The music program requires extensive equipment, all of which should be stored in orderly fashion. Series books should have their definite place on shelves or in cabinets if they are not in the children's desks. Recordings, autoharp, bells, song flutes, record player, percussion instruments, and charts have their special places, too. Children share in the storage of these items, and are taught to take responsibility for keeping this equipment in order and in good condition. It is assumed that by pupil-teacher planning, children will learn to take pride in orderliness, cleanliness, and beauty in the classroom—a pride and interest they will take with them outside the school.

It should be added that an attractive room is not very effective if the people in it do not have good posture and do not exemplify cleanliness and good taste in their own appearance. Good singing implies good posture, and clean and attractive surroundings imply clean and attractive individuals.

FLEXIBLE USE OF ROOMS

The varied activities in music make movable furniture a necessity. Seating (or temporary standing) will be changed at times for singing in large and small groups, playing instruments, creative interpretations, rhythmic responses, and dance. Some children may need special seating if they have difficulty hearing or seeing. The manner in which the children will move from one activity to another is established by clear instructions from the teacher and by teacher-pupil planning, which needs well-planned questions from the teacher that stimulate the children to plan and take responsibility for this part of classroom routine. Leaving and entering a music room, going to and from a music room or assembly room, and moving books, instruments, and other materials are other aspects of school routine that need planning, reminders, and repetition so that good habits are formed that may prevent problems from arising.

Another use of the room is in connection with listening to recordings, when, to reflect the mood of compositions, shades might be drawn, lights turned on, color employed, or objects placed in a way to heighten the aural effect.

SELECTION AND HANDLING OF MATERIALS

When series books are selected, the teacher considers such things as print size, clarity of notation, a good grade of paper that is free from eye-straining high gloss, ease of handling by children, color, illustrations, and general attractiveness, a well organized and comprehensive index, content that appeals to the age group, general durability, quality of the cover, simplicity and musicality of accompaniments, helpfulness of the teachers' manuals, and quality of the recordings.

When instruments and equipment are selected, the teacher chooses those that produce excellent tone quality, that are durable, attractive, and easy to store, that are suitable for the age group; instruments meeting these qualifications are often those designed and sold for school use. Chairs and desks should be selected to fit the varying sizes of children found in a class.

When songs are selected, the teacher seeks both simplicity and variety in the melody, repeated parts that assist rapid learning, content interesting to the age group, proper range for the voices, appropriate length for the age level, rhythmic appeal, and a suitable, attractive accompaniment. He examines the song to find what teaching purpose it can serve, such as those associated with rhythmic response, listening, tone matching, playing instruments, dramatization, assembly singing, relationship to material studied in other areas, and usefulness for public performance. It must pass these tests: "Is this song worth learning?" and "Is it a worthy art song or a folk song that is authentic?"

Teachers should have necessary materials assembled, should know how to use them, and should plan necessary routine with the children. A system of distributing materials and collecting them should be planned with and executed by the children, who should know where and how to store them. For example, if tonettes are used, each should be labeled with the child's name; they should be placed in the plastic bags that are made for them in order to keep them clean; they should not be taken home until the child can play reasonably well; a place should be selected to store them, such as a box on a shelf, and they should be played and treated as musical instruments, not as noisemakers. For sanitary reasons children should not exchange instruments, but if this is necessary, a disinfectant that can be placed on plastic must be used; the instruments must be cleaned periodically with disinfectant, and a small brush or cotton swab.

Standards must be established, preferably with the children, for proper use of the room in viewing television and films, listening to radio programs, and using the music center. Provision should be made for displays of music materials other than at the music center, and for the filing or storing of music charts when they are not on display. A classified card file of recordings, a card file of available books about music, and a vertical file of pictures should be placed conveniently for the teacher as he prepares lesson plans.

ROUTINE AND SYSTEMATIC PROCEDURES

While over-routinization can stifle creativity, the proper amount saves time and assists the orderly procedure of events in the music period. Experienced teachers have found certain ideas helpful.

A chord played on piano or autoharp, or a tone played on the bells can be a signal for a change of activity in the classroom. Such musical means to give directions are much more conducive to pleasant feelings than the teacher's voice directing children to do something.

The art of asking questions. Teachers should plan questions in advance. They should be formulated in such a way that a topic will be developed sequentially and consistently before introducing another one. These questions should require creative thinking and discussion rather than "Yes" and "No," or memorized answers. The teacher should be prepared to follow such questions with others that ask *how, why, when, who, what, where,* and for *explanation, comparison,* and *to what extent.* Such questioning stimulates reasoning and problem-solving. Questions should be formulated and distributed in such a way that both slow and fast learners can participate. Children should not be hurried into replying to questions by the teacher calling on the first child who raises his hand, because the purpose of asking questions is to stimulate the thinking of all. A general rule is to wait until several children are ready to reply. Questions should be brief, explicit, and challenging so that little or no restating is necessary. To communicate with children, one must use a vocabulary that is understood by them. To involve the children further, to stimulate discussion, and to develop the topic at hand, the teacher should encourage them to help clarify or express their opinions concerning the answers given to questions by their classmates.

When a student asks the teacher a question that is suitable for class discussion, it is good practice to refer it to the class. Then, if the class cannot give an adequate answer, it is the teacher's responsibility either to answer it or to provide time for the class to find the answer. Aggressive children should not be permitted to dominate discussions. The teacher should do his utmost to help children succeed in class discussion, and to save them from possible embarrassment. If a child cannot answer a question, the teacher might ask the other children how they might help him. Children who are having difficulty in phrasing answers should not be interrupted by the teacher, nor should the teacher permit ridicule. It is possible that these children may know the answer, but their command of oral expression is not yet adequately developed. A particularly effective type of question is one that involves the child in a more personal way, by having him imagine that he is in certain situations, or that he is a famous composer, and asking him what he would then do in certain circumstances. An example of this is the question one teacher asks: "If you were a little boy named Wolfgang Mozart, and were five years old, what kind of music would you write for the keyboard?" . . . "Why?"

Questions to avoid include, "Who knows . . . ?" and "Who wants to . . . ?" For example, "Who wants to take the autoharp to Miss Palmer's room?" can upset the entire class. What the teacher should do is not ask, but say calmly, "Mary, please take the autoharp to Miss Palmer's room."

In conclusion, ask pertinent, provocative, and concise questions; then give time for the group to think through their possible answers carefully; designate the child who is to answer; establish a classroom environment in which the child's ideas are respected, and in which helpful, constructive criticisms can be made.

It should be remembered that in music classes little musical learning may take place if talking and discussion predominate, since the skills of musical performance are gained by actively performing music, not by answering questions. Proper questions in music class are based upon music activities, and follow the activity as well as precede it. They stimulate better listening, better singing, better rhythmic responses, better playing of instruments, more creativity, and better understanding and use of notation.

Part of preparation for the music class is the removal of any objects or materials from the desks that could take attention away from the lesson. Proper posture for singing should become habitual (see Chapter Six) for reasons known and understood by the children. Books should be held up in a manner that encourages good singing posture and makes it easy to see the teacher.

Definite purposes and directions should be established with the children. The teacher should occasionally make certain of this by asking a child to state in order the things that were decided upon.

Special music teachers who teach in a music room should assign seats to pupils so the roll can be taken in the shortest possible time. When this is done, children should be given a reasonable choice of seats and a part in the planning of this seating arrangement so that they understand the necessity of it. Children in intermediate grades can take the roll, with the roll-takers alternating each week or so. Other children can be class monitors to distribute and collect books and other materials. Still others can be delegated responsibility for room temperature, ventilation, and lighting. These responsibilities develop needed social skills, self-esteem, and a feeling of contributing to the welfare of others. Teacher and pupils should evaluate their effectiveness from time to time.

In class discussions, it is usually better to call individual children by name rather than always to wait for volunteers. This procedure helps the class progress more evenly and efficiently.

All materials used in a lesson should be assembled in advance. Special music teachers often have some of these on carts that they wheel from room to room. When a teacher makes advance preparations for a lesson by doing such routine things as assembling materials, writing on the chalkboard the titles and page numbers of the songs, words of rote songs, notation for class study, the order of music activities, and other directions, he promotes general efficiency. Through pupil discussion, evaluation and modification of the order and directions of activities indicated, children have a part in the planning, and see meaning and purpose in the sequences of activities included in the lesson. Thus time is saved for developing a variety of creative and significant activities within the lesson. When verbal directions are given, they should be stated clearly and concisely, thus lessening the need for repeating them. The teacher should make certain that every child can see and hear what is spoken, sung, played, danced, or dramatized.

Testing devices in singing, rhythmic responses, and playing, and checklists or other evaluative techniques can be planned to determine readiness for music activities. The teacher needs to know how much the class knows in order to plan music lessons wisely. Thus, finding out how much a group knows about symbols of notation or what its vocal range is will reveal to the teacher what some of his purposes will be, purposes based upon "where the children are" musically at this particular time. Later, the teacher must know "where every child is" in musical understanding and responsiveness in order to plan skillfully.

Children who are in advance of the class musically should be assigned work through which they can continue to grow at their own rate. Such a child might prepare a song to teach to the class, practice an instrumental part to add to a song, create an accompaniment on the piano, play a song on the bells, prepare a descant to add to a song, or present a short listening lesson based upon a teacher-approved recording of his choice.

All teachers should know the *names* of the children. Even before they see the children, names can be learned from photographs in the school records. Special music teachers sometimes have the children wear name tags until they can remember the names. Knowledge and use of names places a teacher in closer relation to children at once, has profound influence on discipline, and is a vital aspect of good classroom management. Thus special effort must be made by every teacher to learn children's names as rapidly as possible.

Interruptions must be expected. These can include visits by the principal, another teacher or pupil, parent, or supervisor. A child should be appointed to be the host or hostess to care for visitors' needs; this responsibility changes each week to another child.   When a visitor comes into the room to observe, the child will see that there is a chair and a music book for him so that he can follow the lesson and perhaps join in the singing.   This procedure eliminates the stopping of the lesson by the teacher.   With children prepared for the possibility of such visits, the class will continue without interruption, not only saving time and confusion, but contributing to the children's learning of social skills and proper human relations.   It is a good lesson in courtesy for the children to take pride in making visitors comfortable.   Unscheduled announcements over intercom systems are another type of interruption for which children should be prepared and for which teacher-pupil planning should result in an agreed-upon response.

A simple technique in teaching rote singing that relates to classroom management is for the teacher to point to himself when he wants the class to listen to his voice, then to point toward the class when it is their turn.   By such simple signals, the teacher is able to convey ideas without having to give spoken directions.

Collecting data for effective music teaching.   Planning for effective music teaching is based upon the knowledge of each child, on knowledge of available music materials and supplies, and knowledge of the curriculum.   Some of this information can come from observing and recording children's musical performance and attitudes in music classes, while some can come from cumulative school records.   Still more of it comes from knowledge of the home environment and general community environment. Obviously, some of this can be accumulated and recorded rather quickly, while other aspects of it may take considerably more time to assemble.   It is also obvious that until a teacher "knows" each child's musical status, it is not possible to plan music lessons that will assist each child's musical growth.   Knowledge of available music materials and supplies comes from school inventories.   Knowledge of the curriculum comes from individual study and participation on committees concerned with curriculum development.

In the classroom the teacher observes vocal ranges, attitudes, social aptitudes, rhythmic ability, evidence of special talents, special interests, and special problems.   After each music class, he should record such information, perhaps in a card file or on a special form that he uses for each child.   At times he will work with individuals and small groups to determine such things as exact voice ranges.

From school records and from questioning teachers who taught the children in prior years, relevant information can be gleaned.   Such information may include significant health records, past musical experiences and achievements, data assembled from parent conferences over the years, family histories, and information regarding social and emotional adjustments. Any pertinent facts should be recorded in the teacher's files and made readily accessible so that it can be used in planning music lessons that contain activities that help each child. Parent conferences and questionnaires given to the children can reveal needed information about the home and community musical environment, such as parents' musical abilities and interests, musical activities of brothers and sisters, radio and television program preferences, and record collections.

The teacher should consult school and classroom accession and inventory records to familiarize himself with available music materials and supplies. Teachers in the entire school should work co-operatively to inventory and make available to each other the materials centered in the general supply room of the school as well as in each classroom. Such inventories should always be current, thus revealing the latest acquisitions.

ENCOURAGING SELF-CONTROL AND DEMOCRATIC BEHAVIOR

Class control is a complicated process, involving many different personalities, each unique. Therefore, there are no specific solutions that will apply in all situations. Every teacher is different, and each must determine what techniques function best for him in terms of both his personality and those of the children. In order for learning to take place, there must be order and control. The nature of the activity determines to an extent the precise type of order and control. Control is evidenced when each child accepts his responsibilities and carries them out without disturbing others. Democratic behavior is furthered through teacher-pupil planning in which the children have a major part in defining the conditions necessary to learn most effectively, and deciding how to achieve them. The feeling is developed that the classroom is the *children's* classroom and that each child has a definite responsibility in helping establish and maintain the standards by which it functions. Such a classroom helps develop the importance of the individual, a sense of respect for others, ability to work with others, and a maximum of self-control. Since the teacher realizes that skill in self-control develops slowly, and that children regress from time to time, he carefully evaluates the standards that the children have set up for each specific activity, their success in maintaining these standards, and what they need to do next time to improve. Standards for a listening activity will be different from those for a singing activity. Until these standards are well established, they might well be reviewed before a lesson. After introducing the lesson, the teacher might say, "Now, let us all think together about the standards we decided we would observe when we listen to music." Time is given for everyone to think about this, then one child is asked to review a standard, and so on, until the class is thoroughly conscious of their earlier decision. After the standards are well learned and incorporated into the behavior of most of the pupils, the teacher works with individuals who have not learned to modify their behavior in accordance with the established standards.

Behavior relates to concepts of learning. If the concepts of learning are incorporated in teaching, behavior problems are at a minimum. These concepts, outlined in Chapter Two, are simply applied common sense. When they are used, learning takes place more rapidly and effectively. However, approximately one child in every 25 may be emotionally and socially maladjusted to the extent that what is being proposed here can have little effect. Such a child may need medical or psychiatric attention.

FACTORS AFFECTING CLASS CONTROL

There are many factors that influence children's behavior. Most classroom misbehavior is the direct result of conditions in the learning environment that could have been prevented, had the teacher given proper consideration to the following:

Physical comfort. Children who are too cold, too warm, too crowded, who must breathe stale air, who cannot see or hear what is going on, who are not comfortably seated, or have been seated too long, or have been physically active for too long, often misbehave. Children should be seated so as to facilitate their participation in and concentration on the activity at hand.

Organization and proper routine. Teachers who are well prepared, and who have made provision for proper directions and routine, usually exemplify a feeling of confidence and security that is reflected in the behavior of the child. Children sense insecurity in teachers, and they are disturbed by it. Therefore, the teacher must make careful plans for the learning activities and assemble all materials needed in developing them. He must also give attention to such details as how to begin and conclude the lesson, how to keep it progressing steadily and thoroughly toward realization of the intended purposes, how to seat or group the children for specific activities, how to distribute and collect materials, when to change or alternate activities, and how to evaluate and summarize with the children the accomplishments of the day. The reader may wish to refer to pages 63–67 in this chapter.

Challenging every child. Children who are engaged in activities that are interesting and worthwhile to them are normally well-behaved. Those who fail to find interest and purpose in what they are asked to do become bored and often disturb others. If children have a part in the planning of activities, they are ordinarily interested in them and believe them to be worth while. Most children are attracted by activities that deal with significant concepts selected in terms of their maturation level and interests.

The social environment and the teacher. Wholesome pupil-pupil and teacher-pupil relationships, including a feeling of acceptance and unity, are basic factors in class control. The teacher builds trust and respect in children by exhibiting these qualities in his relations with children. He also builds trust and respect among the pupils by providing opportunities for each to succeed in some aspect of music and thus gain the approval of his classmates, and for them to develop courtesy toward each other by teaching them how to respect ideas and abilities through mutual assistance and through the use of constructive criticism. Democratic behavior is not innate; it must be learned. The teacher will find ways to recognize and encourage those who show improvements in behavior and in work habits. He shows respect for the personality of each child. The teacher knows that children reflect his enthusiasm, interest, and confidence. This confidence is fundamentally based upon the knowledge that what he is teaching is significant to the physical, social, emotional, aesthetic, and intellectual development of children. A teacher should be happy, well-adjusted, and should truly want to teach. He assists children in solving their own behavior problems, but when unable to do this in specific cases, he seeks assistance. He knows that he loses prestige if he repeatedly sends pupils to the principal, so he does this only as a last resort. His own behavior is consistent, understanding, and firm, and he has a sincere interest in every child. He has a good sense of humor, sees humor in many situations, and knows that humor can help in the solution of problems. He refrains from using ridicule and sarcasm, and is mature in his behavior. As an adult, he is objective, thus is not overly friendly or emotionally attached to the children. If he is in error, or does not know the answer to a problem, he admits it. He retains his self-control, and is a dependable adult in whom children can have confidence and faith. He deals with individuals who have behavior problems in private as much as possible, since this is usually much more effective and is less disturbing to both the troublemaker and the class. The class is not made to suffer for what one or two children may do. He is generous with his praise whenever praise is due, and emphasizes the positive. His speaking voice is pleasant and varies in pitch and intensity. He knows that a voice that reveals tension disturbs children. His singing voice is natural, sincere, and pleasing. He approaches difficult situations calmly, and seeks reasons for behavior problems. In order to accomplish these things, he tends to his own physical and mental health by getting sufficient rest and wholesome recreation. His personal appearance is such that it increases the children's respect and serves to remind them to be neat and orderly in their appearance.

GENERAL CONSIDERATIONS

Know the children's names and use class leaders. Books and materials should be distributed after directions for an activity have been determined, or after the standards established for the activity have been reviewed. Anticipate possible problems, and plan ways to offset them. Intersperse appropriate music throughout the day to relieve tensions and to unify the group. Through thoughtful selection of music, a teacher can calm or stimulate the class as he desires. Small difficulties can be avoided by simple actions. For example, if a teacher sees a child about to trip another in rhythmic movement, or about to throw an eraser, he can ask the child a direct question that brings him back into the group activity at once. To head off trouble such as this, the teacher must keep his eye on the members of the class at all times. For instance, he cannot focus his attention on notation in a music book or on piano accompaniments so exclusively that he cannot see the class. This necessitates complete familiarity with the song being taught and its accompaniment. The division of the class at times into several groups, one singing, one accompanying, and the third evaluating the musical performance of the others, is conducive to class control because it gives every child something specific to do. Other purposeful assignments to keep individual children occupied and therefore "out of trouble" could include tending the record player, pressing the buttons on an autoharp, playing the bells, conducting, or interpreting music creatively through bodily movement or dramatization. The teacher should refuse to talk when children are talking, and when he begins to speak, should do so in a low-pitched, calm, positive, soft but easily heard voice.

All behavior is goal-centered and has specific causes. Teachers must continually collect information about pupils in order to understand the motives for their behavior and to attempt to deal with the causes of it. They should endeavor to treat the causes, and not confuse them with the symptoms, which may be the overt actions of the child. When a child must be corrected in behavior, this should be done with due consideration for his background and motives. Because every child is different, the manner of rebuke appropriate for one may not be appropriate for another.

The ultimate goal of the teacher is to assist the child in developing the skill and desire to assume responsibility for his own behavior. Such competence is necessary in a democratic society.

PLANNING FOR TEACHING

Before a teacher can plan purposeful, significant, and challenging music activities for and with children, he must assemble all available information about the children in the class; he must know any individual pupil's handicaps—such as poor hearing, eyesight, damaged heart—and he must know all special aptitudes, talents, maturity levels and competencies in the skills of music; he must know the pupils' attitudes toward, and appreciation of music, and their types of previous music experiences in the home, community, and school.   Personal needs, interests, and problems should be met by planning a variety of activities and by carefully selecting the materials of instruction.   The teacher should know the level of musical understanding and competence of each child in all areas of music —singing, rhythm, understanding of music notation, playing of instruments, creating, and listening.

THE SCHEDULE INFLUENCES PLANNING

In order for a teacher to make effective plans, he must take into consideration the type of schedule employed by the school.   If the music teacher is a music specialist, he may be scheduled to appear in many different classrooms, or have many different groups of boys and girls come to a music room.   The music periods will be of varying length, usually from 15 to 30 minutes, depending upon the age level.   This teacher needs to know the other school activities and interests of these boys and girls in order to interrelate their music class and their other classes.   He needs to know the type of activity they have been engaged in before he teaches them music, and what type of activity they are to do after the music period is over.   All these things affect to a degree the content of his daily plans.   If the music teacher is a classroom teacher, he may have one of several types of schedules, from a type that is as definitely scheduled as the music specialist's to an exceedingly free and flexible plan that may change almost daily.   Furthermore, the classroom teacher will not only teach music during a music period, but will have music at several points during the day for different purposes, such as alleviating fatigue.

A typical definitely scheduled fifth-grade day might look like this:

9:00–10:00	Planning, news, and social studies
10:00–10:10	Recess
10:10–10:30	Physical education
10:30–11:00	Language arts
11:00–11:10	Recess
11:10–12:00	Reading
12:00– 1:00	Lunch
1:00– 1:10	Stories, rest, listening to music
1:10– 1:50	Arithmetic
1:50– 2:00	Recess
2:00– 2:40	Science
2:40– 3:15	Music and art

Notice that this schedule alternates quiet and active work, and that music can be used in other periods such as social studies, physical education, rest, and language arts.

A typical flexible schedule organized by some classroom teachers for fifth grade would be quite different, because it might change very frequently. Instead of periods, there are *areas* of work, and all class activities are included in seven major areas, or large blocks of time. This type of schedule allows for a higher degree of relationship of content in all areas and for greater flexibility of scheduling. Notice that music appears in some form in each area:

Areas of Work	*Approximate Time Allotment*
I. *Daily Living Activities.* Midmorning and noon lunch, rest (which can include listening to appropriate music), toileting, washing hands, and housekeeping duties.	1/24 of the day (15 minutes)
II. *Social Studies Program.* Group socializing experiences which emphasize problem-solving in history, geography, science and health and which involve such activities as planning and discussing, reading and research; trips, observations, experiments; learning appropriate songs, poems, and dances; using audio-visual aids; creative work —writing poems and songs, creating rhythms and chants, and designing costumes in connection with some unit of work.	1/3 or more of the day (two hours)
III. *Skills.* Small-group or individual instruction in reading, writing, spelling, listening, speaking, music, and arithmetic skills.	1/3 of the day (90 minutes to two hours)
IV. *Aesthetic, Creative, and Recreational Activities.* Art, music, poetry, storytelling, dramatics, rhythms, literature, and play activities. (Time *scheduled* for music in this area.)	1/4 of the day (90 minutes)
V. *Special Interests.* Individual projects, reading, research, and experiments in any worthy area of special interest; special group interests such as band, orchestra, and chorus.	1/24 of the day (75 minutes per week)

The above allotment varies from day to day.   The daily program is flexible in order to provide for the children's varying interests and needs. The different stages in the development of an experience require different lengths of time.   The amount of flexibility varies in accordance with the age of the children, the size of the class, and the personal needs of the group.

In order for music to function properly in the lives of boys and girls, it must be an integral and vital part of this program.   It belongs logically and naturally *in each of the above areas,* and the good teacher sees opportunities for its use and employs it at appropriate times throughout the school day as is shown in the following paragraphs.

Daily living activities.   All phases of a well-balanced school program are closely related in order to provide the balance of activities needed for the children's normal development.   Properly organized daily routine activities establish an environment conducive to a feeling of security and freedom.   Physical needs must be met before learning in music or in any other activity becomes satisfying and worth while.   Daily living needs are taken care of by both the children and the teacher so that work in all areas of learning will be more attractive and effective throughout the entire day. Music can be a part of daily classroom living from the beginning to the end of the day, adding satisfying variety throughout.   A dull dark day can be brightened by cheery music.   Relaxation and alleviation from fatigue can be provided at any needed time through appropriate music activities.   Imagination can be stimulated, and excitement can be calmed and controlled pleasantly by music.

Social studies program.   In this area, experiences center around the personal and social problems of living.   Pupils use many fields of knowledge; therefore, a large block of time is essential for carrying out these activities.   The subject matter incorporated in this program includes history, geography, health, and science, with language arts, art, and music also included whenever they add to the solution of a problem.   In most states, the social studies program for grades one and two concerns problems of living in the immediate community—home, school, and neighborhood.   Children in grades three and four are generally concerned with the community and its relationship to other communities.   In grades five and six the major emphases are on problems of the community, state, and nation, and their relationship to the problems of other countries. Widespread emphasis is presently being given to understanding the people and cultures of the world at all age levels.   For example, the New Social Studies Series published by Silver Burdett includes such titles as *Work in the World, Play and Fun in the World, Pets of the World.* Recent music series books contain song material from all over the world that relates directly to social studies units.   Since the areas of study for the various age levels have been chosen by educators according to the needs, interests, and past experiences of the particular age groups, it follows that combining music with these areas is one of the surest ways to make music meaningful and purposeful. In turn, *music has the power to "illuminate" subject matter, thereby adding interest, understanding, satisfaction, and enjoyment to learning. It motivates learning because it appeals to children's imagination, emotions, and moods.*

Skills. This area provides for the teaching of reading, speaking, listening, writing and spelling, scientific thinking, computation, work-study skills, music skills, and social skills. The need for work on these and other skills may grow out of the social studies program, thus making the activity more meaningful to the children. Ideally, the most effective time for teaching skills in any area is when the need arises. But, since all children do not need the same amount of guidance, a special skills program is necessary. Special assistance in music is thus given to individuals and groups in the class, just as it is given in developing any of the other skills. Activities designed to teach skills can comprise one of the most interesting and satisfying areas of the daily program when the children understand the application of these skills in terms of everyday needs in solving all problems. If music is to become a personal thing to a child, he must possess the skills that will make this possible, such as listening skills, singing skills, note-reading skills, and instrument-playing skills. Then, when the need to respond to music independently arises, the child has the skills he needs and wants.

Aesthetic, creative, and recreational activities. This is the part of the day in which provision is made for the special scheduling of art, music, literature, and physical education. During the time thus provided, interests and abilities in music can be developed. Pupils are encouraged to sing, to experiment with and play various simple instruments, to listen to appropriate radio programs and recordings, to write songs and words for songs, and to participate in rhythms and create rhythmic responses. Experiences in the social studies program often motivate experimentation in the recreational and creative activities area. However, activities in art, music, literature, and physical education need not necessarily be related to other activities of the day; they possess their own value and interest to children. Wholesome learning implies *satisfying* experiences with what is to be learned. During this time, the pupils should feel free to express themselves through many media. *Music can be an important means whereby children experience success, belonging, and aesthetic satisfaction.*

Special interests. Although individual interests are considered in all areas of the daily schedule, not enough time is available, in these areas to develop these special interests and abilities. Therefore, time is provided for children to pursue their special interests in science experiments, in music groups such as band, orchestra, and chorus, in art projects, and in individual research in connection with various subjects (including reading about music and musicians). Special interest groups seldom meet more than once or twice a week. In order for these activities to be of real value in developing genuine special interests, careful planning with individuals and small groups is essential. It is in this area that the children who possess superior interest and ability in music have an opportunity to develop beyond the point ordinarily possible in activities that include the entire class.

This is a time of experimentation in education in which plans of organization and scheduling different from the two discussed above are emerging. For example, an experimental *dual progress plan* is employed in Ossining, New York. This plan combines the graded and nongraded concepts by applying the graded system to language arts, social studies, and physical education and the nongraded system to science, mathematics, arts and crafts, and music. Teachers concentrate their teaching upon those subjects in which they are most skilled, and they do not have the broad subject-matter responsibilities of the teachers in the "flexible" self-contained organization described earlier. There is ability-level grouping in music, science, and mathematics. This has profound effect upon the purposes, materials, and activities in a lesson plan. Music is taught by specialists. The school day appears as follows:

Schedule of the *Dual Progress Plan*[2]

Language Arts-Social Studies	(graded)	120 minutes
Physical Education	(graded)	30 minutes
Science	(nongraded)	40 minutes
Mathematics	(nongraded)	40 minutes
Arts and Crafts	(nongraded)	40 minutes, alternate days
Music	(nongraded)	40 minutes, alternate days

Minimum time allotments for the teaching of music as well as for other basic subjects are usually designated by state law and local regulations. Minimum time requirements are established to provide a balance of experiences in all areas of the curriculum and to protect children from classroom teachers who are inclined to spend excessive amounts of time in areas which are of special interest to them.

Recommended time allotments. Minimum time allotments for the teaching of music vary from state to state. For example, in the *Utah Guide—Kindergarten through Grade Twelve,* State of Utah, Department of Public Instruction, the specified minimum time allotment for music is as follows:

---

2 Glenn A. Brown, "The Dual Progress Plan in Music Education," *Music Educators Journal,* September–October, 1962, p. 62.

Kindergarten	90 minutes per week
First Grade	90 minutes per week
Second Grade	90–100 minutes per week
Third Grade	90–100 minutes per week
Fourth Grade	120 minutes per week
Fifth Grade	120 minutes per week
Sixth Grade	120 minutes per week

Music educators nationally have suggested the following minimum weekly time allotments:

Preschool, Kindergarten, and First Grade	100 minutes
Grades Two and Three	100 minutes
Grades Four, Five, and Six	125 minutes

The responsibility of the American public schools for the scheduling of music is implied in the following pronouncement of the Music Educators National Conference:

The Child's Bill of Rights in Music[3]

I

Every child has the right to full and free opportunity to explore and develop his capacities in the field of music in such ways as may bring him happiness and a sense of well-being; stimulate his imagination and stir his creative activities; and make him so responsive that he will cherish and seek to renew the fine feelings induced by music.

II

As his right, every child shall have the opportunity to experience music with other people so that his own enjoyment shall be heightened and he shall be led into greater appreciation of the feelings and aspirations of others.

III

As his right, every child shall have the opportunity to make music through being guided and instructed in singing, in playing at least one instrument both alone and with others, and, so far as his powers and interests permit, in composing music.

IV

As his right, every child shall have opportunity to grow in musical appreciation, knowledge, and skill, through instruction equal to that given in any other subject in all the free public educational programs that may be offered to children and youths.

V

As his right, every child shall be given the opportunity to have his interest and power in music explored and developed to the end that unusual talent may be utilized for the enrichment of the individual and society.

---

[3] The Child's Bill of Rights in Music (Chicago: Music Educators National Conference, 1950). Quoted by permission.

VI

Every child has the right to such teaching as will sensitize, refine, elevate, and enlarge not only his appreciation of music, but also his whole affective nature, to the end that the high part such developed feeling may play in raising the stature of mankind may be revealed to him.

THE DAILY LESSON PLAN

There are many different kinds of lesson plans, and they vary from subject to subject, from day to day, and from lesson to lesson. However, all well-prepared plans contain certain essential parts. These are purposes, materials, procedures, and evaluation.

Purposes. Experienced teachers do not confuse long-term and short-term purposes in daily plans. Long-term purposes are stated in *general* terms while purposes for a music lesson or activity are stated in *specific* terms. For example, "To develop enjoyment of music" and "To develop understanding of notation" might be long-term purposes for a month, a year, or for six years. They are examples of the type of purpose that is kept constantly in mind by teachers, but that *is not stated in daily plans.* The specific purposes in daily plans are those that contribute to the realization of the long-term purposes. For example, both long-term purposes of enjoying music and understanding notation are attained through specific satisfying experiences in listening, singing, playing instruments, creating, and responding to music by bodily movement. It is these specific purposes that appear in the daily lesson plan. Examples that build understanding of notation are: "To identify high and low in pitch," "To relate walking and the quarter note," "To hear, then see, identical phrases." Certain long-term purposes were stated in Chapter One, page 3. Certain short-term purposes are suggested in the chapters to follow.

Involving children in establishing their purposes. When children have a part in formulating purposes that are meaningful and significant to them, they are usually highly motivated and interested in working to realize them. Often the purposes of a music lesson will grow naturally and directly from the previous one. For example, children may realize after learning an Indian song that a ceremonial dance is needed to convey its meaning. Thus, a major purpose for the next day's lesson emerges. Purposes less obvious to the children could include analyzing the music for clues that help create the dance, or possibly reading in the library about Indian dances and listening analytically to recordings of this and other Indian dances both in and out of class. *Teachers' purposes and children's purposes are not always identical,* because the teacher sees many more ramifications in subject content and long-term objectives than the children can. The teacher assists the pupils in understanding and seeing a need for these purposes that are obscure to them, but which may be very challenging to the class once they are identified and clarified. Some teachers have difficulty in stating children's purposes. They must ask themselves why the children need to do a particular activity, then write the purpose, which usually states why they should participate in an activity. For example, "To learn the meter signature (identify the meter) in order to direct a song." Notice that the purpose and the activity are united in the child's mind. The specific purposes in a lesson plan are normally few in number, from two to five.

Materials. There are certain considerations in selecting materials. In regard to these, the teacher must answer questions such as the following: Is the song, instrument, or recording suitable in content and in difficulty for the age and ability levels in the group? Is the song or recording the right length for the attention span of the children? Is the music appealing rhythmically? Is there sufficient variety in types of songs, rhythms, and instruments? Is the melody or rhythm a type that can be easily learned? Are there repeated phrases or sections? Is there a simple accompaniment? What opportunities are presented for fulfilling the purposes of the lesson by playing percussion instruments; playing melody instruments; creating introductions, codas, chants or other added parts; dramatizing; responding rhythmically; playing tone matching or pitch games; or learning aspects of notation? Is the song useful for an assembly sing or a public performance? Do other curricular areas relate to this music? Is the music authentic and of good quality? Are the recording and the record player capable of producing the beauty of tone necessary? Are the piano and autoharp in tune? Is the song sufficiently worth while to add to the children's permanent repertoire? Is the song written within the range of the children's voices, or can it be transposed into this range? Do the materials provide quality, contrast, variety, and are they appropriate for developing sequential learning?

Procedures. The procedures are the sequential steps and activities used to realize the purposes of a lesson plan. The introduction or motivation is the first essential item of procedure in a well-planned lesson. It should help children to see meaning and purpose, and should stimulate interest and a desire to learn. One type of introduction is to have the class briefly summarize what was learned in a previous lesson, another is to have the children determine what they need to do with a song to have it ready to sing to parents at a Valentine party. "Do you think we know the words well enough?" "What do we need to do to improve our singing of the song?" Answers to the latter question can be listed on the chalkboard, and specific ways to improve the performance of the song are then briefly planned.

Creative teachers continually think of unique, clever, and meaningful ways to introduce a lesson that capture the interest and imagination of

children and develop a desire to learn.   The alert teacher of music may
secure suggested ideas from courses of study in music, professional music
textbooks, magazines, films, children's music textbooks and their accompanying teacher's manuals, and from suggestions made by music specialists.

Music teachers must avoid extensive introductions to lessons.   Children want to be actively involved in making music; they tend to lose
interest in a lesson in which verbal introductions are lengthy.   Proper
timing is essential to capture maximum interest.

The development of the lesson follows logically from the introduction.
It can include activities and problems listed in order, with motivating
questions or experiences.   Such questions should be carefully formulated
and written into the plan.   A good plan indicates *how* the teacher intends to guide an activity as well as *what* he plans to do.   The person who
is inexperienced in music teaching needs to write such plans in detail.
However, as he grows in experience, much of this detail becomes habitual,
it eventually becomes unnecessary to write it, and he can teach from
brief, undetailed plans.   In preparing to teach from a plan, the teacher
considers many things.   Among them are:

1. A classroom environment that stimulates interest in music.
2. Thorough study of the songs to be used: the meaning and pronunciation of words; knowledge of proper tempo, rhythm, and
   note values; deciding whether the song should be taught by the
   whole or part method; and acquiring such confidence and enjoyment in the songs that the children cannot help sharing the
   teacher's enthusiasm, thus stimulating their interest and learning.
3. Planning ways to involve the children in the lesson as they understand their purposes.
4. Deciding how much motivation a song requires.   (Some songs
   need none because they are easily understood, self-explanatory, and
   self-motivating.   Never waste time with unnecessary questions and
   explanations.)
5. Providing for individual differences by a variety of activities,
   materials of instruction, and types of grouping.   For example,
   musically gifted children can accompany, direct singing, and sing
   or play descants or other added parts; the class can be divided into
   performing and evaluating groups; dialogue songs can be used with
   girls and boys taking "answering back" verses; dramatizations and
   rhythmic responses can be used; a short recording can be played;
   different types of instrumental parts can be added or created.
6. Seeking opportunities for musical experimentation and creation
   by the children at their particular level of development.

7. Finding ways for children to use music notation in activities that are meaningful to them.

8. Exploring the possible uses of different audio-visual aids such as the keyboard, films, filmstrips, tape recorder, and visual aids such as charts, pictures, slides, felt board, magnetized board, posters, and chalkboard.

9. Inviting persons in the community to perform music related to the children's interests.

10. Designing the order of activities so that the lesson concludes with an activity (usually calmly satisfying) that leaves the children in an emotional state conducive to easy transition to their next school day activity in another subject area. Music specialists should observe this carefully.

The conclusion or evaluation of a lesson plan is to be considered from two points of view, the teacher's and the teacher-pupils'. From the teacher-pupil point of view, pupil participation in evaluating the results of their efforts is an important part of the learning process which often sets the stage for the next day's lesson. This can be done very simply, with the teacher asking, "Did we learn more about the songs (or activities) today?" "What did we learn?" "What do you think we did best today?" "Why?" "What do we need to do better?" "All right, we will be sure to work on that at our next lesson." Teachers should emphasize the positive —the real accomplishments—first, then after satisfaction is expressed about these, ask what the children think they need to work on next time. The teacher will, after the lesson is taught, add to the plan a statement describing the extent to which the purposes were achieved, the strengths and weaknesses of the plan, and the implications of what took place for the plan of the next lesson. Planning for the next day's lesson can be done very precisely by listing agreed-upon purposes on the chalkboard.

The exact manner of making out lesson plans is determined by supervisors of student teaching and school supervisory officials. The essential parts of any plan have been described above. However, it is impossible for teachers to guide children in logical and essential procedures necessary for realizing the purposes of a lesson plan unless they thoroughly understand the subject matter and content involved, and unless they possess the required skills to teach them.

In review, the essential parts of a daily lesson plan are:

Purposes   Establish teacher's and children's specific purposes.

Materials   Prepare and assemble all necessary books, instruments, audio-visual aids.

Procedure   Plan the steps and activities needed to realize the purposes, beginning with motivation, and review of plans stemming from the previous lesson, if any; and establish the purposes of this plan with the children.

Evaluation   At the end of the lesson, summarize and evaluate with the children what was accomplished and what needs further emphasis in the next lesson.

After the lesson the teacher analyses the strengths and weaknesses of the plan, and gleans implications from these for the next lesson.

MUSIC LEARNING IN LESSON PLANS

It was stated earlier that only from two to five specific purposes are found in most daily plans, and that these purposes form part of sequential music learnings over weeks, months, and years. The various kinds of musical learning that can be considered in the specific purposes of lesson plans follow. Notice that learning of music notation is a part of several of the classifications.

Learning about melody. Discovering pitch directions: high, low, up, down, the same; the contour of the melody, phrase, or note pattern; tonal patterns such as step, skip, scale or chord-line; the key center or home tone and movement of melody tones in relation to it; chord tones and the movement of melody tones in relation to them; key signatures in relation to melodies; intervals found in melodies; singing names of notes; letter names of the staff; different clefs; accidentals; major and minor modes; the pentatonic and chromatic scales; modal melodies; characteristic melodies of peoples of the world.

Learning about rhythm. Discovering fundamental movements and rhythms; tempos; use of terms such as ritard and accelerando; the beat or pulse; feeling accents and determining the beats in a measure, then finding the meter signature; different kinds of rhythm patterns; different kinds of note values that are found through rhythmic responses; syncopation; conductor's beats; dance steps; characteristic rhythms and dances of the peoples of the world.

Learning about linear music. Rounds, canons, chants, descants, obligatos, ostinato and bourdon; combinable songs; imitation as a device in composition; polyphony; counterpoint; fugue; listening to recordings of linear music; composing and improvising linear music.

Learning about harmonic music. Chords and their uses in accompaniments and in writing parts; part singing in two and three parts; listening to recordings of harmonic music; composing and improvising harmonic music.

Learning about tone quality. Different voices and instruments; tone color; discovering reasons for combinations of voices and instruments to gain desired effects.

Learning about intensity.   Degrees of loud and soft; discovering the function of terms such as diminuendo, accent, crescendo.

Learning about form.   Discovering the phrase and its identical and contrasting forms; balance and contrast as artistic principles; cadences; tension and release; two-part and three-part song forms; rondo, variation, concerto, opera, oratorio, and other large vocal and instrumental forms; thematic development.

Learning about styles and types of music.   National and racial styles in the music of the world; individual styles of composers; music of different periods and historical times; mood music, descriptive music, story music, and music written without nonmusical implications but for purposes of beauty or intellectual design.

REFERENCES AND MATERIALS

Byers, Loretta and Elizabeth Irish, *Success in Student Teaching.*   Boston: D. C. Heath & Company, 1961.

Hubbard, Kenneth, *Teaching Elementary School Subjects.*   New York: The Ronald Press Company, 1961.

Michaelis, John U., and Enoch Dumas, *The Student Teacher in the Elementary School.* Englewood Cliffs, N.J.: Prentice-Hall, Inc., 1960.

Wiles, Kimball, *Teaching for Better Schools.*   Englewood Cliffs, N.J.: Prentice-Hall, Inc., 1959.

Chapter Four

RESPONDING TO RHYTHM

It is the aim of the good teacher to teach children to hear, feel, and see rhythm. They will learn to listen to rhythm with their ears, to feel it and express it in movement with their bodies, and to see it in the world around them—in the motions of people, in the movements of waves against the shore, in art and architecture, and in notation, man's remarkable way of recording rhythm on paper. A true sense of rhythm comes from the innermost parts of the body and seems to extend beyond the fingers and the toes into space. Teachers of dance have always known this. Teachers of music have not always had this insight. A Swiss musician, Emil Jaques-Dalcroze,[1] found in the early part of this century that unless rhythm is first felt by the whole body, the would-be musician may produce music mechanically, without feeling, thus never developing the responsiveness essential to genuine musicianship.

Expressing rhythm through movement is an activity that music shares to an extent with physical education and creative dramatics. Music assists physical education by helping the physical movement be more rhythmic; it assists creative dramatics by heightening the dramatic expression. When physical education gives children more control over their bodies, and when creative dramatics helps to free them to interpret what they hear in music, these areas contribute to understanding music. By moving to music, children learn to hear music with perception, to respond to it with imagination, and to explore the expressive ideas it contains. An understanding of the values of rhythmic experience in the natural growth of boys and girls is an essential part of the teacher's professional preparation.

---

[1] Emil Jaques-Dalcroze, *Eurhythmics, Music, and Education.* New York: G. P. Putnam's Sons, 1921.

Of primary concern is listening to music in order to respond to it with physical movement. Singing will be actively engaged in but will not be stressed here. In the authors' opinion there is good reason for this initial emphasis upon active listening, particularly in the primary grades. When children aged five, six, and seven begin their school year, a great many of them will not be able to match tones (i.e., sing in tune). Therefore there is logic in first listening to music, then responding physically to what is heard, and in the process becoming oriented to rhythm, pitch, and mood. This builds a background of experience for better singing a little later.

However, there are important values in rhythmic responses other than the building of a background for successful singing. Among these are the development of bodily control, imagination, willingness to experiment, emotional responsiveness, and concepts of fast and slow, heavy and light, long and short, in terms of bodily movement. Furthermore, rhythmic response is a necessity in carrying out a balanced daily program of activities for children. As stated earlier, it is unnatural for boys and girls to sit quietly for long periods of time. There is evidence to show that teachers who guide their pupils in appropriate rhythmic responses, and who know the proper time to use them, can by so doing reduce pupil fatigue to a marked degree.

SUGGESTED PURPOSES FOR TEACHING RESPONSES TO RHYTHM

Children use rhythm creatively for purposes of their own. These include the sheer pleasure of moving; help in tasks such as lifting, carrying, moving their bodies, and manipulating objects; imitation of the movements of people, machines, and animals; the portrayal of imaginative ideas; expression of mood and emotion, and nonverbal communication. Teachers plan guided opportunities to assist children's rhythmic development. When they do this, they develop their plans in accordance with purposes such as those listed below. However, it should be realized that only one or two of these appear in a typical daily lesson plan. They are to be developed consistently and sequentially according to the maturity level of each child in the class. (See Chapter Two, pages 19–41, concerning learning and developmental characteristics of children.)

This list will be of assistance in writing lesson plans.

1. To develop listening skills through specific activities.
2. To develop muscular co-ordination and control (a) for large muscles, (b) for small muscles.
3. To teach specific fundamental rhythms as basic means of movement.
4. To develop creative self-expression through interpretive actions.
5. To develop the ability to sing songs with rhythmic precision.

6. To develop comprehension of musical concepts, terms, and symbols such as tempi (slow, fast); pitch (high, low); accent; ritard (gradually slower); accelerando (gradually faster); decrescendo (gradually softer); crescendo (gradually louder); pause; hold; repetition, and contrast.
7. To introduce a percussion instrument.
8. To learn to express mood through appropriate choice of percussion instruments.
9. To provide a means of participation other than singing for children who need this.
10. To teach note values through movement; to introduce notation.
11. To discover the metric accent, the rhythm of the meter, the rhythm of the notes or words, and to write a percussion score from these rhythms.
12. To discover rhythm patterns, respond to them physically or through the use of percussion instruments, and learn how to notate them.
13. To stimulate creative power to improvise and to refine the percussion score and to devise aesthetically suitable "sound effects" for appropriate songs.
14. To learn a characteristic dance.
15. To learn specific rhythm patterns related to dances and to employ percussion instruments to play these rhythms in connection with a song or a dance.
16. To develop comprehension of aspects of music structure such as rhythm patterns, the phrase, repetition, and contrasts.
17. To stimulate interest in instrumental music through use of percussion instruments.
18. To utilize rhythm for social and therapeutic reasons, such as for developing group feeling, enjoyment, relaxation, co-operation, self-discipline, and to relieve tensions.

INITIATING RESPONSES TO RHYTHM

Responses to rhythm can be initiated with limitless variety. The inventive teacher is always finding "new" ways. Certain basic approaches will be presented here, to which the teacher will eventually add his ingenious variations. Teachers respond to children; children respond to teachers, and when they motivate and stimulate each other in an environment that offers freedom to experiment and to create, many thrilling innovations can occur.

ECHO-CLAPPING

Echo-clapping is one of the simplest introductions to rhythmic instruction because normal children of school age have the physical co-ordination to do it with ease. If children can imitate the teacher's clapping perfectly, the teacher knows that the children are hearing the rhythms clapped. Children of all ages are interested when the teacher suddenly says, "Listen; can you clap what I clap?" For example:

Soon children will be able to clap improvised rhythms to be echoed by the class.

Beginning with very simple rhythm patterns, the complexity and length can grow with the increasing skill of the children in this rhythmic imitation. The activity can relate to song material and to the teaching of notation by use of a pattern or patterns that are outstanding in a song. Then, after the imitative clapping has helped the children feel the rhythm with their bodies, they can be shown what this looks like in notation, and asked if they can discover, find, or see this rhythm in the song. Perhaps the rhythm or rhythms can be played on percussion instruments to enhance the song and written on the chalkboard for use with the instruments. Thus, beginning with rhythm, the activity unfolds to include notation, singing, and experiments in creating a percussion score that, if properly guided, will increase musical sensitivity and discrimination. Particularly in the upper grades teachers can relate clapping to notation quite directly by first doing the clapping, then showing the class a chart of the rhythms clapped, and finally learning to read a song based on these rhythms. In such an instance, the rhythm patterns used would be found by the teacher by analyzing the song as a part of his preparation for the daily music lesson, and the rhythmic exercise would be a part of learning the song, and of understanding and using music notation as well as to develop good rhythmic responses.

Another interesting type of echo-clapping is the question-and-answer, in which the teacher or a child claps a rhythmic question to be answered creatively, such as:

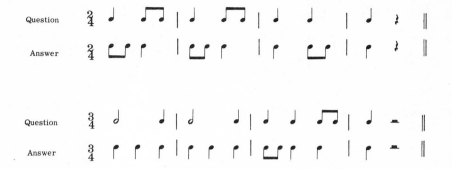

This activity leads to discovering and creating questions and answers in melody, and to increasing comprehension of the phrase.

RHYTHMIC EXERCISES

Beginning in grade two with very easy movements, teachers help children to feel basic rhythm by having them perform knee-slapping, finger-snapping, desk-tapping, and heel-stamping first as exercises, then in connection with songs and recordings.   This builds comprehension of metrical rhythm, described by the meter (time) signatures of 2/4, 4/4, 3/4, and 6/8.   After some attempts guided by the teacher, children can discover the meter rhythm themselves, and they can also devise interesting rhythms of their own.

Examples: March rhythms, as in "This Old Man," "The Caisson Song," "Pop Goes the Weasel."

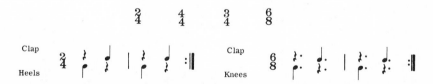

Waltz rhythms such as "Ach du lieber Augustin" ("The More We Get Together").

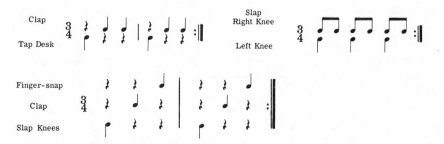

Other rhythmic exercises:

Percussion instruments can be played by teacher or children to accompany such responses or to enhance them.   Even tone bars or bell sets can be used.   While the class does one response softly in unison, one child can improvise rhythm patterns by clapping, or by using a percussion instrument or a bell set.   If the basic beat is felt and understood, intermediate grade students should be able to place these in notation if they have been taught notational concepts through experiences with fundamental movements.   (See page 76.)

Conductor's beat patterns are another rhythmic response to the meter. The entire class can do these with songs or recordings as another rhythmic exercise.   The primary (heavy) accent of each measure is indicated by a down-beat, as illustrated.   A drum or other percussion instrument played on this beat (marked *1*) will help the children hear and feel this accent. A secondary accent appears in 4/4 and 6/8 meters in beats 3 and 4, respectively.   It sometimes receives more volume also, as indicated by the italics below:

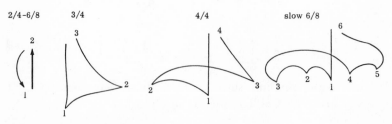

Down-Up   *Down*-Right-*Up*   *Down*-Left-Right-*Up*   *Down*-Left-Left-*Right*-Right-*Up*

Left-handed children will conduct all left and right motions as right and left—the reverse of the drawings.   Such an exercise by children while singing a song will assist them in giving each measure the correct number of beats.   They can also use them in determining the meter of a song sung or played for them by the teacher or reproduced on a recording.

WORD-RHYTHMS

The use of word-rhythms is an excellent simple and natural way to introduce rhythmic response. There is rhythm to be discovered in the spoken word, and children use and enjoy this rhythm in their play. The *sound* of words attracts children in the early primary grades, and people of all ages react to them, as testified by the rhythmic cheers at collegiate and professional athletic events. Also, the rhythms of both simple and complex note values can be assimilated with ease when teachers relate these to familiar words.

Examples:

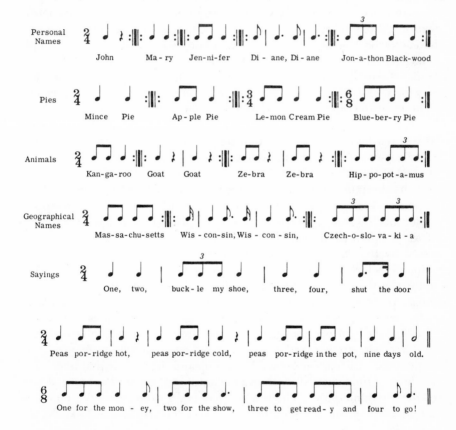

Percussion instruments, clapping, and the use of feet can be added to enhance the rhythm and add to the interest, for names can be "said" with the feet and with instruments. The teacher should be alert to the fact that most of these word-rhythms can be altered according to different ways of accenting words. For example, "Lemon cream pie" might be:

Several different rhythms can be correct for one word. The rhythms of some television and radio commercials are sometimes interesting to work with.

FUNDAMENTAL MOVEMENTS AND FREE RHYTHMIC PLAY

"Fundamental movement" is a term used in physical education. It describes simple, basic movements such as walking, running, skipping, and galloping. Series books for kindergarten and first grade contain helpful song and piano material as well as suggestions for teaching such movements. Also, teachers can quickly learn to use percussion instruments or a few notes on the piano keyboard to improvise rhythms for the simple fundamental movements to which children learn to respond.[2] In these grades the teacher should not expect every child to respond in the same way for a while; some children need time to experiment before being able to do what the others do. It is necessary that children learn fundamental movements because command of them is essential to being able to engage in free rhythmic play, some action songs, and singing games and dances. Excellent recordings are available to assist the teacher; some are listed at the end of this Chapter.

As has been indicated, music is not always required to initiate rhythmic response. For example, words for walking can be chanted, then clapped, then walked, before appropriate music is added in the tempo and rhythm of the children's walking. Other fundamental movements can be introduced by the teacher's drum beat or by word rhythms and learned by clapping before the children move to them with their whole bodies. The music can then be brought in after the rhythm is learned. The words of songs can be learned first in rhythmic speech, and the melody added later.

In primary grades further understanding of fundamental movements can be gained by using songs that suggest impersonation (imitative play). Children who are five and six years of age tend strongly to *be* what they impersonate, such as the horses that gallop and the rabbits that hop. The teaching of fundamental rhythms can continue also from the point of view of free rhythmic play. The teacher may tap a drum, play the piano, or use a recording, and ask the children what it "makes them feel like doing."

---

2 Suggestions for improvising easy piano accompaniments for rhythmic activities are found in *The Kindergarten Book*, Music for Young Americans Series, New York: American Book Company; in *Basic Music for Classroom Teachers*, 2nd ed., Englewood Cliffs, N.J.: Prentice-Hall, Inc., pp. 105–6, and in *Singing With Children*, Belmont, Calif.: Wadsworth Publishing Company, pp. 96–8.

From their own experience should come such movements as clapping, walking, running, skipping, galloping, sliding, hopping, and jumping. Through the freedom of children to respond to the rhythms of music they can discover other bodily movements which may include swinging, pushing, bouncing, pulling, bending, stretching, twisting, shaking, dodging, and striking.   Through all of this the teacher controls and guides the learning situation by helping the children relate familiar physical responses to the music they are hearing.   The teacher, while guiding the children, should do so in such a manner that each child feels he has made his personal contribution.

Walking is commonly done to 4/4 and 2/4 meters, depending on the tempo.   It is relaxed and swinging, never tense and jerky.   Children may develop different types of walking by pretending they are different characters or animals.   Marching is an outgrowth of walking.

Running is done to 4/4, 2/4, and 6/8 meters, depending on the tempo. Running on tiptoe is commonly stressed, and the movement should be kept light.

Skipping is generally done to fast 6/8 meter.   It is a step, hop, first on one foot and then on the other.   Children enjoy a large fast skip that gives them the feeling of moving high in the air.

Hopping and *jumping* are done to several meters, depending on the tempo.   Hopping is done on one foot while jumping is done with both feet together.   Children can imitate jumping rope, kangaroos jumping, and playing hopscotch.   Overly heavy movements are avoided.

Galloping is ordinarily done to fast 6/8 meter.   One foot is kept ahead of the other throughout, and the back foot is brought up to meet it. Heels never touch the floor.   Children pretend they are ponies or horses.

Swinging, swaying, and *rowing* can relax the children after the stimulation of the more active movements.   Swaying trees, branches or flowers are often imitated, as are swings, the pendulum of a clock, rocking a baby to sleep, and rowing a boat.

These and other fundamental movements are taken up in detail in physical education books.

RESPONSES RELATING TO NOTE VALUES

Note	Clapping	Chanting	Stepping
Whole	clap-flick-flick-flick*	who-o-ole-note	step-point-point-point
Dotted Half	clap-flick-flick	half-note-dot	step-point-point
Half	clap-flick	half-note	step-bend

* Some prefer to rub palms or to squeeze the hands rather than to "flick."

Note	*Clapping*	*Chanting*	*Stepping*
Quarter	clap clap	q́uart-er q́uart-er	walk walk
Eighth	clap-clap clap-clap (faster)	eighth-eighth eighth-eighth	run-run run-run
Skipping Pattern	clap—clap clap—clap	śkip-ty śkip-ty	śkip-ping śkip-ping
Galloping Pattern	clap-clap-clap clap-clap-clap	gal-lop-ing gal-lop-ing	same rhythm as skipping, therefore respond verbally, "galloping, galloping."

After children have learned to respond to note values in these ways, they can analyze the notation of simple songs by clapping, chanting, and stepping. Songs such as "Hot Cross Buns" are done by second grades late in the year, and third grades will do such songs as "Come Thou Almighty King" and "Clocks." When using this approach to notation the teacher should never forget that the primary purpose of the activity is to help children explore rhythm and sound by using their bodies. Learning the note values is important, but it is secondary to this. For example, stepping the note values is more than learning notes and rhythm; it is a means of exploring the rhythm, and even a means of creating a dance for the song being analyzed. The activity should be illustrative of the music being studied, not simply a drill on notes.

In the first grade the terms "walking note" and "running note" make sense to the child because they represent bodily movement he knows. It is recommended that the conventional note names not be emphasized here. Children in this grade do not know fractions, thus terms like "quarter" and "eighth" are usually without meaning. However, these terms are part of the vocabulary of music and learning them should follow learning the "movement terms."

When fundamental rhythms are properly taught they are invariably enjoyed by children. It takes time to develop skill in these activities; the beginning teacher is likely to try too many things at first and thus meet with some initial discouragement. As in so many other areas of education, he should "make haste slowly." Therefore, the teacher should strive for a simple and thorough approach. By the end of the first grade most children will have learned to walk, skip, run, and hop in time to music. During the second grade most children will have learned to slide, jump rope, and bounce a ball in rhythm. In third grade the ability to leap and step-hop is generally acquired.

Occasionally teachers take a rhythm from something a child is doing, or from nature or machines outside the classroom, and repeat this on a percussion instrument or on a piano. For example, they may clap or tap the rhythm of such sounds as those made by a train, hoof beats, the rain, footsteps, sawing, or a clock. The children are then asked to move to the rhythm they have heard. Percussion instruments may be selected to accompany or to represent the rhythm.

Children should not be asked to respond to rhythm until they have had the opportunity to listen carefully. Teachers often ask them to close their eyes while they listen. After this comes the question, "What did the music tell you to do?" There may follow a discussion, then the music will be repeated and the children will begin to contribute ideas to the group. The teacher will often help free rhythmic responses to grow naturally by asking such questions as, "Does the music make you feel like walking or running or skipping?" "Is it happy, sad, fast, slow?" "Is it high or low?"

Free rhythmic responses are so numerous that it is doubtful that any listing of them can ever be complete, particularly since each of them can be varied almost endlessly. Some, in addition to those already mentioned, are:

trotting	tapping	stroking	swaying
dipping	reaching	patting	rolling
tripping	grasping	creeping	hammering
stamping	banging	rocking	whirling
tossing	circling	crawling	tumbling
skating	beating	turning	sliding

Others are rising and falling in terms of crescendo (gradually louder) and decrescendo (gradually softer) and in terms of rising and falling pitch, bouncing a ball and jumping rope. For example, one way in which crescendo and decrescendo can be acted out is by a circle of children coming together at the height of the crescendo, and being at the farthest point apart at the lowest level of the decrescendo. Also, accelerando (gradually faster) and ritard (gradually slower) can be felt and seen when two children throw and catch a large ball as the music changes tempo. In this, they come closer together for a more rapid bouncing of the ball, and farther apart for the slower tempo.

Space is needed for freedom of movement, and it must be admitted that it is at a premium in some classrooms. However, excellent work can be done despite admitted handicaps, by keeping the following suggestions in mind. First, rhythmic activities need never be boisterous or unruly. Second, activities requiring space may be arranged in some larger room. However, this room should seldom be the size of a gymnasium because this can destroy the intimate feeling necessary for this type of music work. Third, many substitute responses can be made. Children seated quietly at their desks can "walk" with their hands in the air above their heads, and they can "march" with their heels while their toes remain on the floor. When clapping is required, it can be done in quiet ways such as striking the tips of the fingers of both hands together rather than using the palms, or striking the fingertips of one hand on the palm of the other hand. Fourth, part of a class often can do the rhythmic activity while others sing, chant, clap, evaluate, or perform a quiet substitute for the activity.

To sustain interest, variety is essential. No child enjoys skipping to the same music over a long period of time. A variety of accompaniments is also recommended. The teacher may use recordings, the piano, various percussion instruments, and the chanting of the voice. Still more variety may be attained by changing the tempo of the music. When song material is used, more effective results are often obtained when part of the group sings while part does the rhythmic responses—a division into performing and accompanying groups. Jumping ropes, bouncing balls, scarves, flags, and balloons may be used to make appropriate activities more colorful and impressive. These often aid the self-conscious child by focusing attention on the object, and assist the development of big, free movements. Scarves for this purpose are made of silk or lightweight nylon, longer than the child. Such length permits many uses, including dramatization.

It is important that teachers know the physical limitations of the various age groups they guide in activities that require some physical exertion. For example, if a student teacher is unaware that to "waddle like a duck" during a song about a duck is a strenuous exercise for children in first grade (or any grade), he might easily continue this activity for too long a time and eventually see children fall down from exhaustion. It may be well for any teacher who intends to ask children to do some of these things to try them himself in advance. The developmental characteristics chart in Chapter Two is helpful in learning about the physical development of children.

There is a great deal of good recorded music to use with rhythmic activities. Besides special albums relating directly to rhythm such as "Rhythmic Activities" in the *RCA Victor Record Library for Elementary Schools* and those made by Bowmar Records, American Book Company and others, appropriate recordings of the finest symphonic music can be used. Another interesting source of rhythmic motivation is in the ethnic recordings of such firms as Folkways Records and Columbia, by means of which children can listen to and perform with the rhythmic music of both primitive and sophisticated peoples from all over the world.

PERCUSSION INSTRUMENTS

When children begin to control their responses to rhythm, their growth in rhythmic accuracy and precision can be furthered by the use of percussion instruments. An introduction to them can be made through certain basic experiences in percussive sounds. Children in kindergarten and first grade should be helped to experiment with miscellaneous objects made of wood, metal, glass, and stone by tapping, shaking, and striking them. A leading music educator once said that the purchase of commercial sets of rhythm instruments should be delayed until children have exhausted the surprising potentialities of scrap lumber, iron pipes, oatmeal boxes, gourds, ice cream cartons, and various other items found in homes, alleys, and junk piles. Even the human body can produce interesting sounds that have rhythmic value. Hand clapping of various kinds (flat-palmed for loud, cupped-palm for lower pitches, fingers only for soft) has an important place in purposeful sound-making. The sound made in pulling the tongue away from the roof of the mouth (to imitate a clock's ticking, or a click) can be done in ways to produce high and low pitch. Snapping fingers and stamping feet add their effects too. These and the other body sounds can be made in rhythm with a song, a piano piece, or a recording, just as percussion instruments will be used a bit later.

In the beginning, this activity is of necessity teacher-directed. That is, it is the teacher who tells the children rather completely what they should do, and how to do it. As soon as possible the teacher directs the child's attention to what instrument or instruments sound most appropriate with different kinds of music or with contrasting sections of the same song, and the building of a sense of musical discrimination and of good musical taste is begun. This sense of discrimination develops until in the second grade the children should be able to make their own value judgments of their sound effects, and as a group make their own selection of the instruments most appropriate to the mood and form of the music. For example, they have learned that the tinkling sound of the triangle is suited to light and dainty music while the heavier sound of a drum is best suited to louder music of sturdy rhythm.

THE RHYTHM BAND

Percussion instruments are used in day-to-day classroom rhythmic activities. Any public presentations should be outgrowths of this classroom work and not performances of specialized "bands" that have been organized and rehearsed (in forced imitation of adults) specially for such a presentation. Rhythm bands or "kiddie" bands as organizations that perform regularly in public are contradictory to sound educational principles for this age group. The classroom rhythm band might have the following instrumentation:

5 jingle bells	3 triangles	2 tambourines
3 jingle sticks	5 pairs of sticks	1 small drum
1 large drum	2 pairs of cymbals	3 pairs of sandblocks

A first-grade teacher made these comments concerning activities in her classroom that culminated in the successful use of this instrumentation:

> The children are given many opportunities to initiate their own rhythmic activities. Duration, volume, accent, tempo, and moods are felt with hands, fingers, feet, and moving bodies. Percussion instruments are but extensions of tapping feet and clapping hands. Thus the children *gradually* use drums, bells, woodblocks and sticks to accompany or to create rhythm patterns. By careful listening children find one drum lower or higher in pitch than another. They discover differences in quality as well as in pitch by tapping different places on their instruments. They suggest that part of a song reminds them of a bell or a gong. Tambourines and other instruments can be used for spontaneous self-expression and interpretation during story time.

In this first grade the children had done "drum talk"—beating out the rhythm of words in "drum language," and they had walked, run, or tapped instruments as they spoke their names, thus had learned to respond to the rhythm of names, and they had used scarves, streamers, and balloons to help to feel and see other rhythms. Instruments were introduced slowly over several weeks, one at a time. Clapping generally preceded playing at first. Early playing was very informal; each child played each instrument at one time or another. When most of the class learned to beat in time with rhythmic songs, they all played together with songs like "The Mulberry Bush." They were instructed to play so that the group would sound "pretty," not noisy, and they were helped to feel that the first beat of the measure sounded louder than the other beats. After this experience was well absorbed, the players were divided into two sections, the wooden instruments and the metal instruments, and songs such as "Little Miss Muffet" were used, in which the light-sounding metal instrument section would play first, then the heavier-sounding wooden instrument section would take its turn as the climax of the song approached, and the two sections would be combined in a concluding climax. Among the many other steps in learning to play the instruments well was to have the wooden instrument section play on the primary accent and the metal instruments on the other beats. Then further divisions of the instrumentation were made, in accordance with the message of the music—sometimes to a song, sometimes to a piano piece played by the teacher, and sometimes to a recording. The children then suggested and created their own rhythm band scores in terms of individual instruments as well as the wood and metal groups.

In the series books for kindergarten and first grade there are songs that introduce percussion instruments one or two at a time. Some of the books and recordings listed at the end of this chapter include songs with good suggestions for using these instruments. Since the emphasis today is upon children's growth in creative ability and in musical discrimination, fully written published scores for percussion instruments that the teacher dictates to the children are used only infrequently today. It should be made clear that there is nothing wrong with a teacher using such scores to introduce children to the potentialities of this type of instrumental performance; it is wrong only when this is continued to the exclusion of opportunities for the children to grow in listening, discrimination and taste through learning to create their own scores.

PERCUSSION INSTRUMENTS IN GRADES 3–6

In the third grade there is often less emphasis on the mass use of these instruments. However, their use as an element contributing to song interpretation continues through the intermediate grades and junior high school. Sound effects heard on radio, television, and in the movies form a very real part of everyday living. Children in *every* grade enjoy the challenge of adding or creating appropriate "sound effects" to heighten the message of the song. One or two drums can add immeasurably to an American Indian song; a tambourine or two can lend real atmosphere to a Gypsy song; a combination of tambourine, drums, and maracas can vitalize a Latin American song. At times a characteristic rhythm played on percussion instruments can be both experimental and creative to the children who are led to discover it. This experience can relate to the teaching of note values if the rhythm pattern is written on the chalkboard or flannel board in notation so that "we can see what we did" and so that "our work can be saved and remembered for tomorrow's music period." This helps develop associations between playing and feeling the rhythm and visualizing it. Children should create aesthetically satisfying rhythmic patterns for songs suggested in the indexes of series books. Such percussion accompaniments may be constructed on the rhythm of the meter, or a different pattern may be invented which will be combined (by another instrument) with the meter rhythm. Contrasting rhythms can be played on two or more different instruments or groups of instruments. Combinations of two or more patterns with the rhythm of the meter are done in the intermediate grades.

PERCUSSION INSTRUMENTS DESCRIBED

The successful use of percussion instruments demands a variety of sounds and pitches. Thus the teacher knows the different instruments, how each is played, and the type of tone that can be produced by each instrument. In general, commercially made instruments are superior to those made by teachers and children, although some of the latter can be quite suitable for temporary use, and some can be of permanent value.

PERCUSSION INSTRUMENT SOUND CHART

Wooden instruments that "click"	Types of tone
Sticks	Light
Claves	Not as light
Castanets	Not as light
Coconut shells	Heavier
Wood blocks	Heavier
Tone block	Depends on size
Xylophone	Depends on size and pitch

Metal instruments that ring or jingle	
Finger cymbals	Delicate
Triangle	Light
Jingle bells	Light
Jingle clogs	Not as light
Tambourine	Varied, depending on way it is played
Gong	Heavy
Cymbals	Heavy

Instruments that swish or rattle	
Sandblocks	Light
Strip rattles	Light
Maracas and other rattles	Varied

Instruments that "scratch"	
Sticks	Light (when grooves are scratched)
Guiro (notched gourd)	Not as light

Hawaiian instruments	
Pu 'ili (slit bamboo sticks)	Light
'Illi-ili (stones)	Not as light
'I pu (large gourd)	Heavier, depending on size

Instruments that "boom"	
Drums	Varied, depending upon size and method of striking

WOODEN INSTRUMENTS

Rhythm sticks can be made from dowel rods of from 3/8″ to 5/8″ in diameter, purchased from lumber yards. They are usually cut in 12″ lengths.

Rhythm Sticks
RHYTHM BAND, INC.

Claves
RHYTHM BAND, INC.

Hardwood produces the most resonant sounds and will not break as easily as softwood. Ends can be smoothed with sandpaper; they can be enameled any desired color. Children hold one in each hand and strike them together. They should explore differences in pitch and sound by tapping different places on the sticks, and by tapping the sticks on suitable objects such as the floor and desk.

Claves are paired resonant sticks about an inch in diameter. They can sometimes be satisfactorily made from six-inch lengths of a broom stick or from doweling that is an inch in diameter. While the professional method of playing is to hold one clave loosely in the partly closed left hand, resting on the heel of the hand with the other end resting on the fingernails and on the thumb and index finger, and to strike this one with the other clave held sticklike in the right hand, many play them in a manner similar to rhythm sticks, by simply holding them sticklike in each hand. This instrument is seldom used in primary grades. It has its major place in Latin American songs of the intermediate grades. A favorite example of claves rhythm that can be learned through speaking the rhythm of words is:

Shave, hair__ cut, six bits!

A more intricate claves rhythm is played in 4/4 meter on the underlined numbers representing eighth notes: <u>1</u> 2 3 <u>4</u> 5 6 <u>7</u> 8 <u>1</u> 2 3 <u>4</u> 5 6 <u>7</u> 8.

Castanets used by children and by adult orchestra players are mounted on a handle. The instrument is made of a pair of cupped pieces of resonant hardwood, usually chestnut, attached by a cord. Of Spanish origin, the adult Spanish dancer holds a pair of unmounted castanets, one in each hand. The skilled dancer-player produces a variety of

Castanets
RHYTHM BAND, INC.

exciting effects from a sharp click to a sustained muffled rattle. Those played by children will produce only the sharp click. One castanet is sufficient, because of its penetrating sound. A recording of Chabrier's *España* rhapsody will illustrate its use in the adult orchestra.

Coconut shells are useful to imitate hoofbeats of horses. Ripe coconuts can be purchased at food stores and the outside fibers can be removed, if desired, by a coarse kitchen "scratcher." They are then cut in half with a saw and the meat is scraped out. The two halves are then struck together to make a "clip-clop" sound. Children should explore the variety of sounds possible by striking them together in different ways including inside out, and striking them with sticks. Two paper cups can imitate coconut shells with a softer sound.

Coconut Shells

Woodblocks
RHYTHM BAND, INC.

Woodblocks are best obtained from commercial sources, although imitations can be made from sections of old baseball bats. Woodblocks are sometimes held suspended by a cord to increase vibration, and struck lightly with a stick at the hollow side near the edge. They can also be played resting on a desk (not suspended). Children should experiment by striking them at other places, and with different beaters. They are useful to enhance songs about such subjects as ponies, cowboys, and clocks.

Tone block
RHYTHM BAND, INC.

The *tone block* is produced commercially. The instrument is held in the left hand with the cut side toward the player. It is struck lightly on top with a stick, above the cut opening. Different sizes have different pitches, and this fact can be useful in song accompaniments.

The *xylophone,* a keyboard instrument, should be purchased for best results although it has been made experimentally by teachers and students in upper grades from redwood strips or one-inch doweling resting on ropes. In early primary grades it is often used for a special *glissando* effect to describe such incidents in songs as "The mouse ran up the clock," in "Hickory Dickory Dock." Later on it is used as a melody instrument. The *marimba* is a xylophone of Latin American origin that has metal tube resonators. (Illustrations of these instruments are shown on page 125.)

METAL INSTRUMENTS

Finger cymbals
RHYTHM BAND, INC.

Finger cymbals are tiny replicas of the larger cymbal, and are usually obtained commercially rather than made by teachers. One is usually held in each hand, and they are struck together lightly at the edge or flat together for different effects. They can also be played with one hand, with the two cymbals fastened to fingers that can strike the instruments together. This latter way enables a dancer to accompany his own dancing with delicate metallic punctuations. Finger cymbals are useful for subtle effects in Oriental songs and to portray elves or angels.

Triangle
RHYTHM BAND, INC.

The *triangle* is struck lightly by a metal rod on the inside corner of the base of the instrument. A large nail or spike will sometimes make a satisfactory substitute. It is held suspended by a cord. The tone can be continued by moving the beater back and forth rapidly on the inside edges of the two sides. It can be silenced by touching it.

Jingle bells are purchased. They are played by shaking them vigorously. Some are mounted on sticks while others are worn around the wrist or ankle. A small tinkling sound can be produced by holding them toward the floor and moving them back and forth with a gentle motion of the wrist.

Jingle bells
RHYTHM BAND, INC.

Jingle clogs are more easily purchased than made. Their major use is in primary grades. They are held in one hand and tapped against the palm of the other hand in a manner that leaves the jingles free to sound. When teachers make them from metal discs used in roofing, fastened loosely on a stick, they will gain added resonance if the discs are bent slightly. Sometimes the discs are alternated with bottle caps.

The commercially produced *tambourine* is best. It is held at the place on the instrument where there are no metal jingles. To play it, the head is struck against the heel of the hand, or it is shaken. Experimental effects can be obtained by tapping it on the knee, tapping it with fingers, and using a rubbing motion with fingers followed by striking, tapping,

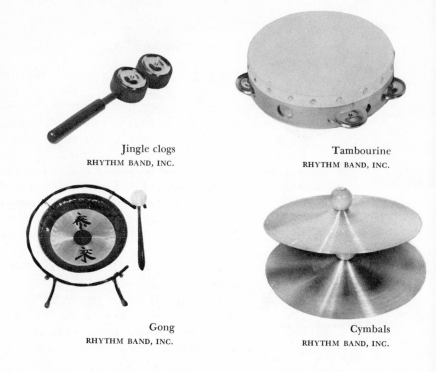

Jingle clogs
RHYTHM BAND, INC.

Tambourine
RHYTHM BAND, INC.

Gong
RHYTHM BAND, INC.

Cymbals
RHYTHM BAND, INC.

or shaking. Tambourines lend atmosphere to Gypsy, Hebrew, Spanish, and Italian songs.

The true *gong* is relatively expensive. A large one could be borrowed from the high school band, perhaps. A gong can be made from German silver about one foot square. Cut a circle from this. Drill holes for the cord that will suspend it. Then hammer the edges, testing the sound from time to time, until the edges curve inward about two inches. A substitute can be found in the metal lid of the heavy barrel-like cardboard containers often used as waste baskets in schools. Ask the school custodian to save one of the containers (to use as a drum) and the lid to use as a gong. Drill a hole by which to suspend it. A suspended length of iron pipe can be another substitute. This instrument is used with songs about cathedral bells, huge clocks, and the Orient.

Cymbals of the best tone are commercially made, although some teachers have found good tones in aluminum pan lids. They are held one in each hand and struck together with hands moving up and down in contrary directions. Other effects can be found by striking the cymbal on its edge, and with different beaters or sticks.

INSTRUMENTS THAT SWISH OR RATTLE

Sandblocks, used largely in primary grades, can be made from any soft wood from 3/4" to 1" thick and about 3" by 3" square. Handles can be door or drawer pulls, spools, leather, or small pieces of wood. Fasten the handle with screws, and place No. 1-0 sandpaper or emery cloth (this lasts longer) on the rubbing side of the block with thumb tacks. Hold a block in each hand and rub the rough surfaces together. Some teachers believe that the motion of the arms required to play sandblocks is a superior means by which the five- and six-year-olds can achieve rhythmic control in a very short time.

Sandblocks
RHYTHM BAND, INC.

Maracas
RHYTHM BAND, INC.

Maracas can be purchased or made from a pair of gourds by placing in them a suitable amount of dry seeds, pebbles, or bird shot. They are necessary for many Latin American dance songs. Maracas are held either by handles or by the neck of an elongated gourd, and are usually shaken in a steady eighth-note rhythm. For a soft effect they can be tapped by the fingers rather than shaken. Gourds from which to make maracas and guiros can be purchased from the Pearson Gourd Farm, 1409 North Merced Avenue, Box 310, El Monte, California. The catalog of this firm gives directions for the construction of these instruments. A single maraca on a long handle is used as an American Indian rattle. It can be decorated with feathers and furs. The *cabaca* is a large enameled gourd that has small wooden beads strung loosely around it. This form of rattle is a Latin American instrument. *Strip rattles* can be made from walnut shells and bottle caps suspended alternately on 3" to 4" cords suspended from a band. They are worn on the wrist or ankle in American Indian dances. *Other rattles* can be made from spice cans, typewriter ribbon cans, pill boxes, ice cream and cottage cheese cartons, salt boxes, etc. A maraca-like rattle can be made from a large electric light bulb. Cover it with papier mâché; when dry, break glass.

INSTRUMENTS THAT "SCRATCH"

Rhythm sticks make a light scratching sound when they are stroked across notches. The notches appear in most commercially made sticks, and can be added to teacher-made ones by making a row of shallow saw cuts on one of each pair of sticks. These can be filed to the proper depth and smoothness, and the smooth stick is then stroked over the notched stick.

A *guiro* is a large gourd with ridges cut along its side. It is played with a small stick or a wire scratcher scraped back and forth across the ridges. It is a Latin American instrument.

HAWAIIAN INSTRUMENTS

Pu 'ili are slit bamboo sticks. They can be made from two 18″ bamboo sticks that are 1″ to 2″ in diameter. The lowest large joint is the handle. It can be drilled out and sanded. Holes 1/4″ to 3/8″ in diameter are drilled above this joint to serve as guides for cutting out corresponding slices from the holes to the tip. The sticks are struck softly together and used in graceful motions as an extension of the arm. *'Illi-ili* are pairs of small rounded volcanic rocks to be held in the palm of the hand and clapped or rubbed together. Using many players gives an interesting effect. The *'I pu* is a "drum" made from a wide, jar-shaped gourd. The top of the stem end is cut off and the seeds and pulp are removed. It is played by slapping the side of the gourd with the palm of the hand.

DRUMS

There are many kinds and sizes of drums, manufactured and teacher-made. Some have one head, others two. They come singly and by two's and even three's. For different effects they can be struck off-center or in the center, with the fingertips, the heel of the hand, or with various types of padded beaters. There should be at least two drums in every classroom; one of low pitch and one of high pitch. The many types of commercial drums include the tom-tom, tunable drums, bongo, and conga drums. Homemade drums of varying quality may be devised from chopping bowls, wooden kegs, lard cans, and wastebaskets with goatskin (soaked 24 hours), real calfskin or heavy rubber thumbtacked, nailed, or laced on. Old drumheads can be used, salvaged from stores or from the high school band room. To paint skin drumheads, use

Conga drum
RHYTHM BAND, INC.

Bongo drums
RHYTHM BAND, INC.

water-color paint applied on the *wet* head.   Color is an important element in constructing any of the instruments because it makes them more attractive to children.   Smaller drums can be devised from oatmeal boxes or other cardboard containers, used as they are or with ends covered with a rubber sheet or very heavy paper.   Flowerpot "drums" can be made by stretching and taping wet heavy paper across the opening; the paper tightens as it dries.   Ready-made drums of fair quality are found in the very heavy cardboard barrel-like cartons used to ship china-ware, seed, ice cream mix, and sweeping compound.   These are stood open-end-down on two books (to raise them off the floor in order to increase resonance) and pounded.   They can be very useful as drums, and have added utility in that the metal cover can be used as a gong.   These potential drums are often found as wastebaskets in school corridors.

Drum beaters can be purchased.   They can be made from sticks of doweling of sufficient diameter cut to proper length, and soft rubber balls.   The doweling is glued into a hole made in the ball.   Instead of the rubber ball, a ball of cotton, covered with muslin and tied, can be used, or a ball can be made of aluminum foil covered with muslin and painted with two or three coats of the nitrate liquid used by airplane manufacturers.

The *conga drum* is a large Cuban drum played with the hands or beater, usually with the left hand with flat fingers striking the edge of the head and the right hand also with flat fingers striking the center of the head.

The *bongo drum,* another Latin American instrument, is a double drum; one is larger than the other. Held between the knees with the small drum on the left, it is played with the tips of the fingers. The bongo is used in Latin American music.

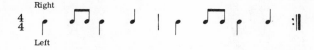

PERCUSSION INSTRUMENTS IN THE EDUCATION OF CHILDREN

The study of the different types of percussion instruments, their pitch, tone quality, and source of resonance, relates logically to acoustics, the science of sound. Many musical concepts (and a few social principles as well) can be taught through the use of percussion instruments in the rhythmic education of children. Among them are:

1. Keeping time with the meter (basic rhythmic response).
2. Differences in dynamics (degrees of loud and soft); strong beats and weak beats (primary and secondary accents); crescendo and diminuendo.
3. Musical form (the phrase, repetition, and contrast).
4. Mood expressed by choice of instruments in the percussion score.
5. Awareness of notation and its use.
6. Tempi (degrees of slow and fast).
7. Pitch (degrees of high and low).
8. Relation of rhythm patterns to appropriate instrumentation.
9. The relatedness of tempo, dynamics, mood, form, melody, pitch, and percussion instrumentation.
10. Creative power and self-expression on the child's level to invent and refine the percussion-instrument score and to devise "sound effects" to accompany songs.
11. The importance of co-operation of people in groups.
12. Self-discipline.

ACTION SONGS, SINGING GAMES, AND DANCES

Action songs and singing games are emphasized in the primary grades, and dances are emphasized in the intermediate grades because children aged nine to eleven have gained the physical control and co-ordination that enables them to perform and enjoy this more patterned social activity. However, each of these responses appears to some extent in all the grades.

Although many action songs can be done without first acquiring a background of fundamental movements, this is not true of most singing games and dances. The title of this section is stated in an order that implies increasing complexity. *Action songs* are those to which children can add appropriate motions. *Singing games* are those that involve elements of game, chance, and sometimes dance. *Dances* are more formalized. Teachers and children who have imagination will find that they can transform some "ordinary" songs into action songs, singing games, and dances of their own invention.

Most folk dances are easily taught in the intermediate grades. Some of them are taught to primary grade children in simplified versions. The easiest "dance" would be the American Indian type in which six-year-olds do a thumping walk or hop. Occasionally a simplified waltz is introduced in those grades also. However, most basic dance steps are taught in grades four and five, and they are embellished in grade six. Children in these grades can easily learn the polka, schottische, minuet, polonaise, and mazurka.

When children sing and at the same time do extensive bodily movement, the result is usually detrimental to either good singing or good rhythmic action or both. Consequently it is best to divide the children into two groups that alternate in singing and in doing the game or dance. The group that does the singing frequently adds hand clapping and percussion instruments to its accompaniment.

Many singing games and dances contribute to organized play on the playground. The song forms the accompaniment. As previously implied, these activities whether indoors or out are valuable in relieving pent-up energies, in developing muscular control, in developing good citizenship habits and sportsmanship, in releasing emotion and by identifying the child with his group. When these activities take place indoors, the piano and recordings provide variety.

One of the major values of certain singing games and folk dances is the contribution they can make to social studies, for through them children can come to a better understanding of the peoples of the world and their customs.

While children need rhythm, and lots of it, there is some danger in identifying folk dancing too closely with the music program. Granting that it is a part of a balanced music program, it should be acknowledged that it is essentially a part of physical education. Therefore, any extensive development of this activity removes it in a sense from the objectives of a balanced music program. Teachers need to clarify their aims concerning this point. Because the time available for the education of children is limited, and because there are so many aspects of music to be taught, it is not logical to consider any large amount of time spent in dancing as time spent in music class. However, because dance songs invite rhythmic responses, including dance, any teacher of music needs to be able, when necessary, to teach folk dances.

TEACHING FOLK DANCES

There are folk dances from all over the world. The four American types are (1) play-party games, (2) round dances, (3) long-ways and circular formation dances, and (4) square dances. The origin of the *play-party game* is interesting: at a time in American history when dancing and musical instruments were sometimes frowned upon, people sang dance accompaniments instead of playing them, and called the dance a game, thus getting around the restrictions of those days. *Round dances* are done with partners. They were "round" because to move easily about a crowded hall, the partners danced in the same circular direction. Examples of this type include the waltz, polka, schottische, rye waltz, and the varsovienne ("Put Your Little Foot . . ."). *Long-ways* and *circular* formation dances include the Virginia Reel. The *square dance* is one in which eight dancers (four couples) salute, curtsy, and change partners in a square formation while performing many interesting figures. Possible steps in teaching a folk dance follow:

1. In preparation, study the directions of the selected dance. It should be one of which the children already know the basic movements required, but if they do not, be sure to teach these as separate rhythms as a preparatory step to their learning the dance.
2. As you study the dance, practice the steps without the music. Then listen to the music or learn the music, and do the steps in rhythm to it.
3. If necessary, write any difficult part of the directions on a small pad or card that can be carried inconspicuously in the hand.
4. Teach the song (if it is a dance song) so that the children know the melody and words well before attempting to learn the dance.
5. Direct the children into the proper dance formation.
6. Have the children practice the first set of steps with no music. Then have them do these steps while speaking the rhythm of the words of

the song, and guide them to associate the word-rhythm with the steps. Repeat until the steps are learned.

7. Do this much of the dance with the music.
8. Repeat Steps 6 and 7 with the next set of steps. Continue this process until the entire dance is learned.
9. Do the entire dance with the music.

RHYTHM AND MUSIC STRUCTURE

Both in physical response to music and in the choice of appropriate percussion instruments to accompany music, comprehension of musical phrases and of contrasting musical ideas should gradually grow in the children's minds. Although in kindergarten and first grade much of this is done rather spontaneously and without emphasis, children in the second grade ordinarily are advanced enough to be able to understand that music "swings" in two's and three's, that it is put together in sections, and that these phrases, sections, or parts can be discerned if one listens carefully.

In making a simple analysis of songs from the standpoint of rhythm, one of the first questions is, "How does the music swing—in two's or in three's?" The children are taught to feel the *loud* beats (accents) and to respond to these strong accents with a downward motion of the arm. The arm then comes up on the beats that are not as strong. If in response to

the music the arm moves $\underset{\text{down}}{\downarrow}$ $\overset{\text{up}}{\uparrow}$, the music "swings in two's"

(duple meter). If it moves $\underset{\text{down}\ \uparrow}{\downarrow}$ up $\overset{\text{up}}{\uparrow}$, the music "swings in three's"

(triple meter).

The question, "Is the music the same, or is it different now?" illustrates the basic principle underlying *form* in music. Children can be led to discover that in songs like "Au Clair de la Lune" (At Pierrot's Door), the first section of the song is repeated, a new melodic idea is brought in, then the original section is again repeated. It is therefore learned there are four phrases identifiable as A A B A. Other familiar songs that have similar contrasting phrases are "Blue Bell of Scotland," "Marines Hymn," "Massa's in de Cold Cold Ground," "Long Long Ago," and "Oh Susanna." These form a good starting point for phrase analysis. Simple rondo form can also be analyzed in this way. Most of the songs in the series books for second and third grades are printed with one phrase on each line of a page. When songs are not printed that way, commas in the text or rests in the melody line often mark the length of the phrase.

Children in the second grade and above are sometimes guided to "act out" phrases in several ways, which include the following arm movements:

 Moving the arm in a curved horizontal pattern for each phrase

Moving the arm in a circular direction for each phrase

Moving both arms in a heart-shaped design

One method of teaching recognition of phrases or of contrasting sections of larger pieces of music is to have children *change direction* when they are moving to this music.

Children do not always agree in their physical responses to a phrase, some feeling the phrase to be half the length that others may feel it to be. In certain songs it is interesting to note that adults are more apt to feel long phrases than are children, who often feel twice the number of phrases that the adults do. When this occurs, the children usually divide each long phrase into two shorter ones. In the opinion of the authors, this is not of particular importance, the real point being that children learn to sense that music is divided into logical sections. In view of individual differences in musical background, unanimity of response to phrase length cannot be expected. However, the simplicity of most of the songs found in music series books makes for fairly obvious phrase lengths.

In some songs, and in free rhythmic response to recordings and piano selections such as those used for rhythm band, there are obviously contrasting sections of the music, each of which may be composed of a number of phrases. In rhythm-band work these contrasting sections call for differences in the percussion score.

The child should gain certain definite benefits from his experiences with rhythm: sensitivity to rhythm as an element in music; bodily control and grace; an increased understanding of the world's peoples through folk dances and games; and a growing concept of form in music. Important by-products of the above benefits are an understanding of note values (as they emerge from physical responses to music and from forms of rhythmic notation such as long and short dashes), and a knowledge of dance forms and rhythms, which can lead to a more enlightened understanding when they are found in the works of the great composers.

INDIVIDUAL DIFFERENCES

Since children are different in physical make-up, the teacher can expect that what is an easy rhythmic response for one child may be a difficult one for another.   To assist the child who finds the rhythm difficult, the teacher seeks to guide him to success either in the same rhythm at a slower tempo, or with a different and more simple rhythmic action to which he can respond at his own natural tempo.   When he succeeds, then the child should be helped to synchronize his movement with gradually slower and faster tempos.   It helps some children to produce the sound of the rhythm by clapping, singing, speaking, chanting, or making up sounds; their sounds and actions are then more easily synchronized and a habit of doing an action with a sound begins to develop.

Sometimes a six-year-old does not understand that there is supposed to be a definite relation between the sound he hears and what his muscles are to do.   Therefore, he cannot march in time with music until he is guided to discover this relation, possibly by the example of other children.   Teachers should remember that when children are asked to move in time with music, they are being expected to (1) control a specific movement, (2) listen to the music, and (3) synchronize the two.   It is natural that some children find the teacher's request to do three things at once confusing, and that the teacher must help the child by permitting him to learn the movement well first before asking him to add the two other aspects.   Sometimes the use of a paper streamer or a scarf will help a child to comprehend a motion that he cannot understand by use of the arm alone.   The teacher should remember to emphasize use of the large muscles, for such children are probably not sufficiently developed physically to control the small muscles well.

When some children cannot clap their hands in time with music, they can sometimes succeed by striking both hands on the thighs. Some teachers slow the speed of recordings for action-responses of subnormal children.   When this is done with songs, it should be remembered that this also lowers the pitch.   Thus, the pitch must not be lowered out of the natural vocal range if the recording is to be used for singing with the action.   For children who are above average in physical control, the teacher encourages responses of a creative nature of which they are physically capable.

NORMAL EXPECTATIONS

KINDERGARTEN:

Rhythmic activities in the kindergarten are primarily free and informal; they emphasize use of the big muscles in large, free motions.   The children do imaginative and creative play in imitation of the movements of men, animals, and things. They become able to respond to simple rhythmic patterns played on the drum, piano, tone block, or record player with actions such as walking, running, jumping, hopping, skipping, galloping, and tiptoeing. Concepts of high-low, heavy-light, long-short, and soft-loud are acquired. Simple directed action songs and singing games are played, such as "The Elephants," "Eensy Weensy Spider," "Hey Diddle Diddle." Such activity songs are found in quantity in kindergarten and first-grade series books. Dramatizations, finger plays, and hand movements are done. Children learn to use percussion instruments to tap in time with the music and for certain sound effects that add interest and variety to musical experiences.

GRADES ONE AND TWO:

Ability to respond to fundamental movements with large free motions: walking, running, jumping, hopping, skipping, and combinations of these.

Performance and enjoyment of action songs (such as "If You're Happy") and singing game songs (such as "Wee Little Man," "My Pretty Little Miss," "Looby Lou," "Clapping Land," and "Pony Land").

Ability to respond to rhythm with movements such as swinging, bending, twisting, swaying, stretching, pushing, pulling.

Creative response to rhythm (rhythmic dramatization).

Ability to do simple dance steps, skills, and formations including galloping, sliding, skipping, bowing, circling, singing circle with partner on the right.

Understanding of the relation of rhythmic movement to quarter, eighth, and half notes (walking, running, and step-bending or bowing), and ability to use these rhythms by playing them on percussion instruments.

Growth in ability to create suitable percussion scores for piano pieces and for recorded music.

Comprehension of whether the music "swings" in two's or three's (duple or triple meter).

Ability to combine movement and percussion instruments with greater skill and for more specific purposes in grade two.

Awareness of repeated rhythm patterns and repeated and contrasting phrases or sections of music in grade two.

GRADES THREE AND FOUR:

Mastery of rhythmic understandings taught in kindergarten through the second grade.

Knowledge of many action songs, singing games, and simple play-party games and dances such as "Bow Belinda"; the dance from Hansel and

Gretel; the schottische; "Old Brass Wagon"; the simple waltz; "Turn the Glasses Over"; "Heel and Toe"; the varsovienne; and the Virginia Reel.

The transfer of rhythmic understanding gained from bodily responses to note and rest values, including the dotted note.

Continued development in understanding beat, patterns, accent, meter, and form through bodily response.

Development of more awareness of the difference between descriptive music and pure music ("pattern" music) through creative rhythmic dramatization; introduction of longer forms in music in this way through recordings.

Knowledge of conductor's beat patterns for the following meters: 2/4 and fast 6/8, 3/4, and 4/4.

Ability to perform combined movements of walk-run, step-hop, skip-hop, step-slide, slide-hop, and to use these steps in dances such as the waltz and schottische and in creative dances and dramatizations.

Ability to march to duple and quadruple measures, accenting the first beat of each measure.

Recognition and identification of 2-, 3-, and 4-beat measures in recordings or in the singing and playing of the teacher.

Ability to step the note-rhythm of selected familiar songs.

Ability to clap, step, and write in notation simple rhythm patterns played by the teacher.

Recognition of the musical phrase through bodily movement.

Ability to create percussion accompaniments to songs and recordings.

Ability to interpret songs and recordings with rhythmic movement.

GRADES FIVE AND SIX:

Mastery of all rhythmic skills taught in kindergarten through the fourth grade.

Ability to dramatize work songs and ballads.

Ability to notate common rhythm patterns.

Knowledge of notation, rests, and meter signatures in relation to rhythm.

Some creative interpretation of music's feelings and structure through movement.

Ability to use conductor's beat patterns including slow 6/8 meter.

Ability to select and use percussion instruments for appropriate "sound effects" with music.

Understanding syncopation through movement and through use of percussion instruments.

Increased skill in moving to and in reading the notation of more complex rhythm patterns.

A repertoire of many American play-party games and of folk dances of the world such as the gavotte, Mexican Hat Dance, minuet, polka, schottische, square dances, and the Virginia Reel.

Understanding and use of Latin American percussion instruments such as the bongo, claves, tambourine, and guiro.

SELECTED SONGS

DOWN AT THE STATION

English Song for Kindergarten through Second Grade

SOME SUGGESTED RHYTHMIC ACTIVITIES

CHILDREN

1. Clap the meter, four beats to the measure, as in measure 7, "Chug, chug, puff, puff."
2. Clap the word-rhythm.
3. Combine 1 and 2 by selecting appropriate percussion instruments for these rhythms.

TEACHER

4. Select a rhythm pattern such as the note values in the first measure and have this played on a percussion instrument throughout the song. Children can learn it by repeating the words "Down by the station" in the rhythm of the first measure.
5. The second grade can step the note values.

SAILING

Italian Melody for Grades Two and Three

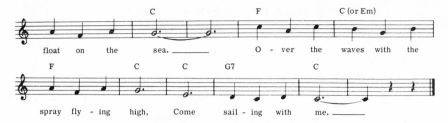

float on the sea. _____ O - ver the waves with the spray fly - ing high, Come sail - ing with me. _____

SOME SUGGESTED RHYTHMIC ACTIVITIES

CHILDREN

1. Sway in time with the music.
2. Clap hands or use percussion instruments on the first beat of each measure and in the rhythm of the meter in three beats to the measure.

TEACHER

3. Guide the children to invent with hand clapping or percussion instruments an appropriate way to mark the end of each of the four phrases, thus teaching phrase awareness.
4. Have the class conduct 3/4 meter.
5. Teach a simple waltz run or step. Examples: L R L   R L R
   After this simple accented walk is learned, have the children take a long step on the accented beat, followed by two short steps in each measure.

L R skip   L R skip   R L skip   R L skip

OLD MACDONALD

American Song for Grades Three and Four

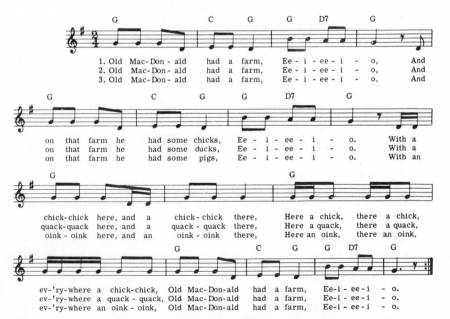

1. Old Mac-Don - ald had a farm, Ee - i - ee - i - o, And
2. Old Mac-Don - ald had a farm, Ee - i - ee - i - o, And
3. Old Mac-Don - ald had a farm, Ee - i - ee - i - o, And

on that farm he had some chicks, Ee - i - ee - i - o. With a
on that farm he had some ducks, Ee - i - ee - i - o. With a
on that farm he had some pigs, Ee - i - ee - i - o. With an

chick-chick here, and a   chick-chick there, Here a chick, there a chick,
quack-quack here, and a   quack-quack there, Here a quack, there a quack,
oink - oink here, and an   oink - oink there, Here an oink, there an oink,

ev-'ry-where a chick-chick, Old Mac-Don-ald had a farm, Ee-i - ee-i - o.
ev-'ry-where a quack - quack, Old Mac-Don-ald had a farm, Ee-i - ee-i - o.
ev-'ry-where an oink - oink, Old Mac-Don-ald had a farm, Ee-i - ee-i - o.

SOME SUGGESTED RHYTHMIC ACTIVITIES

CHILDREN

1. Create a percussion score and notate it.
2. Invent actions each time "Ee-i-ee-i-o" is sung.

TEACHER

3. Review the basic beat by having the class conduct the meter.

THE PAW-PAW PATCH

Kentucky Singing Game for Grades Three through Five

1. Where, O where is pret-ty lit-tle El-lie? Where, O where is pret-ty lit-tle El-lie?

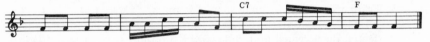

Where, O where is   pret-ty lit-tle El-lie? 'Way down yon-der in the   paw-paw patch.

2. Come on,   boys,   let's find   El - lie,   etc.

3. Pick-in'   up   paw - paws,   put'n' 'em in   a   bas - ket,   etc.

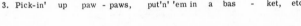

4. Here she   comes,   we'll   all   go   with   her,   etc.

SOME SUGGESTED RHYTHMIC ACTIVITIES

CHILDREN

1. Create a dance-dramatization of the song.

TEACHER

2. Use the song to teach the relation of word-rhythms to note values; use the different word-rhythms of the verses in a percussion score for the song.

RIG-A-JIG-JIG

Song for Grades Four and Five

Verse

1. As I was walk - ing down the street,
2. A pret - ty maid I chanced to meet,

down the street, down the street, As I was walk - ing
chanced to meet, chanced to meet, A pret - ty maid I

down the street, Heigh - o, heigh - o, heigh - o.
chanced to meet, Heigh - o. heigh - o, heigh - o.

Refrain

Rig - a - jig-jig, and a - way we go, a - way we go, a - way we go;

Rig - a - jig - jig, and a - way we go, Heigh - o. heigh-o,__ heigh - o.__

SOME SUGGESTED RHYTHMIC ACTIVITIES

CHILDREN

1. Create a dance; learn and compare 2/4 and fast 6/8 meters in the process.
2. With percussion instruments, enhance the leisurely walking effect of the verse and the excited skipping effect of the refrain.

TO PUERTO RICO

R. E. N.

Song for Grades Five and Six

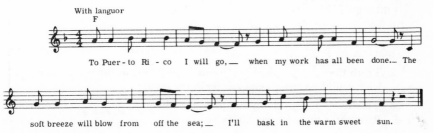

With languor

To Puer - to Ri - co I will go,__ when my work has all been done.__ The

soft breeze will blow from off the sea;__ I'll bask in the warm sweet sun.

SOME SUGGESTED RHYTHMIC ACTIVITIES

CHILDREN

1. Devise a Latin American percussion score and notate it.

   Possibilities include:

TEACHER

2. Teach the concept of syncopation.

THE COUNT

Brazilian Song for Grades Five and Six

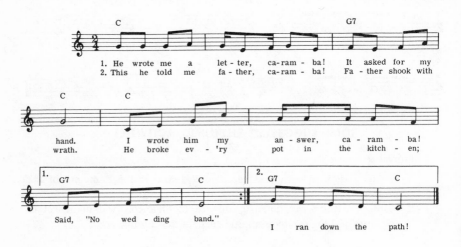

1. He wrote me a let-ter, ca-ram-ba! It asked for my
2. This he told me fa-ther, ca-ram-ba! Fa-ther shook with

hand.   I   wrote   him   my   an - swer,   ca - ram - ba!
wrath.   He   broke   ev - 'ry   pot   in   the   kitch - en;

Said, "No   wed - ding   band."

I   ran   down   the   path!

SOME SUGGESTED RHYTHMIC ACTIVITIES

CHILDREN

1. Devise a Latin American percussion score.

TEACHER

2. Teach the ♪♫ rhythm pattern through use of the word "caramba," which children enjoy emphasizing in the song.

3. Teach ♫♪♫ by comparing it with ♪♩ ♪♩ ♩ in "To Puerto Rico"; it is the same rhythm twice as fast.

THINGS TO DO

1. Experiment with simple echo-clapping as described on pages 71–2 and with question-and-answer echo-clapping as described on pages 72–3. Then try a rhythmic *canon* in which the leader, with a drum or a wood-block, begins a more lengthy rhythmic exposition which the class answers by clapping one measure later. This is a form of rhythmic round, and requires more intensive listening and memorization because as the class listens to the teacher or leader it must at the same time keep in mind the previous measure and be playing it. Examples of echo-clapping and of rhythmic canons are found in *Music For Children, I,* Orff-Keetman-Hall, pages 80–2.

2. Play recordings produced by series book publishers of songs that appear in series books. Identify the meter by listening. Every meter contains natural accents as follows:

   2/4, fast 6/8   ONE two ONE two ONE two
   3/4   ONE two three ONE two three
   4/4   ONE two *three* four ONE two *three* four
   6/8 (slow)   ONE two three *four* five six

   These accents identify and establish the meter. It should be noted that 4/4 and slow 6/8 have besides the primary (heavy) accent on the first beat, a secondary (less heavy) accent on another beat. A question that helps in identifying the meter is, "Does the music swing in two's or three's?" (See page 95.) Find songs which are particularly rhythmic. Try the bodily responses (clapping, knee-slapping, tapping) suggested on pages 73–4 and try to evaluate children's reactions to these responses. Remember that meter is the plan of accents that establishes the basic rhythm of music.

3. Referring to the preceding activity, practice conductor's beats with these recordings. This is another type of rhythmic response which children learn. Practice the conductor's beat patterns at home in front of a mirror; this is necessary to be certain that you are making the type of motions you desire. Study the Columbia recording, *Lead a Little Orchestra,* which deals with conducting, and plan how you would present this to children in an elementary school classroom.

4. Explore the rhythm of names. In the college class, arrange the class cards in order of rhythmic complexity, with the most simple name-rhythms on top and the most complex name-rhythms on the bottom of the pile. Some classmates' names will have the rhythm of walking (Bob Smith), running (Ellen Dillon), walk and running (Tom Adams), running and walk (Susan Fry), skipping (Marie McCann), and galloping (Gwendolyn Armitage). Clap the names, play them on percussion

instruments, "step" them, and write them in notation. (See page 75.) Do this with other words, such as geographical names and names of cakes and pies.

5. Organize a repertoire of "rhythm words" to use to teach rhythm patterns and note values. Examples:

Line Notation	Words	Music Notation
—— ——	train, train	𝅗𝅥 𝅗𝅥
— — — —	rail-road, rail-road	♩♪ ♩♪
– – – – – – – –	Chat-ta-noo-ga, Chat-ta-noo-ga	♬♬ ♬♬
—— — —— —	choo--ka, choo--ka	♩. ♪ ♩. ♪
– – — – – —	straw-ber-ry, straw-ber-ry	♪♬ ♪♬
– – — – – —	cho-co-late, cho-co-late	♬♩ ♬♩
– – – – – –	ca-rol-ing, ca-rol-ing	♬♩ ♬♩

6. Study Young People's Record 619, *Little Indian Drum,* in which a little Indian boy sends a message to his father on his drum. This recording can motivate children's interest in word-rhythms. Classroom teachers may have the children write creative stories in which drum talk has a part.

7. A variant of drum talk consists of the teacher playing on a drum the rhythm of the words of parts of a familiar song and the children answering by playing instruments or clapping the rhythm of answering words. Examples for primary grades:

Teacher drums: "Mary had a little lamb,
Children: Little lamb, little lamb,
Teacher: Mary had a little lamb,
Children: Its fleece was white as snow."

Example for intermediate grades:

Teacher drums: "Oh Buffalo gals won't you come out tonight?
Children: Won't you come out tonight, won't you come out tonight?
Teacher: Oh Buffalo gals won't you come out tonight?
Children: And dance by the light of the moon?"

8. Using percussion instruments and the words

(a) have one group play the rhythm of the meter (the basic beat); (b) have another group play the rhythm of the words while *walking* across the floor in this rhythm; (c) have the first group play while walking across the floor in its rhythm while the second group plays in place; (d) try to evolve a simple dance from these two rhythms.

9. Try stepping word rhythms (melody rhythms) as mentioned on page 75, using familiar nursery rhymes as a beginning experience. After stepping these rhythms, write them in rhythmic notation, then in music notation. Try some of the following:

   (a) Hot cross buns, hot cross buns,
       One a penny, two a penny, hot cross buns.
   (b) Bah, bah, black sheep, have you any wool?
       Yes sir, yes sir, three bags full!
   (c) Sing a song of sixpence a pocket full of rye,
       Four and twenty blackbirds baked in a pie!
       When the pie was opened, the birds began to sing,
       Wasn't that a dainty dish to set before the King?

Now refer to the Music Series Guide, page 110, and step the melody rhythms of songs indicated for use in this activity in the music series books.

10. It is said that characteristics of rhythm include tempo, meter, rhythm of the melody, and accent. Using a song as an example, explain these terms.

11. Play a guessing game by tapping or clapping the rhythm of the melody of familiar songs, having the class, or members in the class identify the song by its rhythm.

12. Listen to the Childrens Record Guild recordings for kindergarten through grade three, *A Visit to My Little Friend* (1017), and *My Playful Scarf* (1019). Have a group from your class or the entire class act them out and evaluate them for use in the primary grades.

13. Ask a teacher of dance to demonstrate fundamental movements and creative dance with a small group of children.

PERCUSSION INSTRUMENTS

14. In every song there are ordinarily three distinct rhythms: the rhythm of the first beat of the measure (the primary accent), the rhythm of the meter, and the rhythm of the melody (or words). Try orchestrating a familiar song on this basis. Have the low-pitched heavy-sounding instruments play on the rhythm of the first beat and select others to play on the remaining two rhythms. Experiment by dividing the instruments into groups of similar pitches, and also into groups of similar type. Find out which of these instruments are most appropriate to each rhythm.

15. Make up a story and use percussion instruments for sound effects. Example: The alarm clock (triangle) awakes us in the morning. The

clock (gong) strikes eight. Mother calls, "Are You Sleeping?" (Sing the song to the accompaniment of the clock ticking—woodblocks, rhythm sticks.) On the way to school we hear a train (sandblocks) and horses (coconut shells). Such a story is another way to teach the appropriateness of individual percussion instruments.

16. Learn how to use recordings prepared for rhythm band such as the RCA *Music for Rhythm Bands:* Primary Grades, Album WE-90; American Book Company Albums AS-27 and AS-28, for Primary Grades.

RHYTHM BAND PATTERNS

17. Play a recording of a march such as "National Emblem." As a class project, create and notate a percussion score to play with the recording as children in intermediate grades might do it.

18. Pretend you are in a classroom that contains no percussion instruments. Find what the potentialities of the materials around you may be. Examples: the sound of paper held in the air and tapped with a pencil, buckles or heavy costume jewelry, the radiator, and objects found in handbags. Use these in creating a rhythm score to a song.

19. Using the RCA Basic Library for Elementary Schools, listen to *Minuet from Don Giovanni,* Mozart (Album E-75), and *Andante from the Surprise Symphony,* Haydn (Album E-80). Develop percussion scores to accompany these recordings. After you have done this, refer to *This Is Music, Book 3* to compare your scores with those suggested in a series book.

ACTION SONGS, SINGING GAMES, AND DANCES

20. Invent an action song to use in the intermediate grades to alleviate fatigue by using the verse of "Tavern in the Town" for the tune and the words, "Head and shoulders, knees and toes, knees and toes" followed by "Eyes and ears and mouth and nose." In this action song, have the singers touch the part of the body stated in the words. Begin the song slowly, then gradually increase the tempo, but not to the point where children cannot continue to do the actions together in good rhythm.

21. Dances can be created from common rhythm patterns. Guide a group of class members in creating an Indian circle dance from the note

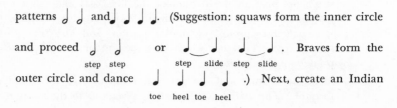

patterns ♩ ♩ and ♩ ♩ ♩. (Suggestion: squaws form the inner circle

and proceed ♩ ♩   or ♩ ♩ ♩ ♩ . Braves form the
           step step   step slide step slide
outer circle and dance ♩ ♩ ♩ ♩ .) Next, create an Indian
           toe   heel toe heel

line dance with the pattern   ♩ ♩ ♩ ♩ ♩ . (Suggestion:

step step step step bow

count off. Even-numbered dancers may step while odd-numbered dancers may bow, and vice versa.) Other members may provide a percussion instrument accompaniment for these dances.

Invent a rhythm pattern, write it on the chalkboard in notation, and create a dance.

22. Examine state and city courses of study in physical education. Many of these have excellent lists of recordings of dances classified according to national origin.

23. Develop a repertoire of mixer dances in which the dancers are continually changing partners. Such dances are useful in situations where children are reluctant to have only one partner throughout an entire dance. Examples are "The Old Brass Wagon" (*This Is Music, Book 3, Music Across Our Country, Singing With Children*), "The Caller's Song" (*American Singer, Book Four*), and "Red River Valley" (*Singing With Children*).

24. Learn how to teach commonly-used dances by means of directions from various sources—the series books, physical education books, and courses of study. For example, the schottische step is step-step-step-hop, and the polka, which is faster than the schottische, can be step-slide-step-turn or step-slide-step-hop. The waltz can be introduced by a walk in which first a large step then two smaller steps are made as the dancers move in a circle.

25. Learn a Hawaiian stick dance such as "My Boat" (*Singing With Children,* pages 57–58).

26. Create or find singing games for such songs as "Did You Ever See a Lassie?" (also an action song), "Skip to My Lou," and "Looby Lou." Teach the class these "singing game" dances.

RHYTHM AND MUSIC STRUCTURE

27. Play a recording accompanying one of the series books that has several songs on it. As you listen, find out by your arm movements (page 95) whether these songs "swing in two's or three's." Decide what the meter signature may be.

28. Learn about the *rondo* form through imaginative listening and bodily response. Listen to "Amaryllis," by Ghys, in RCA Album WE-90, *Music for Rhythm Bands.* Do you hear the different sections? What do they sound like? Invent characters to fit the different sections and dramatize the music. Call the first section A, the next different section B, and so on. What is the form of the piece? This same procedure can be carried on in intermediate grades with Ravel's "Pavan for a Dead Princess."

29. Examine the songs in series books and find identical, similar, and con-

trasting phrases. Call the first phrase A and its exact repetition A also.
Should A appear in an altered form, call it A1, A2 and so on. When
phrases occur that are different from A, the first of these will be
called B, the second C, and so on. See how many different arrangements of phrases can be found. Which can be identified as two-part
and three-part forms?

30. Class members may sing the familiar song, "Row, Row, Row Your
    Boat," standing in rows as they sing. They may walk forward on the
    words "Row, row, row your boat, gently down the stream," then back-
    ward on the remaining words. This dramatizes the division of the
    song into two phrases. Another way of doing this is to have odd-
    numbered rows wait until the second phrase to begin their movement.
    Try this with other simple songs.

31. With marching or simple dance steps, floor patterns can be developed
    in accordance with the phrase structure of the music. Line or circle
    formations can be used. After deciding on the basic beat and foot
    pattern, the participants can move forward, backward, in, or out from
    the line or circle or go around a partner on suitable short phrases, or
    directions of the movement can be reversed on contrasting long
    phrases. Dancers will invent other ways to "act out" the phrase. Try
    this with marches and dance-type songs.

32. Write a percussion score to a song. How does the form of the music
    influence your selection of instruments?

33. The study of different types of marches can be made interesting by
    the types of bodily movement each type suggests. Contrast the marches
    found in the RCA-Victor Basic Record Library for Elementary Schools,
    The Rhythm Program, Albums 74, 75, and 76 (for grades four, five,
    and six), and gather examples from other sources. For what purposes
    are these various kinds of marches used? How does one march to
    them? Select the marches you believe appropriate for this activity in
    the intermediate grades and gather information for planning a unit of
    work on this subject. Types of marches include military, concert,
    funeral, wedding, triumphal, religious, processional, descriptive, and
    singing.

34. Read the Teachers Book for *Music Through the Year* (Follett), pages
    vii-ix, on the phrase and how to teach this concept.

GENERAL

35. Write a lesson plan that emphasizes the teaching of rhythm, following
    the steps outlined on pages 63–67 in Chapter Three.

MUSIC SERIES GUIDE

The following Guide leads the reader to rhythmic activities found in the books used
in student and professional teaching. The Guides found in this textbook are designed
to assist the student in his study and use of music series books. They help reveal the

content of both the children's books and the teacher's books. Teacher's manuals are identified by the abbreviation TM.

BIRCHARD MUSIC SERIES (SUMMY-BIRCHARD COMPANY)

KINDERGARTEN

Classified Index: chants, 156; finger plays, 157; games, 157; rhythm instruments, 158; rhythms 158-9
Games, 39-47
Rhythm instruments, 5
Rhythmic activity, 4
Rhythms, 134-55

BOOK ONE

Chants: see poetry, 187
Charts for rhythm patterns, 5
Finger plays, 19, 22
Games, 185-6
Rhythm instruments, 186
Rhythms (fundamental), 188

BOOK TWO

Charts, TM 25
Form, TM 25
Rhythm instruments, how to play, TM 10-14; songs for, TM 207
Rhythmic movement, TM 186-97, 209
Singing games, 152-3

BOOK THREE

Games and dances, 153
Rhythm instruments, TM 11-15, 207
Rhythm patterns, TM 204, 208
Rhythmic movement, TM 210-11
Rhythms, TM 8

BOOK FOUR

Games and dances, 169, TM 247-8
Rhythm instruments, TM 13-19, 253
Rhythm: glossary TM 40; patterns, TM 254
Singing games: glossary, TM 39

BOOK FIVE

Creating rhythm patterns, TM 315-6
Dramatization, TM 316
Games and dances, 183, TM 312
Rhythm instruments, TM 13-19, 318

GROWING WITH MUSIC (PRENTICE-HALL, INC.)

The teachers editions for Books 1, 3, 4, 5, and 6 were not available when this Guide was compiled.

MUSIC FOR LIVING (SILVER BURDETT COMPANY)

Drums, scores for (and other rhythm instruments), TM 164
Instruments (rhythm, native, use of), TM 163

MUSIC IN OUR COUNTRY

Instruments, native, TM 188; use of, TM 188
Rhythm instruments, 217, TM 186

MUSIC AROUND THE WORLD

Instruments, TM 204
Rhythm instruments, 232
Songs for playing instruments, TM 201

MUSIC FOR YOUNG AMERICANS (AMERICAN BOOK COMPANY)

KINDERGARTEN

Action songs, 47–58
Creative movement, 32, 35, 61, 62
Developing understanding of rhythm, 148–9
Finger plays, 10–12
How to improvise for guided rhythms, 156–60
Index of rhythmic movements, 164
Piano selections, 95–109
Rhythm instruments, 76–9

BOOK ONE

Action songs, 57–76
Developing understanding of rhythm, 180–1
How to improvise for guided rhythmic activities, 188–92
Index of rhythmic movements, 196
Piano selections, 114–33
Rhythm band, 97–101

BOOK TWO

Dance directions in TM, 16, 27, 28, 34
Games and dances, 177
Natural movements, 177–8
Rhythm instruments, 178
We sing, play and dance, 108–31

BOOK THREE

Dance and singing game directions, TM 10, 11, 27, 38, 39, 42
Rhythm activities, 195–6
Rhythm instruments, 195
Rhythm and melody instruments, TM 4
We study rhythm, 22–31
We sing, play and dance, 108–31

BOOK FOUR

Dances and games, TM 9, 13, 15, 19, 41, 42, 44
Play-party songs and dances, 195
Rhythm activities, 195

Rhythmic games, songs and dances, 32–48
Square dances, 137, 138, 139, 141

BOOK FIVE

Dance directions, TM 7, 15, 39, 42, 43; waltz, 45
Play-party songs and dances, 202
Rhythm activities, 203

BOOK SIX

Dance directions in TM 20, 50
Play-party songs and dances, 211
Rhythm activities, 211

OUR SINGING WORLD (GINN AND COMPANY, 1951 EDITION)

KINDERGARTEN BOOK

Action songs, 9b, 21b, 30ab, 33ab, 36b, 37a, 49ab, 50abc, 51ab, 117b, 127abc, 134ab
Singing games, 39ab, 40a, 40b, 41ab, 42a, 43ab
Rhythm instruments, 137, 138abcd, 138e, 139ab, 140ab

FIRST GRADE BOOK

Action songs, 7ab, 21b, 34ab, 44b, 59a, 60ab, 78c, 105, 125ab, 132a, 159a, 171a
Singing games, 45, 46ab, 47ab, 48, 49ab, 50ab, 51, 52ab
Rhythm instruments, 134b, 173, 174ab, 176ab

SINGING ON OUR WAY

Action songs, 26, 42, 43, 45b, 54, 55b, 133, 153
Singing games, 7, 9, 31, 32, 33ab, 34, 35ab, 36, 37, 38ab, 38, 44
Rhythm instruments, 46b, 50, 77, 78, 101, 103b, 155b

SINGING AND RHYMING

Action songs, 9, 10, 24, 25, 28, 60, 154, 161, 165
Singing games, 11, 13, 16, 41, 42, 43, 44 (TM directions, 128), 45, 46ab, 47, 48, 49a, 51ab
Rhythm instruments, 154ab, 155b, 156, 160, 164, 165, 168ab

SINGING EVERY DAY

Action songs, 7, 17, 22b, 56
Dances, 12, 54, polka, 59
Singing games, 45, 46, 47, 49ab, 50ab, 51, 52, 53, 57, 58, 60, 61, 158b (refer TM for
    directions and song index)
Rhythm instruments, 43, 55, 170, 172ab

SINGING TOGETHER

Dances: varsovienne directions, 31, 33 (TM, directions); polka, 40
Singing games with directions, 29, 30, 32, 34, 36; without directions, 186
Rhythm instruments, 45, 48, 58, 92, 138, 139, 188, 189

SINGING IN HARMONY

Action songs, 35, 38
Dances: square dance, 37 (TM, directions), 40 (TM, directions), waltz, 41

Singing games, 39, 44 (TM, directions)
Rhythm instruments, 7, 9b, 38, 40, 43, 52, 53, 56, 62, 68, 146, 200

THIS IS MUSIC (ALLYN AND BACON, INC.)

BOOK ONE

Dances, 188
Instrumental activities, 189
Making instruments, 181–3
Movement, 8
Percussion instruments, 189
Piano music for movement, 189
Rhythmic activity, 189
Scores for percussion instruments, 189
Verses to dramatize, 189

BOOK TWO

Learning to play instruments, 164–5
Rhythm of words, 54
Rhythm patterns, 164
Singing games: TM 85, 95, 101
Songs with movement (fundamental movements), 166
Speech and rhythm patterns, 164

BOOK THREE

Creative dances, 163
Percussion instruments, 164
Singing games and dances in TM, 2, 6, 8, 10, 25, 28, 30, 81, 94, 102, 106, 109, 112
Songs with movement (action songs, folk dances and games, hand clapping, heel tapping, imitative rhythm, natural rhythm), 165

BOOK FOUR

Conducting, TM ix
Rhythm activities (arm motions, clapping, dances, singing games, and fundamental movements), 189
Rhythm instruments, 189
Singing games and dances in TM, 1, 10, 67, 78, 79, 84, 127–8

BOOK FIVE

Percussion instruments, 211
Rhythmic activities (clapping, conducting, dances, dance songs, singing games, marches, waltzes), 212
Singing games and dances in TM, 11, 61, 66, 68, 76, 91, 92, 93, 104, 105, 117, 122

BOOK SIX

Percussion instruments, 235
Rhythmic activities (clapping, tapping, conducting, dances, rhythmic patterns), 236
Singing games and dances in TM, 10, 11, 64 (and references to many recorded dances)

TOGETHER WE SING (FOLLETT PUBLISHING COMPANY)

REFERENCES AND MATERIALS

BOOKS AND ARTICLES

Action Songs (P–89). New York: National Recreation Association.
Andrews, Gladys, Creative Rhythmic Movement for Children. Englewood Cliffs, N.J.: Prentice-Hall, Inc., 1954.
Bauer, Lois and Barbara Reed, Dance and Play Activities for the Elementary Grades: Vol. I for Grades 1–3; Vol. II for Grades 4–6. New York: Chartwell House, Inc., 1952.
Buttolph, Edna G., Music in Motion. Cincinnati: Willis Music Co.
Cole, Natalie Robinson, The Arts in the Classroom. New York: The John Day Company, Inc., 1940. Chapter 4, "Free Rhythmic Dancing."
Coleman, Satis, The Drum Book. New York: The John Day Company, Inc., 1931.
Driver, Ann, Music and Movement. London: Oxford University Press, 1947.

Driver, Ethel, *A Pathway to Dalcroze Eurythmics.* New York: Thomas Nelson & Sons, 1951.

Dykema, Peter, *Twice 55 Games With Music.* Evanston, Ill.: Summy-Birchard Company, 1924.

Geri, Frank H., *Illustrated Games and Rhythms for Children: Primary Grades.* Englewood Cliffs, N.J.: Prentice-Hall, Inc., 1955.

————, *Illustrated Games, Rhythms and Stunts for Children: Intermediate Grades.* Englewood Cliffs, N.J.: Prentice-Hall, Inc., 1956.

Hood, Marguerite V., and E. J. Schultz, *Learning Music Through Rhythms.* Boston: Ginn & Company, 1949.

Jenkins, Ella, *This Is Rhythm.* New York: Oak Publications. (Recorded by Folkways Records: *This Is Rhythm* FC 7652.) Nursery and early elementary.

Kraus, Richard, *The Recreation Leader's Handbook.* New York: McGraw-Hill Book Co., Inc., 1955.

LaSalle, Dorothy, *Rhythms and Dances for Elementary Schools,* rev. ed. New York: A. S. Barnes & Co., 1951.

Mandell, Muriel, and Robert E. Wood, *Make Your Own Musical Instruments.* New York: Sterling Publishing Co., Inc., 1957.

Marsh, Mary Val, "An Exploration in Percussion," *Music Educators Journal,* June–July, 1962, pp. 37–40.

Mason, Bernard S., *Drums, Tomtoms, Rattles.* New York: A. S. Barnes & Co., 1938.

McMillan, L. Eileen, *Guiding Children's Growth Through Music.* Boston: Ginn & Company, 1959. Chapter 3.

Miller, Mary, and Paula Zajan, *Finger Play.* New York: G. Schirmer, Inc., 1955.

Morales, Humbert, *Latin American Rhythm Instruments.* New York: H. Adler Publishers Corp., 1954.

Mukerji, Rose, "Visit to a Workshop on Rhythm," *Elementary School Journal,* Vol. 60, December, 1959, pp. 132–6.

Murray, Ruth L., *Dance in Elementary Education.* New York: Harper and Row, 1953.

Mursell, James L., *Music Education, Principles and Programs.* Morristown, N.J.: Silver Burdett Company, 1956. Chapter 9, "Rhythm and Music Growth."

Orff, Carl, and Gunild Keetman, *Music for Children, I-Pentatonic,* English adaptation by Doreen Hall and Arnold Walter. New York: Associated Music Publishers, 1956, pp. 66–87. Also see *Music for Children* recording (Angel Records 3582 B) and *Music for Children* film (Contemporary Films, 267 West 25th Street, New York 1, N.Y.)

Pitcher, Gladys, *Playtime in Song.* New York: Music Publisher Holding Corporation.

Rohrbough, Lynn, *Handy Play Party Book.* Delaware, Ohio: Cooperative Recreation Service. Also *Handy Square Dance Book* and *Handy Folk Dance Book* from same source.

Saffran, Rosanna B., *First Book of Rhythms.* New York: Holt, Rinehart & Winston, Inc., 1963.

Sheehy, Emma Dickson, *Children Discover Music and Dance.* New York: Holt, Rinehart & Winston, Inc., 1959. Chapters 7 and 8.

FILMS

Building Children's Personalities with Creative Dancing, University of California Extension Division Film No. 5844. For teachers.

Percussion, the Pulse of Music, National Educational Television, Audio-Visual Center, Indiana University, Bloomington, Indiana. Three professional percussionists demonstrate instruments and involve children in playing them.

Rhythm is Everywhere, Carl F. Mahnke Productions, 215 E. Third St., Des Moines,

Iowa. A small boy hears rhythm in nature and his teacher helps relate these to rhythm in the classroom. Primary Grades.

PERCUSSION INSTRUMENT DISTRIBUTORS AND MANUFACTURERS

Conn Corporation, 1101 E. Beardsley St., Elkhart, Indiana.

Educational Music Bureau, 434 S. Wabash Ave., Chicago 5, Illinois.

Lyons Band Instrument Company, 223 W. Lake St., Chicago 6, Illinois.

Pearson Gourd Farm, 1409 North Merced Ave., Box 310, El Monte, California. A source of gourds for instrument-making.

Peripole, Inc., 51–17 Rockaway Beach Blvd., Far Rockaway 91, New York.

Rhythm Band, Inc., 407–409 Throckmorton St., Fort Worth, Texas.

Walberg and Auge, 86 Mechanic St., Worcester 8, Massachusetts.

	Suggested Grade Levels
RECORDINGS	
Bassett-Chesnut Records	
Childrens Music Center	
5373 W. Pico Blvd.	
Los Angeles 19, California	
Basic Rhythmic Activities: album of 3 records	Primary
Holiday Series: album of 4 records	
Bowmar Records	
4921 Santa Monica Blvd.	
Los Angeles 29, California	
Albums:	
Holiday Rhythms	1–5
Mexican Folk Dances	4–6
Rhythm Is Fun	K–2
Singing Games and Folk Dances (6 albums)	K–6
Singing Square Dances—Album 1	4–5
Album 2	6–7
Children's Record Guild and Young People's Records	*Suggested Grade Levels*
The Greystone Corporation	
100 Sixth Avenue, New York 13, N.Y.	
"Do This, Do That!"	K–1
"Drummer Boy"	K–3
"Eensie Beensie Spider"	K–2
"Folk Songs for Singing and Dancing"	2–5
"I Am a Circus"	K–2
"Let's Dance"	1–4
"Little Indian Drum" ("drum talk")	K–2
"Little Red Wagon"	K–2
"Merry Toy Shop"	K–3
"My Playful Scarf" (creative)	K–3
"My Playmate the Wind" (creative)	1–4
"Nothing To Do" (fundamental movements)	K–2
"Out of Doors"	K–3
"Ride 'Em Cowboy"	K–3
"Skittery Skattery"	K–2
"Slow Joe" (fast and slow)	K–2

"Strike Up the Band" (percussion)	K–3
"Swing Your Partner" (create dances)	2–6
"Sunday in the Park"	K–2
"Trains and Planes"	N–1
"When I Was Very Young"	N–2
"Visit to My Little Friend" (fundamental movements)	K–3
The following albums contain many of the above:	
EAD 2005: *Things To Do*	K–3
EAD 2006: *More Things To Do*	K–3
EAD 2017: *Let's Play Rhythms*	K–3
EAD 2027: *Rhythm, Fun, and Songs*	K–2

Columbia Records, Inc.
Educational Department
799 Seventh Avenue
New York 19, N.Y.

Participation Records	
"Jum-A-Jingles" (rope skipping, ball bouncing)	1–3
"Lead a Little Orchestra" (conducting)	1–3
"Let's Have a Rhythm Band"	1–3

World Library of Folk and Primitive Music
(ethnic recordings)

Folkways Records
117 W. 46th St.
New York 36, N.Y.

"Adventures in Rhythm" (Ella Jenkins)	4–6
"American Play-Parties"	3–6
"Calypsos for Children"	3–6
"Dance Along"	K–3
"Folk Songs for Young Folks" (animals)	K–3
"Jamaica Songs and Games" (calypso)	3–6
"Rhythms for Children"	K–3

	Suggested Grade Levels
"Skip Rope Games"	K–3

(Note: The Folkways Catalog contains ethnic recordings from all
   over the world.)
Kay Ortman's Productions, Ltd.
1644 W. Broadway
Vancouver 9, B.C.

Set 1: *Basic Rhythms*	K–2
Set 2: *Music for Movement and Space*	3–6

Methodist Church Publishing House
417 Church St.
Nashville 2, Tennessee

World of Fun Folk Dances
New World of Fun Series
   (Booklets of dance instructions available.)

Phoebe James
Box 904
Mentone, California

Album 1: *Animals*	K-3
Album 2: *Free Rhythms*	K-3
Album 3: *Animal Rhythms*	K-3
Album 4: *In the Garden*	K-3
Album 5: *Fundamental Rhythms*	K-3
Album 6: *Trains*	K-4

	Suggested Grade Levels
Album 7: *Boats and the Harbor*	K-4
Album 8: *Branding Cattle* (creative Mexican dance)	4-6
Album 9: *Dramatic Play* (Billygoat Gruff, Gingerbread Boy)	K-2
Album 10: *Indian Rhythm* (creative dance, drum beats)	1-6
Album 11: *Fire! Fire! and a March*	K-3
Album 12: *Favorite Action Songs*	K-3
Album 13: *Farm Animals*	K-3
Album 14: *Christmas Rhythms*	K-3
Album 15: *Hallowe'en Rhythms*	K-3
Albums 16, 17, 18: *Interpretive Rhythms*	2-6
Album 20: *Rhythm Orchestra*	K-2
Album 21: *Nursery School Rhythms*	N-1

RCA-Victor Records Division
155 E. 24th Street
New York 10, N.Y.

RCA-Victor Basic Record Library for Elementary Schools
The Rhythm Program

Six albums, one for each grade	1-6
Music of American Indians (album)	1-6
Music for Rhythm Bands (album)	1-3

	Suggested Grade Levels
The World of Folk Dances	
A series, from easiest to most difficult, of 85 dances from 26 countries	
Let's Square Dance!	
Album 1	3-4
Album 2	5-6
The Ballet	4-8

Ruth Evans Records
Box 132, P. O. Branch X
Springfield, Massachusetts

Childhood Rhythms	
Albums 1, 2, 5, 7	1-3
Albums 3, 4, 6, 7, 8	4-6

Chapter Five

PLAYING MELODY AND HARMONY INSTRUMENTS

Making music by playing an instrument, no matter how simple the instrument, his highly pleasurable to most human beings of all ages. It follows that if teachers can learn to direct this natural interest and enthusiasm properly, this type of music-making can be a source of important musical learnings.

USES OF MELODY AND HARMONY INSTRUMENTS

When melody instruments are used to invent introductions, codas, interludes, and to play tonal patterns, aspects of the structure of music are being experienced. The concept of the interval can be made clear by seeing intervals on keyboard instruments, and by seeing and feeling them on blowing-type instruments and comparing them to the written intervals on the staff. The effect of the key signature is relatively unimpressive from the vocal standpoint, but undeniably significant in connection with playing an instrument. Note-reading becomes clearly practical and functional when the player must relate notation to the keyboard or to fingerings on a small wind instrument. Instruments can assist in part-singing. Chording instruments are useful in helping children hear chord changes—a listening activity that is preparatory to part-singing. They are also useful in introducing the study of simple theory. The melody and harmony instruments are used to accompany songs, dramatic play, rhythmic movement; they enhance the moods of these activities. They can comprise special interest projects. They are important both to music and social studies by lending atmosphere to songs of the American Indian (flute-type instruments), folk songs of Europe and the Americas (autoharp, Harmolin, guitar, concertina, and occasionally the ukulele), the Orient (plucked strings of autoharp, psaltery, ukulele), and Latin American songs (the marimba). Furthermore, children can compose tunes and songs with the aid of instruments. The variety of instruments assures that every child can take part regardless of ability. The instruments are easy to play; they can be taught by the classroom teacher. They induce good discipline by requiring co-operation and precision.

WATER GLASSES AND BOTTLES

Many teachers use water glasses and bottles as introductory experiences to keyboard instruments such as bells, xylophone, and piano. There are tuned glasses that can be used without water, obtainable from various sources on order, even from some variety stores. Other teachers employ glasses with water, knowing that this probably means some spilling and evaporation, both of which necessitate retuning because of the change in water levels. Some teachers use bottles with water, often corked or capped to keep retuning at a minimum.

One of the first listening activities in primary grades is the experimenting with sounds made with metal, wood, glass, and stone. These early experiences lead to experiments with water glasses and bottles. By striking glasses and bottles when they are empty and when they contain water, children can make certain scientific observations. They discover that the pitch and tone quality are affected by the size and thickness of the glass or bottle. They may also discover that decreasing the amount of water raises the pitch and increasing the amount of water lowers the pitch—except in some glasses and bottles that will not tune lower no matter how much water is added. They may also discover that striking glasses or bottles with soft objects such as felt-covered mallets produces soft tones.

After experimenting with glasses and bottles, children and teacher may decide that bottles are superior because if one can seal them, the pitch will remain stable. However, the most important element of comparison should be the beauty of the sound, which could be determined by the quality of the glass in either of these instruments. Paint or paper strips can be placed on them to show the water level that produces the desired pitch. Numeral names, note names, or syllable names can be painted on or written on paper stickers. Some teachers put vegetable dyes or other coloring in the water to add interest. Placing the glasses on a thick cloth will result in a better tone.

Interest in playing melodies on bottles may prompt the teacher or the children to make or obtain a rack from which to suspend the bottles. When this is done, each bottle is suspended by two loops of string, one on each side of the bottle neck, to help it to hang with more stability.

The first experience in playing songs on glasses or bottles is generally with only three pitches: 3-2-1 (mi-re-do). However, it is good to compose a song with only one pitch, that of 1 (do); then a song with scale tones 1 and 2;

and, finally, a song with tones 1, 2, and 3, arriving at the three-pitch stage in a logical way.   Favorite songs in the three-tone category are "Hot Cross Buns" and "Mary Had a Little Lamb" (slightly altered).   After this, the next step is to use four- and five-tone melodies.   Teachers usually devise their own three-, four-, and five-tone songs, and encourage the children to compose others.   After songs such as these have been learned, more scale tones are added and eventually melodies are played using all eight tones of the major scale.[1]   It is advantageous to transfer the skills acquired on glasses and bottles to wooden or metal xylophones.   In this book the term *bells* will be used to denote metal types of xylophones, which are good preparation for the piano keyboard.

THE BELLS

When the bells are introduced to the children, the children will soon feel at home with them if the teacher asks questions such as: "Can you find a high pitch?"   "Can you find a low pitch?"   "Can you find pitches that are near each other?"   "Can you find pitches that are far apart?"   "Can you play the same pitch twice?"   "Three times?"

Perfection Song Bells
WALBERG & AUGE

[1] Every major scale conforms to the following pattern:
whole-step   whole-step   half-step
whole-step
whole-step   whole-step   half-step
F major scale:

Notice that this scale consists of whole-steps with the exception of the intervals between 3 and 4, and 7 and 8, which are half-steps.   One of the best ways to learn the major scale is to see it and play it on the keyboard.   A major scale may begin on any note the player chooses, and its name is the same as that of the beginning note.

Playing of simple songs on the bells often begins in the key of C so that children are not confused by the black keys. However, with guidance and careful listening, children in first grade can play songs or parts of songs in keys such as F and G major where one black key is necessary. The general procedure at first is to learn a song well by rote before attempting to play it (*listen, sing,* then *play*).

Before children understand music notation, teachers guide them to play by ear and by numeral notation.[2] The scale-tone numbers can be written on the white metal keys with black crayon, or they can be placed on tagboard in back of the bells. Numeral notation could appear as follows. Notice that the "fast notes" are circled.

Hot Cross Buns	*Mary Had a Little Lamb*
3 2 1 – 3 2 1 –	3212 333– 222– 333–
1111 2222 3 2 1 –	3212 3333 2232 1——
five-note tune	six-note tune
Jingle Bells	*Are You Sleeping?*
333– 333– 3512 3——	1 2 3 1 1 2 3 1 3 4 5 – 3 4 5 –
4444 433333223 2–5–	56543 1 56543 1 1 5 1 – 1 5 1 –
333– 333– 3512 3——	
4444 433335542 1——	

Use C major or G major to avoid black keys. Use F major to introduce one black key (B♭). *Hot Cross Buns* and *Mary Had a Little Lamb* can be played on the group of three black keys. Some teachers prefer to introduce the piano keyboard in this way to overcome possible hesitation about the black keys later.

Although children may begin playing songs with the aid of numerals, they are soon looking at notation the teacher has prepared for them that includes the numerals written beneath (or above) the note they represent. Later, teachers prepare notation in which the numerals appear only with the beginning note of each measure, then only with the beginning note of each phrase, and finally they are abandoned altogether because the children have made the transition from numerals to the notes on the staff.

The bells have many uses. If a classroom teacher has a "low" voice or lacks confidence in his singing voice, the instrument can be used to teach rote songs. Difficult tonal patterns in songs can be isolated and studied by means of the bells. They are often employed to establish the pitch of songs by sounding the keynote, playing tones of the tonic chord (I), then

2 A well-known book that introduces numeral notation in kindergarten and first grade in *Timothy's Tunes* by Adeline McCall (Boston Music Company). The *Psaltery Book* by Satis Coleman (John Day Company) is another. *Fun with the Melody-bells* by R. J. Staples (Follett) further develops the use of numeral notation.

playing the starting pitch.   Special sound effects such as chimes, church bells and sleigh bells can be produced to enhance songs.   Children can create tunes and songs with the aid of the bells; they can play simple parts of songs involving a single tone up to an entire scale, and they can play complete songs.   Introductions, codas, and interludes—all created on the bells—can be added to songs.   Older children can write descants and other added parts to songs and play them on the bells.   Bells can assist part-singing.

The "suggestions to the teacher" in one of the music series books states that if children had access to keyboard instruments, many of the problems in teaching understanding of pitch differences, of the interval relationship of tones, and of music notation generally would be minimized.   The reason is that the keyboard constitutes a highly significant *audio-visual* tool for learning.   Children enjoy "picking out tunes" and in doing so on the bells or piano they *see* and *feel* and *hear* the interval relationships of tones.   This can lead to a real comprehension of the meaning of the notes on the staff—a comprehension frequently lacking in children whose musical experiences have been confined to a singing approach.   In every elementary classroom there should be a music corner that includes bells and easy music to play on them.   Some teachers regularly have a "song of the week" which children learn to play in the music corner before school, after school, and during the school day.   When played with a padded mallet or a pencil with a rubber eraser, this soft-toned instrument seldom disturbs other classroom activities.   See *Keyboard Experience* on page 134 for more uses of bells.

The *xylophone* is similar to the bells, but made of wood instead of metal.   *Xylo* is the Greek word for wood.   Because its wood strips do not vibrate as long as the metal bars of the bells, it has a more percussive quality.   A more attractive xylophone is the *marimba*, which has resonators, usually metal tubes, beneath the wood strips.   German music educators use the term xylophone, but prefer the terms *glockenspiel* or *metallophone* to bells.   The metallophone is often lower pitched than the glockenspiel.

Xylophone
EDUCATIONAL MUSIC BUREAU

Marimba
EDUCATIONAL MUSIC BUREAU

Resonator bells are individual tone bars that can be used and arranged in different ways, some relating to chording. These uses will be discussed later.

Bells and xylophones in pentatonic composition. The resonator bells and certain German-made glockenspiels and xylophones are particularly useful in creative work within the pentatonic scale, which is one consisting of five pitches. The reader can understand the organization of the pentatonic scale easily if he thinks of it as scale tones 1 2 3 5 6 of a major scale. Scale tone 8, which is 1 an octave higher, completes the scale, producing six different pitches, with the first and last being the same note an octave apart.

The study both of children and of primitive cultures reveals a natural preference for the use of the pentatonic mode. An increasing amount of children's musical improvisation and composition is being done within this framework today. It is based upon the fact that the harmonic sense of children is not well developed until the upper elementary years, and the theory that young children therefore need melody and combinations of melodies without the type of harmony in which chord changes appear. Since the pentatonic mode contains no dissonances when parts are combined, because it has no half-steps, its use can provide the kind of music that children are assumed to need in earlier phases of their musical development.

Resonator bells can be arranged in pentatonic formation by simply removing the bells that are not part of the scale to which the teacher desires the improvising and composing to be restricted. German-made xylophones and glockenspiels designed by Carl Orff are constructed so that the bars of wood or metal can be easily removed. Many bell sets and xylophones do not have this feature, and the teacher must then devise some way, such as fastening paper over the unneeded bars, to keep the children from playing the nonpentatonic pitches.

Discussion of pentatonic composition will be found in Chapter Nine. Few true pentatonic songs are found in series books; teachers and children can and should create their own.

Resonator Bells
B. F. KITCHING & CO., INC.

THE AUTOHARP, HARMOLIN, AND OTHER CHORDING INSTRUMENTS

The autoharp is an instrument of ancient lineage which has come to be popular in elementary and junior high schools, and is used by ballad singers on radio and television. The model most commonly used has 12 push-button bars with felts that prevent the vibration of strings other than those that sound the chord tones desired. It is usually preferred to the five-bar model, which has value in primary grades, because it can be played in more keys, and is thus generally more useful. While "Autoharp" is the registered trademark of the manufacturer, common usage of the word has led Webster to place it in the English language as an uncapitalized familiar word.

Autoharp
OSCAR SCHMIDT-INTERNATIONAL, INC.

Although exceptional children in primary grades are able to play the instrument satisfactorily, it is not until the fourth grade that most children can do well with it. In early primary grades teachers often press the buttons while children strum the strings. It is believed that guiding children to listen carefully to autoharp chording assists the development of a feeling for harmony, which is part of the preparation for part-singing in intermediate grades. It is something of a substitute for the piano in situations where no piano is available, as well as being valuable for enrichment in rooms that have pianos. Hearing chord changes and playing the correct chord at the proper time are valuable for ear-training purposes, and teachers should emphasize these as listening experiences in their efforts to develop children's musicianship. The act of chording is a rhythmic response. A child who is yet unable to sing beautifully may be able to make as beautiful music on the autoharp as anyone else; thus success on this instrument can help individual children feel a sense of accomplishment essential to good social and emotional growth. Chording on the autoharp is an effective way to stimulate interest in the study of chords on the piano. Another use of the autoharp is to establish the tempo of a song by playing introductory chords in the desired rhythm.

The autoharp is placed on a desk or table, with the corner between the two straight ends of the instrument pointing somewhat toward the player. Fingers of the left hand press firmly on the appropriate button while the right hand strokes the full range of the strings from left to right with a pick. Sometimes the player may choose to stroke the strings on the left side of the bridge to produce a deeper-toned effect than is obtained on the right side. *Finger forms* are important, and the player needs to analyze the chord progressions he is to play, then plan the most simple and efficient way to place the correct finger on the button. In most of the music suggested for autoharp chording there will be no more than three chords, the tonic (I), the dominant seventh (V_7), and the subdominant (IV). The finger form for these chords in the 12-bar autoharp keys of C major, G major, F major, D minor, and A minor is as follows:

IV V_7 I

left hand

fourth finger   middle finger   first finger

Try this finger form in the above keys, and find the straight position and the triangular position of the fingers in this basic finger form.

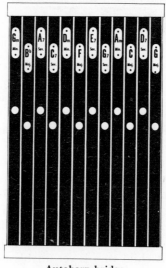

Autoharp bridge

The strings are strummed with a pick held in the right hand. The loud tone produced with a celluloid pick is needed for most classroom singing, while the soft tone produced with a felt pick is good for solo and small ensemble singing. The pick is placed on the pointer finger of the right hand with the long side covering the nail. Men teachers often use their finger nails instead of a pick.

When teaching children to play the autoharp, it is the usual practice to begin with songs that require only one chord to accompany, proceed to those requiring two chords, then to songs in which three chords are necessary, and so on. It is desirable to play at least part of the time by rote to be sure that the children are *hearing* the chord changes, not simply pushing buttons mechanically. Such songs follow:

I–chord songs:	*key:*
Little Tom Tinker	C major
Are You Sleeping?	F major
For Health and Strength	F major
Canoe Song	D minor
Zum Gali Gali	G minor

I–V$_7$ chord songs:	
Mary Had a Little Lamb	G major
London Bridge	F major
Oats, Peas, Beans	C major
Billy Boy	C major
Down in the Valley	F major
Nobody Knows the Trouble I've Seen	G major
Nobody Home	G minor

I–IV chord songs:	
Lovely Evening	F major
Wayfaring Stranger	D minor

I–V$_7$–IV chord songs:	
Silent Night	C major
Brahms' Lullaby	C major
Marines' Hymn	C major
My Bonnie	G major
Camptown Races	G major
Red River Valley	F major
Home on the Range	F major
Go Down, Moses	A minor
Old King Cole	D minor

A summary of the chord resources of the 12-bar autoharp is as follows:

Two-chord songs	I, V$_7$	C major, G major, F major, D minor, A minor, B♭ major, G minor
Three-chord songs	I, V$_7$, IV	C major, G major, F major, D minor, A minor
Four-chord songs	I, V$_7$, IV, II	C major, G major, F major
Five-chord songs	I, V$_7$, IV, II, VI	C major, F major

Since some two- and three-chord songs are not written in these common keys, using the autoharp to accompany them requires *transposing* them into the above-listed keys. This involves only placing the fingers in the finger form of the key nearest to the original key of the song and following the I, V_7, and IV designations or their equivalent in letter names. The teacher should be certain that the range of pitches in the new key is suitable for the children's voices.

A major problem in the use of autoharps is that of tuning them. There is no universally accepted method. Ordinarily, one tunes to a piano that is in proper pitch. The strings sounding the C major chord may be tuned first (all the C's, E's, and G's), then the strings of the G_7 chord (all B's, D's, and F's—the G's having been tuned as part of the C chord), and next the F major chord (all A's—the F's and C's having been tuned as pitches belonging to the other chords). These three chords should then be played slowly to hear whether any of the strings need further adjusting. After this, the other strings may be tuned as individual tones of the chromatic scale (all the half-steps). Then every chord of the instrument is played slowly to determine possible need for further tuning. A child can play the pitches on the piano while the teacher adjusts the strings. As a general rule, the teacher must do the adjusting of the strings, not the children. The only cases the authors know where strings have been broken are those in which elementary school children tighten strings to the breaking point because they think they hear the pitch to which they are tuning one octave higher than it actually sounds. To keep the instrument in tune and to protect it, it should be kept either in the box it comes in or on a covered shelf, and out of the sunlight and away from sources of heat, cold, or dampness. When the instrument is subject to changes in temperature, the expansion and contraction of the strings cause changes in their tension, hence changes in pitch.

Some European music educators who strongly recommend an emphasis on creative pentatonic music in the primary classroom do not look with favor on chording instruments such as the autoharp at this level, claiming that children do not possess sufficient harmonic sense at this age to profit from it. However, many American educators believe that chording instruments can provide a valuable listening experience for this age group. Children can learn to recognize the I-chord as the "home" chord, the V_7-chord as the "away-from-home" chord, and the IV-chord as the "longing-for-home" or "leaning" chord. They can identify them by appropriate motions: the "home" chord with folded arms, the "away-from-home" chord with outstretched arms, and the "leaning" chord by raising both arms to the left or to the right. Children can create other interpretations of the characteristic sound of each of these chords, and create their own related bodily responses.

Types of autoharp accompaniments. Like any other musical instrument, the autoharp should be played with good taste, and there should be logical reasons for the particular style of the accompaniment played.

The mood of the song indicates whether the player uses a slow relaxed stroke (as for lullabies and quiet songs), or a strong fast stroke (as for marches and rhythmic, exciting songs). For some waltzes, an um-pah-pah style is called for. This can be made by playing the first beat of each measure with low-pitched strings and the other two beats with high-pitched strings. A deeper, richer effect is obtained by playing on the left side of the bridge. This brings out the sound of the lower strings and omits a few of the highest pitches. The player can make an appropriate accompaniment for some Spanish-type music by chording in the rhythm of ♩. ♪♩ ♩ . A bagpipe or bourdon effect is made by holding down major and minor buttons at the same time: G major and G minor, D_7 and D minor, and A_7 and A minor. This effect is useful for pentatonic music, for some Scottish music, and for folk songs based upon the open fifth of the bagpipe or musette. Individual strings can be plucked to simulate Oriental-type music. A zither or tamburitza effect that accompanies some Eastern European folk music attractively can be produced by two players on the same instrument. One player presses the buttons while the other strokes the strings rapidly with wooden mallets. A metal bar or object placed across the strings will produce a steel guitar effect. Minor seventh chords can be sounded when two instruments are used. For example, G-minor and B♭-major chords played simultaneously on two autoharps, each sounding one of these chords, will sound the G-minor seventh chord. A minor plus C major will sound the A-minor seventh chord, and D minor plus F major sounds the D-minor seventh chord. For songs of slow tempo, a skilled player can produce both the melody and the harmony. To obtain this effect, a chord is played for each tone of the melody, and the player strums the strings only as far as the melody pitch. A harp effect is obtained by reversing the usual stroke, the player beginning the stroke with the high strings and moving the pick toward the low strings.

"Autoharp chords" appear in many recent music books, and are commonly found in music series books. Besides the many references to the instrument in such books, there are other helpful publications concerned with both the autoharp and the Harmolin,[3] a somewhat similar instrument. Some examples are:

Autoharp Accompaniments to Favorite Songs, by Lillian Mohr Fox. Summy-Birchard Publishing Co., 1834 Ridge Ave., Evanston, Illinois.

Autoharp Song Folio, by Evelyn Waldrop. William J. Smith Music Company, 245 W. 31st St., New York, N.Y.

Fun with the Classroom Harps, by Rj Staples. Follett Publishing Company, 1010 W. Washington Blvd., Chicago, Illinois.

Golden Autoharp Melodies, by Sigmund Spaeth. National Autoharp Sales Co., 560 31st St., Des Moines, Iowa.

---

[3] Harmolin, Inc. P.O. Box 244, La Jolla, California.

Harmony Fun with the Autoharp, by Beatrice Krone. Neil A. Kjos Music Co., 525 Busse Highway, Park Ridge, Illinois.

Singing With Children, by Robert E. Nye, Vernice T. Nye, Neva Aubin, and George Kyme. Wadsworth Publishing Company, Davis Drive, Belmont, California. Chapter 6, "Songs with Autoharp and Ukulele."

Teachers Guide for the Golden Autoharp, by Lorrain Watters. National Autoharp Sales Co., 560 31st St., Des Moines, Iowa.

Ukulele and guitar. If the desirability of chording experiences on the autoharp has gained wide acceptance in elementary music education, it follows that there should be similar values in other chording instruments such as the ukulele and guitar. The ukulele has supporters from the fourth grade on, and chording on the steel guitar is used by some teachers. It is urged that teachers and children experiment to find the comparative advantages of each instrument.

Standard tuning on the ukulele was once G-C-E-A. In recent years a preference for tuning the instrument one whole step higher, to A-D-F♯-B,

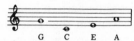

has developed. Thus, the ukulele beginner finds two tunings in current use. Fingering for common keys is on page 133. Notice that if the teacher employs both tunings, the fingering for the common chords in G major and F major become the same, as does that for D major and C major.

Most ukuleles are made of wood, and need the same protection against dropping, cold, heat, and sun that the autoharp needs. Extreme dampness, dryness, or temperature changes will change the tuning and could crack the body of the instrument. Children need to be informed about how to strum the instrument or they may break strings by pulling them.

Spanish guitars are changed to steel guitars by installing a small steel piece at the edge of the peg-box. This can be done at most music stores at small cost. The steel piece can easly be removed when desired. As some teachers use the steel guitar, it is tuned to pitches that form the

A-major chord. The chord names are marked by placing stickers between the frets with printed chord names written on them. Each is covered with Scotch tape to keep it clean. In order, from the peg-box, the chord names are B♭, B, C, D♭, D, E♭, E, F, G♭, G, A♭. The instrument is placed on a table, and the children stand to play it. They move a steel bar from chord to chord, and strum with the fingers, although picks can be used. The steel bars should be simple and of light weight. The bar is held in

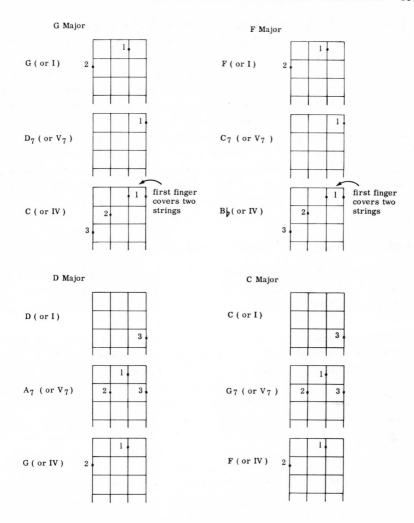

the left hand between the thumb and first finger, and must be pressed firmly enough against the strings so that they sound clearly when the player strums.   The other fingers of the left hand should rest on the strings to muffle the metallic noise caused by lifting the steel and sliding from one chord to another.   Advantages of this instrument include its ease of playing and its appeal for children.   Among its disadvantages are the doubtful aesthetic effect of the parallel construction of every chord, the absence of seventh chords, and the difficulty in playing minor chords, which can be sounded in incomplete fashion by strumming only the four largest strings.

The standard guitar (not the steel guitar) has long been accepted in

Europe as an instrument of quality. As such it is taught in schools of music and as a part of teacher education in music. This has not been true in the United States, perhaps owing in part to radio and television personalities who sing and play "Western music" to the discredit of the instrument. However, the American public now enthusiastically attends and appreciates the performances of professional artists such as Segovia, thus a trend toward acceptance of the guitar seems to be in the making. The Spanish guitar is a six-stringed instrument. There are two common types. One has a round sound-hole, is strung with either steel or nylon strings, and produces a mellow tone. The other has F-shaped sound-holes, is strung with steel strings, and has a brilliant tone. Elementary school children might play a three-quarter size instrument, in keeping with their stage of physical growth. Instruction books are available at music stores.

KEYBOARD EXPERIENCE AND THE PIANO

The term "keyboard experience" is defined as a use of the piano that makes a substantial contribution to the program of general music. It does not stress performing skill in the traditional sense. The piano can be used by children in the primary grades in connection with songs in the same informal ways the percussion instruments and bells are used. Children in intermediate grades can use it for chording in the way they use the autoharp. Like the bells, the piano keyboard provides an audio-visual tool to help the child gain keener perception of the interval relationship of tones, and of many other aspects of music, all of which can develop into a thorough understanding of notation. Through piano chording a foothold in comprehending the science of music theory is gained in a logical way. The piano can be used as an instrument of percussion, melody, harmony, and for any combination of these. Hence it is a superior means through which to teach the fundamentals of music.

Classroom teachers do not have to be pianists to teach music through keyboard experience. They need only to be introduced to it so that they can proceed in the same way the children do. In the beginning a child can play a tone that sounds "one" when the clock strikes "one" in *Hickory Dickory Dock,* just as he may have done earlier on the bells. In a song that has words of importance on one or two tones, children may play these at the time they occur in the melody. The same little three-note melodies played on water glasses, bottles, and bells can be played on the piano keyboard. As time goes on, four- and five-finger patterns can be used in an incidental way in both ascending and descending forms. Here are some examples of such usage:

one finger   The child plays repeated single tones such as the beginning of *Jingle Bells* and in many chants (pages 214–219). He can play a tone-matching game by striking a pitch that is within his voice range, then trying to match it vocally.

two fingers The child plays repeated motives in songs and can also match tones, playing as well as singing such scale tones as 5 and 3 ("so" and "mi").

three fingers The scale tones 3 2 1 can be played whenever the words "three blind mice" occur in the song of that name. The tonal pattern 1 2 3 1 can be played with the words "Are you sleeping?" in the song of that name.

four fingers Scale tones 4 4 3 3 2 2 1 in *Twinkle, Twinkle, Little Star* can be played when the following words appear: "How I wonder what you are," and "Twinkle, twinkle all the night." Scale tones 5 5 4 4 3 3 2 can be played along with the words, "Up above the world so high," and "Like a diamond in the sky."

five fingers Scale tones 5 43 21 are used at the end of *Row Your Boat* with the words, "Life is but a dream," and the scale tones 5 443 2 1 are used with the words "Ten little Indian boys" at the end of that song. Complete songs requiring only five fingers can easily be played. Such songs include *Aunt Rhodie, Mary Had a Little Lamb,* and *Jingle Bells.*

scales Many songs are based on scales and parts of scales that can readily be played on the keyboard.

A book of piano duets for a child and an older person, *The Two of Us* (Summy-Birchard), contains examples of the above usages of the keyboard and is applicable in the classroom. A natural outgrowth of such piano-song relationships is the composing of little songs within the limitations of three, four, and five scale tones—songs that children can both sing and play. Eventually this activity will lead to the use of more scale tones in song composition.

The resourceful teacher will gain pleasure and satisfaction in finding songs to which these simple uses of the piano are suited, knowing that by such processes children learn to listen and thus improve their singing ability at the same time. This type of keyboard experience merges with the listening process of tone-matching and makes it more of a game because of the added variety.

Another simple use of the piano is the playing of the notes according to the chord names to provide an easy added part to songs. Example: play F with the F chord, G with the G chord, and so on. (See *Chord Roots*, Chapter Seven). Still more of the almost limitless things for children to do with the keyboard instruments include playing the rhythm of children's names with one tone or a series of tones; playing two tones that illustrate in correct pitch the concepts of high and low pitch in connection with songs; playing short tonal patterns for tone-matching purposes or to add interest to songs; playing octave intervals in songs that emphasize this interval; playing other intervals in songs that feature them; playing running notes, walking notes and other note values or rhythm patterns for other children to respond to; playing entire characteristic phrases as in the beginning of "The Caisson Song"; aiding part-singing by playing part-songs from the series books with two hands, one on each part; and using the piano to accompany songs by chording.

The playing of the bells, a small instrument, logically comes before the playing of the piano, a very large instrument, but whatever is done on the bells applies directly to the piano because the keyboard is virtually the same.

PIANO CHORDING

Since the 1 3 5 note pattern becomes a familiar one to children, being used both in their songs and in the procedure that enables the class to have a feeling for the key before singing (Chapter Six, page 187) this is a logical note combination to use in beginning to teach chording. This 1 3 5 chord (a major *triad* in *root position*) is also an initial concept in the formal study of music theory. From chording experiences will come understandings of elementary theory.

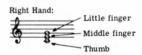

Should a child be unable to exert equal pressure through these three fingers or in any other way be unable to control them at first, he may use any combination of fingers of both hands to accomplish the playing of this chord, or he may play only the two highest notes of a three-note chord, a procedure often employed in primary grades. The teacher may help the child to play the chord in a steady walking-note rhythm, then while he continues playing in rhythm, have the class sing "Row, row, row your boat." To a child who has never played the piano, the discovery that he can accompany a well-known song in this simple manner is thrilling. There are few songs that can be accompanied by the lone 1 3 5 chord. Some were listed earlier in this chapter on page 131.

Songs that rightfully require two chords (I and V_7) but that might be usable as one-chord songs include "Old MacDonald," "Farmer in the Dell," "Three Blind Mice," "Goodbye Old Paint," "Swing Low Sweet Chariot," "Taps," and "Shortnin' Bread."

ROW, ROW, ROW YOUR BOAT

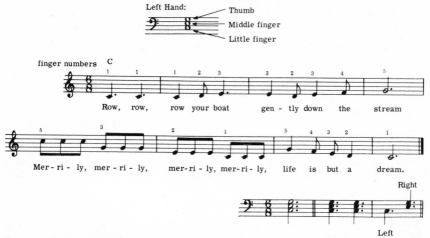

Summary of possibilities:

Play the melody with the right hand.

Play the melody with the left hand.

Play the chord with the left hand.

Play the chord with the right hand.

Play the chord with both hands.

Play the melody with the right hand and the chord with the left hand.

Play the melody with the left hand (in bass clef) and the chord with the right hand (in treble clef).

Play the chord in other forms, such as one note at a time.

How often the chord is sounded depends on how the individual feels about the song. One child may play a chord on every beat (the rhythm of the meter). Another may choose to sound the chord every other beat. Still another child may alter the steady pattern of chord-sounding by a pause at the end of a phrase. Children should be free to be as individually creative as possible in this simple way. The teacher will recognize many individual differences in the ways that children react to keyboard experience.

When a child has learned how to build 1 3 5 chords on different pitches such as C, F, G, and has learned to recognize the distinctive sound of the major chord, the 1 3 5 chord in minor may be easily taught. A child can soon learn that the minor chord has its own characteristic sound and that he can build both major and minor chords at will. Experience will expand the child's feeling for the difference in sound between major and minor. The mechanical difference between major and minor 1 3 5 chords is merely that the middle finger, which plays scale tone 3, is placed one half-step lower in minor than in major. Very few commonly known songs can be accompanied by the lone minor 1 3 5 chord, but children can compose such songs easily. An example follows:

SLAVE SONG

Fourth Grade Four-Part Round

Piano chording:

Suggested rhythmic responses:

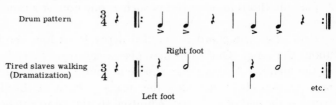

Singing and playing:

A piano part invented later which can be sung as a chant:

The children discovered that their song could be sung as a round.

A song of Israeli origin that can be accompanied by the G-minor chord is "Zum Gali Gali."[4]

When numerals are used to designate scale tones, the home tone in minor is "6." When syllables are used for this purpose, the home tone in minor is "la" while the home tone in major is "do." See footnote, p. 304.

If children have used the autoharp with songs requiring two or more different chords, the addition of the V_7 chord[5] to permit improvising a piano accompaniment to many familiar songs is relatively easy. A simple form of the chord change from I to V_7 and back to I is as follows:[6]

Using the hand position for the 1 3 5 chord as a starting point, the following directions apply in *all* major keys:

right hand: The little finger remains on the same key. The fourth finger is placed one half-step higher than the third finger was. The thumb is placed one half-step lower than before.

left hand: The thumb remains on the same key. The index finger is placed one half-step higher than the middle finger was. The little finger is placed one half-step lower than before.

Many familiar songs can be harmonized with the I and V_7 chords. Some of the most familiar are "Chop Sticks," "Put Your Little Foot," "Billy Boy," "Listen to the Mocking Bird," "Singing in the Rain," "Clementine," "Shoo Fly," "Alouette," "Deaf Woman's Courtship," "Ten Little Indians," "Long Long Ago," "Skip to My Lou," "Where Has My Little Dog Gone?," "Polly-Wolly-Doodle," "Hot Cross Buns," "Lightly Row," "Oats Peas Beans and Barley," "Mary Had a Little Lamb," "London Bridge," "Down in the Valley," "Farmer in the Dell," "Three Blind Mice," "Did You Ever See a Lassie?," "Old Texas," "Looby Lou," "Buffalo Gals," "Lavender Blue," and "Bow Belinda."

Since most songs in minor keys are based on a scale in which the seventh

---

[4] This song is in *Open Road Song Book* (Cooperative Recreation Service, Delaware, Ohio, *Music in Our Country* (Music for Living Series) p. 169, *Voices of the World* (Together We Sing Series) p. 132, *This Is Music: Book Six*, p. 167, and *Singing With Children*, p. 175.

[5] See page 147 for an explanation of the origin of the hand position for playing the V_7 chord.

[6] A more simple form used in primary grades omits the lowest note of each of the chords.

tone is raised one half-step, practically all minor I-V$_7$ chord songs will have the V$_7$ chord played exactly the same as it is played in the major keys of the same name, i.e., the V$_7$ chord in G minor is usually the same chord as in G major. Thus, the only difference in chording would be in the I

CLEMENTINE

Piano chords:

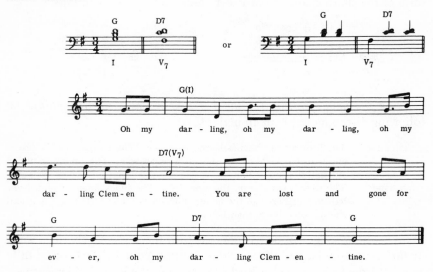

chord, which in minor would have its third (the middle note) one half-step lower than in the major chord. It is a simple matter, then, to play "Nobody Home" in G minor:[7]

NOBODY HOME

---

[7] Some musicians abbreviate G minor by writing "g," and G major by "G."

Piano chording:

or

or yet another way:

Suggestion: Try making up an introduction using the style of Example 3. Also, improvise an ending for this round.   Add suitable percussion instruments and hand clapping.

Other interesting songs in minor that use these same chords are the French carol "Pat-a-pan" and the English carol "Dame, Get Up."   Percussion instruments go well with "Pat-a-pan."

The hand position for the IV chord is easier than the hand position for the V_7 chord.   The "rule" for the change from I to IV is as follows:

left hand: The little finger remains on the same key.   The index finger is placed one half-step higher than the middle finger was.   The thumb moves up one whole step.

right hand: The thumb remains on the same key.   The middle finger is placed one half-step higher than before.   The little finger moves up one whole step.

The round "Christmas Bells" provides a good introduction to this chord change.   Use the above chords as marked.   See page 148 for an explanation of the origin of the hand position for playing the IV chord.

The familiar round "Lovely Evening" and the cowboy song "The Railroad Corral" (*This Is Music: Book 6*, page 23) are other examples of songs that require only the I and IV chords for their harmonization.

CHRISTMAS BELLS

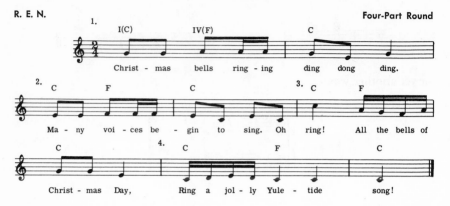

The IV chord in minor is played by lowering the highest of the three tones of the major IV chord one half-step. An American folk song that can be harmonized with only I and IV chords is "Wayfaring Stranger":

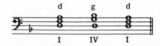

WAYFARING STRANGER

Examples of the many songs in major keys easily chorded with I, IV, and V₇ chords are "The Caisson Song," "Oh Susanna," "He's a Jolly Good Fellow," "The First Noel," "Camptown Races," "Home on the Range," "America," "Night Herding Song," "Eyes of Texas (I've Been Working on the Railroad)," "All Through the Night," "Sing Your Way Home," "Jingle Bells," "Deck the Halls," "Happy Birthday to You," "Old Oaken Bucket," "Auld Lang Syne," "Annie Laurie," "Old Folks at Home," "Old Black Joe," "Reuben and Rachel," "Silent Night," "Santa Lucia," "The Muffin Man."

CINDY

Appalachian Mountains Song

This use of the piano in the classroom can result in a teacher's learning to play comparatively well. Should any teacher desire to hasten this learning process, there are beginning piano books that employ and expand the method of chording used in this chapter; by means of these an adult can teach himself to play with more skill. A list of such books is found at the end of the chapter. Music textbooks that exemplify the different types of simple classroom piano chording include *Singing With Children* (Wadsworth Publishing Company), Chapter 8: "Songs With Simple Piano Chording," and *Basic Music for Classroom Teachers, Second Edition* (Prentice-Hall, Inc.).

Teachers should use the loud pedal of the piano very sparingly. A common fault of piano players is overuse of this pedal, which results in a blur of tones rather than in the clarity and distinctness children need to hear.

If one can chord with I, IV, and V_7 chords in major keys, it is not difficult to chord in minor keys with I, IV, and V_7. Incidentally, minor keys are not as important as major keys as far as common usage in the United States is concerned. While peoples of Eastern Europe find in minor tonality a natural expression, the people of the United States lean rather heavily toward the major tonality. American children should be able to identify minor and major and to enjoy hearing the changes from minor to major and vice versa in songs such as "We Three Kings of Orient Are," "When Johnny Comes Marching Home," and "Minka," but it is not necessary in the elementary school to do much with technical matters such as the different kinds of minor scales.

OTHER INSTRUMENTS FOR CHORDING

The "piano chords" can be played on resonator bells effectively. Teachers use these individual tone bars in many ways. The bars can be distributed among numbers of children, each having a bar and a mallet with which to strike it. In the key of C, for example, all children who hold bells marked C, E, or G, will sound them when the C-major chord is needed, and when the F-major chord is required in the harmonization of the song, all children holding bars that sound F, A, and C will strike them. Of course, they must be struck at the same instant, and this demands the close attention of the players. To produce an interesting shimmering effect, the player needs two mallets with which he strikes the bell in rapid alternation. Playing chords in this manner with appropriate songs can make truly beautiful music. Motivating a fourth, fifth, or sixth-grade class to harmonize a song in this way can initiate a study of chord structure that includes learning note names and their relation to the staff and key signature.

The *Melodica,* a two-octave chromatic harmonica-like instrument, can play either melody or chords. Some teachers use it to guard against overuse of their singing voices, or to substitute for a below-range or otherwise inadequate singing voice. Some teachers have attached rubber tubes to the mouthpiece to permit the child to place the instrument on his desk, thus having a better view of the keyboard.

Melodica
M. HOHNER, INC.

From fourth grade on the teacher must be prepared to answer certain questions. Let us try to forecast some of them.

    1. From where do the V_7 and IV chords come, and why are our fingers in the positions they are on the keyboard?

A 1 3 5 chord can be built on every step of the scale. We could chord by using only 1 3 5 chords, but it would be very awkward to do, and it would not sound well. What we are trying to do with our chord positions at the piano is to move our fingers as little as possible. It is something like being "intelligently lazy"—which in this case is also being efficient. Here are the I, IV, and V chords in 1 3 5 position in the C-major scale:

These chords can also be called.C, F, and G, because they have two names, one being the Roman numeral that corresponds to the Arabic number name of the scale tone on which the chord is built, and the other being the letter name of the note that is "1" when the chord is in 1 3 5 (root) position. Here is the V_7 chord in root position.

We are still in the key of C major. Compare the V_7 with the V above. This chord is called V_7 because a note has been added that is seven lines and spaces above G. The notes from the bottom to top in this chord are G, B, D, and F, or 1 3 5 7. It is V_7 because G is the fifth step of the scale of C, and we are using that key in this illustration.

The following illustration shows where we obtain the simple three-finger hand position for chording:

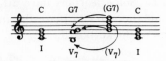

By rearranging the G 1 3 5 7 chord into another *position,* and by omitting the note D, which is the one we can most easily eliminate without injuring the sound of the chord, we can keep the hand in the same place as it was in playing the I chord and move only the fingers.

The IV chord that we use in piano chording is another position of the original 1 3 5 arrangement of the notes:

Common chord positions are:

The first inversion is called 6–3 because if one counts from the lowest note to the highest, numbering the lowest note "1," the *interval*[8] is found to be that of a *sixth*. Counting in similar manner, from the lowest note to the middle one, reveals that this interval is a *third,* hence this is a 6–3 chord. The origin of the name of the 6–4 chord can be counted out in the same way. The two intervals here are a sixth and a *fourth,* hence the name 6–4 chord.

2. Why do we have sharps or flats in major keys?

Every major scale has the same structure, being built of whole-steps except for the intervals between scale tones 3 and 4, and 7 and 8, which are half-steps. The teacher can explain this by holding up the bells and showing the class by sight and sound why sharps or flats are in all major keys except the key of C—and why the key of C needs no sharps or flats.

3. Why is the key of G minor in the same key signature as B♭ major?

---

[8] For an explanation of the term "interval," see Chapter Ten, p. 307. Also see Appendix C.

Every minor scale begins on the sixth step of some major scale. Since G is the sixth step of the B♭ major scale, G minor is therefore *related* to B♭ major and they both have the same key signature. C minor is the *relative* minor to E♭ major; E minor is the relative minor to G major. Again, the bells are useful in explaining this, as is the piano keyboard.

4. Where does the sharp or natural come from when we play the V_7 chord in minor keys? What are the minor scales?

There are three kinds of minor scales: the natural, the harmonic, and the melodic. When the natural minor is used, there are no accidentals (sharps, flats, cancel signs). (See "Wayfaring Stranger," p. 144.)

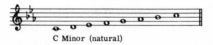

C Minor (natural)

If one listens carefully as this scale is played, he will find that there is a whole-step between scale tones 7 and 8. This is unlike the major scale, which always has a half-step between 7 and 8. Possibly in order to make this scale sound more like the major scale does, people raised that seventh step by one half-step. The new scale was called the *harmonic* minor scale. It is this raising of the seventh step that gives us our sharp or natural in the V_7 chord, and makes that chord the same as the V_7 in the major key of the same name—in this case C major. C minor is called the *parallel* minor to C major since they both begin and end on the same note.

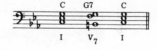

People changed the minor scale again so that its highest four notes would sound just like those notes of the major scale. To do this, they raised one half-step the sixth step of the minor scale along with the seventh step. This resulted in making the IV chord in the melodic minor scale (ascending) just like the IV chord in the parallel major key. An interesting difference about the melodic minor scale is that when it descends, it changes back to the original natural minor.

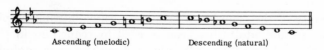

Ascending (melodic)   Descending (natural)

RECORDER-TYPE AND FLUTE-TYPE INSTRUMENTS

These instruments are used most frequently in the fourth and fifth grades. However, some third grades do well with them, and the recorder and the Melody Flute are acceptable in the sixth grade as well as in earlier grades.

The recorder is the ancestor of the present-day flute, and composers of the past such as Bach, Purcell, and Telemann, as well as some present-day composers, have written music for it. There has been a revival of interest in the instrument to the point that there are a great many adult recorder groups all over the United States, and there is a quarterly magazine called *The American Recorder*. Players unite in an organization called The American Recorder Society, Inc., 114 East 85th Street, New York 28, New York. All this is motivated by the facts that the recorder is not difficult to play, although it is not the easiest small instrument to master, and that a great volume of fine literature is available for it—a statement that cannot be made of the other "small winds." The soprano recorder is the instrument used in elementary school classroom situations, and the alto recorder is added to the soprano in ensembles that meet as special groups. Adults play the tenor and bass recorders too, thus making a complete quartet. There is also a sopranino that is smaller than the soprano.

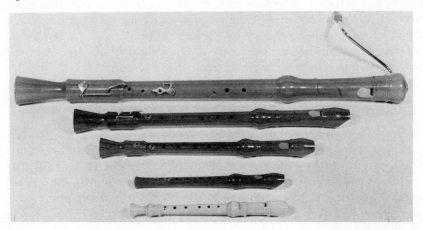

A Family of Recorders
RHYTHM BAND, INC.

Acceptance of the recorder, a genuine musical instrument played by both children and adults, has been speeded by reductions in price that have permitted the soprano to be sold for from two to three dollars each when purchased by schools in quantity. The range of the soprano instrument permits sounding a low of middle C, continuing upward as high as the vocal range. The soprano recorder is widely used because it is built in the key of C and thus has immediate use in playing the music children sing directly from series books; also, it costs less than the larger-sized instruments. Helpful information can be obtained from music dealers and companies that specialize in the recorder such as the Hargail Music Press, 157 West 57th Street, New York 19, New York, a concern that imports recorders and publishes recorder music. Some teachers suggest requesting special tips on recorder mouthpieces because the wooden mouthpieces of low-pitched instruments sometimes fray.

While the recorder is the preferred instrument for classroom use from the standpoint of tone quality, availability of good music to play on it, relation to adult players, and acceptance by musicians, there is currently much wider use made of plastic imitations. These instruments cost from 75c to $1.50 each, thus average one-half the cost of the lowest-priced soprano recorders.[9] Representative of these are the Song Flute, the Tonette, and the Flutophone.

Song Flute   CONN CORPORATION

Tonette   CHICAGO MUSICAL INSTRUMENT CO.

Flutophone   TROPHY PRODUCTS CO.

These instruments have a range of a ninth:

The Tonette can be tuned by lengthening the instrument by pulling out the mouthpiece. Advantages of tuning are offset by the fact that the plastic material wears when the mouthpiece is pulled in and out frequently, and that the teacher must be sure that all Tonettes are tuned alike when they are played by a group. After a mouthpiece has become worn, it can be kept from falling out by placing a thin strip of paper between the mouthpiece and the body of the instrument where they join. Some teachers use tape to hold the parts together. The Song Flute cannot be tuned. This disadvantage is offset by having all instruments in the same pitch, and by the assurance that no mouthpiece will fall out. Both the Song Flute and the Tonette are constructed so that children's fingers fall naturally in place on the

---

9 The Aulos Recorder, a Japanese plastic product, is available for $1.00 in either German or baroque fingering. Imported by Empire Music Publishers Ltd., Empire Building, 934 Twelfth Street, New Westminster, British Columbia, Canada.

finger-holes, which are set in a curved line, while the Flutophone has finger-holes that are set in a straight line.

The sound of these instruments is essentially soft, as is necessary for classroom use. Because all three instruments are limited to the range previously mentioned, their most common use is in connection with songs within the range of the ninth beginning on middle C. A ninth is the interval of an octave plus one whole-step. Two frequently used instruments have a larger range—each of about two octaves beginning on middle C: the Symphonette and the Melody Flute. These instruments are a little more difficult to play than those of smaller range, and, in the opinion of the authors, should seldom be used below fifth grade. Of all these simple instruments, the one with the most pleasing tone is the Melody Flute. All of these instruments except the Melody Flute finger like the saxophone, the flute, and the upper register of the clarinet. The Melody Flute's fingering is one finger removed from that of the standard instruments. This seeming defect does not seem to bother children who later change to a real flute, clarinet, or saxophone, which, for example, fingers G with three fingers while the Melody Flute fingering for the same note requires only two fingers.

Melody Flute
MELODY FLUTE COMPANY

There are music supervisors who object to the use of these little instruments in the classroom. Their major objections are two: (1) the children enjoy them so much that unless a teacher knows how to control the situation they may be overemphasized to the neglect of other aspects of the music program—particularly singing; (2) they are played so badly out of tune that their use constitutes a poor musical experience. It follows, then, that the teacher who uses the easy-to-play instruments must avoid these pitfalls. It is suggested that three rules be followed:

1. Use such instruments on a mass basis no more than once a week.
2. On the day the instruments are used the children should be using their singing voices *in connection with playing the instruments* approximately one-half of the period, as will be explained below.
3. The teacher should devise ways for the children to play the instruments in tune; otherwise they should not be used.

While out-of-tune playing is a grave disadvantage, this need not occur. A convention of music educators was startled by the perfection of pitch and the beauty of tone exhibited on the Flutophone by primary grades children under the direction of a classroom teacher.   When the musicians asked her how she had achieved this excellent result, she replied that she had instructed the children in blowing through soda straws into glasses of water before she had given them the instruments to play.   The children blew bubbles in the water at her direction, starting and stopping them at her signal, and they had taken the straws home with them to continue such exercises.   Other teachers have agreed that breath control is their "secret" in gaining mastery of pitch and tone quality with these little instruments.   Some have used exercises employed by teachers of wind band instruments, such as having children hold sheets of thin paper on a wall with their exhaled breath for increasing lengths of time. Others have profited from suggestions of vocal music supervisors who learned certain breath control exercises in their voice training.   The teaching procedure described below in connection with the *Melody Fun* book includes another approach to the problem of playing in tune that should be considered in the serious study of the small winds.

If a teacher can learn to teach these instruments properly, he will find that through this playing experience he can teach listening, note-reading, sight-singing, part-singing, and music composition as well as playing.

After the teacher decides to use the little instruments, his first task is to choose the one best suited to his group.   If possible, the children should participate in the choice by experimenting with several of them.   Of course, when two or more children blow the same instrument the teacher should have available a sterilizing agent.[10]   The teacher should learn to play the chosen instrument well before attempting to teach the class how to play it.   Skill on any of them is easy to acquire, so this is not an obstacle.

The present music series books do not contain a sequence of beginning lessons of these instruments, so it is best to use instruction books written for this purpose.[11]   There are many of these on the market, but few of them are suited to the general music class because the approach is not a song approach—it is the technical approach of the instrumentalist.   A good beginning book of the desirable type should contain many well-known songs for children to sing and play, including some to sing and play in parts.   A book that fills these requirements is *Melody Fun,* distributed by the Lyons Band Instrument Company, Chicago.   Its subtitle is "For Singing and Playing with the Tonette."   This implies that the playing should supplement the singing—not dominate it.

The following teaching procedure is implied by the subtitle of

---

[10] A variety of disinfectants is available at drug stores.   One should be selected that will not affect plastics adversely.

[11] *This Is Music: Book 3,* pp. 116–20, and *Book 4,* pp. 151–55, are helpful.

Melody Fun. On page two of this book we find the first fingering to be learned by the children, the note B on the middle line of the staff. Before attempting to play this note the children should first *hear* the pitch and *sing* the pitch. The teacher plays the note several times while the class listens to the pitch and to the tone quality. Then the teacher sings the pitch. The class sings the pitch—singing the note name B, for the children are going to learn the note names in a highly purposeful setting. There may follow more answering back and forth from the teacher to the class (teacher plays and sings B) and from the class to the teacher (class sings B until everyone has matched the pitch vocally and has really "absorbed" it). Thus, when the children finally play B on their instruments, they will tend to match the pitch they have heard to the extent of adjusting their lips and mouths automatically to produce it with some accuracy. Next, this book presents the note A, and we recommend that it be taught in the same manner that B was taught. Following the presentation of B and A is a little song constructed on these two pitches. Here the teacher asks the children to sing B and A again. When this is accomplished (i.e., when the children have matched tones again and remember each pitch distinctly), they are asked to sing the song "On Tip Toe" using the note names as words. This done, they next sing the song with the words. Then they play the song on the instruments. Thus the children have had, first, meaningful experiences in listening (tone matching), then in sight-singing, and finally in playing the instruments. Some of them will be truly concentrating on notation for the first time in their lives.

On page three the note G should be learned in the same manner that B and A were learned. The children then sight-sing the next song, "A Safety Song," which employs the three pitches. They sing them first with the note names, then with the words. Lastly, they play the song.

At the bottom of page three there is a song called "My First Duet." Words can be invented by the children when they have learned to sing it with note names and to play it. It can be sung one line at a time and as a rudimentary duet introducing part-singing. It is then played a line at a time and as a duet. To aid the part-singing, one instrument can remain on each part when the class sings.

Proceeding from this very simple introduction with the above method, F♯, B♭, and the other tones of the C scale are learned. Keen listening for proper pitch, sight-singing, music notation study, and part-singing are combined in this type of instrumental experience. Appropriate songs to play can be found in the series books, and listening and singing based on the instrumental activity can be continued from this source of material.

THE SINGING CLASSROOM ORCHESTRA

When children have learned to play recorder-type instruments, to chord on the piano and autoharp, and to play the bells and percussion instruments, the possibility of the singing classroom orchestra presents itself. When in the series books, in *Melody Fun,* and other supplementary books, the teacher finds a melody line in the range of the recorder-type instruments with the chords named, there are opportunities for combining various instruments with voices, or alternating instruments and voices. Here is a creative activity developing musical discrimination, for the children and the teacher will have to orchestrate the song according to their own judgment. Children can also have experiences in conducting such orchestras. Songs that are not found in books at hand can be presented by means of an opaque projector or can be drawn on large (two by three feet) sheets of heavy paper or light cardboard and placed where all the children can see them. Music can be quickly drawn on such paper. A staff liner with chalk is used to mark the staff. These chalk lines are drawn over with black crayon, freehand. When two-part songs are written, the melody part may be in black crayon while the harmony part is in another color for easier reading. Examples follow:

Theme from NINTH SYMPHONY

Beethoven

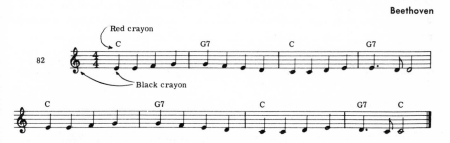

(Children may make up appropriate words around the concept of the brotherhood of man, which relates to this symphony. See *This Is Music: Book 6,* pp. 38–9 for a three-part arrangement.)

The *Theme from the Ninth Symphony* is an example of the very simple beginning music a classroom orchestra uses. Ordinarily, themes from the great symphonies are not applicable to this type of work. This particular theme, however, has the simplicity of folk music and is understood easily by children. It can be extended to include more of the original melody than appears here. An interesting and thrilling event after words have been set to it and the song is learned is the teacher playing a recording of a section of the last movement of the *Ninth Symphony* and watching the reaction of children who are fascinated listeners to "their song" as Beethoven used it. It is possible for appreciation to be at an extremely high level of effectiveness at this point. The key of C was chosen because it is easiest for the playing of the instruments. The key of F is preferable as soon as the fingering of B♭ is learned, because it places the singing voice in a better range.

"Come, Ye Thankful People, Come" is much more difficult and represents a later experience in the development of the classroom orchestra.

COME, YE THANKFUL PEOPLE, COME

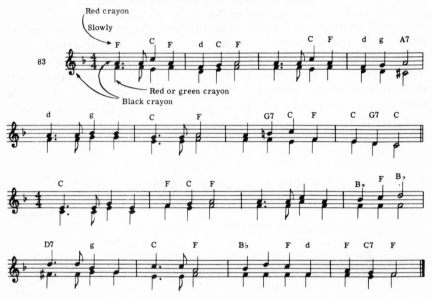

(Children will probably know the words for this familiar song.)

While some classroom teachers will be able to write their own classroom orchestra arrangements, and make their own charts, others may not be able to do so. In these cases the music specialist becomes the helper, the arranger, and perhaps the chart-maker who assists the room teacher.

In summary, instrumental music activities in the general music program constitute not an end in themselves but an important aid in the teaching of better listening, singing, musical discrimination, creativity, part-singing, and note-reading, and serve as an introduction to simple music theory—all in a setting that children enjoy, understand, and know to be purposeful. Instrumental activities in general music are both psychologically and physiologically sound in their appeal to the natural impulses of young Americans to be active and to manipulate a variety of things. Dangers of this approach have been stated: (1) children's interest in this one segment of the general music program may cause undue emphasis on instrumental activities to the detriment of other aspects of balanced musical growth, and (2) children's playing the instruments out of tune can make such experiences worthless. In this chapter a method of teaching recorder-type instruments has been described that helps children to play in tune. It is essential that *all* instruments used in combination in the classroom be in tune with each other. It has been suggested that instruments be used en masse only one period during the week; on that day the teacher should so organize the lesson that the children are using their singing voices approximately half the time.

THE PLACE OF BAND AND ORCHESTRA INSTRUMENTS

Few of the standard "big" instruments blend well enough with children's voices to be usable in singing-classroom orchestra activities. But the flute and the stringed instruments can be welcome additions. The cello provides a simple bass part. Classroom teachers should request the aid and advice of the teacher of instrumental music before adding these instruments to the classroom group.

Clarinets, trombones, cornets, saxophones, and other large instruments can be played by children in the intermediate grades. However, their tones are too powerful to blend with the light voices of children, thus they are ill-suited for inclusion in a classroom orchestra that is associated with the singing program. The authors of the music series books have nonetheless included some interesting uses for these instruments. These include instrumental solos, duets, descants, and true orchestrations of some of the songs. It appears that the best use for these orchestrations is in the playing of instrumental introductions and/or accompaniments for songs on special programs or for large vocal groups. Music series books should be examined in order to be aware of and to evaluate the uses suggested for the band and orchestra instruments in the general music program.

Lessons given on these instruments by the teacher of instrumental music should be scheduled in the special interest period when possible. The temporary withdrawal of some children from the classroom is a disruption unless the teacher can make plans in accordance with it. Much of the irritation that sometimes comes when children leave the classroom for these lessons can be avoided if all teachers concerned have an opportunity to plan the instrumental music schedule co-operatively.

Teachers of general music in grades four, five, and six can encourage membership in band and orchestra classes. Preliminary steps toward this end can include bulletin board displays of instruments and instrumentalists; presenting recordings, films, and film strips that illustrate instruments and families of instruments in ways that attract the interest of the age group; displaying attractive catalogues obtained from instrument manufacturers; displaying commercially produced charts of orchestra instruments by such concerns as RCA Victor, 155 East 24th St., New York 10, New York; Bowmar Records, 4921 Santa Monica Blvd., Los Angeles 29, California; and Keyboard Junior, 1346 Chapel Street, New Haven 11, Connecticut; and making available to the children books that include pictures of children playing instruments, such as *Tune Up: Instruments of the Orchestra and Their Players,* by Harriett Huntington (Doubleday and Company). The general music teacher and the specialist in instrumental music should together plan times when the specialist can speak to the class and when he and children can demonstrate instruments. The sending of notices to parents and the planning for parent-teacher conferences about the selection, rental, or purchase of instruments should also be done by joint consideration of the general teacher and the specialist. A time should be decided upon when the specialist will bring instruments to the class and permit children to try them. (This will necessitate use of a germicide.) The specialist should explain to the class why certain children are suited to the playing of certain instruments, but not for others. He should demonstrate the importance of finger size, length, and flexibility in playing the clarinet, for example, and the importance of being able to "buzz" the lips in playing the trumpet. Teeth formation should be revealed as important. For instance, a small overbite is preferable for small brass instruments while a large overbite is acceptable for bass and baritone. The instrumental teacher should avoid teaching fingering in a way that confuses "finger numbers" with scale-tone numbers. To say that A is played with the first and second fingers is correct, but to say that "A is two" is confusing to the child who is learning numeral names of scale tones. Both the general music teacher and the specialist can utilize good instrumental scores in series books, and they can plan some of these correlated activities together. Singing in the instrumental class can assist in pitch accuracy on the instruments and in the growth of balanced musicianship. To sing, then play rote melodies demands and teaches musical skills. The instrumental score can at times be sung.

The child most likely to succeed in band and orchestra will be one who is sufficiently mature physically to play the instrument, who is generally musical, and who possesses reliability and perseverance.

INDIVIDUAL DIFFERENCES

The variety of possible instrumental music experiences in the general music class can accommodate all the types of individual differences resulting from physical development that affect the manipulation of instruments, as well as variations in physical co-ordination resulting from deviant growth patterns or disease, and degrees of musical ability. For some children, manipulating an instrument is an important physical release. For others it is an intellectual challenge. For those unable to sing well, it is an opportunity to succeed in another important aspect of music. Since instrumental music experiences can range from the very simple to the complex, they constitute activities suited to satisfy certain needs of every child.

NORMAL EXPECTATIONS: PLAYING MELODY AND HARMONY INSTRUMENTS

KINDERGARTEN

Playing activities in kindergarten are very simple, because five-year-olds have poor control of their small muscles. There is exploration of the sound, pitch, and feel of bells, piano, autoharp, wood, metal, and stretched skin. The autoharp is not played by the children as a rule, but they feel it, watch the teacher play it, and learn to recognize its sound. There can be very simple rote playing experiences on the bells, such as sounding only one bell, or a few bells in a scale-line. Bells constructed in the form of stair-steps help teach concepts of high and low in pitch.

GRADES ONE AND TWO

In first grade there is an extension of the exploratory activities of kindergarten. *Timothy's Tunes,* by Adeline McCall (Boston Music Co.), presents an introduction to the keyboard that is understood by six-year-olds. After numbers are comprehended, some of the children will be able to play simple bell parts written in numeral notation such as those suggested in *This Is Music: Book One.* The autoharp can be strummed if the teacher or another child presses the buttons. By second grade children are able to play the bells, and some can play the autoharp without the teacher's assistance. Children enjoy seeing and touching band and orchestra instruments. They can learn to identify many of them by sight and by sound. Some can play small wind instruments and some will be taking piano lessons.

GRADES THREE AND FOUR

Most of these children are able to play the autoharp, bells, and small wind instruments. The fourth-grade child is able to learn to play these instruments somewhat more rapidly and efficiently than the third-grade child. Children are capable of playing these instruments from notation, improvising introductions and codas, and playing harmony parts. In third grade children can play half- and three-quarter-sized string instruments. In fourth grade they can also play the more common brass and woodwind instruments of the band and orchestra. Class piano and private piano lessons can be taken by many, and all children can learn to do some simple piano chording. The children have the ability to recognize all band and orchestra instruments by sight and by ear, if they are helped to do this.

GRADES FIVE AND SIX

Any of the instruments can be played by these children. Discriminating use of instruments can be made in expressing the characteristics of various national or ethnic musical styles. Band and orchestra instrumental groups will be popular, and many players will be able to play the instrumental scores in the series books. Some children can play piano accompaniments to songs and for instrumental solos and ensembles. Piano chording can be done in various appropriate styles, and duets can be played on soprano and alto recorders.

THINGS TO DO

1. Learn how to use water glasses and bottles in the activity discussed at the beginning of this chapter. Compose three-note, four-note, five-note, and scale-line melodies to play on them. Also arrange a pentatonic scale (C, D, E, G, A), and compose songs and tunes with it. Transpose these to the black keys of the piano.

2. Write in numeral notation familiar songs such as "America" and "Twinkle, Twinkle, Little Star."

3. In series books, find and collect songs that contain easy melody-instrument parts, particularly for bells.

4. Distribute resonator bells that comprise a scale among a group of classmates. Give each classmate one resonator bell, being sure that the distribution results in a "scrambled" scale. Then ask the students to stand in a line and play their bells according to direction as they try to arrange themselves in a line from low (left front of the room) to high (right front). Tell two at far left front to tap bells in turn. The

"low" student moves down. The same is done for the next two. Then all four play in turn and arrange themselves from low to high. Continue until the scale is complete. This is a listening game enjoyed by children. It helps them to learn to listen to the related pitches of the scale.

5. Compare the 12-bar autoharp with the Harmolin as to tone quality, rhythmic vitality, number of available chords, the tonal range, ease of tuning, durability, and price.

6. Bring ukuleles to class and demonstrate how children can learn to play them. Teach the chords by a method that does not conflict with the chord designations given in this book.

7. Examine recently published series books and the companion teacher's manuals to be able to report on the suggested uses of the piano for enrichment and for teaching music fundamentals.

8. Collect and compose songs that can be accompanied by one chord only, and compile them in a notebook to be used for introducing chording on autoharp, piano, and ukulele. Such songs are also valuable for introductory part-singing activities, as will be discussed in Chapter Seven.

9. Investigate at local music stores the popularity of the recorder and other small wind instruments in your schools and community. Try to learn what the school discount prices are, and what music is ordered for these instruments to play.

10. Review the songs in the preceding chapter on pages 100–4, adding to the percussion accompaniment:
    a. autoharp, piano, and ukulele chording in styles appropriate to the character of the song.
    b. recorder or flute-type instruments playing the melody.

11. Practice transposition of autoharp and piano chording as described in this chapter by using autoharp finger forms and piano chord fingerings with the following songs from pages 101–4: Transpose the accompaniment of "Old MacDonald" from G major to F major, and the accompaniments of "Paw Paw Patch" and "To Puerto Rico" from F to G, and that of "Down at the Station" from C to F. Then create chording accompaniments in the key of C major for two songs written in Eb major: "Go 'Way, Old Man," in *This Is Music: Book 6,* page 72, and "Clickety-Clack" in *Singing With Children,* page 63.

12. The black keys of the piano form a natural pentatonic scale beginning on the lowest of the group of three keys. Compose a song or piano piece on the black keys. Add a bagpipe (open-fifth) bass for an accompaniment.

13. Learn to identify songs that are in minor keys from the notation of the song. If the song's final note can be identified as scale tone six in

the *major* scale derived from the key signature, then the song is in minor, and this final note is the name of the minor key in which the song is written. Of course, the most important clue is simply how the song sounds, for it is more important to be able to recognize minor tonalities by the ear than to have to depend upon notation to determine whether the song is in a minor or major key.

14. Learn how to chord songs that do not have the chords marked. "Clementine," page 143, exemplifies how, by analyzing the notes of a melody line, one can decide intellectually which chord is required. In measure 1 all melody notes are part of the I (tonic) chord; therefore it is the accompanying chord. In measure 4, two of the three different notes are members of the V_7 (dominant seventh) chord; therefore this chord is probably the one needed. Notes on accented beats of a measure are more likely to reveal the chord than those on unaccented beats. Try this procedure with songs from the series books. The better you know your piano chords and can see them in the melody-lines of songs, the easier this becomes. Let your ear decide whether your "intelligent guesses" are correct by playing the songs with the derived chords to test whether they sound right.

15. A fifth-grade boy asks, "Why are there two flats in the key of B♭ major?" Explain this to the class, using the bells or a cardboard keyboard. Clue: build the scale beginning on B♭, and remember the half-steps between scale tones 3 and 4, 7 and 8.

16. Find and play on a small wind instrument songs of suitable range in series books for grade three, four, five, or six. Are there many such songs? Classify them according to difficulty and by keys.

17. Make up a tune on a small wind instrument and write it in music notation. Children can compose in this same way.

18. Make piano duets from classroom songs by having one class member play the melody while another plays the chords.

19. Direct the singing and playing of "Nobody Home," page 140, as a three-part round. Add percussion and harmony instruments.

20. List ways in which playing simple instruments can aid the classroom teacher who has difficulty with his singing voice, and ways in which they can assist all teachers of music in helping children to listen, to learn notation, and to understand chord structure.

21. For further information on piano chording and improvisation for the teacher and how to teach these to children, study *Music For Young Americans: Book One,* pages 186–92, and *Singing With Children,* Chapter 8: "Songs with Simple Piano Chording."

22. Find and state specific purposes for lesson plans in which melody and harmony instruments have a part. A source is the list of "uses" on the first page of this chapter.

MUSIC SERIES GUIDE

BIRCHARD MUSIC SERIES (SUMMY-BIRCHARD COMPANY)

KINDERGARTEN

Keyboard experience, 10a, 19a, 22, 33b, 35b, 40a, 141b
Melody instruments, 5–6

BOOK ONE

Autoharp, 186
Charts, 5
Melody instruments, 186

BOOK TWO

Autoharp accompaniments, TM 206
Charts, TM 206
Melody instruments, how to play, TM 17–19; songs for, TM 207
Playing instruments, TM 9

BOOK THREE

Autoharp, TM 18–20, 205–6
Autoharp-bells or piano easel, TM 205
Melody instruments, TM 16–17, 206
Playing instruments, TM 10

BOOK FOUR

Autoharp, TM 22–24, 251–2
Autoharp and instrumental easels, TM 251
Melody instruments, TM 20–21, 253
Playing instruments, 12
Ukulele, TM 25

BOOK FIVE

Autoharp, TM 22–24, 317
Autoharp and instrumental easels, TM 12
Melody instruments, TM 20, 318
Playing instruments, TM 12
Ukulele, TM 25

GROWING WITH MUSIC (PRENTICE-HALL, INC.)

(The teachers edition for Books 1, 3, 4, 5, and 6 was not available when this Guide was compiled)

BOOK TWO

Accompanying with melody bells, 161, TM 173
Accompanying with rhythm and melody instruments, 161, TM 173
Autoharp, 161, TM 173
Playing instruments, 118–120, 122, TM 169–170

BOOK THREE

Autoharp, see entry in classified index, p. 170
Bells, see entry in classified index, p. 170
Piano, see entry in classified index, p. 170
Playing instruments, 76–78, 80–85

BOOK FOUR

Autoharp, see entry in classified index, p. 186
Bells or piano, see entry in classified index, p. 186
Flutes or recorders, see entry in classified index, p. 186
Playing instruments, 69–79
Ukuleles, see entry in classified index, p. 186

BOOK FIVE

Autoharp, see entry in classified index, p. 218
Bells or piano, see entry in classified index, p. 218
Playing instruments, 122–138
Stringed instruments, see entry in classified index, p. 218
Trumpets, see entry in classified index, p. 218
Wind instruments, see entry in classified index, p. 218

BOOK SIX

Playing instruments, 146–165

MUSIC FOR LIVING (SILVER BURDETT COMPANY)

MUSIC THROUGH THE DAY (including children's primers *I Like the Country and I Like the City*)

Instruments, 147; index of, 151

MUSIC IN OUR TOWN

Instruments, 153–4, TM xi; index of, TM 133
I and V_7 chords, identifying, TM 14, 43, 49

MUSIC NOW AND LONG AGO

Instruments, 169, TM xi, 132

MUSIC NEAR AND FAR

Instruments, TM 163
Melody instrument scores, 165
Piano music for children to play, 165
Songs for instruments, 184

MUSIC IN OUR COUNTRY

Autoharp, TM 187
Harmonic instruments, TM 186, TM xvii
Instruments, easy to play, TM 188, TM xviii
Playing instruments, 217

MUSIC FOR YOUNG AMERICANS (AMERICAN BOOK COMPANY)

OUR SINGING WORLD (GINN AND COMPANY) 1951 EDITION

THIS IS MUSIC (ALLYN AND BACON, INC.)

BOOK THREE

Learning to play instruments (autoharp, keyboard, bells, descants and songs with small winds), 164
Small winds, 116–20

BOOK FOUR

At the keyboard, 144–9
Instrumental activities (autoharp, bells, keyboard experience, small winds, trumpet, cornet, bugle, ukulele, violin), 189
Small winds and autoharp, 151–5

BOOK FIVE

Instrumental activities (autoharp, bells, keyboard, small winds, cello, clarinet, cornet, trumpet, flute, string bass, trombone, ukulele, violin, xylophone), 211–12

BOOK SIX

Instrumental activities (accordion, autoharp, bells, cello, clarinet, cornet, flute, keyboard, oboe, recorder, saxophone, small winds, string bass, trombone, ukulele, violin, xylophone), 235–6

TOGETHER WE SING (FOLLETT PUBLISHING COMPANY) REVISED

MUSIC 'ROUND THE CLOCK

Autoharp and/or piano chords given for every song
Songs with instrumental parts, 95
Use of the autoharp, TM xi–xii

MUSIC 'ROUND THE TOWN

Autoharp and/or piano chords given for every song
Chording, 139
Songs with parts for instruments, 142
Use of the autoharp, TM xi–xii
Violin, 94, 95

MUSIC THROUGH THE YEAR

Bells and other melody instruments, 23, 26, 27, 30, 33, 34, 36, 40, 43, 53, 65, 67, 68, 71, 79, 81, 99, 106, 108, 116, 120, 125, 126, 130, 141, 143, 147, 150
Chording for autoharp, piano, guitar throughout
Recorder, 71, 101, 123, 126
Violin, 126

MUSIC ACROSS OUR COUNTRY

Parts for instruments, 189

VOICES OF AMERICA

Parts for instruments, 220–1

VOICES OF THE WORLD

National instruments, 209–17
Parts for instruments, 220–1

REFERENCES AND MATERIALS

REFERENCES

Jones, Archie, ed., *Music Education in Action*, Chapter 2, pp. 51–6. Boston: Allyn and Bacon, Inc., 1960.

Nye, Robert E., "The Elementary Classroom Orchestra," *Educational Music Magazine*, November–December, 1946.

CLASSROOM ORCHESTRA BOOKS

Buchtel, Forrest, *Melody Fun for Singing and Playing with the Tonette*. Neil A. Kjos Music Company.

Cheyette, Irving, *Songs for Camp and Campus with Recreational Instruments*. Pro Art Publications.

Cheyette, Irving, and Albert Renna, *Songs to Sing with Recreational Instruments*. Theodore Presser Company.

Slind, Lloyd H., *Melody, Rhythm, and Harmony for the Elementary Grades*. Mills Music, Inc.

Snyder, Alice M., *Sing and Strum*. Mills Music, Inc.

MUSIC FUNDAMENTALS

Nye, Robert E., and Bjornar Bergethon, *Basic Music for Classroom Teachers*, 2nd ed. Englewood Cliffs, N.J.: Prentice-Hall, Inc., 1962.

FILMS

The Autoharp. Johnson Hunt Productions, 6509 De Longpre Ave., Hollywood, California.

Keyboard Experiences in Classroom Music. American Music Conference, 332 South Michigan Ave., Chicago 4, Illinois.

BELLS, SOURCES OF

Educational Music Bureau, Inc., 434 South Wabash Ave., Chicago 5, Illinois.

Harmolin, Inc., P.O. Box 244, La Jolla, California.

G. C. Jenkins Company, P.O. Box 149, Decatur, Illinois.

G. F. Kitching and Company, 9047 Monroe Ave., Brookfield, Illinois.

Lyons Band Instrument Company, 223 West Lake St., Chicago 6, Illinois.

Peripole Products, Inc., 51–71 Rockaway Beach Blvd., Far Rockaway, Long Island, New York.

Rhythm Band, Inc., 407–409 Throckmorton St., Fort Worth, Texas.

Viking Company, 113 South Edgemont St., Los Angeles 4, California.

Walberg & Auge, 86 Mechanic St., Worcester 8, Massachusetts.

ORFF-DESIGNED, IMPORTED INSTRUMENTS

M. Hohner, Inc., Andrews Rd., Hicksville, Long Island, New York.

Rhythm Band, Inc., 407–409 Throckmorton St., Fort Worth, Texas.

STRUMMING INSTRUMENTS

Autoharp. Oscar Schmidt-International, Inc., 19 Ferry St., Jersey City 7, New Jersey.
Harmolin. Harmolin, Inc., P.O. Box 244, La Jolla, California.

SMALL WIND INSTRUMENTS

Flutophone. Trophy Products Company, 744 Bolivar Rd., Cleveland 15, Ohio.
Harmonica and *Melodica.* M. Hohner, Inc., Andrews Rd., Hicksville, Long Island, New York.
Melody Flute. Melody Flute Company, Laurel, Maryland.
Recorder. Hargail Music Press, 157 West 57th St., New York 19, New York. (Also see Educational Music Bureau, Peripole Products, and Rhythm Band, Inc.)
Song Flute. Conn Corporation 1101 East Beardsley St., Elkhart, Indiana.
Symphonette. Handy-Folio Music Company, 7212 West Fond du Lac Ave., Milwaukee 18, Wisconsin.
Tonette. Lyons Band Instrument Company, 223 West Lake St., Chicago 6, Illinois.

PIANO BOOKS FOR CHORDING

Easy:
Eckstein, Maxwell, *Play It Now.* Carl Fisher.
Frisch, Fay Templeton, *The Play-Way to Music, Book Two.* Heritage Music Publications, Inc.
Nevin, Mark, *Tunes You Like,* Books 1, 2, 3, 4. Schroeder and Gunther, Inc.
Steiner, Eric. *One, Four, Five.* Mills Music, Inc.
Slightly more difficult:
Bermont, Georges, *Play That Tune,* Books 1, 2, 3, 4. Musicord Publications.
115 Easy Piano Pieces and Folk Songs, Hansen Publications.
Richter, Ada, *Songs I Can Play.* M. Witmark and Sons.
Stickles, William, *Easy Hymns and Sacred Songs for the Piano.* Hansen Publications.

MISCELLANEOUS PIANO BOOKS:

Burrows, Raymond, and Ella Mason Ahearn, *Young America at the Piano.* Books 1, 2, 3, based on the I, IV, and V chords and the five-finger pattern.
DuBois, Charlotte, *The Keyboard Way to Music.* Summy-Birchard.
Egbert, Marion S., *A Suggested Keyboard Experience Lesson Plan.* American Music Conference, 332 South Michigan Ave., Chicago 4, Illinois.
————, *Keyboard Experiences: A Handbook for Classroom Teachers.* Bourne, Inc.
Howard, Elizabeth, *Around the World on Ten Fingers.* Robbins Music Corporation. Pieces in the five-finger position.
McCall, Adeline, *Timothy's Tunes.* Boston Music Company. For the first grade.
Meier, Guy, and Mary Jarman Nelson, *The Two of Us.* Summy-Birchard.

SPECIAL SUPPLIES

Carl Vandre Interlocking Keyboard. Plastic, with raised black keys. Mills Music, Inc.

RECORDER, METHODS FOR

Katz, Eric, *Recorder Playing.* Clarke and Way, Inc., 35 West 21st St., New York 10, New York.
Krainis, Bernard, *The Recorder Song Book—A Recorder Method for Beginners of All Ages.* Galaxy Music Corporation, New York, N.Y.

Lanahan, Walter O., *Melody Method for the Recorder.* Melody Flute Company, Laurel, Md.

Newman, Harold and Grace West Newman, *Music Shall Live—Singing and Playing with the Recorder.* Hargail Music Press, New York, N.Y.

Trapp Family Singers, *Enjoy Your Recorder.* Magnamusic Distributors, Inc., Sharon, Connecticut. Book M-1 for soprano or tenor, Book M-2 for alto, sopranino, or bass.

Chapter Six
LEARNING TO SING

In Chapter Four it was stated that a background of pleasurable rhythmic experience helps provide a basis for better singing. When rhythm is felt in terms of bodily movement, an individual develops sensibilities that are essential in understanding musical expression. It is believed that the ability to hear music and thus to grasp tonal relationships can improve through these experiences and the playing experiences discussed in Chapter Five. However, granted that these contribute to better singing, *good* singing is the result of special effort made by teachers to help the child to hear musical pitch and to reproduce vocally what he hears with accuracy, understanding, and good taste.

THE CHILD VOICE

The child voice is often described as light in quality as well as in volume. It is also an extremely flexible mechanism, as illustrated by the strident cries of the playground. The teacher, then, is confronted by a voice that is capable of expressing many moods in song. Since there are many moods to express, this child voice can be sweetly soft and ethereal as it sings "Lullaby and goodnight" and can be momentarily harsh as it sings "David *killed* Goliath!" A logical way of deciding upon the voice quality desired in any song is for the teacher and children to discuss what manner of voice should be used to express the meaning of the words properly and to evaluate this continually when they sing. Although the child voice is light in quality, it should not sound weak or overly soft.

Many of the problems related to singing are soon solved when one adds to the above idea the following:

1. To make a generally pleasing sound (simple, natural, and clear).

2. To sing in a manner that avoids strain and tenseness.

3. To take breaths where one does when speaking the words (usually as the punctuation indicates); do not interrupt the phrase by breathing in unnatural places.

4. To enunciate clearly, but pronounce r's as Southerners do [ah(r)], and sound final consonants distinctly and in unison.

VOICE RANGE AND VOICE PRODUCTION

The child voice in first grade was traditionally described as being within the range from D below the staff to F on the top line. The child voice in second and third grades was considered to have a range from middle C up to G above the staff. This remained approximately the same in the intermediate grades.

Many classroom teachers insisted over the years that songs that observed these ranges were pitched too high. It can be noted today that in the more recently published series books the range is lower than in earlier publications. Furthermore, the more recent books on all grade levels include a large number of songs in the rather limited range of from middle C up to fourth line D. The writers of this book have the following comments to make regarding this range:

1. When used at the beginning of a school year, it is suitable for practically every voice in grades two through six.

2. It should be considered a range that is to be expanded rather rapidly into the following ranges for class singing:

3. Although the singing of middle C is not injurious to the voice of the child in the primary grades, the consistent singing of melodies that have most of the pitches near middle C may be injurious, for such songs are believed to be pitched lower than is natural for most child voices.

4. This range is apt to be comfortable for the teacher who has not used his singing voice for some time. However, the teacher's voice should increase in range with use in the same way the children's voices will, for it has essentially the same range when developed.

The range of the voice as referred to above applies to the range of children's voices *in a group*. Individual ranges vary, particularly in ability to sing high pitches. Many children can sing *far* above the top line of the staff, and this highest line should not be considered as the upper limit of the child voice. However, in *group* singing, it can be considered as being at or near the upper limit. When series books print a song in a particular key, the writers have selected that key with the vocal range in mind. While it is indicative of a proper range for children's voices, there are considerations that lead teachers to change this range by pitching some songs higher or lower than written in the books. Most of the songs in recent books are usually pitched in an easy, fairly low range. Therefore, after a song has been learned, the teacher should pitch it and other songs gradually higher, by half-steps, until teacher and children have extended their range into that considered normal for voices that have had help in developing the range to its natural span. Other songs will be printed in keys that demand a high range. Should a class be as yet unable to reach this range, the teacher will pitch these songs somewhat lower—usually not more than two whole steps at the most— then gradually pitch them higher as the singing range of the children improves. In today's music fundamentals classes for classroom teachers, simple transposition of the key by simply building the tonic chord (1 3 5) on bells or piano or singing it from a keynote sounded on a pitchpipe is commonly taught. Every teacher of music needs to be able to change the key of a song when the stage of development of the children's voice range makes this advisable.

The matter of correct pitching of songs becomes more complex in the sixth grade, where some of the boys may be in the first stage of the voice change. The full range of these voices will normally fall approximately a fourth; thus a well-developed singing range of B♭ below middle C up to top line F will drop to a range of from F on the bass staff extending up to an octave above middle C. Since the highest and lowest pitches of any range are somewhat more difficult to sing than the middle pitches, teachers select music that does not stress these extremes. The implications

of this are two: first, that many of the melodies in sixth-grade song books cannot be sung by these boys—at least they cannot reach the notes written above this range—and second, that part-singing thus becomes a necessity.

To sustain interest in singing, the teacher plans vocal parts these boys can sing easily in their range, and takes special care to provide for this type of individual difference. Low harmony parts and chord root parts are helpful in this instance; these will be discussed in the next chapter.

A successful music specialist declares that the natural range of the voice —both the children's and the classroom teacher's—is fairly high when properly developed, and that normal voices should be able to sing the F on the top line of the staff with ease. She states that vocal range is largely a matter of correct breathing, breath support, and voice production. In her intermediate grades classes, the children enjoy standing, then bending deeply with arms hanging limply, taking breaths—inhaling and exhaling—while noting the fact that the diaphragm, not the chest, is primarily involved in breathing. Then, remembering to breathe with the diaphragm, they stand erect, closed fists held near the shoulders with arm muscles taut, inhale, then pretend to "chew" the air while slowly exhaling at the teacher's signal. At other times, instead of "chewing" air, they place the index finger of the right hand on the lips, and slowly and steadily exhale against the finger. These and other exercises, such as holding a piece of thin paper against a wall with the breath for gradually longer lengths of time, are done to develop breath control. The teacher's approach appeals to the boys, for she emphasizes that they should take part in sports and in physical development to acquire the muscles they need in order to sing! There is truth in this, and the trained vocalist will not use the word "relax" that is employed in this chapter, but substitute "flexibility" instead, a word having somewhat different connotations.

To extend the range further, the teacher has the children vocalize up and down the first five tones of the major scale with vowels such as "ah," "oh," and "oo," one-half step higher each time, as one hears adult vocalists practice. When the higher range is reached, the children are instructed to relax their faces to look as if they "had no sense at all," with the jaw held naturally and loose. The teacher takes special care not to injure voices by vocalizing them too high or too low, and she can tell by the facial expression when a child attempts pitches beyond his range at a given stage in his vocal development. In this way, this teacher extends the vocal range of her students to one believed suitable by the vocally trained.

A problem of some classroom teachers is that they have not learned to use their singing voices properly, and therefore hesitate to sing pitches they consider high. Many have used only a chest voice which they try to force upward in an attempt to sing higher pitches. They need to learn how to sing in their high voice. Usually when these teachers try singing high pitches softly in what can be termed a "half-voice" (i.e., it feels as though one is using only half the voice he is accustomed to using; it is the head voice without the chest voice), they find that they can soon sing in a high voice that is very comparable to the child voice, and that eventually they will sing the high pitches with ease.

The classroom teacher needs a clear, natural voice, not a highly trained one. In fact, children are not attracted by singing that sounds artificial and insincere to them; they prefer voices that seem natural and normal. The male teacher's voice is no longer as rare as it once was in elementary school music. Most children are well oriented to listening to and singing with this octave-lower voice on recordings, television, and radio, as well as at home with their fathers. Once in a while a child will be confused by this voice. When this occurs, the male teacher should explain that his voice changed, and that he cannot sing as high as the children can. He should play the song on an instrument that gives proper pitch, or have a child who knows the song sing it. In instances where teachers believe they cannot sing well enough to use their singing voices in teaching music, they can employ substitutions such as recordings, musical instruments, and children who sing well.

The following are physical requirements for good singing:

1. *Posture.* Place feet on the floor with the weight of the body somewhat forward, not on the back of the chair. Sit up straight, but not in a stiff or tense way. If standing, place the weight of the body toward the toes, not on the heels.
2. *Breathing.* Fill the abdominal region with air first (i.e., breathe "low," not high in the chest). This is the kind of breathing we do when lying flat on the floor or flat in bed. The goal in breathing is a controlled, continuous flow of breath. A husky or breathy sound indicates wasted breath.
3. *Open Throat.* Use the open, relaxed throat one has when about to yawn. Sing with the mouth open wide, but not so wide that it causes tension. Use the neutral syllables "loo" and "ah" to relax the throat.
4. *Good Enunciation.* Open the mouth and use lips *generously* in pronouncing words. Be sure to pronounce final consonants distinctly.

Poor results often come from singing too loud, singing too soft, not opening the mouth sufficiently, a slouching posture, a stiff and tense posture, a lack of interest, an unhealthy room temperature, and failure of the teacher to let the children comprehend the pitch and harmonic background of a song before asking them to sing it.

SINGING IN TUNE

The fact that at a certain stage in his development a child does not sing in tune in no way proves that he is not musical. Instances can be cited to illustrate that it is possible for an out-of-tune singer to be an excellent musician. Among the examples known to the authors are the concert master of a symphony orchestra—a superb violinist—and a boy with a very high I.Q. who played Bach with understanding and composed music of some quality in the second grade. Let us remember that inability to match tones with the voice does not necessarily mean lack of musical ability. Among the reasons for not singing in tune are:

1. *Immaturity.* These children are generally behind their classmates in all respects. They need more time in which to grow and therefore should have a variety of simple musical experiences.
2. *Lack of a background of musical experience.* If the teacher will provide this background, children in this category will eventually sing normally.
3. *Emotional and psychological blocks.* Many adults today suffer from emotional and psychological blocks to singing which were formed in the home and in the classroom. The parent who points out to a six-year-old girl that she can't sing in tune like her older brothers and sisters may be developing in the child a sense of failure, frustration, and inferiority. The parent may not recall that the older brothers and sisters who now sing well could not do so at the little girl's age, and the girl is thus called upon to compete with them before she is able to do so. The teacher who tells a child that he can't sing and that he is spoiling enjoyment for others and therefore had better be only a listener from now on, can by this act turn a music lover and potential singer into a hurt person who may try to shut music out of his life from that day on.
4. *Lack of interest, failure to try.* Among these children are those who are underfed, overindulged, and lacking in sufficient sleep. The teacher is expected to try to improve the environment of these children even though this is often difficult. Occasionally a child has so rich a musical background that it leads him to believe the activities at school are childish and unworthy of his attention. A case in point was the musically advanced first-grade girl whose teacher confused her persistent attempts to make up harmony parts to songs with inability to sing on pitch. In this instance, the little girl knew she could sing the simple songs, and was always trying to do something more challenging than just sing the melodies. Among suggested solutions are the assigning of responsibilities to the ad-

vanced children to help those less mature, and the providing of various music materials in the time allotted to special interests that allow them to pursue musical interests on their own level. Of course, if the music activities are ill-planned and uninteresting, many children will fail to try. Failure to try to sing because of fear can sometimes be remedied through use of dramatizations. Young children, particularly, can so lose themselves in dramatic play that they forget their fears and sing characterizations of animals or people freely.

5. *Physical disabilities.* This is rare, but a few children require the help of physicians, the school nurse, and speech, specialists. Adenoids, tonsils, speech defects (but not stammering), and congenital defects can interfere with singing properly.

6. *Unsuitable accompaniments.* Out-of-tune accompaniments, accompaniments in faulty rhythm, and overly complex accompaniments can so confuse children that out-of-tune singing will result.

7. *Muscular tension.* Tension of throat and neck muscles can cause out-of-tune singing. Laughing and yawning often relax these muscles.

Inability to sing in tune should disappear during the elementary school years if children are given consistent and continuing help. This inability can be expected at the beginning of the year in primary grades, since from one-half to two-thirds of the first-grade children cannot sing in tune. With help from teachers and growing maturity, this proportion is sharply reduced in grades two and three until by grade four there should theoretically be no out-of-tune singers. There are skilled music specialists who insist there should be none by the end of the second-grade year. However, in most schools today there are a few out-of-tune singers in each of the upper elementary grades, and teachers should be prepared to assist these students toward pleasurable and accurate singing in whatever grade they find them. An occasional child does not find his singing voice, or cannot learn how to control its pitch, until he is in high school. Therefore, teachers strive to sustain the interest of these children through a varied program of activities—rhythmic responses, listening, playing instruments, creating, reading about music and musicians, and continuing to try to sing.

To help the out-of-tune singer there are three major points of emphasis: he should be a participant in music activities that are happy, interesting, and satisfying; he should be given many experiences in which he will listen carefully to pitches and to pitch differences; and because he learns to sing by singing, he should be encouraged to continue to try.

During some stages of their development, these children do not hear

the pitch of their own voices and often sing loudly (and happily) off key.
There arise the following problems: (1) how to help them to listen, (2)
how to keep these voices from hindering other children who are trying
to keep on pitch, (3) how to help them to make as real a contribution
to the group as the children who sing well, and (4) in the intermediate
grades, how to tell them of their errors in such a way that they are encouraged to try harder and remain confident of eventual success.

For young children who have not yet learned how to sing, the chanting
of old rhymes such as "Humpty Dumpty," "Mary Mary Quite Contrary"
and "Rub-a-Dub-Dub, Three Men in a Tub" can be helpful. Children
like the *feel* of rhythmic or repetitive words; they enjoy saying them
together. If the teacher will establish the pitch of a low note such as
middle C and help them to *chant* the words on that pitch, a beginning
can be made in singing such one-pitch songs. In a few days the words
can be sung to the pitches of two tones, C and D, as follows:

Ma - ry, Ma - ry, quite con-tra - ry, How does your gar - den grow?—

To accomplish this, the teacher will conduct in pitch levels, helping by
the ups and downs of the arm to indicate the low pitch and the higher
pitch. Next, this might be done on three pitches—and soon the children
will have learned not only to find their singing voices but to sing a song as
well.

Ma - ry, Ma - ry, quite con-tra - ry, How does your gar - den grow?—

THE CONCEPT OF HIGH AND LOW

In guiding children to listen, one of the first duties of the teacher is to
establish concepts of high and low in pitch. At first, only repeated
identification of these will build meaning in the minds of children.
Eventually they can be low, up, and down in terms of bodily response,
which builds a background for understanding the ups and downs of notes
on the staff. Children are taught to play little action games in first grade
such as:

I can reach high; I can reach low.

The above example relates high and low to widely spaced pitches illustrating these words and dramatizing them in terms of physical movement.

The following example is relatively more complex:

Clouds are up high;   rain - drops fall   down.

Many simple examples of song material useful in teaching these basic concepts are to be found in the series books and in other supplementary books, particularly those on the first-grade level. However, any teacher can improvise his own songs for this purpose.

Acting out the melody line of songs in terms of pitch levels is a device that aids people of all ages to be more conscious of differences in pitch. The hand is used with a generous motion to move up, down, or to stay the same according to differences in pitch. When children are guided to respond in this manner their concepts of pitch relationships often improve to a remarkable degree. In the above example the hand would move vertically as follows:

Clouds are up high;   rain-drops fall down.

Many of the children who cannot yet match tones try to sing with the same voice they use when they speak. Therefore, it is the task of the teacher to help such children find their "high" or singing voices. This is usually done in a game situation. A favorite device is to have the children pretend to be the sound of the wind, of a bird, or of a siren. Children often sense pitch differences more keenly through actions such as the teacher's lifting a child's hand up high, or the children's starting from a squatting position (low) and moving to a standing position (high). Another popular device is to have a child pretend he is calling someone who is far away, or pretend he is someone's mother calling him to come home from a great distance. When this is done, a sustained speech results—and when speech is thus sustained (vowels held out) singing takes place.

When a child sings, but sings low and does not match the pitch expected of him, if the teacher and class will match the child's pitch and sing the song with him in the key of his own choosing, there often begins a procedure that brings success with the gradual raising of the pitch by singing this song in successively higher keys.

LISTENING TO MATCH TONES

The use that follows of the traditional term "tone-matching" is not intended to convey emphasis upon an isolated drill technique. It is the authors' intention that it be thought of as "songs and games for helping uncertain singers." Such a song or game may be sung by a class and a child may be selected to sing his part at the correct time. The part will be sung at the right time because the teacher will sing with him in case he is not yet ready to sing independently. Little or no attempt is made to correct faulty pitch or rhythm while the song is being sung. It takes patience and faith on the part of a teacher to wait weeks and months for some children to sing correctly.

A commonly used device for listening and tone-matching is the calling of the roll in song and having each child sing his answer. If someone is absent, the entire class responds by singing "absent," thus adding variety to this game. The teacher varies the pitch of these conversations-in-song, singing to each child in the range in which he will be most likely to succeed. Later, the purpose of the teacher will vary according to the progress of each child, and for some he will be working to extend the range of already successful singers.

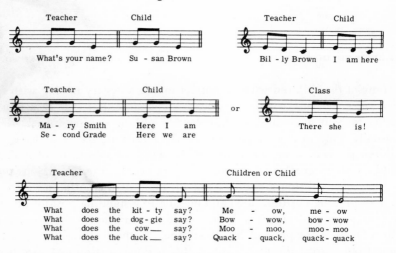

Another well-known tone-matching game is one in which the teacher places various objects in the hands of the children, who may be told to put their heads down on their desks and close their eyes. The game is played by the teacher singing, "Who has the _____?" and the child who possesses the object sitting up and singing, "I have the _____." An additional listening experience is to ask the class to identify the child by the sound of his voice.

Teacher   Child

Who	has	the	pen	-	cil?	I	have	the	pen	-	cil.
Who	has	the	pen	-	ny?	I	have	the	pen	-	ny.
Who	has	the	thim	-	ble?	I	have	the	thim	-	ble.

After learning to play this type of song-game, the teacher can sing questions such as, "What did you do last Sunday?" and "What did you have for breakfast?" and the child can create his own answer with rhythmic and melodic variety. When a child has difficulty in matching tones with the teacher in any of these tone games, matching tones to another child's singing may do the trick. It is not wise to remain working with any one child too long in any of these procedures. To do so would make the other children restless because the progress of the game would be stopped, and it would unduly draw the child's attention to the fact that he is somehow not as successful as others in his class. This refers to primary grades. A further aid to listening is the suggestion that the children "tune in" their voices just as they tune in radio stations. This is a concept children can understand because they know that the dial must be in exactly the right place for the station to "come in" properly. Another suggestion is to sing a familiar grouping of tones (or even a single pitch) for the children while they listen. Then ask them to listen with their "inner ears" while this is repeated for them. Next, ask the children to sing it. Finally, ask them if they sang exactly what they heard. Some of the children who cannot yet match tones will know that they have not sung what they heard. This process when repeated over weeks and months has notably improved the ability to listen and to match tones, especially when the teacher organizes his presentation so that part of the class listens to and evaluates the singing of groups of children within the class, thus involving every child in the room with either singing or listening. Spontaneous tone games such as creating a "song" from children's words—i.e., "Johnny has a hair cut, a crew cut, too,"—and having children sing these words or additional words of their own in turn can sometimes help.

Picking out melodies or parts of melodies on the bells or piano can be a listening experience of value. These instruments can be used with songs that contain tones or tone patterns which are both played and sung. Listening for the proper time to play the instrument, and being sure the correct pitches have been sounded constitute a good listening experience in a situation of challenge and interest, and it helps build the background that leads to eventual singing on pitch.

There are certain tonal groups that are particularly easy for children to sing. It follows that if the teacher selects songs that contain these tonal groups, especially if they are repeated in the songs, and if these songs are pitched in easy singing range, there should be more than average success in group singing as a result. Among these are:

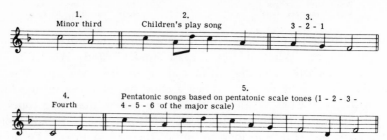

Number 1 is the easiest interval for children to sing; it is the descending minor third (5–3 or "sol"-"mi"). Number 2 is sung by children all over the world in their natural, undirected play. Number 3, a descending series of three tones in whole-step arrangement, and number 4, the ascending fourth, are easy to sing. Number 5, the pentatonic mode, has been mentioned earlier as an important part of the music children create by themselves, and as a type of music easy to sing because there are no harmonic changes involved. "The Caisson Song" emphasizes the minor third and the children's play song, "So Long" emphasizes the minor third and the ascending fourth; "Three Blind Mice" and "Mary Had a Little Lamb" stress the 3 2 1 note group, with the former also stressing the ascending fourth. The popularity of many songs can be traced to their utilization of these easily sung tonal groups. It follows that if easy-to-sing songs are pitched in easy-to-sing keys for the individual child as well as for the class, they can speed the progress of children in becoming more skilled in tone-matching, which is simply hearing what is sounded, and reproducing this pitch with the voice.

At times it is impossible to prevent the voices of out-of-tuners from hindering to some extent the progress of those children who are farther advanced in singing skills. A solution that is only of temporary value is to select out-of-tuners to make such contributions as the "zz" of a bee, the "tick tock" of a clock, the "ding dong" and other sound effects instead of singing. However, since faulty singers learn to sing by singing, this device is no solution to their problem. Furthermore it would be unwise to make any obvious division of a class into singers and those who do something else. Careful listening is essential, but listening and never singing will not produce singers. Out-of-tuners should have many opportunities to listen to good examples of singing. Safeguards in this include the use of small groups or solo singers as examples to be listened to and constructively evaluated so that there is no obvious division of the class into singers and out-of-tuners, and the inclusion of some good singers with the out-of-tuners when such temporary groupings are made. When out-of-tuners respond rhythmically to music, when they play the autoharp, bells, and percussion instruments, and when they offer ideas for interpretation, dramatization and experimentation, they are making real contributions to group music even though they do not yet sing well. Teachers should give them full credit for what they contribute so that they feel they are first-class members of the group—never second-class members.

The traditional seating arrangement for music classes, much in vogue some years ago, was dictated by concern for the out-of-tuners. They were seated in a group in front of the room, with the good singing voices of other children behind them and with the good singing voice of the teacher in front of them. It was supposed that this seating arrangement, which gave them correct pitches from both behind and in front, was of great aid to them. Its disadvantage seems to have been that the obvious segregation of the out-of-tuners was a greater psychological block than the seating was an aid. It has been very largely abandoned today. If present-day children are seated in this manner, such seating is done in some way that presumably makes the children unaware of its purpose. Actually, the increasing informality of seating in today's elementary classrooms tends to make any rigid seating plans for music work unlikely.

In the intermediate grades a problem of some teachers is how to continue to help the out-of-tuners without discouraging them. One fifth-grade teacher begins each year with what she terms "making a joyful noise." Her entire emphasis at first is upon the joyous participation of every child with no regard as to whether or not he is in tune, although she is learning and studying the capabilities and problems of each child during this time. As soon as her first objective is achieved, she begins her work of helping every child to sing on pitch. She walks among the children as they sing, helping the ones who need her. While the singing is in progress she unobtrusively tells Jimmy that he is singing lower than the song is sounding, and to listen to her as she sings. She may tell him to sit with his good friend Billy and tell Billy to help him. All of this is done in good spirit, without setting anyone apart from the group and always emphasizing to Jimmy that he is going to sing in tune soon— to listen hard and to keep on trying. Usually this teacher has eliminated the out-of-tune singer in her room by January.

Children in grades four, five, and six who cannot sing in tune know very well that they cannot, and they appreciate any help that adults can give them as long as they are not embarrassed before their peers. There-fore small-group work apart from the class is desirable and can be very beneficial. A plan that has proved helpful is for the teacher to work with out-of-tuners in groups of two or four, with each child paired with another of like voice quality and range. With four, the teacher will place each child at a far corner of the room. He may begin with a story of children who have become separated in the woods or in the hills, and who are trying to find (call to) each other. One out-of-tune singer is then asked to call in sustained speech (which is singing) to his partner across the room as though he were a city block away. He will ordinarily call his partner's name in the two pitches of the descending minor third pattern (number 1 on page 180). Then his partner will answer on the same pitches; this is the "game." When this contact through tone matching has been established, they next begin singing other information back and forth, such as "Where are you?" "I'm over here," and so on. The two children in the other corners of the room first listen to the pitches sung by the first two, then take their turn. Most of these children will find that they can hear the pitch given them in this way, and that they can answer it with surprising accuracy. After this introduction comes the repetition and extension of this singing back and forth, then eventually the singing of easy-to-sing songs pitched in a range comfortable to the voices, and soon four more accurate singers have been added to classroom music.

Time in which to practice hearing only one voice seems necessary for some as a prerequisite for group singing. That this has not already occurred may indicate a lack of singing in the home. The singing of a mother to her baby and to her young children is highly important in musical development. Music education begins at home, in the cradle.

Some boys have psychological difficulty that stems from attempting to imitate their father's low voices and wanting to sound like men, not like their mothers, their female teachers, or girls. This can be overcome by explaining to the boys that their voices ordinarily change in grades seven through nine, and that shortly before the change begins, they will have better high voices than the girls', a voice that signals the change to come. In fifth and sixth grades this is important to boys, and their understanding of this may determine whether they will use their still unchanged voices naturally or whether they will attempt to sing "down in their shoes." It is best to avoid using the adult terms "soprano" and "alto" and use instead "high" and "low." In three-part singing the parts are "high, middle, and low" rather than the terms descriptive of adult voices.

ESTABLISHING PITCH FOR SINGING

One of the most common failings of teachers of music is that of not giving the children sufficient time in which to hear the beginning pitch of songs a class is reviewing.   This is because the teacher will "hear with his inner ear" the song in its proper harmonic setting, but will forget that the children, or many of them, are not hearing this.   Too often these teachers sound a pitch and start the singing long before children have had time to orient themselves to this pitch, its relation to the scale in which the song is to be sung, and the harmonic setting of the first tones of the melody.   This failure of teachers to help the children get a good start automatically puts some of the children at such a disadvantage that they are out-of-tune singers when they need not be.   When reviewing a song with a class that includes children who need this help, the following procedure is recommended:

1. Sound the 1 3 5 chord built from the keynote[1] of the song by means of the piano, the song bells, or by singing it. Sound 1 3 5 3 1. This is to establish a feeling for the key, that is, a feeling for the home tone with relation to the scale. The playing of the chord sequence I V_7 I on the piano or autoharp does this excellently.
2. Sound at some length the keynote of the song. This should be sounded on an accurate instrument such as the piano, song bells, or pitch pipe.
3. Sing the keynote with the neutral syllable "loo."
4. Ask the children to sing this pitch, helping those who have difficulty. They can also sing 1 3 5 3 1 and 1 5 1 if the range permits.
5. Sing or otherwise sound the first note of the song if it is a note other than the keynote.
6. Ask the children to sing it and help them to match it.
7. Set the tempo by counting, directing, or clapping the rhythm of the meter and saying "Sing!" or, in rhythm, "Ready, sing!", after which the singing begins on the beat following the instruction "sing."

SELECTING SONGS FOR TONE-MATCHING

The teacher finds that he must examine and analyze the melodies of songs to determine whether or not they may be useful in "listen-then-sing" activities. Besides selecting songs of genuine appeal to children, he looks for easily sung repeated-note patterns and phrases that are obvious and

---

[1] The keynote or home tone is found in keys having sharps in the key signature by calling the last sharp to the right "7" and counting up to the next line or space. This will be "8" (1), the keynote. The keynote or home tone is found in keys having flats in the key signature by calling the last flat to the right "4" and counting up or down to "8" or "1." Also, in keys having two or more flats in the key signature, the next to the last flat to the right *is* the keynote.

clear. He seeks songs which have parts that can be echoed, songs with a limited range, and songs with final measures that can be repeated to create aesthetically satisfying codas. He also seeks question-and-answer songs, and dialogue songs in which children can take turns in singing and in constructively critical listening to the singing of others. He will use these songs to help children sing on pitch, with good tone quality, and with good taste.

Three song examples follow, the first two for primary grades, and the third for intermediate grades. The tone-echoing opportunities in the first and second songs are obvious. Other songs of this type include "Kagome," in *Music 'Round the Clock,* page 36; "Calling Song," in *This Is Music: Book One,* page 15; "Guess Who Is Calling," in *Music for Young Americans, Book One* page 4; and a number of songs in *Singing With Children,* Chapter One, "Songs To Begin With." The third song example, "When the Saints Come Marching In," has a tone pattern repeated twice in the original melody, and can be used in this form. However, it is printed here in a specially arranged form to repeat this tone pattern four times, and to add another repeated tone pattern near the end through an extension of the melody by repeating the tone pattern twice. It is an example of how teachers arrange songs to adapt them to tone-matching. This song has a small range, and rhythm and spirit that children enjoy. The second group must listen carefully to the first group, and is challenged to echo the tone pattern perfectly. Other examples are "Old Texas," page 206, which is an echo-type song when sung as a canon; "Three Blind Mice," which has several echo parts; "Hole in the Bucket"; "Deaf Woman's Courtship," and "The Keeper," page 205. These and others are in *Singing With Children* as well as in many series books.

I HAVE A LITTLE BIRD

Peggy Burgess

Elementary Education Class
University of Oregon
Arr. R.E.N.

97

Teacher

F

I have a lit - tle bird, who is well - known to

C7   F

you. He lives with - in a clock, and each hour he sings cuck - oo.

CODA

Class or Group   Teacher   Group   Child

Each hour he sings cuck - oo. Cuck - oo cuck - oo cuck - oo.

THE ECHO

Kate Forman   Old Children's Air

Teacher   Class   Child

1. Ech- o I can hear you,   hear you, hear you,
2. Now the rain is fall - ing,   fall - ing, fall - ing,

though I can't get near you,   near you, near you,
So I'll stop my call - ing,   call - ing, call - ing,

Teacher   Group   Child

You're so far a - way,   a - way,   a - way.
Won't you say good - day?   good - day?   good - day?

WHEN THE SAINTS COME MARCHING IN

New Orleans Song
Arr. R.E.N.

Group One
March tempo
Oh when the saints come march - ing

Group Two
Oh when the saints

in, come march - ing in, Oh when the saints come march - ing

in, Lord, I want to be in that num - ber.

Group One When the saints march in,

Group Two When the saints march

Everyone
in, When the saints come march - ing in.

MUSIC SERIES GUIDE

BIRCHARD MUSIC SERIES (SUMMY-BIRCHARD COMPANY)

KINDERGARTEN

Pitch recognition, 158
Singing, 3–4

BOOK ONE

High and low, 186
Pitch recognition, 187
Uncertain singer, 189

BOOK TWO

Pitch recognition and range, 209
Singing, TM 7
Uncertain singer, 96, 75a, 118

BOOK THREE

Pitch recognition, TM 211
Preparation for part singing, TM 211
Range, TM 211
Singing, TM 7

BOOK FOUR

Helps for uncertain singers, TM 256
Range, TM 257–8
Singing, TM 8

BOOK FIVE

Help for uncertain singers, TM 321
Range, TM 322
Singing, TM 8

GROWING WITH MUSIC (PRENTICE-HALL, INC.)

This 1963 series was not completed when this Guide was compiled. Only the Book Two Teachers Edition was available.

BOOK TWO

About singing in your classroom, TM ix–x

MUSIC FOR LIVING (SILVER BURDETT COMPANY)

MUSIC THROUGH THE DAY (including primers *I Like the Country* and *I Like the City*)

Pitch chart, 149
Singing, 146

MUSIC IN OUR TOWN

Use songs such as 14, 25, 29, 31, 48, 83, 91, 101, 104, 109, 134
Singing, TM x

MUSIC NOW AND LONG AGO

Echo Effects, 132

Phrase and tone echoing, 2, 3, 4, 10, 26, 30, etc.
Singing, TM xi

MUSIC NEAR AND FAR

Phrase and tone echoing, 2b, 3, 12, 14, 17, 26, 27, 30, etc.
Singing, TM xii

MUSIC IN OUR COUNTRY

Singing, TM xii

MUSIC AROUND THE WORLD

Singing, TM xii

MUSIC FOR YOUNG AMERICANS (AMERICAN BOOK COMPANY)

KINDERGARTEN

Heritage songs, vi
How to present a song to children, 143–4
Songs for young children, 138–40
Uncertain singers, 140–3

BOOK ONE

Heritage songs, 102–13
How to present a song to children, 176–7
Songs for young children, 170–2
Uncertain singers, 140–3

BOOK TWO

How to present a song to children, TM 3
Music lesson, TM 2
Suggested lesson plan, TM 3–4
Teaching songs from recordings, TM 3

BOOK THREE

How to present a song to children, TM 3
Music lesson, TM 2
Suggested lesson plan, TM 4
Teaching songs from recordings, TM 3

BOOK FOUR

Lesson planning, TM 4–5
Teaching a rote song, TM 2–3
Tone matching, TM 7

BOOK FIVE

Lesson planning, TM 5–6
Singing, TM 1
Teaching a rote song, TM 3

BOOK SIX

Enunciation, TM 8, 9

Expressive singing, TM 10, 14, 31, 40, 46
Introducing a new song, TM 3–4
Tone quality, TM 12

OUR SINGING WORLD (GINN AND COMPANY) 1951 EDITION

KINDERGARTEN BOOK

Tone-matching games, 5r, 19a, 21b, 25a, 56b, 64a, 65b, 126a, 132a, 133, 136c, 144

FIRST GRADE BOOK

Tone matching, 4b, 5, 6a, 53, 54a, 68a
Animal imitations, 154
Mechanical imitations, 163, 174a, 176a, 178

SINGING ON OUR WAY

Tone-matching, 30, 53, 97, 143, 144b, 150

SINGING AND RHYMING

Tone-matching, 53a, 54a, 125, 138, 139, 160, 170

SINGING EVERY DAY

Tone-matching, 8, 9, 14, 21r, 22arb, 33r, 70b, 153, etc.

SINGING TOGETHER

Tone-matching, 23, 25, 26, 27, 28a, 29, 31, etc.

SINGING IN HARMONY

Tone-matching, 16, 28, 33a, 34a, 36, 42, 46, etc.

THIS IS MUSIC (ALLYN AND BACON, INC.)

BOOK ONE

Answering back, 15, 31, 42
Chants for the day's activities, 20
Singing, 7–8, 189–90

BOOK TWO

Learning to sing (answering back, tongue twisters, fun songs, pentatonic songs), 164

BOOK THREE

Learning to sing (answer-back songs, descants and chants, fun songs), 164–5

BOOK FOUR

For average or slow children, TM vi
Pentatonic songs, 190
The teacher who has difficulty singing, TM vii

BOOK FIVE

Chants, 25, 40, 98, 115, 167, 210
Humming, 88, 99
Low-voice parts, 40, 44, 145, 177, 183

TOGETHER WE SING (FOLLETT PUBLISHING COMPANY)

TEACHING ROTE SONGS

A rote song is a song that is learned by ear. The basic principle in teaching songs by rote is repetition. Among the earliest experiences of children in kindergarten and first grade is listening to a song sung by the teacher—a song the teacher hopes will soon be sung by the children. The teacher selects a song that has content which is interesting and meaningful to the children, and which is easy to sing. Ideally, any song is taught to children from the point of view of sharing with the children something a teacher loves and enjoys. The teacher learns the song *thoroughly* before attempting to teach it. Next, he sings the song to the children, not suggesting that they join with him but only that they listen. This is repeated over a number of days during which time the children gradually join in the singing. Songs are taught in a relaxed and informal manner, with the thought of enjoyment foremost in mind. To initiate singing in kindergarten and first grade, teachers can ask the children which of the several songs he will sing to them they would like to learn.

This encourages careful, interested listening, and improved participation in learning the song of their choice. It is better for the teacher to sing the song from memory than to teach directly from a book. Recordings may be used with this process as a substitute for the teacher's voice.

When rote songs are taught to older groups, the teacher again selects songs with content that is meaningful to the children and with musical features that are suitable to the ability of the group. The exact method of presentation depends upon the song itself, and it is rare that any two are presented in exactly the same manner, since no two songs are exactly alike. Generally speaking, a short song is taught by the "whole method," i.e., singing the entire song to the children and teaching it as a unit. Longer songs are generally taught in a manner that combines the "whole method" with the "part method." The trend today is to teach as far as possible by the whole method and to introduce every song in its entirety. However, after some songs are thus presented, it is necessary to employ the part method, which means that the teacher will ask the children to repeat after him certain logical sections of the song, usually phrases, after which the entire song is sung again. This process goes from the whole to the parts and back to the whole again.

There are many variations in the procedures of teaching rote songs. The children's imaginations can be appealed to by an explanation or a discussion of the content of a song. (Warning: If the teacher's purpose is to provide singing experiences, talking should be reduced to a minimum.) In certain songs the words can be spoken in the rhythm of the note values of the melody. In working with these songs the teacher can make use of rhythmic speech, having the children repeat after him, or say with him, the word-rhythm of the melody, then add the melody after the words are learned.

Basically, rote learning of songs is accomplished through *guided repetition which is always kept interesting* by having children respond in a *variety* of ways—by initial listening to the story of the song as it is sung, by repeated listenings while responding with suitable bodily movement, by singing an easy part of the song while listening to the rest of it, and by dramatic actions. The rather lengthy song on pages 192–3 which appears in a third-grade book is used here to exemplify this learning process—a process that appeals to the inventive mind.

Step one. After arousing the children's interest in the song, the teacher sounds the pitch of the keynote, F, on the pitchpipe, bells, or piano. He has learned the song so well that this pitch brings to his mind the key feeling of the song. He then sounds the pitch of the first note of the song, third-space C, and sings the song to the children as dramatically and expressively as possible. An alternate way is to play the song on a recording, with its words on the chalkboard.

Step two. This is the part of the procedure in which the children continue to listen to the song while it is repeated as many times as is necessary for them to learn it. In primary grades this repetition may take place over many days while in intermediate grades some songs may be learned in a few minutes. The teacher contrives to keep interest high by leading the children to do something different almost every time the song is sung or played. The following suggestions are some of the possible ways to provide interesting variety in an essentially repetitious process. They are given here to illustrate the almost limitless variety of activities the teacher may employ in his own plan of presentation. *Only several would ordinarily be used in one lesson.* They are not listed in order of recommended use.

1. Listening and responding rhythmically
   a. Children clap hands (tips of fingers) soundlessly to the rhythm of the meter.
   b. Children clap hands soundlessly to the rhythm of the melody or words.
   c. Children stand in place and with bodily motions discover what fundamental movements might reflect the rhythm of the meter or of the melody or words.
   d. Children act out phrases in heart-shaped movements of the hands and arms.
   e. Children conduct the meter as the song is sung or played. This is highly important in establishing correct tempo and a feeling of onward rhythmic flow.
   f. Children determine whether the music swings in two's or three's.
   g. Children act out pitch levels of the song in the rhythm of the melody. This aids in comprehending the direction of the melody (high, low, skips or a succession of scale tones).
2. Listening and responding vocally
   a. After singing the song to the children twice, at the next repetition the teacher acts out the pitch levels every time each of the five pumpkins sings. He searches for five volunteer "pumpkins" each of whom can sing his respective part. The song is eventually sung by the teacher and the class with solo responses from the children representing the pumpkins. This aids tonal memory and develops individual singing. (In many songs there are characteristic repeated motives or phrases which can be treated in a similar but even more simple manner.)
   b. The teacher sings the "story" part of the song and all the children sing the pumpkins' parts.
   c. Children sing the "story" part of the song and the teacher sings the pumpkins' parts.

    d. Children are divided into two groups. One sings the story and
the other sings the pumpkins' parts.

    e. The teacher sings the song in individual phrases (the part
method) and the children echo each phrase after listening to it.

    f. Children hum the melody softly while the teacher sings or the
recording is played.

3. Listening and responding in other ways

    a. Children dramatize the story as the song is sung or played.

    b. Individual children who are capable take turns playing the
pumpkins' parts on a keyboard instrument when each part
occurs.

    c. Children mouth the words (pretend to sing or whisper) while
the teacher or the recording sings the song.

FIVE LITTLE PUMPKINS*

Unknown

L.B.P.

* From *Singing and Rhyming* of OUR SINGING WORLD series. Used by permission of Ginn and Company, owners of the copyright.

five   lit - tle pump - kins   rolled __   out   of   sight.

   d. One child who sings well sings the song while the class listens.
      Several children may do this together rather than one doing it
      alone.
   e. Children listen to determine the number of phrases.
   f. Children listen to determine whether or not phrases are alike,
      unlike, or almost the same as other phrases.

Step three. Everyone sings the entire song *without the aid of the
teacher,* unless his voice is needed to help individual children who require
special attention.   One of the teacher's aims should be to lead the children to achieve confidence in singing without the support of his voice
or that of a recording.   He uses his singing voice at first as a helpful
example; later he needs to hear the singing of each child in order to
guide him better, and *he cannot hear individual voices in the group distinctly when his own voice is sounding.*   In the transition from children's
dependence upon the sound of his voice to independence of its support,
the teacher may mouth the words silently, pretending to sing, so that
children will not at first realize that his vocal support is no longer there.
On succeeding days the teacher will seek different ways for the children
to find new interest in the song, such as:

   1. Developing more dramatic actions from the children's suggestions.
      (Some songs can develop into interesting action songs.)
   2. Encouraging the children to experiment with adding their own
      sound effects, employing percussion instruments if they are appro-
      priate.
   3. Encouraging the children to make suggestions for better musical
      interpretation.
   4. Suggest to the children that they bring to school their own words
      to this song, possibly about five little puppies or chipmunks.

A final word of advice is: 1) learn a song *well* before trying to teach it,
and 2) use the pitchpipe, bells, piano or other reliable instrument for
establishing the pitch: *don't guess.*

Seeing what we hear.   The above description has considered the teaching of songs through a variety of repetitions in the absence of music
notation—a purely rote approach.   It should be added that notation can
be used effectively in teaching songs from the series books.   Realizing
that their suitability depends upon children's level of experience, the
teacher may use some of these suggestions:

1. Children follow the words in the book as the teacher sings. Then as the teacher sings the song again, they silently mouth the words.
2. Children are encouraged to watch the melodic line and to follow it on the page with their first fingers, and to relate the up-down-same position of the notes to the pitches the teacher sings.
3. Children look at the phrases to find if they are similar or different.
4. Children seek familiar note patterns in the melody, or find important new ones.
5. Children observe the note values, find out what kinds are used, and why they are needed.
6. In connection with the song example above, place on the chalkboard the tune each pumpkin sings, but not in the order in which the tunes occur in the music. Let the children try to find the tune for each pumpkin.

THE USE OF RECORDINGS

A recording can be used in place of the teacher's voice in the teaching of songs. As in every instance, the teacher interests the children in the song to be learned. Activities to use with recordings that are appropriate to a particular song can be selected from Step Two on page 193. The children must sing softly in order to hear the recording. The volume of the record player can be gradually turned down as the children learn a song so that they will become increasingly independent of the recording. Another test to determine how well the children have learned a song is to have them begin singing with the recording, then lift up the needle and have them continue without its help. When children are challenged like this, they are highly motivated to learn.

It is well to emphasize teaching the words when songs are learned by rote from recordings; they are frequently written on the chalkboard. Another technique, useful as a later step in the learning process, is to have small groups of children, no more than six, stand by the record player and sing with it while the remainder of the class listens to evaluate their efforts constructively and awaits their turn at doing the same thing.

The recordings that accompany the series books as well as some other song books, can be of much value in teaching songs. They usually provide worthy examples for children to hear and imitate; they often bring to the classroom fascinating instrumental accompaniments that could be provided in no other way. They aid the teacher who studies them even though he may prefer not to use them in the classroom, because with their assistance he learns songs correctly, both rhythmically and melodically, thus builds confidence in the use of his own voice. Beginning teachers should study the recordings that accompany the series books they are to use in their classrooms.   Before the fall term begins, if they hear these recordings over a period of days they will have absorbed a repertoire of songs they need to know, and will have saved time by not having to pick out each song on a keyboard instrument and learn it without a model to follow.   In class when a child tends the record player the teacher is free to move about the room to listen to individual voices and to direct class activities.   The teacher does not have to lead the singing, thus he can stop singing and listen to the children—something every teacher of music needs to do.   No matter how well qualified a music specialist may be, there are times when a recording will provide the most effective way to teach some songs.   However, in primary grades recordings cannot completely take the place of the teacher's voice; these younger children sometimes find it difficult to understand the diction of voices strange to them.   And in all of the grades, a machine is not a substitute for the personality of a teacher who sings.

THE USE OF THE PIANO

The piano or bells may be substituted for the voice or recording by teachers who lack confidence in their singing voices and do not have recordings of songs they need to teach.   Words for such songs may be learned by rote or written on the chalkboard.   The teacher will then play the melody of the song.   This may be repeated while the children do several of the activities listed in Step Two of the rote singing process already described in this chapter, the instrument thus taking the place of the voice or recording.   For a song of some length the phrase method may be desirable.   After the playing of the entire song, the melody of the first phrase will be played; the children will mouth the words silently as it is played again.   Then the children may sing this phrase with the piano; and next, sing without its support.   This can be continued throughout the remaining phrases, combining some of them along the way.   As the song is learned, the support of the instrument is gradually withdrawn to gain independence from it.   If a child in the class is a good natural musician and has a pleasing voice, he may be an excellent teacher's assistant by singing to the class phrases or entire songs that he has learned from the teacher's playing the piano or bells.   Recorder- and flute-type instruments are sometimes employed also in this approach to teaching singing.

Although it is highly desirable to have a piano in every classroom, the piano is not essential in teaching or in accompanying songs.   In a normal situation where the teacher uses his singing voice, the piano has its greatest use at two points in the learning process—at the beginning and at the end.   A song may be introduced by playing it on the piano in a simple manner. Since younger children find it difficult to hear a melody when an elaborate accompaniment is played, a simple accompaniment, permitting the melody to predominate clearly, is the most effective style of playing. During most of the learning process involved in teaching songs the piano has little use, for two reasons: (1) when the teacher is playing the piano he cannot hear the children well enough to tell if each child is singing correctly, and (2) he is in a stationary position and is unable to move through the class to hear and to help individual children with their problems. Another commonly stated reason for not using the piano at this time is that if it is used constantly the children cannot sing independently and may become semi-helpless without it. However, after a song has been learned, the addition of a piano accompaniment can be a thrilling and satisfying experience, adding greatly to the singer's enjoyment and to the musical effect of the performance.

Although the piano is not an absolute necessity, it is an important means of enrichment. It is also a very important tool for learning many things about music, as was shown in Chapter Five. Thus, the piano has its rightful place in the well-equipped classroom along with the radio, the record player, the autoharp, the bells, and the percussion instruments —but not as a dominating instrument.

MUSIC ASSEMBLIES AND CUMULATIVE SONG LISTS

Many elementary schools compile cumulative song lists[2] which suggest that certain songs be taught at various grade levels. These lists are compiled for the purpose of providing the students with a commonly known body of song material that is part of their cultural heritage. Teachers plan co-operatively which songs should be on such lists, taking careful consideration of the songs most enjoyed by children. These lists should be under constant revision. The songs they include are ordinarily used in student assemblies and at other times when mass singing is of value to school morale. They are divided into classifications that assure variety, such as *patriotic and service songs* (important in the national tradition), *songs of religious and ethical value* (important in character development), *fun songs* (for group morale), *special-day songs* (Christmas, Thanksgiving), *American folk songs* (our nation at work and play), *folk songs of other lands* (the lands of our forefathers). There are many other possible classifications. Care should be taken to keep the

---

2 A suggested list for classroom, assembly, and community use is found in *Music in American Education,* published by the Music Educators National Conference, Chicago (1955), p. 319. A list of community songs is in Appendix B.

concept of the song list sufficiently flexible so that songs of immediate and temporary value can be used.

Nothing is as effective as good group singing in building group spirit and the feeling of unity every school needs. It is, therefore, an essential element in the total school program. Singing in conjunction with assemblies should be carefully planned so that the children as a group know many songs they can sing well together. However, pleasing variety is attained when the primary grades sing a new song for the upper grades and vice versa, or when one class sings and dramatizes "something special" for the assembly in an informal way.[3]

INDIVIDUAL DIFFERENCES AND NORMAL EXPECTATIONS

Individual differences must be expected, identified and accommodated at all levels of instruction, as stated in Chapter Three. The following list concerns only normal expectations, and does not identify many of the variants present in every classroom. Teachers of all levels should be prepared to assist the out-of-tune singer in becoming an in-tune singer through special uses of song material in the music class, and through small group and individual instruction. Experience in singing in the large group, in small groups, and alone is needed by each child at all levels, providing he is mature enough vocally to do this in a way in which he does not lose status with his peers.

KINDERGARTEN AND FIRST GRADE

Many children need help in learning to listen. They need to be helped to match tones. Some need help in finding their singing voices, and some need help in identifying high and low pitches. Ordinarily all songs are taught by rote. There should be much use of the descending third, easy tone patterns, and pentatonic melodies. Much of this comes from "singing conversations" and spontaneously created songs, song fragments and chants. Careful listening to good examples is necessary.

SECOND GRADE

With a background of good music teaching in kindergarten and first grade, only a small minority of the children will be unable to match tones. However, in schools that do not provide good music instruction, this minority may be sizable. After the summer vacation children normally need a period of review and reorientation in careful listening to

---

[3] The article "Everyone Sings Together," Music Educators Journal, January, 1956, pp. 46–8, describes the organization of assembly sings in a Massachusetts elementary school.

pitch and in singing in tune. They should make rapid improvement after a rather slow beginning in the fall term. Music series books will be placed in the hands of the children when they are ready for them in terms of their background of experience and their physical maturity. While many songs are learned by rote, others are learned with the books in hand; the ear and the eye are co-ordinated in comprehending the notation (the music picture). Simple rounds can be sung when the children sing well on pitch. Some children may lead singing.

THIRD GRADE

Almost all children should be able to sing well on pitch. Therefore the singing of chants, descants, and rounds (see Chapter Seven) assumes increasing importance. Tone quality and range improve under guidance of the teacher and evaluation by the children. There is an emphasis on increasing understanding and use of notation with songs.

FOURTH GRADE

Tone quality, range, and interpretation should show further improvement. Children should try to blend voices to sound like one person singing. Chants, descants and rounds lead to two-part singing by the end of the year. Increasingly complex song material can be learned by rote; some of it requires note-reading, particularly in part work although part-singing is introduced by rote. The study of notation is emphasized in connection with songs, with some note reading of songs.

FIFTH GRADE

Two-part singing is emphasized; otherwise this grade continues in the pattern of the fourth grade. There is emphasis on singing well in unison as well as in parts, with good tone quality, articulation and diction. Voice blending is a goal. When two-part singing is done well, three-part singing can be introduced. Knowledge of notation assists enlarging the repertoire with some sight-singing of songs.

SIXTH GRADE

There is continuation of the work of the fifth grade, but with added emphasis on three-part singing. While many boys will have soprano voices of high range and good quality, some boys' voices in the first stage of the change may become lower. They will sing in a range from the middle of the treble clef down to the highest part of the bass clef.

Their voices need to be accommodated by the assigning of parts within this approximate range.   There is sight singing of one- and two-part songs.

GENERAL AND SPECIFIC PURPOSES OF TEACHING SINGING

Examples of general purposes of teaching singing include learning to sing, learning to sing in tune, learning to sing with good tone quality, learning to sing expressively, learning to sing a culturally significant and socially useful repertoire of songs, and finding satisfaction and enjoyment in singing.   Examples of specific purposes for lesson plans include providing well-planned opportunities for children to listen carefully for proper pitch, expression, and tone quality in singing, providing experiences in tone-matching or tone-echoing, and using songs for purposes that might include any of these.   Possible additional purposes include extending voice range, learning a song for an assembly sing or other performances, relating a song to other curricular areas, using the song to teach conducting, dancing to it, teaching notation, form, and music vocabulary through its use, and stimulating creative aspects such as interpretation, rhythmic responses, dramatization, adding vocal or instrumental parts, and adding appropriate percussion instruments.

THINGS TO DO

1. Ask several classmates to pretend to be inaccurate singers and help them to match tones by means of little song-games, using parts of songs, or other special techniques.

2. Collect songs that can be taught in ways that give the out-of-tune singer pleasurable participation and experiences that lead to his eventual singing in tune.

3. Select an easy-to-sing song and prepare to teach it to your college class by rote as suggested in this chapter.   Write your plan or steps for teaching it, remembering that the content, form, and type of melody of the song tend to dictate your method.

4. Select a recording of a song from a series book.   Teach this song by rote to the class with the aid of the recording and the notation in the book as suggested in this chapter.

5. Practice conducting songs that begin with an upbeat.   Examples: "Auld Lang Syne," "Star-Spangled Banner," "Believe Me If All Those Endearing Young Charms."

6. One way to add interest in classroom singing is to employ songs in which girls sing one verse or part of the song and the boys sing another.   Find such dialogue songs and teach them to your class.   See Music Series Reference Guide to Part Singing, Chapter Seven.

7. Plan a community sing for a PTA meeting. Include a greeting song, a fun song, a sentimental ballad, a patriotic song, and a closing song. See Appendix B.

8. Practice the physical requirements of good singing as outlined in this chapter so that you can convey them to the children you will teach.

9. Bring a tape recorder to class. Tape a song that the class sings well. Play it back and ask your fellow students to suggest how their singing may be improved. When might you use the tape recorder in your music teaching?

10. Know "America" and "The Star-Spangled Banner" and in what keys to play and sing them. "America" is pitched usually in G or F. "The Star-Spangled Banner" is pitched in B♭ in elementary grades and in A♭ from the seventh grade on.

11. Demonstrate how tone-matching is done in the intermediate grades through the use of songs such as those mentioned in this chapter.

12. Some classroom teachers feel insecure in the use of their singing voices. What aids are available to help these teachers to teach singing, and how are they used?

13. Select a song and make a tape recording of it designed to teach it to an elementary class by rote. Plan carefully what children need to hear in order to learn it. Ask an elementary school teacher to use it with his children, and ask for his evaluation of it and also for its evaluation by the children.

14. Investigate the teaching methods of the German composer Carl Orff. Refer to the book *Music for Children, I-Pentatonic,* by Carl Orff and Gunild Keetman in the English language edition distributed by Associated Music Publishers, Inc., 1 West 47th Street, New York, N.Y. The Orff method stresses rhythm and the singing and playing of melodies based on the pentatonic scale. Major and minor tonalities are avoided or minimized in the musical activities of the young child. Percussion instruments including xylophones and metallophones are employed. Since few songs in series books are genuinely pentatonic in conception, creating such songs is necessary. This is easily done within the limitations described in *Music For Children, I-Pentatonic.* Books II and III are also available; these deal with minor and major. The film *Music For Children* is available from Contemporary Films, 267 West 25th St., New York 1, N.Y.

REFERENCES AND MATERIALS

SINGING IN PRIMARY GRADES

Bailey, Charity, *Sing a Song with Charity Bailey.* New York: Plymouth Music Company, 1955.

Coleman, Satis N. and Alice G. Thorn, *Singing Time,* 1929; *Another Singing Time,* 1937; *The Little Singing Time,* 1940; *A New Singing Time,* 1952. New York: The John Day Company.

Crowninshield, Ethel, *Mother Goose Songs,* 1948; *Sing and Play Book,* 1938; *Stories That Sing,* 1945. Boston: Boston Music Company.

Grant, Louise, *Your Book of Poems and Art Songs,* Vols. 1, 2. Rockville Centre, New York: Belwin, Inc., 1960.

Landeck, Beatrice, *Songs to Grow On,* 1952; *More Songs to Grow On,* 1954. New York: Marks and Sloane. Recorded by Folkways Records.

McCartney, Laura P., *Songs for the Nursery School.* Cincinatti: Willis Music Company, 1937.

Seeger, Ruth Crawford, *American Folk Songs for Children,* 1948; *Animal Folk Songs for Children,* 1950; *American Folk Songs for Christmas,* 1953. New York: Doubleday and Company, Inc.

Songs Children Like. Washington, D.C.: Association for Childhood Education, 1954.

Wood, Lucille F. and Louise B. Scott, *Singing Fun,* 1954; *More Singing Fun,* 1961. St. Louis: Webster Publishing Company. Recorded by Bowmar Records.

SINGING IN INTERMEDIATE GRADES

Boni, Margaret B., *Fireside Book of Folk Songs.* New York: Simon and Schuster, Inc., 1947.

Smith, Fowler, and Harry Robert Wilson, *Songs We Sing.* Minneapolis: Schmitt, Hall, and McCreary, 1941.

Snyder, Alice M., *Sing and Strum.* New York, Mills Music, Inc., 1957.

Tobitt, Janet E., *The Ditty Bag.* Pleasantville, N.Y.: J. Tobitt, Box 97.

Zanzig, Augustus, *Singing America.* Evanston, Ill.: Summy-Birchard, 1950.

GENERAL

Nye, Robert E., Vernice T. Nye, Neva Aubin and George Kyme, *Singing With Children.* Belmont, California: Wadsworth Publishing Company, 1962.

RECORDINGS FOR SINGING

RCA-Victor Basic Record Library for Elementary Schools. *The Singing Program:* one album each for primary grades, fourth, fifth, and sixth grades. New York: RCA-Victor Educational Sales, 155 East 24th Street, New York 10.

Children's Record Guild and Young People's Records. New York: The Greystone Corporation, 100 Sixth Avenue, New York 13.

	R.P.M.	Suggested Grade Level
Around the Campfire (community singing)	78	3–9
Hooray! Today Is Your Birthday (six songs)	78	1–4
Mother Goose (two records)	45–78	N–2
Sing Along (echoing)	45–78	K–3
Another Sing Along	45–78	1–4
Yankee Doodle (six folk songs)	78	2–6
Every Day We Grow-I-O (two records)	45–78	N–2
Albums:		
Let's Sing	78	1–5
Folk Songs	78	1–5
Songs to Sing (activity songs)	78	1–4

Recordings That Teach Singing
Ginn and Company, Back Bay Post Office, Box N,
Boston, Massachusetts

Albums:

Let's Sing and Play and Dance	33	1
Let's Sing of Fun and Frolic	33	2
Let's Sing and Be Merry	33	3

Let's Learn Productions, *Let's Learn to Sing*, Vols. 1, 2. Champaign, Ill.: Box 207, Station A.

33   K-2

Bowmar Educational Records, *Songs for Children with Special Needs*. North Hollywood, California: 10515 Burbank Blvd.

FILMSTRIPS WITH RECORDINGS

Young America Films, Inc., 18 E. 41st Street, New York 17, New York. *Songs to Sing* Series: four filmstrips in color with Mother Goose songs.

K-2

Chapter Seven

LEARNING TO SING PART SONGS

One of the characteristics of children as they mature physically and musically is that they become capable of hearing harmony well enough to learn to sing parts other than the melody of a song. They enjoy part-singing because of its increased aesthetic appeal, its social and group activities and connotations, and because it is challenging, emotionally satisfying, and evidence that they are "growing up." A prerequisite to learning to sing parts is that children must be able to sing melodies with confidence, independence, and with accuracy of pitch. The purpose of this chapter is to present many different ways to teach part-singing.

The concept of part-singing is one that has expanded and changed in this century, particularly as it applies to the primary grades. Today, as in the past, an emphasis upon readiness for and an introduction to part-singing is included in the music program of the fourth grade, two-part singing is emphasized in the fifth grade, and three-part singing is of major concern in the sixth grade. However, there are ways to sing in parts that are not dependent upon the harmonic sense, and some of these can apply at the primary level.

HOW SKILL DEVELOPS

Skill in musicianship develops rapidly when children learn to "hold" one part while another part is being sung or played at the same time. This can be introduced with piano accompaniments at all levels when, after a song is well learned, the teacher plays an accompaniment consisting of rhythmic and melodic patterns that are different from those of the melody the children sing. Some accompaniments of this type are in the piano books that are provided by series book publishers to be used with their books. Added parts that will be sung later can be introduced first in conjunction with the children's singing of the melody

203

by playing them on instruments such as bells, recorder, flute, and violin.

It was stated earlier that the harmonic sense is not generally well-developed until between the ages of ten and twelve. Thus, most of the singing in parts engaged in before this age, and also by children of these ages who have not yet developed skill in part-singing, would be of a type in which melodic lines are emphasized rather than harmonies. This implies the use of simple rounds and chants, combinable songs, combinations of simple chord tones that can easily be held "against" the melody of songs that can be accompanied by only one chord, and employing combinations of melodic lines in the pentatonic framework.

DIALOGUE SONGS, ROUNDS, CANONS, AND COMBINABLE SONGS

Among the several theories about the introduction of part-singing is one exemplified by the dialogue song, a song in which children are divided into two groups taking turns at singing parts of the song. Although this is not part-singing in the harmonic sense, it is assumed that the singers will become oriented to the idea of being divided into groups within the class and of being responsible for singing their particular part at the right time. An example of a dialogue song for intermediate grades is "The Keeper," on page 205.

The singing of rounds and canons[1] is believed to be preparation for part-singing. Whether this opinion can be justified depends upon how such songs are taught. If children are taught to sing them in a manner that leads them to out-shout other parts, or to put their hands over their ears so that they cannot hear the other parts, then no real part-singing is taking place. If, on the other hand, they are taught in a manner that leads the singers to hear how the other parts join with theirs, then the experience can justifiably be called a form of part-singing. The teaching procedure may be outlined as follows:

1. The children learn the melody well.
2. The children learn to hear the harmony upon which the melody is based. The teacher chords this harmony on the autoharp or piano, or uses a recording that provides a clear and simple harmonization. He tells the children how many times they are to sing the song.
3. The hearing of the new part (second entrance) of the round is accomplished by the teacher singing or playing this part while the

---

[1] Rounds and canons are similar. The difference is that a round repeats (goes back to the beginning) whereas a canon does not. A round is a "circle canon."

class is softly singing the first part, and is listening to how the parts join together to make interesting music.

4. Some children join with the teacher on the new part. Listening to all the parts and how they join together in the harmonic setting is stressed. Balance of the parts so that all singers can hear all of the parts is essential.

5. If the round is of more than two parts, the new parts are added in the same general manner as above.

After children have learned to sing rounds in this way and have acquired a good understanding of this type of singing, a procedure can be used that repeats the first two points above. Then the children can be divided into two groups, and a leader who sings well is selected for each group. Each group practices singing the song while the other group listens and evaluates. Then the round is sung according to the teacher's instructions, with careful attention directed to tone quality and balance.

Rounds and canons are emphasized in fourth and fifth grades and are used less frequently in the primary grades because many of the children are not of sufficient musical maturity to be able to sing them well and to hear with understanding what they are doing. It is possible, however, for exceptional first-grade children to sing simple canons like "Old Texas" because they are echo-type songs.

Frequently sung rounds include "Are You Sleeping?", "Three Blind Mice," "Little Tom Tinker," "Row Your Boat," "Scotland's Burning," "Sweetly Sings the Donkey," "Kookaburra," and "The Canoe Song."

THE KEEPER

Unknown

Old English
Dialogue Song

The keep - er did a - shoot - ing go, And un - der his cloak he car - ried a bow, All for to shoot at a mer - ry lit - tle doe, A - mong the leaves so __ green, O!

OLD TEXAS

Canon

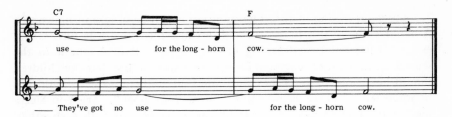

use _____ for the long - horn   cow. _____

_____ They've got   no   use _____ for the long - horn   cow.

Other useful songs of this type are "Susan Blue" (*Singing Every Day*, page 176), "A Thankful Song" (*New Music Horizons Book Five,* page 125), "Taps" (*American Singer Book Six,* page 124, and "Oh the Deacon Went Down," (*This Is Music,* Book 5, page 17).

ROUND OF THANKS

Traditional   Four-part round

For   health   and   strength   and
dai - ly   food   we   give   Thee   thanks,   O   Lord!

PRAY GOD BLESS[2]

Four-part round

Pray   God   bless   all   friends   here,   A
mer - ry   mer - ry   Christ - mas   and   a   hap - py   New   Year.

---

[2] From *Singing Together* of *Our Singing World* Series (Ginn and Company).   Used with permission.

Some songs having identical harmonization can be sung simultaneously. A major value of this is recreational, because the attempt is fun. However, this has value in learning to sing in parts if it is taught in the same general manner suggested for rounds remembering that the children should hear both parts as they sing, and that aesthetic values should not be forgotten. "Three Blind Mice," "Row Your Boat," "Are You Sleeping," and "The Farmer in the Dell" can be combined with each other. Other combinations are "Ten Little Indians" and "Skip To My Lou"; the choruses of "Blue-Tail Fly" and "Shoo Fly"; "Solomon Levi" and "A Spanish Cavalier"; "Darling Nellie Gray" and "When You and I Were Young, Maggie"; "Goodnight Ladies" and "When the Saints Come Marching In"; "Keep the Home Fires Burning" and "There's a Long, Long Trail"; "Humoresque" and "Old Folks at Home"; and "Ring the Banjo" and "The Girl I Left Behind Me." Frederick Beckman has developed this idea cleverly in his two collections, *Partner Songs* and *More Partner Songs*, published by Ginn and Company. They can be used in intermediate grades.

ADDING HARMONIC ENDINGS

This simple and effective way to develop a feeling for part-singing may be initiated in third grade, where two-part harmonic endings may be used, and expanded in the fourth grade to three-part endings. In this activity the teacher adds a part or parts to the final note or notes of a song. For example, "Three Blind Mice" ends with scale tones 3 2 1. The children would be told to sing or hum those tones softly while they listen to the teacher as she[3] sings the words on scale tones 3 2 3. Next, the children who believe they can sing the new part will join with the teacher while the others continue singing the melody. It has been the experience of many teachers that some children may never before have been conscious of their ability to hear two different pitches at one time in this fashion. These children may ask to sing such a harmonic ending again and again in order that they may fully enjoy what is to them a new comprehension of beauty.

---

[3] A woman teacher is referred to here because the female voice has the same pitch as the unchanged child voice. A man teacher would probably play the new part on the Song Bells, piano, or a melody instrument to avoid using his octave-lower voice.

This idea can be expanded as follows:

Examples of harmonic endings may be found in the music series books by using the Music Series Guide in this chapter and the indexes of some of the books. When once understood, they can be easily created by teachers and children. It is recommended that these be taught first by rote, since the aim at this juncture is to develop harmonic feeling. Notation can then be used to show how the already experienced harmony looks. Eventually this can lead to an understanding and purposeful use of the notation of part-singing. This activity develops a helpful background for improvising parts ("barbershop harmony") and for singing in thirds and sixths.

CHORD ROOTS

The singing of chord roots as an approach to part-singing is assuming new importance in the thinking of some music educators. In order to present this point of view, it should be stated that it is believed that the musical background of elementary school children is quite different today than it was a comparatively short time ago. Now children are brought into a world brimming with music with which they are in direct contact almost from the hour of their birth, due to the prevalence of radio, recordings, and television. Furthermore, this music with which they are daily associated does not consist of a single melody line; it is more apt to be rich and full-bodied. Dr. L. H. Slind describes this music as vertical in structure as compared to the horizontal melodic line. The music the children hear out of school is built of rhythm and harmony as well as of melody. Consequently, they may find less interest in isolated melody than did the children of 25 years ago. This leads to the theory that kindergarten and first-grade children need first an emphasis on rhythm, then upon singing simple melodies to which simple harmony is later added by means of the teacher's chording on autoharp or piano and using selected recordings. It follows theoretically that if children have this rich background in rhythm and harmony they will be better able to understand, sing, and enjoy melody because of their understanding of its place in combination with the other two major components of music. There may be logic in the claim that many children are bored with music programs that are confined largely to melody because such music suffers by comparison to the more complete music heard outside the classroom.　Dr. Slind advises, "Let the children have *all* of the music, not only the melody!"　Another implication of this is that if children are taught rhythm, melody, and harmony, rather than mostly melody, part-singing will become a much more evident and successful part of the music program than it is now.

The singing of chord roots is one of the easiest parts to add to a song because of the harmonic strength of the root, which is the foundation tone of each chord.　Although this activity is primarily of intermediate grade level, it is possible for some younger children to take part in it. The song materials employed are those that are best harmonized by only two or three chords—I, IV, and V_7.　(See Chapter Five, pages 142–143, for listings of such songs.)　The following example consists of the first section of a dance, the varsovienne.　It can be harmonized by two chords, G (I) and D_7 (V_7).　After the song is well learned, and after the harmony is taught by chording an accompaniment or by the children's hearing this song from a recording, the chord roots may be added.

The words can be sung in melody rhythm on the pitch of the chord root, or numerals, note names, or syllables can be sung on those pitches.

VARSOVIENNE
(Put Your Little Foot)

Traditional

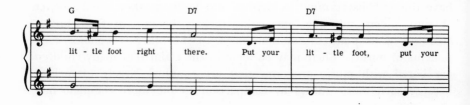

lit - tle foot,   put   your   lit - tle foot   right   there.

"Wait for the Wagon" illustrates how one of the music series books applies this principle.

WAIT FOR THE WAGON[4]

R. B. Buckley

5 (sol)

109

Brightly

1. Will you   come with me, my   Phyl- lis,   To   yon blue moun - tain
2. Where the   riv - er   runs like   sil - ver,   And   birds they sing   so
do (1)....................   do....................   sol (5)....................

free?   Where   blos - soms smell   the   sweet - est,   Come,   rove a - long with
sweet,   I   have   a   cab - in,   Phyl - lis,   And   some- thing good to
do................   do.............................   do......................   fa (4)...... sol..........

me.   It's   ev - 'ry   Sun - day   morn - ing,   When   I   am   by   your
eat.   Come,   lis - ten   to   my   sto - ry,   It   will   re - lieve my
do................   do.........................   do......................   so..................

side,   We'll   jump in - to   the   wag - on,   And   all   take   a   ride.
heart,   So   jump in - to   the   wag - on,   And   off   we will   start!
do................   do.........................   do......................   fa......... sol............   do..........

Chorus:

Wait   for   the   wag - on,   Wait   for   the   wag - on,
do........................   do....................   do....................   fa......................

Wait   for   the   wag - on and we'll   all   take   a   ride.
do........................   do............................   fa......... sol...............   do...............

---

[4] From *Singing Together* of *Our Singing World* Series (Ginn and Company). Used by permission.

FROM CHORD ROOTS TO OTHER ADDED PARTS

To provide for individual differences and to support the new part, children can play the chord roots on bells, piano, or recorder-type instruments. In singing-classroom orchestra work, the viola and the cello can make a good bass part by playing the chord roots. The type of bells that separate into individual tone bars can be employed very profitably in this activity.

The adding of this part to songs that are of simple harmonic structure can be the beginning of much meaningful activity. Let us assume that the children are going to build a score for the singing and playing of "Put Your Little Foot," a score that will reveal their ideas about rhythm and harmony as well as about melody. The teacher has placed the melody on the chalkboard. He has also written the two chords that accompany this song. The children's first task is to find where in the song each of the chords is needed, if it is to be sounded on the piano or autoharp to accompany the song. Since they have been taught that the note that receives the heavy accent or accents is ordinarily a tone of the required chord, they have an important clue on which to work. They know that the first beat of the measure in every meter signature is the most heavily accented beat, and that in 3/4 meter there is only one primary accent (the first beat) in each measure. (In 4/4 meter there are two—a primary accent on the first beat and a secondary accent on the third beat.) The children find that in the first three measures of "Put Your Little Foot" the note on the first beat is B. Looking at the chords, they notice that B is a member of the tones of the G (I) chord, but not of the D_7 (V_7) chord. Therefore, the chord needed for those three measures (or at least at the beginning of them) is the G chord. The note at the beginning of the fourth measure is A. The children find A to be a member of the D_7 chord; therefore this is the chord needed in the fourth measure. They proceed in this manner to the end of the song, then "try out" their harmony with the melody to see if it is correct. In some songs, the note D may be on the first beat of a measure. In this case, the children will decide by listening which of the chords is the right one to use. They can also tell by analyzing all the notes of any measure to find to which chord most of the notes belong. This is an important clue whenever students are determining chords for songs for which chords are not designated.

Now that the children have found the chords, they may write these on a staff below the melody, later creating a more interesting piano part derived from these chords. If one knows the chord, he knows the note that is the chord root, because the note G is the root of the G (I) chord and the note D is the root of the D_7 (V_7) chord. These notes are placed on a staff below the other music already written. Next, the children may invent rhythms for the song, which they will play on suitable percussion instruments. If they know how to write chants[5] they may add one to their song. There will be continual experimenting which will involve singing and playing of parts, a use and understanding of harmony, and different ways of presenting the melody. The beginning of the score may look like this:

To add to this simple melody, harmony, and rhythm, children may create more parts in the form of chants and simple countermelodies:

---

5 The writing of chants is discussed on pp. 214–219.

lit - tle foot   right   there,   Put   your   lit - tle foot

lit - tle   foot,   Put

The opportunities for creative experiences are very great in this approach to music. Creating and experimenting with such a score can provide a truly basic experience for understanding part-singing. Singing chord roots constitutes learning a new part. Learning this part contributes markedly to the further comprehension of harmony because it forms the foundation tones of the harmonic structure that supports the melody. Since understanding chord roots comes from understanding the chords (and chording) on the piano and autoharp, it stimulates the addition of other rhythmic and harmonic parts. All of this is assumed to result in musical growth particularly conducive to part-singing.

CHANTS

Chants[6] have been defined as recurring rhythmic or melodic patterns or figures. As in the case of chord roots, knowledge of the harmony forms the basis for understanding chants. These added parts have value as rhythmic, creative, and part-singing activities as well as being music that some immature singers can sing in tune. Easy chants, particularly of the one-pitch (one-note) type, can be sung in the primary grades.

Initial experiences in writing simple chants may be gained through the use of well-known songs that can be accompanied by only one chord such as "Row Your Boat," "Are You Sleeping?" and "Little Tom Tinker." The first tone to be used would be the chord root. Instead of using the chord root as in the preceding pages, invent a rhythm pattern that contrasts with the melody. The regular recurrence of this rhythmic pattern is sung on the pitch of the chord root (i.e., the home tone, "1," or "do"). For example, in the case of "Row Your Boat" (Chapter Five, page 137) the patterns that can be composed to be sung in conjunction with the melody are myriad. A few of them are:

Row, row your boat.   Row, row,   down the stream.

---

[6] A detailed explanation of writing chants may be found in *Basic Music for Classroom Teachers*, 2nd ed., Nye and Bergethon, pp. 109–20.

Life is but a dream. Row, boys, row.

Percussion instruments are frequently used to accentuate the rhythm of a chant, and melody instruments are sometimes of aid in keeping some children on pitch. For dramatic effect those children singing the chant often begin about four measures before the melody begins, thus adding an *introduction* to the song. They also may continue for a few measures after the melody is finished, thus adding a *coda*. "Row Your Boat" may be sung as a melody with an added chant. When sung as a two-part round, addition of the chant results in a form of three-part singing, and when extended to be a four-part round, the chant adds a fifth part. With such simple song material, three- and four-part singing of this type can be done in fourth grade. Furthermore, the chant itself can be extended so that still more parts result.

For example, the above chants are pitched on "1" (C) of the 1–3–5 (tonic) chord. The chanters can be divided into two groups with one group singing on scale tone 3 at the same time the other sings on 1. When this is learned, the chanters can be divided further into three groups singing the chant on scale tones 1, 3, and 5 respectively. This is an example of vocal chording[7] done in the rhythm of a chant. The melody adds a part. If the chant now consists of three parts and the round is sung in four parts, a seven-part song results. The teacher is, of course, limited in the number of possible parts by the musical maturity and size of his group. However, the possibilities present in this simple music are surprising. Chording instruments can be a natural companion activity to this type of part singing. Melody instruments may be used also.

Thus far we have been concerned with the one-note chant. There are other possibilities. For example, "Are You Sleeping?" could have chants as follows:

Ring, bells, ring. Wake up, Jo - hn.

"Little Tom Tinker" could have these:

Tom - my Tink - er. Tom - my Tink - er.

---

7 See Vocal Chording, this chapter, p. 223.

Some Chant Patterns For

I–Chord Harmonization	V₇–Chord Harmonization
5 5 5	5 5 5
5 6 5	5 6 5
5 3 5	5 2 5,5 4 5
3 5 3	2 5 2,4 5 4
1 3 5,5 3 1	5 4 2,2 4 5
1 8,8 1	$\overline{5}$ 5,5 $\overline{5}$
8 5 8	2 5 2,7 5 7
8 7 6 5	7 7 6 5,7 6 5 5
8 5 6 7	5 5 6 7,7 6 5 5
8 5 6 5	7 5 6 5,2 5 6 5
8 7 6 5,5 6 7 8	5 4 3 2

Multiple chants (two or more different ones) could conceivably be employed in the same song. However, if too many different words are sung at one time, the meaning of the words is lost and the effect ceases to be very musical. Experimenting by substituting neutral syllables or melody instruments may be worth while.

When chants are sung with two-chord songs,[8] the initial experiences are usually with scale tone 5 because that tone is common to two chords, I and V₇. This is the only tone of the scale on which it is possible to create a one-tone chant in such songs. Such rhythmic chants for "Three Blind Mice" might be:

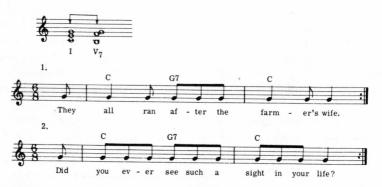

Children often alter the final repetition of such chants in order that the last pitch sung will be the home tone.

Another commonly used chant is one based on the scale tones 5 and 6. Scale tone 6 is a member of neither the I nor the V₇ chord yet it has the unusual quality of not interfering with the harmony as long as it is placed on an unaccented part of the measure. This kind of a chant for "Looby Loo" could be:

---

8 A list of two-chord songs is found in Chapter Five, p. 136.

Loo - by Loo   each   Sat - ur - day   night.

We take a bath on each   Sat - ur - day   night.

This 5–6–5 pattern works very well with songs like "Old Texas," "Ten Little Indians" and "Skip To My Lou," and children can invent many rhythmic variants of it.

LOOBY LOO[9]

American singing game

Here we go loo - by loo__ Here we go loo - by light__

Here we go loo - by loo__ all on a Sat - ur - day night __ I

put my right hand in ___ I put my right hand out __ I

give my right hand a shake shake shake and turn my-self a - bout.__

2. left hand   3. right foot   4. left foot   5. whole self

Although all good chants are essentially simple, slightly more complex chants can be written for songs like "Looby Loo." One way to proceed with writing such a chant is to analyze the harmony of "Looby Loo"

---

[9] This song describes an old American custom before the days of plumbing. The children are taking their bath in a washtub near the kitchen stove which burned wood or coal. They are testing the temperature of the water before getting into the tub.

and chart it to find what this harmony demands of a four-measure-long chant. Looking at the song, we find that it consists of four four-measure phrases. The heart of the problem is to find what chords harmonize each of the measures, and view this in a vertical fashion to find how to write a chant that will fit this harmonic arrangement. We find:

measure	1	2	3	4 (of each phrase)
phrase 1	G	G	G	D_7
phrase 2	G	G	D_7	G^7
phrase 3	G	G	G^7	G
phrase 4	G	G	G D_7	G
	G	G	G&D_7	G&D_7

Looking down the columns it can be seen that a chant for "Looby Loo" must be written in the following harmonic scheme: the first measure of the chant requires a pattern related to the G chord (I); the second measure requires a pattern related to the G chord; the third and fourth measures require patterns related to *both* G and D_7 (V_7) chords. This means that during measures three and four, the chant is restricted to patterns such as those made up of scale tone 5, or scale tones 5 and 6—simple patterns that sound well with *either* chord I or V_7.

The following chart is included for those who wish to pursue more fully the writing of chants and other added parts to songs. It endeavors to picture some of the simple movements of tones possible during common chord changes. It will assist in the writing of descants as well as chants.

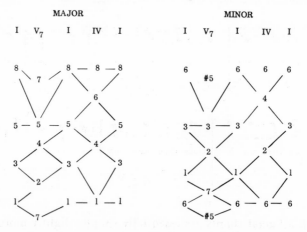

Chants may become monotonous because of their constant repetition. Therefore it is desirable that they be omitted from sections of some songs. The following example of a simple chant for the three-chord song "The Blue-Tail Fly" illustrates this. Although a chant could be used throughout the song, one is used only with the refrain. It is altered at the end of the song to add variety and a feeling of completion.

Chants for three-chord songs are necessarily more complex, since they are based upon the tones of three chords rather than those of one or two. The chant for "The Blue-Tail Fly" employs scale tone 5 for the I and V_7 chords and scale tone 6 for the IV chord. Other examples of chants can be found in the books included in the reference list as well as in the Music Series Guide at the end of this chapter.

THE BLUE-TAIL FLY

Daniel D. Emmett

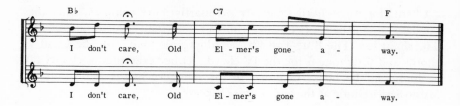

COUNTERMELODIES AND DESCANTS

Singing countermelodies and descants constitutes another of the many approaches to part singing. A countermelody is an added melodic part, usually lower than the original melody, which often imitates it and often moves in contrary motion to it. Ideally, a descant is a melody in its own right although written to accompany another melody. In practice, the descant is subordinate to the melody. It is usually higher in pitch than the melody and a small group of children sing it while the majority of the children sing the melody. The reason for this is that high pitches sound relatively louder than low pitches when they are combined in part-singing; therefore a small group on a high part balances with a larger group on a low part. When the teacher understands the relation between countermelodies or descants and the chords and the original melodies, he can guide children to compose them. The first example is a countermelody to "Down in the Valley." In this case it is of such melodic nature in its own right that it is easier to sing than the real melody. Children in the third grade can sing this part song.

DOWN IN THE VALLEY

American folk song
Arranged by R.E.N.

THE BREAK OF DAY[10]

Czechoslovakian folk tune

Sidney Row

Arranged by Gladys Pitcher

[10] From *Our Land of Song,* p. 74. Used by permission of C. C. Birchard & Company. This appears in a fifth-grade book.

A beautiful traditional-type descant, higher than the melody, and therefore to be sung by a small group, is one composed by Ewald Nolte to "Silent Night." It is designed for sixth grade.

SILENT NIGHT[11]

Franz Gruber

Joseph Mohr

Descant by Ewald Nolte

Ideally, countermelodies and descants should be learned in integral relation to the original melody, because when they are learned as separate songs and then combined, many children fail to hear the real re-

---

[11] From Beattie, Wolverton, Wilson, and Hinga, *The American Singer, Combined Grades.* Used by permission of American Book Company.

lationship of the two parts.   The melody should be well learned first of all, and a feeling for the harmony should be established.

The elementary school chorus may learn a descant or countermelody to be sung while the rest of the children sing the melody; and these elements may be combined in an assembly program.   Likewise, children of superior ability may prepare descants out of school to be combined in class with the melody sung by the other children.   Another use for this type of added part is by certain melody instruments—from song flutes, tonettes, and bells to violins and flutes.   If done with discretion, employing a melody instrument is a way of strengthening either or both parts.

VOCAL CHORDING

An example of one type of vocal chording was mentioned on page 214 in connection with I-chord songs.   Usually, chording of the vocal type consists of the same tones that are often used for piano chording in the treble clef.   The children may be divided into four groups, with one assigned the melody and the other three assigned the three chord tones. This activity would logically begin with one-chord melodies and progress to three-chord melodies.   It may start in a simple way in third or fourth grade.   It is sometimes emphasized in fifth and sixth grades as an approach to three-part singing.   The ease with which children can learn to chord vocally will be determined by their ability to hear harmony; their ability to learn harmony will be favorably influenced by successful experiences in instrumental chording (autoharp, piano) and by guided listening activities that aid the hearing of chord changes.

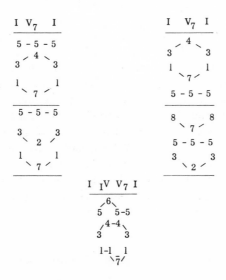

One of the music series refers to the singing of chord roots as "chording." In this book, singing chord roots and vocal chording are two different activities, though harmonically related.

The chords to be sung can be arranged in several positions. The following chart not only exemplifies this but illustrates chord positions that are sometimes used as exercises to introduce children to this activity. Although numbers may be used to introduce this work, humming or the neutral syllable "loo" is used in actual performance.

The following excerpt from "Silent Night" illustrates this activity:

IMPROVISING HARMONY PARTS

The improvising of harmony parts has often been overlooked as one practical approach to part-singing. "Barber-shopping" or "singing harmony by ear" has had a definite carry-over into the natural musical expression of boys and girls when they are on field trips or picnics, at camp and at home. The writers know of an elementary school where the improvising of parts by volunteer neighborhood quartets was an activity of importance, even affecting school and community programs. A list of songs that have had use in this activity includes "Home on the Range," "Down by the Old Mill Stream," "There's a Long, Long Trail," "Moonlight and Roses," "Let the Rest of the World Go By," "Eyes of Texas" (I've Been Working on the Railroad"), "Red River Valley," "Oh My Darling Clementine," "A Bicycle Built for Two." This activity is usually most effective at sixth-grade level, where it develops into three-part singing, although some fifth grades can do well with it.

THIRDS AND SIXTHS

Earlier in this chapter, the singing of chord roots was mentioned as one of the easiest types of elementary part-singing because of the strength of the harmonic elements involved. An approach older from the standpoint of general use is the employment of thirds and sixths. As in other ways to begin part-singing, the children are first assumed to know the melody very well, and to have heard the song on a recorder accompanied by the autoharp or piano in a manner that helps them comprehend the integral relation of the melody and harmony.

The singing of thirds has been introduced in the section on harmonic endings, page 208. This use of thirds can be expanded to include parts of songs and eventually entire songs. Using "Old Black Joe" as a familiar example, the melody accompanying the words, "I'm coming, I'm coming" can be sung softly by the children while the teacher sings (or plays) this same melodic fragment one third lower.

As before, children who believe they can sing the new part will join with the teacher while those who as yet feel more secure by remaining on the melody will sing that part. This section of "Old Black Joe" can be further extended in parallel thirds to include the words, "For my head is bending low." In the music series books will be found songs that rely heavily on parallel thirds to introduce part-singing. A song that can be sung in its entirety in thirds is the well-known "Polly Wolly Doodle."

POLLY WOLLY DOODLE

American Song

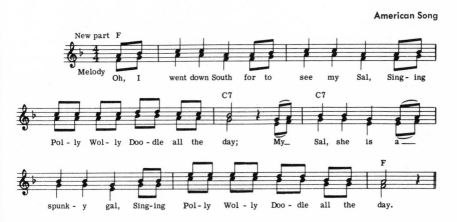

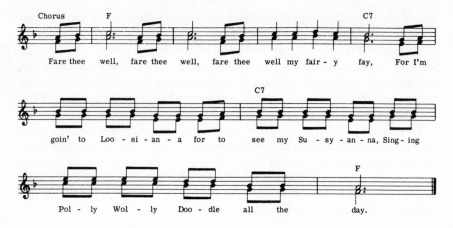

An interval that sounds similar to the third is the sixth, which is the inversion of the third. After children have become accustomed to singing in parallel thirds, they can easily learn to sing in parallel sixths. Any song that can be sung in thirds can be sung in sixths. "Polly Wolly Doodle" illustrates this. However, when the interval is changed in this way the key must often change also to accommodate the voice range.

Songs such as "Lightly Row," "London Bridge," "Goodbye My Lover Goodbye," "Yankee Doodle," "Hand Me Down My Walking Cane," "To Puerto Rico" (page 103), "Catch a Falling Star," and the refrain of "Marching to Pretoria" can be used to advantage in approaching part-singing through the use of thirds and sixths.

LONDON BRIDGE

English game song

fall - ing down,   Lon - don Bridge is   fall - ing down,   My   Fair   La - dy.

There are older methods of teaching part-singing, which emphasize drilling on each part, then putting them together. Today the emphasis is upon helping children to hear a new part in relation to the melody and the harmony so that they hear all of the music. This principle is applicable no matter what type of part-singing is being done, whether it be round, descant, or traditional two- and three-part singing. The general outline of progress in part-singing in grades four, five, and six is as follows:

1. The learning of the melody.
2. The comprehension of the harmony (chord structure) that accompanies the melody by use of autoharp chording, piano chording, or a suitable recording.
3. The introduction of the new part in a manner that permits the children to hear the integral relation of the two parts.
   (Children hum the melody or sing it softly while the teacher sings or plays the new part.) Harmony must be *heard* before it is *made*.
4. The singing of the new part by those children who are ready for part-singing, always working for a balance in volume that permits the hearing of both parts by all of the children.
5. Introducing a third part by repeating Steps 3 and 4, adding the new part to the two parts previously learned.
6. When children have learned to feel secure in part-singing activities, then the sight-reading of part songs can be an interesting and challenging activity. When this skill is developed, Steps 1, 2, and 3 are eliminated. Since sight-singing is a complicated skill, neutral syllables instead of words are generally used at first so that the children can concentrate on the notation. The words are added when children feel secure on the parts.

In general, the voices of fifth- and sixth-grade children are unchanged and have approximately the same range, with the exception of boys in the first stage of the voice change. Therefore each child should experience singing both high and low parts. Technically, it is incorrect to call these immature voices "soprano" or "alto." It is more accurate to abandon these adult terms and to call the children's voice parts "high," "low," and "middle," rather than "first soprano," "alto," and "second soprano." It is the aim of the teacher that every child sing each of these parts, changing from one to another according to the directions of the moment or by being assigned them in different songs.

In each of the music series fifth-grade books will be found a sequence of songs that stresses parallel thirds. Following songs in thirds there will be those that include both thirds and sixths, then some fourths and fifths. Every teacher in the intermediate grades should know the sequence of songs through which part-singing is expected to be learned in the particular series book or books available in his school. This requires the study of the recommendations found in the teachers' manual that accompanies the books of each series.

THE MALE TEACHER

The male teacher is at some disadvantage in teaching part-singing, since his voice sounds one octave lower than the child voice. Therefore, it is necessary that he use some melody instrument instead of his voice when he wishes to illustrate part-singing of unchanged voices. His voice is excellent, however, in the singing of chord roots. There is seldom a changed voice among sixth-grade children, but in case there should be, the singing of special parts such as chord roots by the male teacher along with the boy will help the child adjust to his temporarily unique situation.

TEACHING AIDS

Among aids in the teaching of part-singing are some of the recordings of part songs that accompany music books, both the intermediate grades series books and some other publications. In these, the children may hear the complete song with the parts, then each of the parts singly, then hear them united again.

The value of instrumental music experience as an aid to the background and performance of part-singing has been commented upon several times previously. To summarize, chording on instruments helps children's readiness for part-singing, and the use of melody instruments or the piano in playing one or more of the parts can aid in making the activity successful. But children should not remain dependent upon hearing a part played instrumentally in order to sing it; teachers should use these helpful aids with discretion.

Another aid is the tape recorder. Working with two machines, a child in a cubicle in the classroom or in another room can participate in part-singing and evaluate it. Perhaps the first step would be to record the harmony part (second part) of a two-part song on one of the machines. The child practices singing the melody along with the harmony part, and when ready, records the two parts on the second machine, plays it back and evaluates the result. Then the process can be reversed, with the melody recorded on the first machine, and the child practicing adding the second part to it, eventually recording the "duet" on the other machine. This teaching aid permits individual work, promotes careful listening, and can be a powerful motivating influence.

Classroom teachers who have difficulty with their own part-singing may assign talented children the preparation of part songs to teach to the class. Also, in the preparation of descants, small groups of children can learn the descant outside of class, and be ready to add their special part to the melody sung by the rest of the class.

PROVISION FOR INDIVIDUAL DIFFERENCES

Should any child have an unusual voice range, this range may be accommodated by part songs that are selected with it in mind, or special parts can be written for this child. Those children who are not yet ready to sing parts other than the melody should be assigned the melody most of the time while their harmonic sense continues to develop by guiding listening and repeated attempts at singing simple parts. They can also play the parts on the bells, piano, or other melody instruments as preparation to learning to sing them.

THE ELEMENTARY SCHOOL CHORUS

Among the special interest groups in the elementary school are the orchestra, band, and chorus. The instrumental groups are generally the responsibility of special music teachers but the chorus is frequently taught either by the music teacher or by a classroom teacher who has the interest and ability. Although some schools have a primary grades chorus which sings unison songs, the usual chorus is composed of fifth and sixth graders. Today's teachers are fortunate in having an improved selection of song materials to use, some of which are listed at the end of this chapter. Not only do the series books include chants, descants, and countermelodies in addition to the standard types of two- and three-part songs, but there are valuable supplementary materials. There is no standard seating arrangement for elementary choruses. However, it is best to have the lowest and highest parts seated so that each can hear the other well. In this way the group is able to keep on pitch better. In chorus work which has a goal of public performance, the children are more or less permanently assigned to one of the parts (high, middle, or low).

GENERAL AND SPECIFIC TEACHING PURPOSES

The general purpose is to teach children to sing part songs. Specific purposes for lesson plans include: teaching children to sing a melody while a contrasting piano accompaniment is played; guiding children to discover chord changes by having them accompany a two-chord song "by ear" on the autoharp; encouraging a small group to play or sing a part other than the melody while the class sings the melody; helping children hear all the parts of a round as they sing it; teaching a dialogue song as an early step toward part-singing; helping children hear the parts of a combinable song as they sing it; guiding children to create a harmonic ending as a step toward harmonic improvisation; teaching the singing of chord roots; encouraging children to create a harmonic score to a simple song, and to sing the added parts with the melody; teaching a chant as an experience in holding a simple part against a melody; teaching children how to create chants, how to add a descant to a melody, and how to evaluate the balance of the parts; teaching vocal chording; experimenting with "barber-shop harmony"; teaching the singing of parallel thirds and sixths; teaching the singing of a song containing both thirds and sixths; teaching children to sight-sing a two part song; and providing for individual differences in several specifically stated ways.

THINGS TO DO

1. Study, then teach to the college class chants and descants selected from Beatrice Krone's *Our First Songs to Sing with Descants,* published by Neil A. Kjos, Park Ridge, Illinois. Evaluate them for their use in primary grades. Find similar materials in recent music series books for grades one, two, and three.

2. Select a round and teach it to your class. Become accustomed to directing the entrance of each group of singers. Have the class work with you on the problem of how to sit or stand so that every singer can hear all the parts.

3. Select a two-chord melody and develop a score that provides melody, rhythm, and harmony as suggested in this chapter on page ???, being sure to add chord roots.

4. Write a chant for a one-chord, a two-chord, and a three-chord song. See Chapter Five, pages 129, 136, and 139 for suggested songs, including "Looby Loo," page 217, which includes a staff on which to write. Make use of the chant pattern charts on pages 216, 218.

5. Select a familiar two-chord song in G, F, or C major and demonstrate in the college class how teachers can use the autoharp to improvise an accompaniment, thus helping children to listen carefully for chord changes, and developing the background necessary for part-singing.

6. Improvise "barber-shop harmony" for some of the songs mentioned on page 224.

7. Add a vocal part a third above the melody of "To Puerto Rico," page 103. Arrange "Lightly Row" and "Goodbye My Lover Goodbye" in two-part harmony, employing thirds and/or sixths.

8. Find a recording of a part song and use it in teaching this song to the college class, planning each step of your presentation. Then evaluate the effectiveness of this use of the recording.

9. Evaluate the following part-singing drill. Write the scale of D major on the chalkboard. Use both index fingers, two pencils, or two short pointers. Have half the class follow your right hand and the other half follow your left hand as you point to different notes of the scale as they sing them in harmony. Remember that thirds and sixths sound well.

10. Select from the series books a sequence of songs you could use in helping fifth-grade classes learn two-part singing by the use of thirds.

11. Write descants to "Are You Sleeping," "Hickory Dickory Dock," and to the first half of "Oh Susanna."

12. Make a tape recording designed to teach a two-part song to fifth- or sixth-grade classes.

13. Prepare a short demonstration to show how teachers can use melody instruments to help children learn to sing in parts.

MUSIC SERIES GUIDE

BIRCHARD MUSIC SERIES (SUMMY-BIRCHARD COMPANY)

BOOK THREE

Preparation for part singing, TM 211

BOOK FOUR

Added harmony (by ear), TM 256–7
Conversation songs, TM 257
Descants, TM 257
Part singing, TM 9
Partner songs, TM 257
Rounds and canons, TM 257
Two-part songs, TM 257

BOOK FIVE

Added harmony (by ear), TM 321
Conversation songs, TM 321
Descants, TM 321
Easy part songs, TM 319

Part singing, TM 9
Partner songs, TM 321
Rounds and canons, TM 321

GROWING WITH MUSIC (PRENTICE-HALL, INC.)

The teachers edition for the following books was not available when this Guide
was compiled.

BOOK FOUR

Songs for part singing: rounds and canons, descants, ostinato patterns, two-part songs,
see entry in classified index, p. 186

BOOK FIVE

Songs for part singing: rounds and canons, descants, ostinato patterns, two-part songs,
see entry in classified index, p. 218

BOOK SIX

Harmony in music, 46–68

MUSIC FOR LIVING (SILVER BURDETT COMPANY)

MUSIC IN OUR TOWN

Dialogue songs, TM 133
Echo effects, TM 133

MUSIC NOW AND LONG AGO

Dialogue singing, TM 132
Echo effects, TM 132
Preparation for part-singing, TM 133

MUSIC NEAR AND FAR

Chord roots, 163
Harmony, TM xi
Instruments as aid to part-singing, 163
Rounds, 166, 184
Song conversation (dialogue), 183

MUSIC IN OUR COUNTRY

Conversational songs, 218
Descants, TM 188
Rounds, 218, TM 188
Part-singing, TM xii, TM 188

MUSIC AROUND THE WORLD

Descants, TM 203
Part-singing, TM xii, TM 204
Rounds, 231

MUSIC FOR YOUNG AMERICANS (AMERICAN BOOK COMPANY)

BOOK THREE
Dialogue songs, 196

BOOK FOUR

Combinable songs, 54, 104, 166
Descants, 69, 158
Rounds and canons, 195
Songs with a few measures in two parts, 195
Two-part songs, 92

BOOK FIVE

Descants, 23, 47, 82, 165, TM 8, 27
Dialogue songs, 203
Part-singing, TM 2
Rounds and canons, 203
Songs with descants, 203
Songs with optional second part, 203
Two-part songs, 203

BOOK SIX

Combinable songs, 6, 7, 26, 27, 46, 47
Descants, 212
Dialogue songs, 212
Rounds and canons, 212
Solo-chorus combinations, 212
Optional second parts, 212
Two-part refrains, 212
Two-part songs, 212–3
Three-part songs, 213
Four-part songs, 159, 197

OUR SINGING WORLD (GINN AND COMPANY) 1951 EDITION

SINGING EVERY DAY

Chant, 165ar
Rounds and canons, 121, 165b, 176
Songs harmonized in thirds, 147arb, 157b, 168, 182
Songs with optional harmonies, 40a, 63, 77, 79, 93, 122b, 167
Vocal expression, TM 76–87

SINGING TOGETHER

Canon, 58
Descants, 14, 80, 140a, 154, 159, 163
Improvising harmony, 7, 12, 13, 24a, 31, 93, 95
Introducing part-singing, 10, 60b, 153, 151, 148, 25b, 76b, etc. Other recorded two-

part songs: Album 5–A, 46, 68, 77, 80, 93, 94a, 115, 151, 163, 178, 183, 184. Album
  5–B 24a, 45, 46, 157, 164a, 165b, 179
Rounds, 17, 18a, 69b, 81a, 112ab, 137a, 147a
Singing chord roots, 22, 53, 67, 91, 92, 128
Three-part songs, 188, 192
Vocal expression, TM 205–16

SINGING IN HARMONY

Descants, 8, 33ab, 147, 150, 152, 154
Dialogue song, 36
Improvising harmony, 11, 13, 66, 69
Partial canons, 102, 144
Quodlibet, 201
Recorded part songs: two-part, Album 6–A, 24, 49, 54, 57, 62, 76b, 97, 121, 136b, 144,
  167b, 169, 185, 226, Album 6–B, 27, 38, 40, 53, 59, 100, 137, 151, 167a, 203, three-
  part, Album 6–A, 25, 41, 81, 85b, 142a, 150, 189, 196, Album 6–B, 52, 104, 105, 106,
  114, 116, 118, 33b, 138, 195, four-part, 73
Rounds, 30a, 82a, 136a, 162a, 190a, 199ab
Singing chord roots, 23, 58, 196
Vocal expression, TM 311–6

THIS IS MUSIC (ALLYN AND BACON, INC.)

BOOK THREE

Chants, 165
Descants, 165
Rounds, 165

BOOK FOUR

Canons, 190
Chants, 18, 81
Descants, 190
Rounds, 190
Soprano and alto, 190
Together songs (combinable), 190

BOOK FIVE

Canons, 212
Chants, 212
Chord roots, 212
Combination songs, 212
Descants, 212
Dialogue songs, 212
Humming parts, 88, 99
Low-voice parts, 212
Rounds, 212
Two-part songs, 212
Three-part songs, 212

TOGETHER WE SING (FOLLETT PUBLISHING COMPANY)

REFERENCES AND MATERIALS

BOOKS FOR PART-SINGING

Bampton, Ruth, *Sing With Me.* Byrn Mawr, Pennsylvania: Theodore Presser Company. For grades 4–6.
Beckman, Frederick, *Partner Songs; More Partner Songs.* New York: Ginn and Company, 1958, 1962. Combinable songs usable in grades 5–7.
Bell, Leslie, *The Festival Song Book: One.* New York: Mills Music, Inc. For unaccompanied voices.
Cooper, Irvin, *Songs for Pre-Teentime.* New York: Carl Fischer, Inc. For grades 6–7.
Foltz, David, and Arthur Murphy, *Descants to Sing for Fun.* New York: Mills Music, Inc.

Gearhart, Livingston, *A Christmas Singing Bee.* Delaware Water Gap, Pennsylvania: Shawnee Press.

Grant, Louise, *Harmony and Rhyme.* Boston: Boston Music Company.

Jurey, Edward B., *Mills First Chorus Album.* New York: Mills Music, Inc. For upper elementary and junior high school unchanged voices.

Kent, Willys Peck, *A Book of Descants.* New York: Vantage Press. For use in grades 5–8.

Krone, Beatrice, and Max Krone, *Our First Songs to Sing with Descants* (for upper primary grades): *Very Easy Descants; Songs to Sing with Descants; Descants for Christmas; Our Third Book of Descants; From Descants to Trios; Descants and Rounds for Special Days.* Park Ridge, Illinois: Neil A. Kjos Music Company.

Marais, Joseph, *Marais and Miranda Two-Part Singing.* New York: Charles Hansen Music Corp. With optional obbligato.

Rhea, Lois, *Singing Is Fun.* Bourne, Inc.

Scott, Richard, *Clap, Tap and Sing* (for grades 2–5); *Sevenfold Choral Method* (for grades 5–7). Milwaukee: Handy-Folio Music Company.

Slind, Lloyd H., *Melody, Rhythm, and Harmony; More Melody, Rhythm, and Harmony.* New York: Mills Music, Inc.

FILMS

Harmony in Music. Coronet Instructional Films, 65 E. South Water St., Chicago, Illinois. Introduces harmony and chords. Grades 5–8. Twelve minutes.

Two-Part Singing. Johnson Hunt Productions, 6509 De Longpre Ave., Hollywood, California. Grades 4–6. Twenty minutes.

RECORDINGS

Let's Sing a Round. Los Angeles: Bowmar Records.

Growing Up With Music. Five albums of part songs and descants based on the books of Beatrice and Max Krone. *Our First Songs to Sing with Descants; Very Easy Descants; Songs to Sing with Descants; Intermediate Descants; Songs for Fun with Descants.* Los Angeles: Bowmar Records.

The basic music activity is listening. Children learn to respond physically to beat and accent by listening. Creative rhythmic responses and creative dramatizations are based upon listening, then reacting accordingly. Singing is made possible by listening carefully to a teacher's singing voice, to recordings of singing, to children's voices, to melodies played upon instruments, then attempting to reproduce the pitches with one's own voice. Tone-matching and ear-training experience are based upon listening to pitches and pitch differences. The instrumental activities described in Chapter Five began with listening to songs and singing them before attempting to play them. Percussion and other instruments were added to songs on the basis of listening with discrimination to find out whether the musical effect was what was desired. Thus, all these activities were made possible by listening. Listening is more than hearing; the teacher must establish the necessity of listening attentively *for* something. It may be to discover, to verify, to follow a sequence of events, to answer a question, to examine the music critically, or to seek entertainment. Truly, listening must be taught. Its activities require courtesy because no one should interfere with another's listening.

PURPOSES IN LISTENING TO MUSIC

The list of musical learnings in Chapter Three, pages 67–68 will be helpful in identifying purposes in listening. Examples of the way in which specific purposes are derived from general purposese follow. The list is by no means exhaustive.

General Purpose   *Specific Purpose*

To find pleasure

By preparing for physical responses to music

By enjoying sheer beauty of sound

By resting and relaxing to music

To develop skills

By recognizing pitch changes

By learning to match pitch with voice or instrument

By learning to sing a song

By learning to improve tone quality in singing

By learning to recognize melodies

By learning to respond by physical movement

By learning to recognize specific instruments

By learning concert-audience manners

To develop creative capacities

By planning responses by bodily movements and drawing

By creating dramatizations and stories

To develop knowledge of music literature

By listening to recordings of significant songs

By listening to recordings of significant instrumental music

By evaluating recordings brought from home by children

By listening to school and community concerts

By listening to selected radio and television music

To develop understanding of music symbols and vocabulary

By hearing high and low and associating these with notation

By hearing pitches of long and short duration and associating these with note values

By hearing scale and chord patterns and associating these with notation

By hearing such things as slurs, repeats, accents, ritards, accelerandos, pauses, and associating these with the term or symbol as soon as the maturity level permits

To develop understanding of musical design	By hearing and identifying phrases; by hearing phrases that are the same and that are different By hearing and identifying introductions, interludes, codas By finding out how music communicates ideas and concepts
To develop understanding of humanity	By hearing and identifying childhood emotions expressed in music By hearing interests common to humanity expressed in music of various peoples of the world By learning to co-operate to achieve good musical results

GRADES 4–6

To find pleasure	By preparing for physical responses to music By enjoying sheer beauty of sound By resting and relaxing to music By listening to performances of classmates and others By sharing interesting music with others
To develop skills	By identifying the more unusual instruments By identifying major, minor, pentatonic and other modes By recognizing common pitch intervals By hearing harmony parts in part-singing By becoming increasingly aware of all the component parts of musical design through listening By responding to rhythmic aspects of music with increasing accuracy
To develop creative capacities	By listening in order to respond to music with bodily movement By listening in order to devise an appropriate accompaniment By listening in order to improvise another vocal or instrumental part to a song By listening in order to respond with art media By listening in order to respond with written descriptions or stories

To develop knowledge of music literature	By listening to program music By listening to music that has no story By listening to music of great composers By learning to recognize folk and national characteristics in music By relating music to world history and events
To develop understanding of musical symbols and vocabulary	By identifying by notation the themes that are heard in the music By following notation as children listen to a harmony part sung by the teacher By hearing scale and chord patterns and associating these with notation By hearing such aspects as slurs, repeats, accents, ritards, accelerandos, pauses, and associating these with the term or symbol
To develop understanding of musical design	By identifying two- and three-part song forms when these are heard By identifying forms such as rondo, variation, and fugue when they are heard By hearing and identifying such aspects as contrast, tension and release, polyphony, homophony, and instrumentation By becoming aware of extended musical forms such as classic dance suites, orchestral suites, tone poems, concertos, operas, symphonies
To develop understanding of humanity	By learning of humanity's common needs through listening to music By learning to appreciate through music the characteristic differences in humanity that add interest in and appreciation of other peoples of the world By learning how mankind has used music as a universal form of communication throughout history

Education puts strong stress on *listening skills.* Today's world is so filled with distracting sounds that many children protect themselves from the din by somehow shutting sounds out and by attempting *not* to listen.

Therefore, the responsibility of the teacher is to make listening to music so interesting and challenging that habits of good listening become firmly established. In this chapter, listening to recordings will be emphasized. As in any other kind of teaching, the good teacher knows the background of his class in this activity, knows the material he is to present, knows why it is appropriate for his students, and knows what he expects the children will learn from it.

Children in primary grades enjoy listening to recordings that possess some of the following characteristics: (1) the potential for active physical response; (2) a distinct mood; (3) songlike melodies; (4) beautiful tone quality; (5) a story or message in the music; (6) content that relates to the experience and interest of children, and (7) brevity (because the attention span is short). Children in the intermediate grades have the ability to be more analytical in their responses to listening, even though the above criteria are also applicable to them. Beginning at the fourth-grade level, asking *what, why,* and *how* is a characteristic that assists the teacher in helping the children develop a more intellectual approach.

Formalized listening to recordings is ordinarily planned for only one occasion during any school day, and it is not always a daily occurrence unless for a brief time as a related part of the daily lesson. However, recordings are used for other purposes and at a number of times during a day in connection with rest periods, art, physical education, language arts, social studies, and in singing and rhythmic responses. Incidental playing of recordings can give familiarity to music of quality. There is a repertoire of music every child should know that can be assimilated in part by playing it on the record player in an unobtrusive way during rest periods, and at other times when background music is in order. This music can be of a type that promotes relaxation and emotional stability, as the famed article by Katherine Scott Taylor[1] states. She used such music as Bach's *Air for the G String,* and simple chamber music of Beethoven, Haydn, Schubert, and Schumann to create a calm environment for a first-grade group of children of migrant workers. Discipline problems dwindled while the children learned to love fine music—a love and enjoyment that will last a lifetime. Types of listening differ in accordance with the function of the particular recording. For instance, some recordings that include music are not designed for musical listening, but only to tell a story that is made more enjoyable through the addition of background music. They may be useful in language arts. Some that include music with story-telling may be purely for recreation, while others may offer much learning about music and musicians. The good teacher studies a

---

[1] Taylor, Katherine Scott, "An Autochthonous Approach to Music Education," *Music Educators Journal,* February–March, 1949, pp. 17–19, 50–52; September–October, 1959, pp. 35–39.

recording, analyzes its true function, and uses it in accordance with that function—if he uses it at all.

During listening activities, the teacher is always an example of an interested listener, illustrating by his actions and attitude the mental concentration necessary for such listening.   He listens attentively to hear the things for which he has prepared his class to listen.   When such listening is properly planned, there is no talking while the recording is being played.

If there is an over-all teaching principle involved in listening, it is that the teacher prepares for this activity so thoroughly that he and the children are *always* actively listening *for* something.   If we were to ask about the basic purpose of teaching listening, we might say it is to aid children to lead happier, better lives through enjoying the best of many different types of music.   This teaching is urgently needed today when the school is called upon to help children be selective and discriminating in the midst of the overwhelming amount of music of questionable taste and value being brought to them daily by jukeboxes, radio, and television.

CLASSIFICATIONS OF RECORDINGS

Many efforts have been made to classify recordings so that teachers can find and evaluate them for classroom use.   Music educators and writers have stressed different types of classifications.   For example, one writer considers *types* of music and states the issue in terms of authentic music (such as authentic folk songs or ethnic music), music based upon authentic sources but altered (such as some music based upon American Indian sources but harmonized and arranged in non-Indian ways), music that is stylized by imitating and idealizing older forms or characteristic types of music (such as Maurice Ravel's *Tzigane,* which idealizes Gypsy music, and his *La Valse,* which idealizes the nineteenth-century waltz), music by nationalist composers (such as Chopin, Vaughan-Williams, Wagner, and Mussorgsky), and performances by leading vocalists and instrumentalists that emphasize types of voices and kinds of instruments.   Another writer considers the *content* of music and classifies recordings in terms of relations to nature (with various subdivisions such as animals, weather, and seasons), descriptive fantasy, toys, stories and legends, and instruments of the orchestra.   Most of the classifications mentioned thus far are helpful in relation to both social studies-centered and music-centered units of work.

A simple type of classification is in terms of program music that expresses mood, description, or story, and nonprogrammatic music that expresses concepts such as beauty, form, or an intellectual plan.

Efforts have been made to classify this music according to grade level.

This has been done both in the courses of study in individual school systems and in the compiling of record collections and books such as Lillian Baldwin's *Music for Young Listeners,* books (Silver-Burdett) with companion recordings, and RCA's *Listening Program* Albums of the *Basic Record Library for Elementary Schools,* and *Adventures in Music,* another graded series of recordings (also RCA).   Grade level classifications are made for two primary purposes: (1) to attempt to select music for listening in terms of the general abilities of the age level, and (2) to eliminate unnecessary duplication of listening experiences in the elementary school years.   For example, *Peter and the Wolf* has possible uses in each of the six grades, and for this reason, it can easily be overused.   It is necessary for teachers to plan on what grade level this composition—or any other recording—is to be presented for time is too valuable in today's schools to be wasted by unnecessary repetitions.   While there is unquestioned value in reviewing worth-while music over the years, some of this review can be done at times when this music is useful as a background for other activities or in recreational listening, while the major emphasis should be devoted to enlarging a listening repertoire of culturally significant music.

Catalogs offer valuable assistance to teachers who are seeking music to relate to social studies or other nonmusical units of work, or to relate to units of work in music.   Catalogs of classified educational recordings are obtainable from concerns such as Folkways, RCA-Victor, The Harrison Catalogs,* and the Children's Music Center.   The latter catalog, for example, contains approximately 90 classifications, assisting the busy teacher to select recordings relating to all commonly taught units of work, from Indians to symphonic music based upon American and European themes.   Added assistance is provided by recommending books, tapes, and filmstrips as well.   Thus, highly useful classifications are found in this catalog and in those of other concerns, addresses for some of which will be found later in this chapter.

Still other teachers think of general levels of musical worth through which they will lead children to advance in their enjoyment and understanding of music of quality.   Level 1 would be what is heard frequently on radios—popular songs and gospel tunes.   Level 2 would be "semiclassics," folk music, music from Broadway musical shows, and other easy-to-listen-to music.   Level 3 would be music of undeniable quality—art songs, chamber music, symphonies and operas, and music played or sung by first-rank artists.   Most teachers find little need to use music on Level 1.   If they are judicious in their choice of music, the bulk of it will be on Level 3 from the very beginning of the listening experience.

---

* The Teachers' Record Catalog, 274 Madison Avenue, New York 16, New York.

It would seem that one of the best ways to classify recordings is in accordance with their function as an aid to the teacher in achieving his purposes. The following listing exemplifies this. It is only a beginning; many other recordings and other headings can be added.

DRAMATIZATION	COMPOSER
Nutcracker Suite	Tchaikovsky
Peer Gynt Suite	Grieg
Sorcerer's Apprentice	Dukas
Carnival of the Animals	Saint-Saëns
Little Train of Caipira	Villa-Lobos
The Moldau	Smetana
Danse Macabre	Saint-Saëns
Death Valley Suite	Grofé
Of a Tailor and a Bear	MacDowell
The Witch	MacDowell
The Villain	MacDowell
Clowns	MacDowell

CREATIVE ACCOMPANIMENT WITH PERCUSSION INSTRUMENTS

Music for Rhythm Bands	[RCA-Victor]
Hungarian Dance No. 5	Brahms
"Polka" from *The Age of Gold*	Shostakovich
Country Dance	Beethoven
Second Gavotte	Sapelnikov
"Soldiers' Chorus" from *Il Trovatore*	Verdi
"Toreador Song" from *Carmen*	Bizet
Snowdrops	Tchaikovsky
Spanish Serenade	Bizet
Czarine Mazurka	Ganne
Procession of the Sardar	Ippolitov-Ivanov
"March" from *Love for Three Oranges*	Prokofiev

IDENTIFICATION OF METER

Ruth Evans Childhood Rhythms, Series 3	Ruth Evans
Marches	Sousa

Any waltz, two-step, polka, jig, and folk dance that has strong accents to indicate the meter

PHRASING

Ruth Evans Childhood Rhythms, Series 3	Ruth Evans
Spring Song	Mendelssohn
The Wild Horseman	Schumann
Melody in F	Rubinstein

CHANGES IN TEMPO

Hungarian Dance No. 5	Brahms
Norwegian Dance	Grieg
Golliwog's Cakewalk	Debussy
Boating on the Lake	Kullak

In the Hall of the Mountain King	Grieg
March of the Gnomes	Rebikov

CHANGES IN VOLUME

Soft and Loud (Album)	[American Book Company]
Hungarian Dance No. 5	Brahms
March of the Dwarfs	Grieg

SIMPLE FORM

Music for Rhythm Bands	[RCA-Victor]
Moths and Butterflies	Elgar
Boating on the Lake	Kullak
Norwegian Dance	Grieg
Golliwog's Cakewalk	Debussy
To a Water Lily	MacDowell
March of the Dwarfs	Grieg
Country Dance	Beethoven
Country Gardens	Grainger
Round and Round	[Young People's Record 431]
Hot Cross Buns	[Children's Record Guild 5005]
Turkish Rondo	Mozart
Turkey in the Straw	Guion (Theme and Variations)
Little Pumpkin Eater's Fugue	

Marches such as those of Sousa, "Funeral March of the Marionettes," and "March of the Toys "from *The Nutcracker Suite*

Dance patterns such as polkas, waltzes, minuets, square-dance tunes

MORE COMPLEX FORMS

Opera

A Child's Introduction to Opera:

The Barber of Seville (Rossini)	[Childcraft Records No. 38]
Amahl and the Night Visitors	Menotti
Hansel and Gretel	Humperdinck

Symphony

"Toy" Symphony	Haydn

Suite

Peer Gynt Suite	Grieg
Death Valley Suite	Grofé
Grand Canyon Suite	Grofé
Scheherazade	Rimsky-Korsakov

Symphonic Poem (tone poem)

The Moldau	Smetana
Sorcerer's Apprentice	Dukas
Danse Macabre	Saint-Saëns
Till Eulenspiegel	Richard Strauss

Overture

Overture to *William Tell*	Rossini

Overture to *The Barber of Seville* (Rossini)   [Childcraft Records No. 38]
Overture to *A Midsummer Night's Dream*   [Children's Record Guild 205]
(Mendelssohn)

ANALYSIS OF THE ELEMENTS OF MUSIC

Peter and the Wolf	Prokofiev
Danse Macabre	Saint-Saëns
Sorcerer's Apprentice	Dukas
Mother Goose Suite	Ravel
Clair de Lune	Debussy
The Living Desert	[Walt Disney]
Grand Canyon Suite	Grofé
Death Valley Suite	Grofé
Rhapsody in Blue	Gershwin
An American in Paris	Gershwin
Scheherazade	Rimsky-Korsakov
The Bee	Schubert
Carnival of the Animals	Saint-Saëns

EMOTIONAL AND INTELLECTUAL LISTENING

The illustration on page 247 is an attempt to show the growing amount of analytical listening a child should experience as he progresses from kindergarten through sixth grade. Notice that enjoyment in music listening develops from nonintellectual listening, and that the bases for nonintellectual listening remain present even though the amount of intellectual listening increases. Since music *is* based upon physical responses, feelings, and emotions, these "nonintellectual" aspects should never be forgotten or neglected. However, if the teaching of music listening is poorly guided, and serves only nonintellectual purposes, intellectual enjoyment and understanding can never be achieved. A major criticism of listening as a part of music education is that teachers who do not know how to teach this subject simply "put on a recording," and hope that it will somehow do the teaching. This same group of teachers is often found taking up sizable periods of time doing only this kind of "teaching," to the neglect of the other aspects of music. Such a lack of understanding of the listening program (and of the music program) has deprived some children of the education in music that is their right. Studying this illustration should assist the teacher's understanding of how to teach music listening.

BUILDING READINESS FOR LISTENING

Before children are asked to listen to music, there are physical factors to be considered. These include having the record machine in proper position in the room and set with the correct turntable speed, the record placed on the machine, the children seated in a way that will promote attention to listening, healthy room temperature, appropriate lighting, and freedom from interference of competing noises, interest-catching articles on desks, and irrelevant activities of some of the children that can distract the attention of others.

The teacher should remember that a vocabulary is necessary for listening, and that this vocabulary must be planned and gradually acquired. New words, both descriptive and musical, should be listed on the chalkboard, and discussed and explained when necessary. Motivation sometimes begins with such interesting new words. It might continue with a brief story about the music, about the composer, or dealing with something original created by the teacher. The teacher might relate the composition to the country of its origin, or the country the music might describe. Further motivation could come from relating the music to a

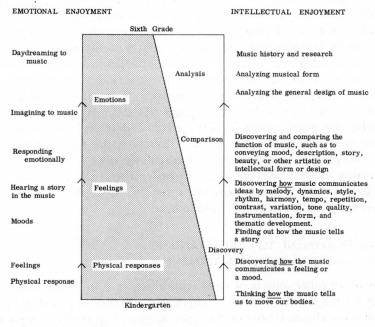

EMOTIONAL ENJOYMENT   INTELLECTUAL ENJOYMENT

Sixth Grade

Daydreaming to music   Music history and research

                            Analysis   Analyzing musical form

                                                    Analyzing the general design of music
            Emotions
Imagining to music

                            Comparison   Discovering and comparing the
                                                    function of music, such as to
Responding   conveying mood, description, story,
emotionally   beauty, or other artistic or
                                                    intellectual form or design

Hearing a story   Feelings   Discovering _how_ music communicates
in the music   ideas by melody, dynamics, style,
                                                    rhythm, harmony, tempo, repetition,
                                                    contrast, variation, tone quality,
Moods   instrumentation, form, and
                                                    thematic development.
                                                    Finding out how the music tells
                                                    a story
                                        Discovery
Feelings   Physical responses   Discovering _how_ the music
                                                    communicates a feeling or
Physical response   a mood.

                                                    Thinking _how_ the music tells
            Kindergarten   us to move our bodies.

concert on radio, television, or local stage, either in anticipation of it, or in reference to a concert that has already been given. The teacher can "set the stage" by relating certain aspects to the general mood or type of the music. These aspects include lighting, objects in the room and their placement, the teacher's tone of voice and facial expression. For example, if Sibelius' _Swan of Tuonela_ were presented in a sixth-grade class, the lighting could be darkened in keeping with the somber mood of the music, a picture of the dark waters of northern Finland might occupy a central location, and the teacher's voice and facial expression could match the solemn overtones of this legend of the ancient past. He might tell part of the story, keeping this tone of voice and facial expression throughout. When children come to realize that such listening is "staged" for their benefit and enjoyment, they can become highly motivated, and intrigued with what they are about to hear. Visual aids such as pictures, slides, transparencies on an overhead projector, pictures and scores shown on opaque projectors, thematic material drawn on the chalkboard or appearing on teacher-made or purchased charts, and charts that relate history and music, either those commercially available or "time-lines" constructed by children on chalkboard or butcher paper motivate interest as well as playing a part in the development of the listening lesson.

Readiness to listen to music is influenced by a child's maturity level and by the music-listening experiences he has had in his out-of-school environment. Thus, the teacher selects music with these in mind. A child's interest in listening is more apt to be keen when he can understand a large part of what he hears. Therefore, a child is more ready to respond to listening when the content of the music relates to past experiences, and when the music itself contains familiar elements, particularly in rhythm and melody. With regard to melody, identifying familiar melodies in settings new to the listener assists motivation. The listing of music of this type is found on pages 250–251. Teachers should remember that genuine interest on the part of children is from the children's point of view, not that of adults. Therefore, the teacher will always assess his plans in accordance with children's interests.

Further motivation comes from teacher's plans that include asking the children to answer specific questions and to solve specific problems by listening carefully to what they are to hear.

FROM ENJOYMENT TO UNDERSTANDING AND TASTE TO FURTHER ENJOYMENT

As in all other aspects of music education, skill in formal listening is built upon a firm foundation of enjoyment. Earlier in this chapter were listed seven characteristics of the types of recordings children enjoy hearing. On the basis of enjoyment, the teacher undertakes to enlarge the children's musical understanding. In the primary grades, owing to the mental and physical make-up of that age group, most listening activities taking place with recordings are of three types: those that produce rhythmic and dramatic responses, those that are associated with different moods, and those that are associated with stories. It is the teacher's task to draw from the children the answers to questions such as the following: "Does the music sound lively, like walking, running, marching, skipping, galloping, goblins, Indians, fairies? Does the music sound happy, sad, quiet? Could it be a lullaby?" Thus the teacher begins formal listening with information already familiar to the children. They have acquired a background of activities through which they can provide the answers to such questions.

In the intermediate grades the questions can become more musically specific, as, for example: "Is this a dance (or waltz, gavotte, polka, minuet, mazurka, march)? What instrument played the melody? Do you think this was a folk song or an art song? What do you think the function of this music could be? Has this music a distinctive style? What does the music tell you about the spirit and culture of these people or of their nation? What do you know about this composer? What did you notice about the form of this music?"

From these understandings come the development of discrimination and taste in listening to music. In this, the child is led to set up his own standards; they should not be adult-imposed. When children have a musical environment which provides many opportunities to choose and judge, their taste is remarkably competent. They *like* good music. The teacher guides listening with appropriate questions such as: "'Do you think this music achieves what it is supposed to do? Is it sincere? Is it true to its type? Is the style one you would expect to hear? Is this music authentic—the real music of Arabia, China, the American Indian—or is it music written by composers of some other nationality or culture? Which recording of this composition do you think is the best one, and why?" Thus the teacher works toward the goal of discrimination and good taste—a goal which should heighten their enjoyment of music.

In recent years there is thought to have been an overemphasis in the use of program music (music which tells a story) and a corresponding neglect of absolute music (music which has no story). Perhaps this is because a "story" recording appears to succeed without much effort or preparation on the part of the teacher, while absolute music requires preparation. However, good program music can serve musical learnings when the children are asked questions that will reveal the musical means by which the composer tells the story. For example, upon listening to the third movement of Ferde Grofé's *Death Valley* Suite, "Desert Water Hole," the experiences the children think they hear described in the music when the pioneers' wagon train crosses the valley can be listed on the chalkboard. Then the teacher can draw from the children through questioning them *how* the music tells of these experiences by means of melody, rhythm, harmony, instrumentation, contrast, repetition, tempo, and dynamics.

Children can be helped to understand almost any type of music if the teacher will "set the stage" for it. The authors once experimented in a

It has been stated above that interest in listening is stimulated when the child can discover familiar melodies in the "new" music to which he listens. In this approach, after the class has learned to sing and enjoy the song, a recording is presented in which the familiar melody forms part of the thematic material of the composition. This approach may speed the discovery by the children of musical forms such as variation and rondo, and also the various methods of *thematic development*, a basic ingredient of great music. The following list includes recordings of this type.

COMPOSER	TITLE	THEME OR SONGS
Beethoven	String Quartet, Op. 59, No. 2	Russian hymn "Praise to God" (*This is Music*, IV, p. 172)
Beethoven	Symphony VIII (2nd movement, 3rd theme)	"The Metronome"
Beethoven	Symphony IX (4th movement)	"United Nations Hymn"(*This is Music*, VI, pp. 38–9)
		"World Anthem"
Beethoven	Wellington's Victory	"For He's a Jolly Good Fellow"
Caillet	Variations on "Pop Goes the Weasel"	"Pop Goes the Weasel" (Victor WE PR 26)
Copland	Appalachian Spring (ballet)	"Simple Gifts" (Birchard Music Series, V, p. 36)
Copland	Billy the Kid (ballet) (4th theme)	"Goodbye, Old Paint"
Copland	Lincoln Portrait	"Camptown Races"
		"Springfield Mountain" (Pesky Serpent)
Copland	Rodeo	"Hoedown"
Dvořák	Symphony V	"Swing Low, Sweet Chariot" (1st movement, 3rd theme)
		"Going Home" (*This is Music*, V, pp. 147–8)
Dohnányi	Variations on a Nursery Tune	"Twinkle, Twinkle, Little Star"
Gould	American Salute	"When Johnny Comes Marching Home"
Gould	Cowboy Rhapsody	"Goodbye, Old Paint"
		"Home on the Range"
Grofé	Death Valley Suite	"Dixie"
		"Old Black Joe"
		"O Susanna"
Guion	Turkey in the Straw	"Old Zip Coon" (same tune)
Haydn	"Emperor" Quartet	"Glorious Things of Thee Are Spoken" (Austrian National Hymn)
		This is Music, V, pp. 54–5)

Humperdinck	Hansel and Gretel, Prelude to Act I	"Prayer" (*Singing Together*, Ginn, p. 205)
McBride	Mexican Rhapsody	"Song of the Gingerbread Children" (*Singing Together*, Ginn, p. 211) "Hat Dance" "Rancho Grande" "La Cucaracha"
Mozart	Variations on "Twinkle, Twinkle Little Star"	*A Junior High School Music Handbook*, p. 46. (Prentice-Hall)
Mussorgsky	Boris Godunov (Coronation Scene)	"Praise to God" (*This is Music*, IV, p. 172)
Nelson	Kentucky Mountain Portraits	"Cindy" "Skip to My Lou" "Paw Paw Patch"
Rossini	William Tell Overture	"Lone Ranger" theme
Sibelius	Finlandia	"Song of Peace" and other titles
Sowerby	The Irish Washerwoman	"Lane County Bachelor" *This Is Music*, VI, p. 76 (RCA Album E 75)
Strauss, Richard	Aus Italien	"Funiculi, Funicula"
Tchaikovsky	1812 Overture	Russian National Hymn (appears under different titles)
Tchaikovsky	Symphony IV (4th movement)	"The Birch Tree" (*This is Music*, IV, p. 108)
Vardell	Joe Clark Steps Out	"Old Joe Clark" (*This is Music*, V, p. 77) "What Child is This?" (same tune) (*This is Music*, VI, p. 65)
Vaughan-Williams	Fantasia on Greensleeves	
Quilter	A Children's Overture	This overture contains ten familiar primary grades songs: "Girls and Boys Come Out to Play," "St. Paul's Steeple," "Dame Get Up and Bake Your Pies," "I Saw Three Ships," "Sing a Song of Sixpence," "Over the Hills and Far Away," "The Frog and the Crow," "The Frog He Would A-Wooing Go," "Oranges and Lemons," "Baa Baa Black Sheep."

fourth-grade class by planning for the presentation of music that they considered unlikely to be accepted by the children—Igor Stravinsky's *Le Sacre du Printemps* (The Rite of Spring). This music, from the layman's point of view, was disjointed rhythmically and even lacked melody in the traditional sense. Furthermore, it was a work of such length that a portion of it had to be taken out of its natural place in the work to have something short enough to use.

It all happened when the fourth-grade teacher was working with a unit on the early history of the earth. The children were fascinated with their research on dinosaurs and other prehistoric life on this planet. This gave the music teacher the idea of presenting a section of the Stravinsky,[2] somewhat as Walt Disney had done it in the film *Fantasia*. He obtained a book of photographs of scenes from the film and showed the children the color illustrations of the animal and plant life and the geological conditions of prehistoric times as Disney imagined them. When the fourth-grade children were told that a composer had written music about prehistoric man they wanted very much to listen to it—so a short part of it was played. The spell was broken when the needle reached the end of the disc. One little girl said, "That music is exciting! It just wears me out!" which was a good description of the effect of the composer's rhythmic complications and dissonances. Questions from the teacher concerning *why* the music was exciting, and what there was about the music that "wore the listener out," developed some analysis of the musical means the composer employed to achieve his purposes. Later on the children asked to listen to the recording again, an indication that the listening experience had been successful. Had a fifth or sixth grade found similar attraction in this music, the teachers might have evoked from the children opinions about certain characteristics of the music of this century, more about the instruments selected to perform it, and more about the composer and his great influence on musical composition in the first half of this century.

ASSISTANCE FOR THE TEACHER

It is obvious that the background of musical knowledge needed by the teacher of musical listening is more than most teachers possess. While music education majors may be held responsible for a rather thorough knowledge of music literature, it would be unrealistic to expect this from the elementary education major who must know much about many fields, of which music is only one. However, important assistance is available to

---

2 For other music by Stravinsky likely to be enjoyed in the intermediate grades, try the ballets *The Firebird*, which is a fairy tale, and *Petrouchka*, which concerns a fair and puppet show.

classroom teacher and music specialist alike. The RCA-Victor *Basic Record Library for Elementary Schools* includes a six-album Listening Program, with one album for each of the six grades. These include teaching instructions and suggestions for each composition in the collection. RCA also provides a new record library, *Adventures in Listening*, with one album for each grade. There are no duplications in the two RCA collections. Comprehensive teachers' guides are provided for each album. The address of RCA Educational Records is 155 East 24th St., New York 10, N.Y. The late Lillian Baldwin is the author of a series of books to read and recordings to hear that extends from the primary grades through grade eight. The books are: *Tiny Masterpieces for Very Young Listeners* (Theodore Presser, Bryn Mawr, Penn.); and Music for Young Listeners: *The Green Book* (grade four); *The Crimson Book* (grade five); *The Blue Book* (grade six); and *Music to Remember* (grades seven and eight). Published by Silver Burdett Company, these books are written so that children can read them; thus they serve as reference books for the classroom as well as books for the teacher. The recordings to use with these books are obtained from the Sound Book Press Society, Inc., Scarsdale, New York, or from Silver Burdett Co., Park Ave. and Columbia Road, Morristown, New Jersey. *The Bowmar Orchestral Library* is obtainable from Bowmar Educational Records, 10515 Burbank Blvd., North Hollywood, California. Suggestions for the teacher are printed on each album. The collection consists of eleven ungraded albums. Each album concerns a subject: Animals and Circus, Nature and Make-Believe, Pictures and Patterns, Marches, Dances, Fairy Tales in Music, Stories in Opera and Ballet, Legends in Music, Under Many Flags, and American Scenes. This collection is accompanied by wall charts of 156 themes printed on heavy artboard, an important visual aid.

It is well that every teacher of elementary school music be familiar with this material and know how to use it. In addition to these collections are various recordings and albums from a number of companies that pertain to lives of composers, instruments of the orchestra, music history, and musical forms.

Other aids include pictures of instruments, composers, and subjects related to the content of music. Pictures of instruments and composers, and recordings are available from sources listed at the end of this chapter. One such source is Keyboard Jr., 1346 Chapel St., New Haven 11, Connecticut, a concern that publishes the magazine *Young Keyboard Jr.* for grades four through six, available at bundle subscription rates. Supplementary materials are provided to assist in classroom use of the magazine. These include recordings, lesson plans, large charts of themes, radio and television guides, and many pictures for the classroom including those of conductors, composers, instruments, and opera. Another visual aid is a "Build Your Own Orchestra" kit by which children place cut-outs of players in symphony formation. Record albums include *Contemporary American Composers, American Composers, Norwegian Album,* and *Opera Record.*

The tape recorder, and opaque and overhead projectors should not be neglected as teaching aids. Recording a class performance on tape, then listening to it and evaluating the performance, can provide excellent motivation.

Films for use in music education are helpfully indexed and evaluated in *Film Guide for Music Educators,* a 1961 publication of the Music Educators National Conference, 1201 Sixteenth St. N. W., Washington 6, D.C. Films are classified under the headings Musical Performance, History of Music and Biographies, Band, Orchestra, Teaching of Music, Visual Interpretation of Music, Acoustics, Music as a Career, and Music Festivals. The catalog of the Children's Music Center, 5373 West Pico Blvd., Los Angeles 19, California, has been referred to earlier as a source of recordings, books, and filmstrips.

Teachers can make card files of recordings and their uses. Such a file of information is an excellent time-saver. There are a number of different ways information can be placed on a card, one of which appears below. It is assumed that this card would be for the individual teacher, and kept in a convenient place on or in his desk. By making duplicate cards, a file useful for an entire faculty can be made, with the titles placed alphabetically behind primary-use headings such as Rhythm, Singing, and Listening.

Title	Number of Album
Composer	Primary Use
Sources of information a) composer b) performer	Other Uses
Motivation, suggestions for	
Comments	

SUMMARY

The classroom environment should be conducive to good listening. Children should be seated where they can easily hear, and those with hearing difficulties should be seated accordingly. Reduce or eliminate competing sounds by closing windows and hall doors. Children must have a purpose for listening; they should expect purpose and meaning in listening to music. The music to be heard should relate to the maturity level of the listeners, to their attention span, interest, background of understanding, and to their previous experiences. Children can set up standards for good listening in the classroom. Listening is dynamic, not passive. Each music period should involve intensive listening for a number of things: pitch, tone quality, singing, playing, evaluation, answering questions, discovering, and analyzing. Children need the opportunity to compare and to analyze music in order to develop ability to discriminate and to make value judgments. They do not fully accept value judgments of music from adults; they must be helped to make their own.

MORE SUGGESTIONS TO AID LISTENING

Devote only a part of the music period to listening to recordings. Plan a variety of music activities, combining different kinds of listening experiences with singing, rhythmic responses, and playing instruments. Remember that children are normally unable to sit still and listen for very long.

Correlate listening with social studies, art, and dance.

Use *good quality recordings* on a *good quality machine*. Even the loveliest music cannot succeed if distorted by poor equipment. Records should be stored vertically in folders to protect them from scratches and dust. The needle should be of high quality and the correct type for the machine. The tone arm should be placed on the record very gently. Because the human skin is oily, and oil damages records, the record should be touched only on the edge and in the center, never on the grooves. Dust should be removed with something clean and lint-free, such as a damp sponge.

Bring *live performers* into the classroom from school and community—but be sure before they are invited that they can perform suitably. Let the young children touch and feel the instruments used, for it is through physical contact that they gain in comprehension.

Use visual aids: an attractive *bulletin board* with pictures, newspaper and magazine write-ups, concert and recital programs, and clever cartoons about music and musicians. If the teacher changes the content of the bulletin board regularly, the children will read it with interest. *Films* and *filmstrips* have an important place. *Write music themes* on the chalkboard or use charts if the children do not have them to follow in their books while listening. Sing these themes before playing the recordings, if they are singable.

Bring listening to life by relating it to current events, motion pictures, radio and television programs outside the classroom, local concerts, and to newspaper and magazine feature stories.

Begin the study of musical form by leading children to discover melodic changes and repetitions, i.e., "Is the music the same now or is it different?"

Use appropriate *radio and television* programs in the classroom, taking care to prepare the children for them fully and to follow up afterwards.

Add a *Listening Post* to the classroom music center. This is a control box with headphones which may be attached to any record player, thus permitting several children to listen without disturbing the class. It is manufactured by A. M. Brooks Company, 1222 West Washington Blvd., Los Angeles, California. There are other similar teaching tools. One is The Listening Corner, devised for both music listening and speech training and accomodating eight sets of headphones and a microphone input. It is manufactured by Caliphone Corporation, 1041 North Sycamore Ave., Hollywood 28, California. These can sometimes be made in high school manual arts classes.

To help direct listening, place a list of key words on the chalkboard before the recording is played. Example: mood, instruments heard, meter, form, sounds of nature.

Prepare the children to understand the music of *concerts and recitals* given at the school or in the community.

Request that special *concerts and programs* for children be given at school and prepare the children to listen to them.

Employ *music notebooks and scrap books* in grades five and six—but use discretion. Children can put into them all the things listed above for the bulletin board. However, if children feel compelled to assemble bulk without true interest, such a project can defeat its purpose. Maybe all of this belongs on a lively bulletin board after all!

Children can bring favorite *recordings from home* to share with the class, explaining why they like them.

Give children the opportunity to play appropriate thematic material on piano, bells, and other instruments.

Children can plan with the teacher a *pretend concert* of recorded music. Such programs can be organized around ideas such as music of other lands, marches of many kinds, musical instruments and soloists, music of certain composers, and American music. A variant of this was done by a student teacher in music who substituted himself and his school-of-music friends for the recordings, and substituted the school auditorium for the classroom. The children "sold" themselves tickets, provided ushers, and planned what their behavior was to be in the intermission. The university students entered wholeheartedly into the idea, dressing in formal clothes. This program was planned so that the children joined with the performers in singing at the close of the concert.

Have appropriate books about composers and music in the music corner and in the school library.

Organize listening sessions by grouping the recordings around unifying themes such as types of instruments (percussion, woodwind, brass, string), elements of music (rhythm, harmony, melody), dances, marches, different composer's concepts of sunrise, sunset, seasons, the sea, day and night, plant and animal life.

Read or tell stories about composers to make them live in children's minds. Especially appropriate are stories about these men in their childhood, and about composers' relations with children. For example, Bach, Mozart, and Mendelssohn composed music when they were very young. Dioramas and puppetry may be employed.

In primary grades a lengthy recording such as *Tubby the Tuba* is too long for playing at one sitting. Make it a continued story and play one or two sides a day, reviewing them before playing another side the next day. In intermediate grades, the *Nutcracker* Suite (Tchaikovsky) is too long for one listening lesson. Therefore, play a section of it a day. Really long compositions have little or no place in elementary school music.

The piano can be used effectively for some listening experiences, particularly in the kindergarten and first grade.

By all means use the tape recorder to record children's singing and playing. Nothing stimulates interest in listening to recorded music as much as making recordings.

Children need *vocabulary* in order to discuss music they hear. This vocabulary is of two types: (1) musical terms such as *ballet* and *suite,* and (2) descriptive words. Musical terms can be written on the chalkboard and explained by the teacher before a recording is played. After the children have listened to a recording, descriptive words can be drawn from them through class discussion and written on the chalkboard as an activity in language arts.

Allow children to respond to music physically when they are listening, as long as this response is of a type that does not interfere with the listening of others. Remember that it is normal to want to move to music. Discover and notate rhythm patterns.

The RCA-Victor Educational Record Catalog contains a section, "Instruments of the Orchestra," suggesting recordings of fine music that features certain instruments.

For an activity in language arts classroom teachers can encourage children to write creative plays concerning lives of composers. These plays might be performed by the class and include playing and singing music of the particular composer.

If children are asked to listen to a recording to imagine a story, the teacher should never reject the story on the grounds that it is not what the composer intended. Music does not communicate with such accuracy; the child's version may be as good as the composer's. The teacher's questions should then draw from the child the musical components—melody, rhythm, harmony, tempo, dynamics, instrumentation—that prompted the story, thus stimulating analysis of the music by the child.

To sharpen listening ability, have the children close their eyes, then guess the name of the child who is singing or the name of the instrument being played.

Appoint a committee to advise the class about significant programs to appear on radio, television, and in local concert halls.

EVALUATION OF LISTENING PROGRAMS

To aid in evaluating pupil progress in listening activities, the following evidences of success are listed:

1. The child enjoys listening to music that has meaning to him.
2. His attitude, questions, and comments reveal that he has listened actively.
3. He listens in out-of-school situations as revealed by his remarks about radio, television, and other musical programs.
4. He brings favorite recordings from home to share with the class.
5. He can hear the recurrence of melodies and rhythms in music.
6. He recognizes various moods in music.
7. He identifies musical instruments.
8. He recognizes musical compositions frequently heard.
9. He recognizes the names of composers and knows something about them.
10. He looks for pictures and stories related to music and composers.

THINGS TO DO

1. Examine the music series book of your choice for listening activities and prepare a short listening lesson for that grade level.
2. Study the different music series and compare them concerning their assistance to the teacher in presenting listening.
3. Plan a "concert" for an elementary classroom, using recordings. Explain how children can help plan this program. Tell of the many things other than music that can be taught through this activity.
4. A music educator said, "Good music is that music which is good for boys and girls at their present stage of development." According to this, when is "music of the masters" good for children?

5. Listen to recordings of authentic music that employs native instruments and native voices. Sources of these include Folkways Records, 121 West 47th St., New York 36, New York, and the *Columbia World Library of Folk and Primitive Music,* Columbia Records Educational Department, 799 Seventh Ave., New York 19, New York. Evaluate them as to possible classroom use.

6. Select a recording to be used in a listening lesson. Draw up a list of "key words" to be placed on the chalkboard to help children know what they might listen for.

7. Find out what impressionist music is, and how this music can be related to impressionism in art. Debussy, Ravel, and Delius are composers who wrote music in this style.

8. For your own cultural background, study various periods in music history. The following dates are approximate only: Renaissance: 1450–1600, Baroque: 1600–1750, Classical: 1750–1820, Romantic: 1820–1900, Contemporary: 1900–. Refer to books such as those listed for the teacher at the end of this chapter.

9. Select appropriate recordings for use in the rest period, or at other times when quiet background music is appropriate.

10. Examine the *Listening Program* record albums of the RCA-Victor Basic Record Library for Elementary Schools and learn how to use them. Note the references to these recordings in the music series, particularly the *Music For Living* Series. Examine RCA's *Adventures in Music* albums in the same manner.

11. Visit a record shop and ask what children's records the parents and the schools are buying. Listen to them and evaluate them for classroom use.

12. Kindergarten and first-grade teachers should study the relationship between playing the piano and listening activities as demonstrated in the series books for those grades. It is clear that the ability to play simple piano pieces is one of the requirements of the professionally prepared kindergarten and first-grade teacher.

13. The classification and evaluation of educational records are greatly aided by some of the catalogs published by concerns that specialize in this area. Evaluate this assistance to teachers provided by catalogs such as those named in the "Assistance for the teacher" section of this chapter.

14. Find what services your state university or state system of higher education offers teachers in supplying 16 mm. films for use in the listening area.

15. Learn how to care for and to store recordings.

16. During repeated listening to a recording that tells a story, first listen for the story. Next, listen to and analyze *how* (by what musical means) the music tells the story. Finally, listen to determine *how successfully* the composer or arranger portrayed the story by means of his music.

MUSIC SERIES GUIDE

BIRCHARD MUSIC SERIES (SUMMY-BIRCHARD COMPANY)

KINDERGARTEN

Music for listening, 158
Quiet listening, 5

BOOK ONE

Music for listening, 186–7

BOOK TWO

Listening, TM 8
Music for quiet listening, TM 198–201
Related recordings found in teaching suggestions in TM

BOOK THREE

Composers, 152, TM 200–1
Listening, TM 8
Recordings, TM 209–10
Songs with related listening, TM 207

BOOK FOUR

Composers, TM 246
Listening, TM 7
Recordings, TM 255–6

BOOK FIVE

Composers, TM 310
Films and filmstrips, TM 316
Listening, TM 7
Recordings, TM 320
Songs with related listening, TM 319

GROWING WITH MUSIC (PRENTICE-HALL, INC.)

The teachers edition was not available when this Guide was compiled.

BOOK TWO

Music by contemporary composers, see entry in classified index, p. 162
Music by great composers, see entry in classified index, p. 162

BOOK THREE

Funeral March of a Marionette, 13
Music by contemporary composers, see entry in classified index, p. 169
Music by famous composers, see entry in classified index, p. 170

BOOK FOUR

Music by contemporary composers, see entry in classified index, p. 185
Music by famous composers, see entry in classified index, p. 185
World of sound, 63–68

BOOK FIVE

Music by contemporary composers, see entry in classified index, p. 217

MUSIC FOR LIVING (SILVER BURDETT COMPANY)

MUSIC FOR YOUNG AMERICANS (AMERICAN BOOK COMPANY)

KINDERGARTEN

Instrumental material index, 164

BOOK ONE

Instrumental material index, 196

BOOK TWO

Integrating the listening program, TM 4–6
Music of great composers, 179
Suggested list of recordings, TM 6
We listen and hear, 132–40

BOOK THREE

Integrating the listening program, TM 4–6
Music of great composers, 196
Suggested list of recordings, 6

BOOK FOUR

Listening program, TM 5
Music by great composers, 195
Suggested list of recordings, 5–6

BOOK FIVE

Listening program with suggested recordings, TM 5–6
Music by great composers, 204

BOOK SIX

Listening program with suggested recordings, TM 5–6
Music by famous composers, 213
Recorded selections, excerpts from, 213

OUR SINGING WORLD (GINN AND COMPANY) 1951 EDITION

THE KINDERGARTEN BOOK

(See IV *Listening* to Music, xix–xx)

THE FIRST GRADE BOOK

(See IV *Listening* to Music, xvii–xviii)

SINGING ON OUR WAY

Suggested recordings: music concerned with rhythm, 24, 29; mood, 56, 58, 73, 118, 120, 147; stories, 67, 73, 81, 132, 147, 156; simple instrumental music, 25, 57, 59, 120

SINGING AND RHYMING

Suggested recordings: music concerned with rhythm, 18, 20, 21, 22, 23, 27, 36, 79, 106, 110; mood, 20, 106, 109, 112, 114, 120, 126, 130; stories, 79, 81, 102, 124, 131, 133, 137, 145, 149, 150, 151, 155, 156 (see TM 163 for additional list); simple instrumental music, 23, 68, 72, 112, 126, 156 (see TM 161 for additional list)

SINGING EVERY DAY

Mozart, Haydn: see Contents, *Music Makers,* 3
Suggested recordings: music concerned with rhythm, 23, 55, 86, 88, 92, 134, 141, 148; mood, 19, 20, 21, 24, 25, 124, 129, 145; stories, 36, 54, 92, 127, 130, 141, 152; simple instrumental music, 21, 65, 68, 71, 85, 90 (see TM 95 for additional list)

SINGING TOGETHER

Bach, Handel: see Contents, *Music Makers,* 3
Humperdinck, 197–213
Suggested recordings: music concerned with rhythm, 66, 67, 100, 192; mood, 136, 148, 153, 174; stories, 51, 107, 136, 139, 178; simple instrumental music, 72, 76, 98 (see TM 223 for additional list)

SINGING IN HARMONY

Beethoven, Schubert: see Contents, *Music Makers,* 4
Grieg, 219–37
Suggested recordings: music concerned with rhythm, 16, 17, 27, 56, 194; mood, 54, 96, 138, 167, 172; stories, 39, 59, 72, 74, 75; melodic music, 27, 29, 43, 53, 84, 85, 87, 88, 175

THIS IS MUSIC (ALLYN AND BACON, INC.)

BOOK ONE

Listening, 6–7
Piano music for rhythmic movement, 184–7
Stories and music of famous composers, 164–83

BOOK TWO

Famous composers, music and stories of, 164; Instruments, stories about, 164
Related recordings in TM teaching suggestions

BOOK THREE

Famous composers, music and stories of, 164
Instruments, 50–7
Music of storyland, 164
Orchestra, 58, 60, 62–4
Related recordings in TM teaching suggestions

BOOK FOUR

Famous composers, 188
Listening suggestions, 189
Related listening for special units, TM xv–xvi
Related recordings in TM teaching suggestions

BOOK FIVE

Famous composers, 211
Listening units (five), 212
Related recordings in TM teaching suggestions

BOOK SIX

TOGETHER WE SING (FOLLETT PUBLISHING COMPANY)

MUSIC THROUGH THE YEAR

MUSIC ACROSS OUR COUNTRY

VOICES OF AMERICA

VOICES OF THE WORLD

REFERENCES AND MATERIALS

BOOKS FOR TEACHERS

Baldwin, Lillian, *Music for Young Listeners: The Green Book, The Blue Book, The Crimson Book.* New York: Silver Burdett Company, 1951. Also *Tiny Masterpieces for Very Young Listeners,* Bryn Mawr, Pennsylvania: Theodore Presser Company, 1958. These books can be read by both teachers and children. Recordings for each book are obtainable from Music Sound Book Press, Box 444, Scarsdale, New York.

Barlow, Harold and Sam Morgenstern, *A Dictionary of Musical Themes.* New York: Crown Publishers, Inc., 1948.

Bibliography of Books for the Music Educator. New York: The Combined Book Exhibit, Inc., 950 University Ave., New York 52.

House, Marguerite, *O Say Can You Hear?* New York: Mills Music, Inc. Five workbooks to use with children.

McMillan, L. Eileen, *Guiding Children's Growth Through Music.* Boston: Ginn and Company, 1959. Chapter 5 and Appendix B.

Myers, Louise, *Teaching Children Music in the Elementary School,* 3rd ed. Englewood Cliffs, N.J.: Prentice-Hall, Inc., 1961. Chapters 6 and 12.

Pierce, Anne E., *Teaching Music in the Elementary School.* New York: Holt, Rinehart & Winston, Inc., 1959. Classified list of recordings, pp. 183–91.

Snyder, Alice M., *Creating Music With Children.* New York: Mills Music, Inc., 1957. Chapter 6.

Swanson, Bessie R., *Music in the Education of Children.* Belmont, California: Wadsworth Publishing Company, Inc., 1961. Chapter 8.

MUSIC HISTORY

Buchanan, Francis, *How Man Made Music.* Chicago: Follett Publishing Company, 1951.

Commins, Dorothy Berliner, *All About the Symphony Orchestra and What It Plays.* Eau Claire, Wis.: E. M. Hale and Company, 1961. The instruments, the conductor, large instrumental forms, and some composers. For older children too.

Kinsky, George et. al., *A History of Music in Pictures.* New York: Dover Publications, 1951. Useful with an opaque projector.

Machlis, Joseph, *The Enjoyment of Music,* shorter edition. New York: W. W. Norton & Company, Inc., 1957.

Miller, Hugh, *An Outline of the History of Music.* New York: Barnes and Noble, Inc.

Stringham, Edwin J., *Listening to Music Creatively.* 2nd ed. Englewood Cliffs, N.J.: Prentice-Hall, Inc., 1959.

Wold, Milo, and Edmund Cykler, *An Introduction to Music and Art in the Western World.* Dubuque, Iowa: William C. Brown Company, 1955.

BOOKS FOR CHILDREN

Albus, Harry, *Music Maker, Johann Sebastian Bach.* Grand Rapids, Mich.: Wm. B. Eerdmans Publishing Co., 1950.

Arnold, Elliot, *Finlandia, the Story of Sibelius.* New York: Holt, Rinehart & Winston, Inc., 1941.

Barne, Kitty, *Introducing Handel.* New York: A. N. Roy Publishers, 1957.

———, *Introducing Mozart.* New York: A. N. Roy Publishers, 1957.

Bulla, Clyde Robert, *Stories of Favorite Operas.* New York: Thomas Y. Crowell Company, 1959.

Burch, Gladys, *Modern Composers for Young People.* New York: Dodd, Mead & Co., 1941.

———, *Richard Wagner, Who Followed a Star.* New York: Holt, Rinehart & Winston, Inc., 1941.

Cross, Donzella, *Music Stories for Boys and Girls.* Boston: Ginn & Company, 1926.

Davis, Marilyn K., and Arnold Broido, *Music Dictionary.* New York: Doubleday & Company, Inc., 1956. An excellent book.

Deucher, Sybil, *Edvard Grieg, Boy of the Northland.* E. P. Dutton & Co., Inc., 1946.

———, *Young Brahms.* E. P. Dutton & Co., Inc., 1949.

Disney, Walt, *The Nutcracker Suite.* Boston: Little, Brown & Co., 1941.

Douty, Esther, *The Story of Stephen Foster.* New York: Grosset & Dunlap, Inc., 1954.

Freeman, Warren S. and Ruth W. Whittaker, *Great Composers.* New York: Abelard-Schuman Limited, 1952.

Higgins, Helen Boyd, *Stephen Foster: Boy Minstrel.* New York: The Bobbs-Merrill Company, Inc., 1944.

Jones, G. K., *Joyous Stories from Music's Wonderland.* New York: St. Martin's Press, Inc., 1956.

Kaufmann, Helen L., *The Story of Beethoven.* Grosset & Dunlap, Inc., 1957.

———, *The Story of Mozart.* Grosset & Dunlap, Inc., 1955.

Kettlekamp, Larry, *Singing Strings.* William Morrow & Co., Inc., 1958.

Kinscella, Hazel, *The Kinscella Readers,* 2nd ed., 8 vols., 1949. Lincoln, Nebraska: University Publishing Company. Vol. 8, *History Sings,* has particular value in upper grades.

Komroff, Manuel, *Mozart.* New York: Alfred A. Knopf, Inc., 1956.

Mirsky, Reba Paeff, *Beethoven.* Chicago: Follett Publishing Company, 1958.

Norman, Gertrude, *The First Book of Music.* New York: Franklin Watts, Inc., 1954.
Peare, Catherine Owens, *Stephen Foster: His Life.* Holt, Rinehart & Winston, Inc., 1952.
Prokofieff, Serge and Warren Chappell, *Peter and the Wolf.* New York: Alfred A. Knopf, Inc., 1946.
Siegmeister, Elie, *Invitation to Music.* Irvington-on-Hudson, N.Y.: Harvey House, Inc., Publishers, 1961. For more mature children. The author's Folkways Recording FT 3603 has the same name. It can be used from fourth grade on.
Skolsky, Syd, *The Music Box Book.* New York: E. P. Dutton & Co., Inc., 1946. Contains stories of popular program music.
Wheeler, Opal, *Frederic Chopin, Son of Poland, Early Years; Frederic Chopin, Son of Poland, Later Years; Handel at the Court of Kings; Ludwig van Beethoven and the Chiming Tower Bells; Paganini, Master of Strings; Robert Schumann and Mascot Ziff; Stephen Foster and His Little Dog Tray; The Story of Peter Tchaikovsky.* New York: E. P. Dutton & Co., Inc., 1941–53.
Young, Percy M., *Music Makers of Today; More Music Makers; The Story of Song.* A. N. Roy Publishers, 1958.

MUSICAL INSTRUMENTS AND THE ORCHESTRA

Balet, Jan, *What Makes an Orchestra.* New York: Oxford University Press, 1951. An excellent book to use in preparation for concerts.
Britten, Benjamin and Imogene Holst, *The Wonderful World of Music.* New York: Garden City Books, 1958. An unusually attractive book.
Edgerly, Beatrice, *From the Hunter's Bow.* New York: G. P. Putnam's Sons, 1942. A child's reference book on instruments.
Frost, Bruno, *A Child's Book of Music Makers.* Chicago: Maxton Publishing Corp., 1957.
Huntington, Harriet E., *Tune Up.* New York: Doubleday & Company, Inc., 1952. Includes illustrations of children playing different instruments.
Lacey, Marion, *Picture Book of Musical Instruments.* New York: Lothrop, Lee & Shepard Co., 1952. Includes historical sketches.
LaPrade, Ernest, *Alice in Orchestralia.* Doubleday & Company, Inc., 1948.
Montgomery, Elizabeth Rider, *The Story Behind Musical Instruments.* New York: Dodd, Mead & Co., 1953.

RECORDINGS

Biographical
Composers Series Albums, Educational Audio-Visual, Inc., 57 Wheeler Ave., Pleasantville, New York.
Period Albums, each on the *Life, Times and Music* of the following composers: Bach, Beethoven, Brahms, Chopin, Haydn, Honegger, Mozart, Schubert, Schumann, Tchaikovsky.
Young People's Records
   The Music of Aaron Copland
   The Music of Igor Stravinsky
Vox Albums, each on the *Story and Music* of the following composers: Bach, Beethoven, Haydn, Mendelssohn, Mozart, Schubert, Schumann, Tchaikovsky.
   General
Bowmar Educational Records, 10515 Burbank Blvd., North Hollywood, California.
   Bowmar Orchestral Library, with 156 wall charts of themes.
Children's Record Guild and Young People's Records. Obtainable from The Greystone Corporation, 100 Sixth Ave., New York 13, New York.
   Music Listening Game (hearing pitches)
   Golden Goose (combining melodies)

Hot Cross Buns (variation form)
Mr. Grump and the Band (instruments)
Clock Went Backwards (history of music)
Let's Dance (creative)
The King's Trumpet (evolution of the trumpet)
The Wonderful Violin
Mozart Country Dances
Said the Piano. to the Harpsichord
Licorice Stick (clarinet)
Round and Round (round, canon, fugue)
Rondo for Bassoon and Orchestra (form)
Muffin in the City (learning to listen)
Muffin in the Country (learning to listen)
Little Brass Band
The Hunter's Horn (French horn)
Albums containing many of the above recordings:
Just Listening
Music Listening (two volumes)
Bands, Orchestras, and Instruments
Musical Instruments
Decca Records, Inc., 50 West 57th St., New York 19, New York.
Tubby the Tuba Album
The Symphony Orchestra, 4 albums: strings, woodwinds, brass, percussion.
Golden Records
Child's Introduction to the Orchestra
RCA-Victor Record Division, 155 E. 24th St., New York 10, New York.
The Basic Record Library for Elementary Schools, Listening Program, six albums, one for each grade.
Adventures in Music, six albums, one for each grade (new).
Album, *Instruments of the Orchestra,* with photographs of each instrument (new).
Sound Book Press Society, Inc., Box 444, Scarsdale, New York.
Recordings to complement the books of Lillian Baldwin, *Music for Young Listeners; Tiny Masterpieces for Very Young Listeners.*
Recordings with Filmstrips
Jam Handy, Organization, 2821 East Grand Blvd., Detroit 11, Michigan.
Music Stories—filmstrips in color with recordings
1. *Peter and the Wolf*
2. *Hansel and Gretel*
3. *The Nutcracker*
4. *Peer Gynt*
5. *The Firebird*
6. *The Sorcerer's Apprentice*
Stories of Music Classics—six filmstrips in color, stories of beloved classics come to life
1. *The Sleeping Beauty*
2. *William Tell*
3. *A Midsummer Night's Dream*
4. *The Swan Lake*
5. *The Bartered Bride*
6. *Scheherazade*
Opera and Ballet Stories
1. Lohengrin
2. The Magic Flute

3. Aïda
4. The Barber of Seville
5. The Mastersingers
6. Coppélia
Instruments of the Symphony Orchestra
1. String Instruments
2. Woodwind Instruments
3. Brass Instruments
4. Percussion Instruments
5. Melodious Percussion Instruments
6. The Orchestra
Great Composers and Their Music
1. Johann Sebastian Bach
2. George Frederick Handel
3. Franz Joseph Haydn
4. Wolfgang Amadeus Mozart
5. Ludwig van Beethoven
6. Franz Peter Schubert
Bowmar Educational Records, 10515 Burbank Blvd., North Hollywood, California.
Meet the Instruments

FILMS

Shetler, Donald J., *Film Guide for Music Educators.* Washington, D.C.: Music Educators National Conference, 1201 Sixteenth St., N.W., Washington 6, D.C.

MISCELLANEOUS

Charts and Pictures
Construction of the Grand Piano; Evolution of the Grand Piano. Baldwin Piano Company, Cincinnati 2, Ohio.
Famous Composers, RCA-Victor Record Division, 155 East 24th St., New York 10, New York.
Great Composers, The Willis Music Company, 124 E. 4th St., Cincinnati 1, Ohio.
Historical Panorama, Schmitt, Hall & McCreary Company, Park Ave., and 6th St., Minneapolis 15, Minnesota. Relates music and world history.
Instruments of the Orchestra Charts, J. W. Pepper and Son, 1423 Vine St., Philadelphia, Pennsylvania.
Meet the Instruments, 25 permanent posters, Bowmar Records, 10515 Burbank Blvd., North Hollywood, California.
Musical Instrument Pictures, C. G. Conn, Ltd., Elkhart, Indiana.
Musical Instruments, York Band Instrument Company, Grand Rapids, Michigan.
Potraits of Great Composers, Schmitt, Hall & McCreary Company, Park Ave., and 6th St., Minneapolis 15, Minnesota.
Portraits of Great Composers, RCA-Victor Record Division, 155 E. 24th St., New York 10, New York.
Story of Recorded Stereophonic Sound, RCA-Victor Record Division.

MAGAZINE AND TEACHING SUPPLIES

Young Keyboard Junior Magazine, pictures, thematic charts, lesson plans, radio and television guide, recordings (produced annually), and "Build Your Own Orchestra" cardboard set, Keyboard Junior, 1346 Chapel St., New Haven 11, Connecticut.

Chapter Nine
RESPONDING CREATIVELY

Creativity is characterized by discovery, imagination, critical thinking, individuality, problem-solving, and scientific thinking. While some creation is intuitive and unplanned, most is closely related to problem-solving and the scientific process. Examples of problem-solving situations include a child's wanting to play a melody on the bells and doing it by his own combination of rudimentary note-reading and listening skills; a committee's critical experiments to find appropriate sound effects to add to a song; and a class that has heard its singing reproduced on a tape recorder seeking ways to improve the quality of its singing. Answers to musical problems are found by listening, comparing, evaluating, exploring, experimenting, and by research. If the procedures leading to the solution of problems are routinized, stereotyped and teacher-dominated, little creative activity will result. If the procedures are characterized by experimentation and discovery, creative work can take place. In creative teaching, skills are related to problem-solving uses. Since ideas can be expressed in many ways—with music, painting, the body, and words, and since all of the senses can be used as well as the intellect, the creative person is sensitive to the world about him, especially to beauty. In the final analysis, creativity and learning pertain to individuals, and this gives further emphasis to the teacher's constant study and analysis of individual differences of children.

The definition of creativeness is difficult, for only God can create; man rearranges, combines and reorganizes what he finds already in existence. In the language of educational writers, creativeness takes place in a learning environment where children are free to suggest and to experiment. To help children become emotionally well-adjusted, the school should provide many and varied opportunities for creative expression. What is creative at a certain time to one child may not be creative to another; it depends on the particular background of experience of the individual

269

child. *Educators consider creativeness to take place whenever the child discovers new relationships and whenever he projects himself into an activity or project and makes it something that at the time belongs uniquely to him.*

One of the tests of creative teaching is whether or not the song or the activity becomes psychologically the possession of the children. They should properly think or say, "This is *our* song," (not "This is the song the teacher has told us to sing"). "*We* found a rhythm to play with our South American song which *we* decided sounded best on the tambourine." "*We* decided that the first part of the song sounded best slow so as to contrast with the last part, which *we* thought sounded best fast." "*We* made up a new dance to a favorite folk song, and changed one of our old dances to a way *we* like better." "*We* wrote a poem today to tell how we felt about the weather we're having and made a song of it." "Johnny made up an Indian tune on the Melody Flute which *we* decided to use with the Thanksgiving play our class is writing." When, under the intelligent guidance of the teacher, there is freedom for children to share in the development of classroom projects, a good measure of creative activity is found. When children create constructively they learn to appreciate; therefore creative activity is one of the best avenues to appreciation. "To appreciate the work of others one needs experience in creating."

Attempts have been made to set forth steps in the progress of a creative act. First, there is a rich, sensory, first-hand experience to which the individual makes an emotional response. This response is such that there is a desire to share emotion with others. Second, the means of expression will be selected; it may be poetry, painting, music, or some other form. Third, there follows the experimenting with the selected means. The enthusiasm and encouragement of the teacher are vital to the success of the creative act in the classroom.

Before children can be active in creative ways, they need to acquire a background of experience, for creative possibilities are directly related to the richness of prior experiences. Some of this necessary background comes from rhythmic activities, dramatic play, and dramatization. Some comes from class activities such as making the classroom a more beautiful place in which to live, observing beauty in nature, feeling the rhythm of poetry, and from listening to music to hear stories, to imagine pictures, and to become aware of music's tone qualities, and harmonies.

The environment that nurtures creative activities includes the physical (space for movement, informal furniture arrangements, many materials including percussion and melody instruments, proper lighting and ventilation) and the psychological (freedom from pressure and from fear of criticism, the existence of a friendly spirit in the classroom, and the approval and acceptance of individuals by the class). The teacher is responsible for enriching the children's backgrounds and for providing the necessary physical, emotional, and social setting. He gives suggestions when they are needed, and he is careful that his suggestions stimulate the children's thinking and do not supplant it. He neither dominates nor dictates. His attitude is one of learning with the learners while guiding them in an unobtrusive way.

Through creative activities children can recognize their possibilities, limitations, and capabilities, find the joy that comes only from developing their creative powers, gain confidence through the satisfaction that comes from creating, feel stronger and less inhibited, learn perseverance, grow in ability to appreciate, develop increased sensitiveness to beauty, find relaxation and release from tensions, learn to respect individual differences, share in the success of others, learn social co-operation as opposed to antisocial competition, and use leisure time wisely in the pursuit of special interests. *All* music activities should be approached in a creative spirit.

Although there are creative aspects in all phases of the elementary music program, it is well to point out here what is not creative. Usually, if it is the primary goal of a teacher in a given activity to teach facts about music such as notation, key signatures, meter signatures and identification of form, the situation is seldom one in which creative elements are present. However, all of these things and many more can be taught as *by-products* of genuine creative activities. The important purpose in these activities, aside from the act of creation itself, is bringing from the children the ideas, judgments, and consequent experiments that help them grow and effectively express their feelings. Happier living results when, in pursuit of this purpose, notation is used in composing or playing a song (and meter and key signatures are found to be useful) and when children are led to discover the form of the song they have written. Then such facts about music take on meaning because of their function in a situation real to children.

The good teacher remembers that although learning the technicalities of music is not the only goal of elementary school music today, these technicalities can be rather easily learned if they serve the children in connection with their music activities. The good teacher will make definite plans for this. He knows that school music can be sterile and uninteresting when the approach to teaching it does not include the creative aspects. Furthermore, he realizes that a primary goal of creative activities is to guide boys and girls to think for themselves.

In order for children to be creative they must be encouraged to be *different* in constructive ways. Usually, when children are found to be conforming to a set pattern it is an indication that creative activities are not present and that the teacher has imposed adult standards upon them.

CREATIVE RHYTHMIC ACTIVITIES

In Chapter Four, "doing what the music tells you to do" illustrates a creative approach to rhythm because in this activity each child is free to make his own interpretation of what he hears. When such responses take place by means of arms in the air when children are seated, the teacher should at times request that eyes be closed. With closed eyes, each child can concentrate upon his own response to the rhythm, since he is not influenced by watching the actions of others. The writing of new words to familiar melodies is considered by some to be a rhythmic activity since these words must have the same rhythm as the original ones in order to fit the melody. However, this activity should be a natural outgrowth of child interest and should not be forced. For example, a first-grade class had been studying the circus when a boy began singing new words to "Hot Cross Buns." He began "Laugh clown laugh, laugh clown laugh." Classmates joined in the fun and added, "You are funny, I am happy, laugh clown laugh." Later, when the group was thinking of the play period to come, other words were invented: "Run boys run, run girls run; You are playing on the ball field, run boys run."

Another creative rhythmic activity is inventing rhythm patterns. These can be done with percussion instruments and hand clapping or in connection with a song. Very interesting rhythmic creations may occur when a class is divided into small groups, supplied with various percussion instruments, and told to invent rhythms and act them out. Often this is done in a large playroom or gymnasium, and each group presents its rhythm before the class.

When rhythm patterns are invented to accompany a song, it is logical for teacher and class to write such patterns in notation on the chalkboard so that they can recall them in the next music period. In lower primary grades such patterns can be notated in line notation (long and short lines) as a preliminary step in learning notation. This provides from second grade on a meaningful use for music notation and is an example of learning music skills as outgrowths of needs established in a creative activity. Special words can be supplied to rhythm patterns; in some songs chants are created from these. Note values can be "discovered" by clapping, chanting and stepping words, and some musical forms and terms can be derived from bodily responses to music.

Still another activity is the deriving of rhythms from words. This can be done with one or two repeated words such as "Mississippi," "merrily," and "blackberry pie," and with names of boys and girls in the class. It is fun for each child to discover the rhythm pattern of his own name, and to see it in notation.

Other creative rhythmic activities are the inventing of singing games, dances, and floor patterns, and the varying of known games and dances. Songs can be created from dance steps, and dances can be created from songs, particularly folk songs. Through dances children can discover aspects of form and mood in music. Interesting rhythmic expressions can be derived from dramatic play experiences. The teacher may observe certain movements which the children can be guided to develop further. Music is then added to enhance the thoughts and feelings expressed rhythmically. Clapping improvised rhythms, and clapping improvised answers to clapped questions were discussed in Chapter Four.

CREATIVE PLAYING ACTIVITIES

The use of percussion instruments as discussed in Chapter Four emphasized the creative processes involved when children listen to music and make their own selection of the instruments and rhythmic playing responses they believe are most appropriate to the music's mood and form. Instruments can also be used to create children's concepts of different types of music. For example, the atmosphere associated with Chinese or Japanese music can be created through use of woodblocks, sticks, a gong, and drums. In addition to these, the black keys of the piano can be used with one or both hands to invent, either by chance or by melodic intent, music based on the five-tone scale,[1] and which represents to our ears some of the music of the Chinese and Japanese peoples. This same scale is characteristic of American Indian music. Children find that an open fifth in the bass of the piano represents Indian drums. To introduce this creative tool, one might play the tones G♮ and D♮ simultaneously with the left hand while the right hand creates an Indian melody on the black keys. Drums, rattles, and sticks are useful in inventing Indian music. For creating Spanish or South American music children need access to sticks, maracas, woodblocks, castanets, and tambourines. The making and testing of simple instruments is another activity that could be included here.

Adding appropriate harmony by means of autoharp, Harmolin, ukulele, guitar, accordion, or piano chording may be taught as a creative playing activity based on listening. Melodies can be composed on the instruments mentioned in Chapter Five.

---

[1] The black keys of the piano are mentioned because they are a ready-made example of the pentatonic scale.

CREATIVE SINGING ACTIVITIES

In Chapter Six several examples of creative singing activities were discussed. The children's responses to many of the activities associated with tone-matching constituted one of them. Included was the response to the teacher's sung question, "What did you see on the way to school?" and the sung responses to other questions such as, "Where do you live?" "What did you bring?" "How do church bells ring?", and pretended telephone conversations such as "Hello," "Hello," "How are you?" "I'm fine." Children can sing their own names, the names of cities, and certain word groupings that grow out of their experiences. They can also create songs—an activity to be discussed later in this chapter.

An activity of major importance is song interpretation. As stated earlier in this chapter, when a song becomes the possession of children, it means that they have been free to contribute to its interpretation and development. The creative approach tends to have children think seriously about the meaning of the words they sing and about the connotations of this meaning in terms of musical expression. Children should be encouraged to enter into decisions as to whether the song should be sung loud or soft, fast or slow, what percussion instruments or chordal accompaniment should be used with it, and many other critical aspects—all of which should lead toward a high degree of musical sensitivity and discrimination.

CREATIVE LISTENING ACTIVITIES

Chapter Eight stressed listening as the basic music activity from which all the others begin. When children discover or are guided to discover for themselves the many different things active listening can give them, their listening is in many instances of a highly creative type because the making of personal choices in imagination, observation, comparison, and discrimination is a creative experience. As mentioned above, adding appropriate chordal harmony to a melody by means of the piano, autoharp, or the so-called social instruments is basically a creative listening activity.

One form of creative listening is the dramatization of instrumental music. In connection with a unit in conservation, children searched for recorded music that represented aspects of the out-of-doors, particularly trees and water, and life in the forest. *The Moldau* (Smetana) gave the mental image of the streams joining together to form a broad river which flowed through the countryside. The children wanted to show through bodily movement the flow of the water, the tall stately trees, and the animals that played in the forest. After listening many times, they dramatized these things rhythmically to the first section of *The Moldau*. Other compositions from which these children chose sections to interpret were *Contrasts* (Bartók), *Symphony No. 6 in F Major* (Beethoven), *Woodland Sketches* (MacDowell), and *Pines of Rome* (Respighi).

Another aspect of creative listening is the artwork children may do when inspired while listening to music.

CREATIVE IMPERSONATION AND DRAMATIZATION

Creative dramatization of recordings of instrumental music has been mentioned immediately above. To this can be added the dramatization of piano compositions played by the teacher. Creative rhythmic dramatization was mentioned in the section on creative rhythmic activities. Impersonation as a means of introducing fundamental rhythms was discussed in Chapter Four. Chapter Six mentioned the creative dramatization of songs only incidentally. It is one of the more important creative activities, and one of the ways in which children can project themselves with great pleasure into a variety of situations.

When children "lose" themselves in such dramatizations, they forget self-consciousness and some may find their singing voices in this manner. Having children in primary grades impersonate animals and people—or having them sing for puppets—is one of the methods used by teachers to get some children started singing. Children in lower primary grades enjoy dramatizing familiar songs such as "Old Mother Hubbard." They can create actions to songs that were not originally intended to be action songs. New singing games can be created.

Some ballads provide dramatizations growing out of interpretations of the text. Examples found in series books include "Old Woman and the Peddler," "Old Woman's Courtship," "Oh, No John," "Wraggle Taggle Gypsies," and "Good King Wenceslaus." Dances are often created to recurring refrains. Folk dance tunes are important sources of materials for creative dramatization. Sea chanties and question-and-answer songs are also useful, as are old songs such as "Old King Cole." The song sources for creative dramatization are unlimited and no listing can do more than direct attention to the immense possibilities at hand.

Many of the series books contain song stories that are small operettas. These should be examined and evaluated in the light of creative elements that might be present. Since the music and words are already written out and often recorded as well, it is possible that few opportunities for genuine creative expression may be present. However, such song stories are valuable in that they provide necessary background for future activities which can be of more creative nature.

CREATIVE MUSIC COMPOSITION

Small children are natural composers of music. If one listens to them
he will find that speech and song are interchanged quite normally in
their unsupervised play.

COWBOYS

Spontaneous Playground Song
First Grade, Sisters, Oregon

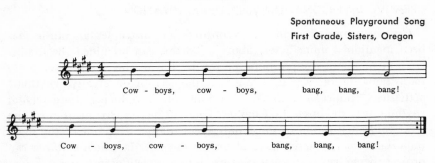

Teachers of lower primary grades continue this natural activity when
they call the roll with their singing voices and the children reply in
like manner. This was described in the section on creative singing
activities in this chapter and in Chapter Six.

One sunny morning a little girl in first grade was holding her teacher's
hand as she left the building to go to directed play. Deeply affected by
the beauty of the day, she sang:

A BEAUTIFUL DAY

First Grade, Washington School
Eugene, Oregon

The teacher asked the child to repeat her song and they sang it together
so that they could remember it when they returned to the classroom
and share it with the others. Another teacher of a first-grade group had
just concluded a reading lesson in which children had learned new
words. It was shortly before lunch, and the children suddenly related the
new words to their interest in food:

1. One   two   three,   come   eat   with   me.
2. Blue   and   red,   will   we   be   fed?

The above examples illustrate the point that creating simple songs is an ability children possess and one that grows under the guidance of good teachers. It is only a short step from spontaneous creative activity to the point where a teacher says of a well-known poem, "Let's sing it today instead of speaking it," and the setting of poetry to music becomes a classroom activity.

Short verse that has a clearly defined rhythm may be used for a type of song improvisation that emphasizes this rhythm. As a background for this activity children should have sung many short poems and simple word rhythms. The words are spoken by the children in a regular beat pattern set by the teacher. The teacher establishes key feeling by chording the familiar I V₇ I sequence in a key of his choice, and when introducing this activity he will sing the first word of the poem, thus suggesting to the children the beginning note of the song-to-be. While he beats time (it is basic to the method that the rhythm never be interrupted) individual children are asked to sing the poem. The other children may be urged to continue to speak the words softly while they listen to the song being born. The rhythm is stressed, the assumption being that if the rhythm is maintained, a melody will appear from each child which can be as spontaneous and uninhibited as speech. It is further assumed that it is as natural for children to have many musical ideas as it is for them to have many ideas expressed in language. This approach to song creation can be effective on any grade level and is believed by some to possess virtues that are superior, from the standpoint of creativeness, to the phrase approach, which will be described later. One finds supposedly well-trained musicians who have little feeling for the onward movement of music; they often "break" the rhythm. It is believed that if children experience this type of creative expression, which keeps the rhythmic flow proceeding without interruption, there might be fewer adult musicians who lack a feeling for rhythmic consistency.

Instruments such as the bells and piano are sometimes of aid in stimulating creative process. A special music teacher brought four tone bars (from a type of bell set that can be separated) into a first-grade room. The children were interested in new shoes, which several of them wore that day, and with the aid of the four tones they created their own special song on the subject, called "New Shoes," which they

NEW SHOES

First-Grade Laboratory School
Wisconsin State College
Milwaukee, Wisconsin

New   shoes,   new   shoes,   nice,   new   clean   shoes.

New   shoes,   new   shoes,   nice,   new   shoes.

also learned to play on the bells. Its repetitious words are typical of first-grade children. This song was sung throughout the term whenever one of the children came to school with new shoes.

Melodies without words are created by children who have opportunities to experiment with tuned water bottles, xylophones, bells, piano, recorder-type instruments, and the instruments of the band and orchestra. When children discover that they have the ability to compose simple instrumental melodies, they will frequently do this at home as a play activity and bring their creations to school.

Teachers save worthy compositions by writing them down in music notation. If a teacher has had special music training, he can "take dictation" when the children create a song—that is, associate at once the tones he hears with degrees of the scale. For instance, the first three song examples in this chapter are based on the same note pattern—the familiar 1–3–5 chord or the *tonic* chord. The recognition of this fact makes notating such songs a simple matter. Since few classroom teachers have had this kind of training,[2] most of them rely on other means to notate these songs. For example, the teacher who heard Julie sing "A Beautiful Day" sang it with her to remember it so that when she returned to the classroom she could find the song on the bells or piano. To help remember the melody of a child's song, the inexperienced teacher can invent pictorial ways to record melodies by such means as drawing a continuous or a broken line showing the directions of the pitches and by drawing short and long dashes to represent comparative note values. Some teachers write melodies with numerals or syllables and determine the notation later. Others have the children help them remember the song until a special music teacher or another classroom teacher has time to help notate it. Some children in the inter-

2 Suggestions for improving one's ability to take musical dictation are found in Appendix C and in *Basic Music for Classroom Teachers, Second Edition,* Englewood Cliffs, N.J.: Prentice-Hall, Inc., pp. 47, 65, 89.

mediate grades can be of help. There is always a way to notate these songs, and any teacher who works with these activities will improve in skill as time goes on.

As soon as children understand and can use notation, the song-creating process in the classroom should include the notating of the song on the chalkboard where everyone can participate in some degree in seeing that it is written in such manner that it correctly pictures what was created. Also, when good songs are notated in or transposed to keys that children find easy to use when playing recorder-type instruments, such songs may be duplicated and given to the children. When children take such songs home to play for their parents on these instruments or on the piano, they are learning about music notation as a by-product of their creative activity.

A SUNSHINY DAY

Second Grade
Eliot School
Portland, Oregon

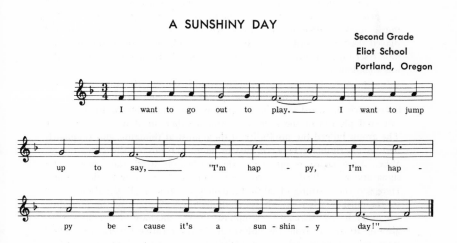

The following excerpt from the *Alabama Education Journal*[3] concerns the writing of poetry and music on the intermediate grade level. The teacher had enriched the children's background for this activity by developing vocabulary through increasing awareness to beauty in the classroom and in nature, and by reading appropriate poetry for the class.

> Until the time when the writing of poetry was found to be an enjoyable activity there had been no particular relation between poetry and music. However, when the time came to try to set some of the poetry to music, the students were eager to try. At the beginning, poems with a very simple and direct rhythm were read by the class so that everyone felt the

---

[3] Vernice Trousdale and Robert E. Nye, "The Fourth Grade Writes Music," *Alabama Educational Journal,* December, 1950.

same rhythmic flow of the words. The children moved at their desks to the rhythm of the words, and they tapped the rhythm. While there was some early hesitance because of the newness of the procedure, this disappeared abruptly after the first experience with it. Children tried "walking out" the rhythm of their poems by walking while they spoke them. As a consequence, the rhythm of the words was a dominant feature of the first songs composed. Later on, the more subtle meanings of words, and the varying moods of the poems became of increasing importance and shared an equal emphasis with rhythm. All that was done with creative music was an outgrowth of the earlier and continuing efforts of the classroom teacher to guide activities in such a way that the children were free to develop their sensitivity to visual impressions, to word meanings, and to sounds.

At first, the children selected from their store of poems they had written those which they felt would be easiest to set to music. The music teacher discussed these with the class and together they examined and experimented to find those with the clearest rhythmic patterns. Then the staff was placed on the blackboard and the words were written beneath it. The music teacher chose the key in which the song would be written and played the tonic chord (1 3 5) on a bell set. This gave the children a harmonic setting in which to start to think tonally. Later on in the year this was abandoned.

No one knew in what way the class would compose its song. Sometimes everyone sang phrases together and the music teacher wrote on the blackboard what he heard as majority opinion. At other times individuals volunteered phrases of the song, one after another, until it was completed. The group judged the suitability of these musical thoughts, and frequently had to discriminate between two or more versions of the same phrase. When the song was completed to the satisfaction of all, the correct meter signature was added, and bar lines and note values were determined. Here was the learning of music fundamentals in a "real" situation. Even so, the music teacher was always ready to hurry this part of the procedure whenever he felt that an overemphasis on the mechanical details was beginning to detract from the enjoyment of the creative experience. These songs were often reproduced on a Ditto Machine so the children could take them home to show to their parents and play them on the piano and on instruments such as bell sets and tonettes. While at the beginning the children had to be encouraged to sing their musical ideas to the class, this early stage of reluctance changed rapidly to one of nearly 100 per cent participation in which the music teacher found it necessary to stress self-control in waiting one's turn. In order to express more completely the meaning of the words, the boys and girls experimented with choric reading in various combinations with singing. Almost from the first they began bringing to the class poems they had written at home, and sharing with the group their musical ideas which had been born along with the words.

Near the end of the year, a college class asked to observe the composition of songs in the fourth grade. The music teacher selected three poems of varying types. The children were not satisfied with their setting of a poem written in strict rhythm. One girl objected that it "sounded too much alike," while a boy stated flatly that "it was monotonous." This led to a revision of the last half of the song which satisfied the group's feeling of what was musically suitable. This discussion and revision revealed to the observers aesthetic discrimination at the fourth-grade level. The second song was a little jingle, "The Funny Instrument." The group found this to be of such obvious tonal suggestibility that everyone began to sing together, and they sang it in unison as though they had known it always.

The third and last poem was one of mood which had no strong rhythm or rhyme to guide the composers. They solved this problem by contributing ideas phrase by phrase. This song seemed to give the children a greater feeling of accomplishment and aesthetic appreciation than any they had done before. After it was completed and on the blackboard, one of the girls suggested repeating the last four notes softly. This was tried and proved to be very effective. A boy contributed the practical thought that putting repeat marks in the right places would eliminate having to write more notes, so this was done.

MOONLIGHT

Fourth Grade
Kilby Training School
Florence State College
Florence, Alabama

Dark is the night as I lie in my bed: The stars and the moon give light. As I lie in my bed rest - ing my head, I go to sleep. —— I

In the course of this creative work each child developed more respect for the worth of each of the other children. The ability to contribute successfully to group action led to a feeling of security which gave, in turn, poise and self-assurance. Some who had not been able to succeed in other things found in the composition of poetry and music the satisfaction of those basic needs so frequently listed by educators: success, acceptance, belonging, and security. Some children wrote poems which showed evidence of being emotional outlets for their worries and troubles.[4]

The class had become more conscious of those intangible elements of beauty inherent in all art. They learned to enjoy many different types of poetry, not only their own, but the poems in the many books which they read voluntarily. Listening to recorded music became active and imaginative listening, perhaps due to the group's experiences in adding to the meaning of words by the use of musical composition.

---

4 "Little Brother"
   My little brother, as you can see,
   Is just as cute as cute can be.
   My little brother makes me mad,
   And that's why I am always sad.

The improvement in the skills of English composition was apparent. The practical use of music notation made music symbols more easily understood.[5] Due to the many socializing experiences found in this form of creative self-expression, there was evidence of improved unity and understanding between the pupils and the teachers.

As culminating activities of some units of work, programs were presented. The original poems and songs made these programs more vital to both students and their parents.

This use of poetry and music was considered successful by those who were in contact with the fourth grade. The teachers believe that knowing the child and providing opportunity and encouragement for him to develop his powers of expression comprise the foundation on which love and enjoyment of poetry and music can be built.

The goal of such group work is not fully accomplished with the successful co-operative composition of songs exhibited by this fourth grade; *the ultimate goal is to develop this creative activity into the successful writing of music by individuals.* In other words, this group process should be a stimulus for each child to write his own songs in the same way that he paints his own pictures. In the situation described in the above article, it would be expected that during the fifth- and sixth-grade years of this same group of children, the bringing to school of songs and instrumental tunes written at home would be commonplace, and that these children would do this because they had acquired in school the skills of a creative act that is fun, challenging, and satisfying to do.

When children can compose poetry and songs, the writing of simple operettas is not beyond the possibilities of the intermediate grades. Another opportunity is more teaching about musical form. Since the form of most of the songs children compose is simple in structure, often being a question-and-answer type with repeated phrases, teachers can guide children to discover elements of form in music by having them examine their own compositions. To analyze song form is interesting to children when it concerns a song they have written.

The procedure many teachers follow when they guide children in song writing in grades three and above is as follows:

1. Choose words that are simple, have steady rhythmic flow, and are understood by children.
2. Write the words on the chalkboard under the staff. Discuss the meaning of the words, seeking ideas that will influence the song writing. Such ideas will include mood and anything that may reflect descending or ascending pitch.

---

[5] One of the favorite pastimes during free periods was going to the blackboard, drawing a staff, and writing tunes. Children who did this were usually those who were taking piano lessons or participating in other types of musical activities outside of school and as a consequence had richer musical backgrounds.

3. Have the class read the words in unison so that a definite rhythm is established. Use clapping or stepping if necessary. The most heavily accented words or word syllables can be underlined. Measure bars can be drawn before (to the left of) these words or word syllables.

4. If this activity is comparatively new to the children, sound the tonic (1 3 5) chord by singing 1 3 5 3 1 (do-mi-sol-mi-do), or by playing it on autoharp or piano. If these instruments are used, it is still better to play the chord sequence I V₇ I to establish a definite key feeling. If the children are experienced in song writing, this step is not necessary because they "hear with their inner ears" what they create, and the arbitrary setting of a key may interfere with the creative process.

5. Ask for suggestions to start the song. There are several approaches to this. In the earliest stages of learning to compose, a teacher may have all or part of the first phrase written and ask the class to finish that section of the song. This can be done by the class *thinking* what the rest of the song might be (after singing the first part several times) and finally singing it, the teacher accepting the majority opinion. Soon individuals will have melodic suggestions to offer, and the process becomes one of both group and individual contribution. The group is the controlling force, however, and exercises musical and poetical discrimination in choosing between versions of parts of the song that are volunteered by individuals. The composition of these songs generally proceeds phrase by phrase with the group singing frequently from the beginning of the song. The teacher notates the song as it grows in length. Those teachers who can take musical dictation will write stemless notes on the staff. Since it is necessary to proceed with rapidity to avoid lagging interest, these are usually little lines (/) instead of filled out notes ( ). Some teachers will prefer to use numerals or syllables and "figure" from these. Others will use the keyboard directly, and still others will employ lines on the chalkboard that indicate high and low in pitch and tonal duration.

6. Have the class decide what the meter signature is. If the bar lines have not already been placed, they can be written before the heavily accented notes. Sometimes the song will need to be transposed to a more suitable key for the voices. The key signature will be determined, as will note values. Stems, flags, beams, and dots will be added wherever necessary.

7. Autoharp or piano chords can be added as desired.

8. The children can now evaluate their song. Does it reflect the meaning of the words suitably? Does it communicate the mood desired?

Can the song be improved?

9. If the song is of good quality, it should be saved by placing it in a class notebook. If it is in a key in which children can play recorder-type instruments, reproduce it on a duplicating machine so that the children may use notation at home in playing the song for their parents.

The good teacher knows that the major purpose of this activity is not to produce composers, but rather to gain the joy and confidence that come from a fascinating creative process. Below are some poems that are included here to be used in building skill and confidence in song writing. This is a satisfying activity that is fun to do. One should forget real or imagined musical deficiencies of the moment and enjoy it!

POEMS THAT MAY BE SET TO MUSIC BY PRIMARY GRADES

"Early to Bed"

Old Rhyme

Early to bed and early to rise,
Makes a man healthy and wealthy and wise.

"Choo Choo Train"

Choo choo train, choo choo train,
Chugging down the track.
Choo choo train, choo choo train,
Clank, clank, clack, clack, clack!

"Robins"

Three baby robins
Have learned a new song;
It's "Tweet-a-tweet, tweet-a-tweet"
All the day long.

"The Snowman"

I'm a little snowman fat and white,
Here is my hat and here is my pipe.
When the sun comes out to play
Then I'll melt and go away.

"Little Chick"

I had a little chick
Who picked up a stick.
He went into his pen
And he sat down again.

He pecked a little worm
And oh! how it did squirm.
He ran and got his mother
To help him find another.

POEMS THAT MAY BE SET TO MUSIC BY INTERMEDIATE GRADES

"The Tree"

The tree outside my window
Is cold and dark and brown.
All the pretty colored leaves
Have fallen to the ground.

"Pioneer Mother"

Composed by a fifth-grade
class for their Westward
Movement Unit

Mother was singing a lullaby
To quiet her tiny babe.
The night was cool and calm and clear;
The child was peacefully sleeping.

"Autumn Leaves"
Pretty leaves of red and yellow,
Colors all so warm and mellow.
Blow, wind, blow, and leaves will scatter
Before the rain comes pitter-patter.

"Dreaming"
As twilight draws her curtain and pins it with a star,
Two sleepy, nodding children that view it from afar,
Are whisked away to dreamland, where streets are paved with gold,
Where trees are ever silver green, and all is safe from cold.

"The River"

Robert Louis Stevenson

Dark brown is the river; golden is the sand.
It flows along forever, with trees on either hand.

RECENT TRENDS

Music educators in the United States have become interested in the theories of the German composer Carl Orff. His methods have developed from his work with children a number of years ago. He sees development of musical creativity as the primary purpose of music education, and believes that this is revealed by the ability to improvise. Orff considers children's traditional rhymes such as the ones in Mother Goose and those used in games to be a natural rhythmic beginning point for a growing comprehension of contrast, dynamics, phrasing, and note values. Echo-clapping, as in Chapter Four, page 71, develops into rhythmic canons and phrase-building with the question-and-answer clapping. From these come melodic canons and melodic phrase-building. These activities are meant to stimulate the children's natural creativeness. For example, use of traditional children's rhymes should result in original verse.

From rhythmic responses and speech patterns come simple types of created melody—the first being the descending third, considered by most adults to be major scale tones 5 and 3 (*sol* and *mi*). Next, scale tone 6 (*la*) is added to the basic melodic fragment. These three tones are the pitches of the "children's chant" that boys and girls use naturally in their play to communicate all manner of ideas. Because it is a natural "play song" it is taken into the classroom. This cluster of three pitches is assumed to be three of the five tones of the pentatonic scale. At first, chantlike songs of two (5–3) and (5–3–6) tones in various combinations are created. When this technique is mastered, more tones are gradually added until the five tones of the pentatonic scale are used in various combinations. Later on, harmonic music that requires chord changes is introduced.

The main advantages of beginning with the pentatonic framework are two: 1) restriction to a small group of pitches assists beginning creativity because the full diatonic or chromatic scales would give the child more resources than he could cope with at this stage of his musical development, and 2) pentatonic melodies require no chord changes to harmonize them; they can be accompanied by bourdons (bagpipe basses) and ostinati (repeated melodic fragments). Since the musically immature person cannot understand harmonic changes very well, the restriction to the pentatonic scale eliminates a formidable barrier to his creativity in music at this stage. Besides designing percussion instruments to enhance the music children create, Orff designed melodic instruments to assist the use of the pentatonic idiom. His soprano and alto xylophones and glockenspiels (bells) have removable tone bars. When all bars are removed except those needed to play the tones of the pentatonic scale, the child is automatically confined to these pitches, and his experimentation will produce no dissonances. Besides these instruments, recorders, lutes, viola da gambas (or cellos) are used in the full Orff instrument ensemble. Orff thinks string instruments are best suited to play the bass lines, and believes the sound of the modern piano to be inconsistent with the tone qualities of the other instruments.

In Orff's scheme, children are to become able to improvise music and to play music from memory. However, notation is introduced and used from the beginning, starting with the word-rhythms.   Accompaniments to songs and instrumental tunes begin with the bourdon or open fifth in the bass.

From these develop "moving bourdons" by alternating the two tones, and growing from this are repeated tonal fragments called ostinati.   It is assumed by followers of this method that it begins where music education should begin—with the creation of music that is truly children's music and is a genuine reflection of childhood rather than music that is basically too adult and too harmonically complex for children to comprehend fully.

Lit - tle Miss Muf - fet   sat   on   a   tuf - fet, etc.

Possible bourdons that would sound one octave lower are played on the alto glockenspiel. Two mallets are used.

Developing ostinati:

Possible ostinati:

The possible combinations of these tones seem inexhaustible, and the above are only a meager beginning of what is possible.   The best pentatonic songs are usually those that are created by children and teachers.   Some of the songs indexed as pentatonic in the series books are pentatonic in a technical melody-line sense but were harmonically conceived and strongly suggest chord changes.   Such songs are not satisfactory for this work.   The reader is referred to three sources of references, each having essentially the same title.   The film, *Music for Children,* is available from Contemporary Films, 267 West 25th Street, New York 1, New York.   The record album of the same name was recorded in England by Angel, and can be ordered from any music store.   The book, *Music for Children I Pentatonic,* is obtained from Associated Music Publishers, Inc., I West 47th Street, New York, New York, in an English adaptation by Doreen Hall and Arnold Walter.   Books II and III refer to major and minor, respectively.   Orff-designed instruments made by Sonor can be obtained from the Sonor Drum Company, Johs. Link, Inc., Aue, Westphalia, Western Germany; M. Hohner, Inc., Educational

Department, Andrews Road, Hicksville, Long Island, New York; Rhythm Band Incorporated, 407–409 Throckmorton Street, Fort Worth, Texas.

Music educators in the United States have varying views about the Orff method. Many schools have obtained sets of the instruments, which are of near-professional quality and possess a high degree of pitch accuracy and tonal beauty. Assembling a group of instruments as suggested seems possible for music specialists who teach in a music room, while specialists who travel from room to room would find it difficult to employ them in any great number. Those specialists who teach in ability-group plans are apt to be enthusiastic about their use with high-ability groups such as those heard in the *Music for Children* film and recordings. A classroom teacher may need considerably more musical training than he now possesses in order to utilize the method in full.

Those who have serious doubts about the Orff method state that while German boys and girls find repetitious melodies having only a few pitches an accepted part of German folk music, American boys and girls may be less apt to accept such limitations because their culture has given them a background of music of richer texture and of more complex harmonic character. They further state that while this method may seem highly creative to German teachers, it appears formula-like to many American teachers. Of course, such opinions prove little. Of real significance is the experimentation with the Orff principles currently taking place in American schools. In some of these, the teachers are attempting to apply the principles vocally, supported by a minimal use of the instruments, a practice of some German teachers. The reader should do his best to be informed about the results of the experimentation, and should try to do his own experimenting as well.

While some American music educators have accepted Carl Orff's basic principles, they are often applying them in their own American ways—with which Orff and his followers might disagree. For instance, they try to use the black keys of the piano and bells simply because these are often already in the classroom, and they form a natural pentatonic scale based on G♭. They sometimes tune the autoharp G chord down one half-step to provide part of the accompaniment to "songs on the black keys." The improvisitory nature of American jazz suggests simple experiments in the classroom leading toward individual vocal and instrumental improvisation. This is being attempted through both rhythmic and tonal variation. It may begin with adding simple passing tones to a melody at about the third-grade year, and slowly work toward simple variations. With American youth this often continues with variations on Stephen Foster melodies and, as an inevitable result by junior high school age, into jazz. This is based upon the American emphasis on simple, but definite, chord changes. Paralleling this style are experiments in melody writing in the old modes. The plan of steps and half-steps of each mode can be exemplified on the white keys of the piano, then transposed like any other scale to the pitch of one's choice. To explore these unfamiliar scales, begin on any white key, and play a scale on succeeding white keys to the octave. The scale beginning on C is the major scale, of course, and the scale beginning on A is the minor scale. All the others are the unfamiliar modes, less commonly used today, but fascinating to explore. Another approach to creativity is the improvising of barber-shop harmony in the intermediate grades, an activity that can carry over into family and community life.

In summary, there is a trend today toward more improvisation and general creativity in music that promises to grow in importance in the future.

THINGS TO DO

1. Compose three melodies, one on the black keys of the piano or bells (pentatonic), one in which most of the pitches are 1 3 5 8, and one in which most of the pitches are scale tones.

2. Compose a melody on a recorder-type instrument.

3. Improvise Oriental- and American Indian-type music on the piano or bells according to the suggestion on page 273. Add appropriate accompanying instruments. The descriptions of instruments and their uses in Chapter Five will be helpful.

4. Select a folk song or a ballad that tells a story that can be dramatized. Present it to the class in such a way that although you guide the activity, the ideas for this dramatization and the making of choices during the process of creating come from the students.

5. Choose recordings of instrumental music for dramatization from the RCA-Victor Basic Record Library for Elementary Schools, *The Rhythm Program* and *The Listening Program,* from RCA's *Adventures in Music* Albums, and from other sources, and try them out in your college class.

6. Listen to recordings of instrumental music that tell a story or that describe a scene, and create a dramatization based on one. A good one is Ferde Grofé's *Death Valley* Suite, the third movement, "Desert Water Hole" (Capitol H-271). The dramatization would include the oxen, the covered wagon, the driver, and the people in the wagon. Let the music dictate the action.

7. Investigate the possibilities of choric reading as an expressive creative activity.

8. Guide the class in creating songs, using poems from this chapter, poems of your own making, or those from other sources.

9. Dramatize one of the song stories from the series books as a class committee project, and evaluate it in terms of teaching creative responses.

10. Create a song from a dance step.

11. Create a dance from a folk song.

12. Create songs and instrumental music based on the pentatonic-ostinati approach described in this chapter, selecting some other medium or media than the black keys of the piano or bells.

13. Choose a mode other than major or minor, and compose a tune in this scale.

14. Review the types of creative accompaniments possible when using the autoharp. See Chapter Five, page 130–131.

MUSIC SERIES GUIDE

BIRCHARD MUSIC SERIES (SUMMY-BIRCHARD COMPANY)

KINDERGARTEN

Creative activities, 156
Creative activity in music, 6
Dramatizations, 156

BOOK ONE

Creative activities, 184
Dramatizations, 184

BOOK TWO

Creative activities, TM 4, 206
Dramatizations, 151, TM 202

BOOK THREE

Creative activities, 39, 45, TM 4–5, 204
Dramatization, 152–3, TM 200–201
Pentatonic scale, TM 24

BOOK FOUR

Creating melodies, rhythm patterns, words, movement and dances, dramatizations, TM 250

BOOK FIVE

Creating rhythm patterns, TM 315–6
Creative movement and dances, TM 315
Creative thinking, TM 316
Dramatization, TM 316

GROWING WITH MUSIC (PRENTICE-HALL, INC.)

The teachers edition for Books 1, 3, 4, 5, and 6 was not available when this Guide was compiled.

MUSIC FOR LIVING (SILVER BURDETT COMPANY)

Dramatization, songs for, TM 164
Dramatizing the music, TM xii
Part-singing (adding unwritten part), TM 163
Piano, creative use of, TM 163
Play, to make a, 181–2
Songs: by school children, TM 166; for drawing and story telling, 183; for acting out, 183; writing down, TM xvi
Writing what one creates, TM ix

MUSIC IN OUR COUNTRY

Creative activities, TM 188
Creative responses, TM xiv

MUSIC AROUND THE WORLD

Creative responses, TM xiv
Dramatizations, TM 201, 203

MUSIC FOR YOUNG AMERICANS (AMERICAN BOOK COMPANY)

KINDERGARTEN

Creativity with music materials, 149–51

BOOK ONE

Creativity with music materials, 181–3

BOOK TWO

Creative experiences, 178
Suggestions with songs in TM

BOOK THREE

Dramatizations, TM 9, 16, 35, 42
Suggestions with songs in TM

BOOK FOUR

Dramatizations, TM 10, 14, 19, 27, 28, 40
Suggestions in TM, 16, 18, 23, 25, 51

BOOK FIVE

Creative activities, TM 8, 43

BOOK SIX

Creative activities, TM 7, 15, 16, 19, 26, 54
Dramatizations, TM 9, 13, 41, 42

OUR SINGING WORLD (GINN AND COMPANY) 1951 EDITION

KINDERGARTEN BOOK

Refer xv C "Imitative Play," xvi D "Dramatic Play," xvi–xvii E "Apparatus," xvii–xix III "Creative Expression"
Song stories, 143–51, 152–62

FIRST GRADE BOOK

Refer xv–xvii III "Creative Expression," xiii C "Imitative Play," xiv D "Dramatic Play," xiv–xv E "Apparatus"
Song stories, 190–8, 199–204

SINGING ON OUR WAY

Dramatic play, 7, 8, 9, 51, 66a, 79, 81, 86, 111, 116a, 124
Instrumental recordings suggested for dramatic play, 66, 73, 81, 132, 156
Song stories, 158–66, 167–75

SINGING AND RHYMING

Dramatic play, 8, 10, 19, 28, 51, 60, 67, 80, 81, 89, 100, 125, 146, 160, 161, 163, 165
Instrumental recordings suggested for dramatic play, 79, 81, 85, 102, 145, 150, 151
Song stories, 170–81, 182–90
Song writing, 20, 32, 94, 115, 131, 157

SINGING EVERY DAY

Dramatic play, 7, 19, 45, 52, 60, 61, 104, 105, 153, 170
Instrumental recordings suggested for dramatic play, 19, 134
Song stories, 180–90, 191–201
Song writing, 18, 94, 115, 127, 133, 139, 171

SINGING TOGETHER

Dramatic play, 36, 38, 39, 42, 44, 45, 49, 50, 53
Song story, 193–213-Album 5-A
Song writing, poems for, 64, 112, 178

SINGING IN HARMONY

Dialogue songs for dramatic play, 45, 46–51
Song story, 219–37,-Album 6-A

THIS IS MUSIC (ALLYN AND BACON, INC.)

BOOK ONE

Creative activities, 188
Creative responses, 6

BOOK TWO

Creative activities with TM song suggestions
Learning to create, 163

BOOK THREE

Creative activities with TM song suggestions
Learning to create, 163–4

BOOK FOUR

Creative activities, 188
Writing of songs by children, TM xiii–xiv

BOOK FIVE

Creative activities, 211
Exploring musical ideas, 32, 122

BOOK SIX

Creative activities, 235
Song composition, 50, 51, 56, 154

TOGETHER WE SING (FOLLETT PUBLISHING COMPANY)

MUSIC 'ROUND THE CLOCK

Words that might be set to music, 10, 17, 29, 33, 44, 61, 71, 79, 82, 84, 86

MUSIC 'ROUND THE TOWN

Dramatization, 133: 5, 13, 14, 30r; 134: 60–7 (circus)

MUSIC THROUGH THE YEAR

Adding instrumental parts, 33 (pentatonic), 90 (drums)
Choric reading, 59, 102
Dramatization 30, 50
Poems that might be set to music; evaluate those listed, 181

MUSIC ACROSS OUR COUNTRY

Poems that might be set to music; evaluate those listed, 191

VOICES OF AMERICA

Creating, TM xix
Creative dramatization, 220
Creative spirit, TM iii

VOICES OF THE WORLD

Creating, TM xvii
Creative spirit, TM iii

REFERENCES AND MATERIALS

Andrews, Gladys, *Creative Rhythmic Movement for Children.*   Englewood Cliffs, N.J.:
    Prentice-Hall, Inc., 1954.
Cole, Natalie, *The Arts in the Classroom.*   New York: The John Day Company, Inc.,
    1940.
Coleman, Satis N., *Creative Music for Children.*   New York: G. P. Putnam's Sons, 1922.
Fox, Lillian M. and L. Thomas Hopkins, *Creative School Music.*   Morristown, N.J:
    Silver Burdett Company, 1936.
Krugman, Lillian, and Alice Ludwig, *Little Calypsos.*   Far Rockaway, Long Island, New
    York: Peripole, Inc., 1955.   Includes instructions for writing calypsos.
Mearns, Hughes, *Creative Power: The Education of Youth in the Creative Arts.*   New
    York: Dover Publications, Inc., 1958.
Niles, John Jacob, and Helen Louise Smith, *Folk Ballads for Young Actors.*   New
    York: Holt, Rinehart and Winston, Inc., 1962.

——————————*Folk Carols for Young Actors.* New York: Holt, Rinehart and Winston, Inc., 1962.

Nye, Robert E., and Bjornar Bergethon, *Basic Music for Classroom Teachers,* 2nd ed. Englewood Cliffs, N.J.: Prentice-Hall, Inc., 1962. Chapter 8, "Improvising Parts to Songs"; Chapter 9, "Creating Your Own Songs."

Nye, Robert E., Vernice Nye, Neva Aubin, and George Kyme, *Singing With Children.* Belmont, California: Wadsworth Publishing Company, Inc., 1962. Chapter 7, "Songs on the Black Keys."

Orff, Carl, and Gunild Keetman, *Music for Children* (English version), Vols. I–III. New York: Associated Music Publishers, 1955.

Ritchie, Jean, *The Swapping Song Book.* New York: Oxford University Press, Inc., 1952.

Sheehy, Emma D., *Children Discover Music and Dance.* New York: Holt, Rinehart & Winston, Inc., 1959. A helpful book for parents and teachers.

Snyder, Alice M., *Creating Music With Children.* New York: Mills Music, Inc., 1957.

Tallmadge, William H., "Teaching Improvisation." *Music Educators Journal,* November–December, 1960, pp. 58–60.

Tobbit, Janet E., and Alice M. G. White, *Dramatized Ballads.* New York: E. P. Dutton & Co., Inc., 1936.

RECORDINGS	Suggested Grade Levels
Angel Records	
Music For Children, Album 3582–13	K–6
Children's Record Guild and Young People's Records	
The Greystone Corporation, 100 Sixth Avenue,	
New York 13, New York.	
Dramatic Play	
Let's Help Mommy	K–2
Emperor's New Clothes (2 records)	2–5
Whoa, Little Horses	N–2
Cap, Spike, and Salty Sam	K–2
Puss in Boots (2 records)	1–5
Indoors When It Rains	K–2
Improvising Dances	
Let's Dance	3–5
Swing Your Partner	2–6
Improvising Songs	
Bring a Song, Johnny	K–3
Where Do Songs Begin?	1–4
Albums	
Pretending	K–2
Let's Act and Sing	2–5
More Act and Sing	2–5

Chapter Ten
UNDERSTANDING MUSIC NOTATION

The symbols of music, like words of a language, convey man's thoughts and feelings. These symbols are a means to communicate ideas. Music reading means the ability to grasp the nature and character of music through understanding its symbols, not merely the ability to identify detail. If music is taught fully, learning to read music is an integral part of it. If music reading is taught rightly, it always has for the children an immediately functional or interesting purpose. Since children differ in the ways they learn to understand notation and since music reading is a complex skill, a variety of approaches should be employed. Every normal child should gain reasonable skill in reading music for social and cultural reasons as well as musical reasons. The efforts to acquire this skill should be both purposeful and pleasurable.

Most of the preceding chapters of this book refer to activities illustrative of the fact that teaching understanding of notation is part of teaching other aspects of music.

RESPONDING TO RHYTHM (CHAPTER FOUR)

Employing bodily movements that eventually become identified with notation, such as:

walking	walking notes	quarter-notes
skipping	skipping notes	skipping-note pattern

Using line notation to describe rhythms of words and melodies
Feeling physically if the music swings in two's or three's, leading toward and understanding of accent and meter
Introducing the phrase by question-and-answer clapping
Developing comprehension of various terms and symbols through bodily response to music
Responding to note values by clapping, chanting and stepping
Using numeral notation
Translating the rhythm of children's names, geographical names, animal names, and old sayings into notation

Conducting the meter

Stepping the melody-rhythm of songs, then translating this physical feeling into note values

Writing rhythm patterns for hand-clapping and percussion instruments in notation on the chalkboard

Writing percussion scores in notation

Acting out the musical phrase in various ways

Discovering similar and dissimilar parts of songs in beginning the study of musical form

PLAYING MELODY AND HARMONY INSTRUMENTS (CHAPTER FIVE)

Learning notation by using it to play on water glasses, bottles, bells, piano, and recorder-type instruments

Learning about chord structure by chording on autoharp and ukulele

Using numeral notation

Using notation in preserving original vocal and instrumental melodies

Seeing and feeling intervals, scales, chords and tonal patterns on keyboard instruments

Sight-singing as part of a method of learning to play recorder-type instruments

LEARNING TO SING (CHAPTER SIX)

Learning concepts of high and low pitch

Relating singing to tonal figures played on keyboard instruments

Singing or playing the tonic-chord tonal pattern to orient singers to the key of a song

Acting out songs in pitch levels

Observing notation of familiar songs while the teacher sings them

Conducting songs

Finding intervals in songs

LEARNING TO SING IN PARTS (CHAPTER SEVEN)

Using notation in part-singing activities of many types

Studying vocal chording and adding chord roots

LISTENING TO MUSIC (CHAPTER EIGHT)

Identifying major and minor modes

Hearing degrees of dynamics and tempo and associating these with musical terms and symbols

Hearing repetition and contrast

Hearing chord changes

Identifying familiar themes by observing their notation

Writing on the chalkboard the themes of unfamiliar music, and singing and playing these when possible

Associating high and low in pitch, intervals, and common tonal and rhythmic patterns with notation

RESPONDING CREATIVELY (CHAPTER NINE)

Notating original rhythm and word patterns
Notating original melodies
Discovering the form of original compositions
Performing notated added parts by voice or instrument
Using notation in the composition of chants and descants and other added parts

Because we have already referred to notation so many times in this book, this chapter will not undertake to review each of the related ways to teach it that have been discussed earlier.

It can be seen that the understanding of notation can be taught in a gradual, informative, and purposeful way when the teacher utilizes it to explain and analyze what is heard, sung, and played. In this approach, knowledge of music symbols grows primarily from the music itself rather than from activities isolated from teaching objectives concerned with developing musical responsiveness through rhythm, listening, singing or playing instruments. The music series emphasize this approach to note reading. As an example, one finds ways to achieve reading readiness outlined on page one of the teacher's manual for Book Two of *Music for Young Americans,* (American Book Company). Continuing in that Series, the teacher's manual for Book Three outlines the first steps in music reading; the manual for Book Four develops this further and expands the uses of notation in playing instruments; and Book Five states the notational concepts children should master at that level. Every music series has an approach to note reading that is similar to this. The reader should study each of them to learn how a given series assists the teacher in helping children to use and understand notation. The suggestions provided by the series should be evaluated in terms of their suitability to specific groups of boys and girls in terms of their current stage of musical growth and their general musical background.

It is generally agreed that normal expectations in the understanding of the symbols of notation are as follows:

NORMAL EXPECTATIONS IN UNDERSTANDING NOTATION

KINDERGARTEN AND GRADE ONE

A rich, happy, and satisfying environment of many varied musical activities. From these emerge such concepts as high and low in pitch, loud and soft in dynamics, mood, the home tone (key feeling), fundamental movements, accent, rhythm patterns, fast and slow. There is increasing understanding of pitch levels by acting out high and low in melody lines and associating these in a general way with notation.

Playing tunes on the bells by ear, by numeral notation, and by some letter names can take place. There is incidental, not direct, teaching of notation.

GRADE TWO

Increasing concern about notation develops, particularly during the last half of the school year when books are commonly in the hands of the children. There is clear association of physical responses to notation (such as up and down, long and short, walking, running, skipping). After this, the notes are named (quarter, eighth, half, whole). Letter names, numbers, and/or syllable names are used. Children are led to notice that melodies are constructed scalewise or skipwise, that notes are sometimes repeated, and that note patterns and phrases are also sometimes repeated. Numbers and/or syllables are associated with note patterns. The bells are played with numbers and with notation. Children come to understand that notation is a picture of rhythms and melodies. They discover that music swings in two's or three's.

GRADE THREE

There is wider use of note names, numbers, and/or syllables, and further stressing of note patterns as "musical words." Melodies are played on bells and piano with notation. Very simple piano chording is introduced. Notation as a picture of a melody becomes a more fully understood concept. Phrases that are alike, different, and almost alike are found in notation, as are scale-line and chord-line note patterns and sequences. Original songs are notated by the teacher while the children observe the results and try them out on voices and instruments. Simple songs are read. Letter names of the staff become known. There is expanding knowledge of musical terms and symbols.

GRADE FOUR

The autoharp, the keyboard, and recorder-type instruments are played from notation. There is understanding of the meter signature, the measure bar, and the dotted note. The significance of the key signature is learned, as is how to find the key note (*1*, or *do*). Notation is used in writing and playing original songs. Intervals are identified in songs that emphasize them, then learned independently and found in other songs. There is increasing independence in the use of notation. There is quick recognition of like, different, and almost alike phrases. Familiar rhythm and note patterns are mastered. There is increasing knowledge of useful terms and symbols of notation. Chording on the piano is a class activity.

Listening activities are made more meaningful by seeing themes or recorded melodies written on the chalkboard or watching them in the series books.

GRADE FIVE

There is more use of notation in playing experiences with keyboard and other instruments. Increased knowledge of intervals plays a more important part in sight-singing. There is chording on the autoharp, piano, and ukulele which, with the teacher's guidance, leads to the understanding of the notation of chords and chord changes. Notation is useful in part-singing. The listening program is assisted by seeing thematic material on the chalkboard, in the series books, projected on a screen, or on wall charts. Knowledge of useful terms and symbols is expanded through their use in a variety of activities. Original songs are notated. There is sight-singing of more difficult songs.

GRADE SIX

The concepts "hearing with the eyes" and "seeing with the ears" are understood and applied. There is independent sight-singing of songs of reasonable difficulty. Intervals are well known. Two- and three-part singing takes place with the aid of notation. Many instruments are played, using notation. Notation is used by the class and by individuals in writing original compositions. Thematic material is employed in the listening program. All common terms and symbols of notation are known through their use in a variety of activities. The grand staff becomes known through piano chording and through the use of some songs that extend into the upper part of the F clef (bass clef).

In grades four, five, and six children should become able to examine and sing selected songs from notation by doing part or all of the following activities:

1. Chant the note values as described in Chapter Four, page 77.
2. Speak the words in proper rhythm.
3. Identify familiar tonal and rhythm patterns.
4. Find like, unlike, and similar phrases.
5. Identify any new or difficult rhythmic, melodic, or interval problem, and find ways to solve each problem. Examples of possible solutions may include finding word-rhythms to solve rhythmic problems, using the bells to solve melodic problems, and singing scale tones leading to the difficult interval in question.
6. Set the tempo and sing the song. This can be done by the entire class, by small groups, or by individuals.

A MINORITY VIEWPOINT

While the majority of teachers plan the teaching of notation in terms of the above discussion, a minority claim that while integrating notation study into all the music activities is proper and commendable, it is not enough. These teachers are convinced that some extra effort must be made if children are to gain the understanding of notation they need to have.

The first point made by these teachers concerns the series books. They claim that these books are multi-purpose books, and that multi-purpose books should not be expected to teach the understanding of notation in a very orderly, sequential, or thorough way. For example, they claim that while the selection of music for the purpose of social studies relationships is a good idea from the standpoint of the curriculum, it may at the same time be a handicap to achieving orderly progress in sight-reading skills. Their second point is that series books are written in terms of *what children's voices can sing* rather than in terms of *what children's minds can comprehend about notation.* Thus, rote singing is overemphasized and the comprehension of notation is correspondingly neglected. Skill in sight-singing develops gradually through use of a large amount of music that is so simple children can grasp it very quickly. The series books fail to provide this simple music in sufficient quantity, thus may promote frustration and slow reading habits by placing before children notation that is too complex for them to understand.

To provide very simple music for this purpose generally means the temporary use of music that does not have much musical worth, a choice most music educators are reluctant to make. The prevailing theory is that selection of music from folk or art sources is mandatory, and that music written for specific notational problems is usually unworthy for school use. Furthermore, this is disturbing to the theory that all music learning should come from a study of good music. The answer made to this problem is derived from a comparison of the usual music-reading approach in the elementary classroom with the approach of the beginning instrumentalist. It is widely acknowledged that instrumentalists as a group are far better music readers than are vocalists. This is attributed to the fact that when a person begins to play an instrument he learns to play only a note or two at a time, and each new note is added gradually along with very simple tunes and exercises based on these few notes. It follows theoretically that if this instrumentalist approach is practiced in vocal classes, the children may become good note readers in the way the instrumentalist does, and would then be able to use notation in the reading of much more music than they now commonly do.

The reader should remember that this viewpoint does not mean the abandoning of the approaches to understanding and using notation stressed throughout this book. It implies the *addition* of other materials of instruction to this approach. The sources of such material are three: 1. commercial; 2. teacher-made; and 3. by research undertaken to find appropriate folk and art music.

Currently, one publisher specializes in easy material for note reading: the Handy-Folio Music Company, 7212 West Fond du Lac Avenue, Milwaukee 18, Wisconsin. However, teachers can plan and organize material of their own in chart form, and use such charts sequentially. They can be mounted on easels or hung on walls. A few have developed mimeographed booklets for specific note-reading purposes. Others are doing research to attempt to find music of some stature for reading purposes in library books, manuscripts and microfilms. Both commercial and teacher-made efforts are based on the principle that the child needs very simple music in which groups of notes can be seen by children at a glance, and that these note patterns should be used repeatedly until they are learned. Such a pattern is scale tones 1, 2, 3. Another could be 3, 2, 1. When these are mastered, they could be combined in a song or tune that uses these notes in both ascending and descending forms. Rhythmic groupings of notes are stressed, as in the concept of identical rhythmic relationships in different tempos, such as ♩ ♩ ♩ ♩ , ♫♫ , and ♬ , and various rhythmic combinations such as ♩ ♩ ♩ , ♫♩ , and ♫♩ . The dotted note can be taught in the same comparative way. One basic rhythm or tonal combination is taught at a time. Music is found or written that uses the rhythm, tone pattern, or interval consistently, and relationships are then found in songs in the series books. Dull drill should play no part in this, and success in note reading should be ever present. In one school system the music supervisor's charts are a popular feature. The classroom teachers evaluate them regularly and suggest changes when they believe improvements can be made. The children in the several elementary schools ask each other the number of the chart hanging in their room, for they know that to have learned the content of one and thus gain a new one is visible evidence of their progress. In another school the music supervisor's collection of songs has been mimeographed to form several song books of specialized nature that assist a step-by-step approach to understanding and using notation. She is doing research to add folk and art songs to her collections that relate to specific problems in understanding notation.

Four guiding principles appear in this type of work that are applicable in all methods of teaching this aspect of music:

1. Begin note reading with *very* simple material, avoiding any difficult rhythm or interval, and teach only one rhythm or note pattern at a time.
2. Use many different materials in which these same patterns appear, including songs in the series books.
3. Present new rhythm patterns, note patterns, and intervals only after the first ones have been learned.
4. Include the review of previously learned notation with the introduction of new material. Use notation consistently, but do not permit it to unbalance a music program. Keep materials for notation study sufficiently simple so that all normal children can read them easily and find genuine success in doing so.

NUMBERS, LETTER NAMES, AND SYLLABLES

Men have long attempted to find practical ways of learning to read music notation. Roughly one thousand years ago two monks sought to improve the skill of their respective choirs in this regard. One of them, Guido d'Arezzo, is said to have invented a system of Latin syllables used as a measuring stick to identify scale tones. This system has evolved to become the *do re me fa sol la ti do* of today. In the United States this is called the *moveable do* system because *do* represents the keynote of all major keys. In France it is called the *fixed do* system because middle C is always *do*. The other monk, Odo of Clugny, chose an instrumental approach, and is said to have had his choir learn to play the monochord, a one-stringed Greek instrument, and then apply this understanding of tone relationships to singing by notation. These approaches to teaching music reading, the Latin-syllable and the instrumental, are both very much alive today.

Lowell Mason, who was appointed to teach music in the schools of Boston in 1838, was the first officially appointed American school music teacher. His method of teaching music reading was a three-fold approach which began with associating the numbers 1, 2, 3, 4, 5, 6, 7, 8 with the degrees of the scale, using the Latin syllables also, and including the regular note names as a third aspect. Mason used numbers in all initial explanations of tonal relationships, and the tonic chord and all the intervals were taught by extensive numeral drills, often from charts. The syllables came to be emphasized by music teachers in part because of their use in ear-training and sight-singing on the college level.

In 1845[1] and 1883[2] methods of teaching music reading were pub-

---

[1] H. M. Beal, *The Boston Numeral Harmony; or Day and Beal's Phonography of Music.* Boston: 1845.

[2] Julian Jordan, *New Method of Sight-Singing.* New York: Bigelow and Main, 1883.

lished that represented revolts against the use of Latin syllables, and
that unsuccessfully attempted to eliminate syllables by substituting
numerals.   The preface of Jordan's *New Method of Sight-Singing* stated
that methods of sight-singing with syllables were too intricate, explaining:

> While some persons overcome the difficulties thus presented [by syllables]
> in reading music, the larger number are left as much in the dark as ever.
> . . . The distinctive features of this [numeral] method . . . are the sepa-
> rating of the two mental processes necessarily employed by the persons
> reading at sight. These processes are, 1st. Reading or comprehending the
> scale number of each tone. . . . 2nd. The production of the tone read.
> The usual custom of using the syllables Do, Re, Mi, etc., is dropped, not
> because it is impossible to teach a person by that method but because ex-
> perience has shown that while a few learn, many fail.

The Jordan Method began with the numbered C scale, then soon transposed the numeral concept to other common keys.   Finally, the neutral
syllable *la* was sung while the student *thought* the numbers.   Chromatics
were avoided.

In the early twentieth century the names of Samuel Cole and Alfred
White stand out as music educators who taught and advocated the use
of numerals rather than syllables.   Still later Howard Hinga discarded
both syllables and numbers in the teaching of music reading in the
schools of Rochester, New York.   A study made by one of the authors

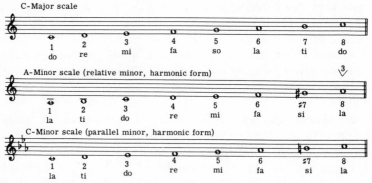

3 When numerals are used in music theory, the first tone of every scale, whether
major or minor, is *1*. However, it is common practice in many schools to teach the
concept of minor in terms of the *relative* minor in a way that equates the Latin syllable *la* with the numeral *6*, thus beginning every minor scale with *6*. An advantage
in so doing is that all scales relate to the major tonality as indicated by the key signature. Another is that the numerals relate directly to the Latin syllable names. A disadvantage is that the chords I, IV, and V$_7$ in minor then appear to be based on scale
tones *6, 2,* and *3*, which is confusing. Thus, one of the less important issues in teaching
the notation of minor scales and chords is whether to do this from the standpoint of
the parallel minor or the relative minor. The authors believe in the use of both as
each is needed to explain scale, chord, and key relationships, with the initial approach
being made through listening.

of the present book at Highland Park, Illinois, in 1948–49 yielded evidence that interest in devices such as syllables and numerals was highest in the third grade, indicating that if teachers chose to employ them, they might consider emphasizing them on that grade level. Another in-service study made at the same school yielded evidence that an approach to music reading consisting of a minimal use of numbers combined with an emphasis on easy-to-play instruments was much more effective than an approach consisting almost exclusively of the use of Latin syllables. Although the children, in this instance, preferred numbers to syllables, slightly more than half of them stated their dislike of singing with either. Their natural inclination was to sing songs with meaningful words, and they had a normal dislike of any substitute unless there was a game aspect to the teacher's presentation.

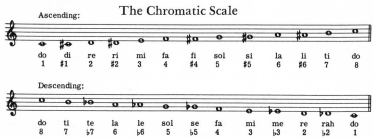

The Chromatic Scale

Ascending:

do	di	re	ri	mi	fa	fi	sol	si	la	li	ti	do
1	#1	2	#2	3	4	#4	5	#5	6	#6	7	8

Descending:

do	ti	te	la	le	sol	se	fa	mi	me	re	rah	do
8	7	♭7	6	♭6	5	♭5	4	3	♭3	2	♭2	1

Numerals and syllables are similar devices. They represent the same idea in that both are "measuring sticks" to help one understand the relationship of the tones of the scale. "1" and "do" are two ways of naming the same thing—the key note in major keys (the home tone). Because numbers are already familiar, they are often preferred by elementary school teachers and children to the Latin syllables, which are unfamiliar. Either device may be introduced in connection with songs that are already well known to children. When syllables are used, some teachers believe that the first grade is the place to begin indoctrination with them, employing them as extra "nonsense" verses to songs. Other teachers believe that syllables should not be introduced earlier than in second or third grade. Gradually *do* or *1* is recognized by the children as the home tone, and other syllables or numbers acquire meaning and position in relation to *do* or *1*. After children have been guided to think tonal relationships accurately in terms of numbers or syllables, the teacher usually has them sight-sing with a neutral syllable such as "loo" while they *think* numbers or syllables. Theoretically, *these devices should be employed only when their use can solve a problem and when they are needed to make music activities more meaningful.* The letter names are learned also, whether the teacher is employing numerals, syllables, or both. Letter names assume real significance when easy-to-play instruments are used by the children.   A comparative analysis of numerals and syllables follows:

Numerals	Syllables
familiar terminology; logical to children	unfamiliar terminology; meaningless when introduced
poor from standpoint of voice production	excellent from standpoint of voice production
favored by music theorists; numbers apply to harmony	not favored by music theorists; syllables do not apply to harmony
chromatics very awkward and are avoided	chromatics easily sung (but elementary school music rarely uses them)
excellent in explaining intervals	poor in explaining intervals
harmful to enjoyment if overused	harmful to enjoyment if overused

Whether or not the prospective public school teacher will employ numbers and/or syllables in his music teaching depends upon a number of circumstances.   The person who can best interpret these is the teacher of the college music education class who has the opportunity to study the trends and traditions of the area served by his institution.   The college teacher and his students are faced with a number of circumstances, trends, and facts, among them the following: (a) the syllable tradition is said to exist most strongly in Northeastern United States; (b) a large number of colleges do not employ syllables in the training of either music majors or elementary education majors; (c) among authors of series books are found those who neither believe in nor practice the use of syllables in their own teaching although their books endorse syllables wholeheartedly; (d) musicians who play musical instruments have no need of syllables or numbers in order to become sight-readers of music; (e) eminent American music educators disagree on the value and use of syllables and numbers, and (f) many distinguished European music educators are said to favor the use of syllables.

This state of confusion is not as serious as it first appears and may be resolved by the knowledge that all of the activities mentioned in this book can be accomplished without the aid of syllables, and that should a teacher find himself in a teaching situation in which syllables must be employed, he can learn them along with the children if he has an adequate musical background that has not included the syllables.   Perhaps most important is the discovery that many teachers use a combination of numbers, syllables, and letter names because they have found each to be of value in helping children understand the relationship of tones.

NOTE PATTERNS AND INTERVALS

To numbers and syllables there has been added another element: the recognition of tonal patterns. With this concept music reading is taught according to the same principles as word reading. When English reading is taught, the children are guided to recognize at once certain familiar combinations of letters that are words. Likewise, the children are taught to recognize in the songs they sing certain common combinations of notes. This approach will be found used in combination with numbers and/or syllables in the music series books.[4]

Examples of tonal patterns:

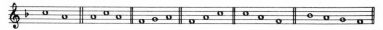

Since experienced sight-readers of music are known to depend in large part upon their instant recognition of the interval relationship of the notes they see, it is believed that an understanding of intervals should be developed in grades four, five, and six. Numbers are of direct aid in the study of intervals.

major second	major third	perfect fourth	perfect fifth	major sixth	major seventh	perfect octave
1 2	1 3	1 4	1 5	1 6	1 7	1 8

All one does to find the interval relationship of two notes is to call one of the notes "1" and count the lines and spaces to the other one. The number of this latter note is the name of the interval.

minor seventh	minor sixth	perfect fifth	perfect fourth	minor third	minor second	perfect unison

Scale tone number:

2 8	3 8	4 8	5 8	6 8	7 8	8 8

Counting lines and spaces to find the above intervals:

1 to 7   1 to 6   1 to 5   1 to 4   1 to 3   1 to 2   1

A common interval is the *fourth*. It is easily sung and occurs frequently in many songs. It is found in the two beginning notes of "Yankee Doodle" (5̄–1) and recurs several times in the course of the tune. The familiar "Lullaby and Goodnight" stresses the *minor third* (three half-steps) at its beginning (3̂3 5 3̂3 5–), and "So Long" repeats this interval

---

[4] Refer to the *Our Singing World* Guide and Teaching Suggestions: Kindergarten and Grades One, Two, and Three (Ginn), 1949 edition, pp. 37–42.

a number of times. The 1–3–5 chord pattern is made up of two thirds, a *major third* (1–3, two steps) and a minor third (3–5). The major scale is composed of *minor seconds* (one half-step) and *major seconds* (one whole-step). The *fifth* is found at the beginning of "Twinkle Twinkle Little Star" (1 1 5 5), and the *major sixth* is popularly identified with the beginning notes of "My Bonnie" (5̄ 3). The *seventh* is found rarely in elementary school songs. The *octave* (1–8) is easily identifiable. It is suggested that intervals be taught in connection with their occurrence in song material. For example, when sixth-grade children know that "My Bonnie" starts with the interval of a sixth, it may be interesting to find that interval in other songs.

INSTRUMENTAL RELATIONSHIPS AND VISUAL AIDS

Instrumental relationships. The reader should review references to notation relating to percussion instruments and rhythm in Chapter Four and melody and harmony instruments in Chapter Five. It should be emphasized that the keyboard is an exceedingly helpful visual aid in building concepts of the lines and spaces of the staff. In fact, a staff drawn on cardboard can be seen, felt, and heard by children when they play them on bells, xylophone and piano. Recent music series contain numerous uses of the keyboard relating to notation. Letter names can be logically learned first on the keyboard, then the pitches bearing these letter names can be found on the lines and spaces of the staff. In fact, staff drawn on cardboard can be fitted to the keyboard to make this relationship exact. Also, certain types of bells can be suspended over the chalkboard, and the lines of the staff are then drawn from each key that relates to the lines. There are *step bells* that both sound and visualize the pitches of the scale, and the Germans make a *bell tower* (see *Glockenturm* on page 322) that relates the tones of the instrument to the staff. One of the easiest ways to help children sense pitch differences and interval relationships is through guided use of the keyboard and other melody instruments. Numeral notation can be an approach preparatory to music notation. This was discussed and illustrated in connection with the bells in Chapter Five.

Visual aids. Besides the real keyboard, the teacher can purchase or make cardboard replicas of it so that all children can have one. When this is done, every child can go through the motions of pressing keys while several children make the sounds by playing on the piano or other keyboard instrument. Series books usually contain drawings of part of the keyboard inside one of the covers. While these are helpful in studying notation, they are often too small for large fingers to use. Some keyboards are manufactured from plastic in a way that provides raised black keys. There are also semiprofessional models having keys made of ivory that press down without sounding. The autoharp bridge is pictured in most series books. This permits every child to go through the act of pressing the correct button while the teacher or a child plays the chords on the instrument.

Teacher-made charts that explain notational concepts are of great value. For example, a simple chart which helps to teach the fact that notes have only three ways to move could appear as follows:

A chart emphasizing steps and half-steps in a common note pattern might appear in this way:

Where is the half step?		
G	A	B - C
So	La	Ti - Do
5	6	7 - 8

Charts containing themes of recorded instrumental compositions accompany the Bowmar Orchestral Library, but any teacher can make such a chart for himself or write the themes on the chalkboard. Good charts, however, are sometimes more attractive and interesting than the chalkboard. A teacher can buy or make flash cards concerned with notation. The Birchard Music Series, the Our Singing World Series, and the This Is Music Series have made charts of some songs. A series of charts containing the notation of common rhythms that can be combined into more lengthy patterns can be purchased[5] or made. Films concerned with the teaching of notation can be found indexed in the Film Guide for Music Educators, published by the Music Educators Na-

---

5 Rhyth-O-Meter Charts, Empire Music Company, 3216 44th Ave., S.W. Seattle, Washington.

tional Conference. Chalkboards, often with staff liner, white and colored chalk, flannel boards, and magnetic boards are useful in the study of notation on the staff. The flannel and magnetic boards have the advantage of clear notation that is sometimes not found when children and teachers write it. The Music-Ease Work Book, published by Visual Education, Inc., 230 West Fifth Street, Dayton, Ohio, is useful for either class, small group, or individual instruction. Plastic symbols adhere to its staff, and the book contains instructions for individuals to follow.

EVALUATION OF NOTE READING

A simple type of written test can be used as early as second grade, even before the children understand the staff. For example, if the teacher's purpose has been to expand concepts of how pitches move in scale-line patterns, he can use the first three notes of "Three Blind Mice" and similar repeated patterns in songs the children have come to know well. Written correctly, this particular pattern could be drawn:

On the Dittoed test paper, however, it might appear with one misplaced note, and the children would be asked to find and circle the error:

Later in the year, this type of test can be written on the staff when the children are able to understand its function. A test that is usable in grades three and above assumes knowledge of the staff. The test paper is so designed that the first two measures of a four-measure phrase are followed by from two to four versions of the final two measures, only one of which is correct. If familiar song material is used, the children may or may not be expected to write the test *thinking* the pitches from the notation with no assistance of any kind. If unfamiliar phrases are used, the teacher must play or sing the phrase and the children would be asked to check the phrase ending that is the one sounded by the teacher. Other questions that might be answered in written tests might include "How many beats are there in each measure of the song I am going to play?" "How many measures are there in the song?" (Teacher plays song again). "How many eighth notes do you hear in the example I will play now?" "Now listen for the number of dotted-eighth and sixteenth-note patterns in what I will play next." When children understand the function of the key signature and why the key signature is important, they can be asked to identify key signatures and key notes in music. An exciting type of test can come from the taping by the children of a familiar song, then the analysis of what is heard when it is played back. In such a test, items could refer to the meter signature, phrase structure, and the notation of important rhythmic and melodic patterns. Recordings can be used this same way. A useful way to test ability to hear and write melody is based upon a numeral system that can be expanded to include more scale tones than illustrated below. Children can write the melody by circling the appropriate numerals. After this, they might transfer the melody to the staff.

2 2 2 2 2 2

1 1 1 1 1 1

7 7 7 7 7 7

Other possibilities for evaluation of learning in notation include observing the use of notation by individual children to play songs on the bells in the music center; using flash cards to find the extent of recognition of terms and symbols, and the speed of this recognition; ascertaining the degree of success in sight-reading easy note patterns and songs; testing ability to recognize phrases that are the same and those that are different by examining the notation of songs; asking individuals to clap or sing notated rhythm patterns; asking children to analyze and explain meter signatures; testing ability to differentiate between two notated rhythm patterns by tapping or clapping them; attempting to notate the rhythm of familiar songs; and attempting to notate parts or all of the melodies of selected familiar songs. Standardized tests should be studied carefully before using them. The teacher should know the purpose of the test and what use will be made of the findings if it is given. The Knuth Achievement Tests in Music, Educational Test Bureau, Inc., 720 Washington Ave., S. E. Minneapolis, Minnesota, have as their purpose the testing of ability to recognize rhythmic and melodic elements of music. It can be used in grades three-eight, with different versions of the test for grades three-four, five-six, and seven-eight.

OTHER SUGGESTIONS

1. Remember that line notation is a step toward learning note values, and that rhythmic bodily movement such as stepping the melody rhythm assists learning to read notes. These were discussed in Chapter Four.
2. A common formula for introducing note reading is: *hear it* sung by the teacher or played on a recording; learn to *sing it* by rote

and to *act it out* in pitch levels; *play it* on the keyboard or other instruments by ear; *see it* on the chalkboard, chart, or printed page. Remember that music notation is essentially a picture of what the ear has heard and the body has felt.

3. Music reading is seldom a separate and special study; it is an integral part of listening, moving to music, singing, and playing instruments. When it is taught in relation to these, it takes on meaning and purpose that motivate the learning of notation.

4. Beginning experiences in music reading should be so simple that success is virtually assured.

5. Emphasize only one aspect of note reading at a time.

6. Children see the five lines of the staff but sometimes fail to comprehend the concept of *space*. The function of the spaces should be made clear.

7. Some teachers begin note reading using only a one-line staff. They place notes on, above, and below this line (*do, re,* and *ti,* or *1, 2,* and *7*). They gradually add more lines as they need them until the five-line staff emerges.

8. Music terms and symbols should be learned in context, i.e., in connection with the music with which the children are working.

9. "When phrases sound alike they look alike" is a valuable concept to teach children.

10. When the interval of a third appears in a melody, the note moves either from a line to the next line, or from a space to the next space (line-line, space-space). When a 1–3–5 chord pattern occurs in a melody, the notes are either line-line-line or space-space-space. Concepts such as this help children to visualize intervals and note patterns.

11. Progress from rote singing to note singing should be so gradual that the child never feels that note reading is a new activity. In other words, he should always have an adequate background for the next step undertaken in understanding notation.

12. The answer to the question "When should I teach children to understand notation?" is "When they have need of it in their daily music activities." If a teacher plans a rich and varied program of music activities, the children are certain to have need of notation, and they will try to learn it because it will have functions that are useful to them and understood by them.

13. Teach first the comprehension of phrases and patterns of notes. After these are grasped, teach the smaller details. Good note reading is based upon the recognition of patterns of notes or note groupings rather than seeing one note at a time.

14. Use a variety of approaches to music reading because of the many individual differences among children and because there is no *one* right way to teach it.

15. The goal is to teach children to "see with their ears" and to "hear with their eyes."

16. The simultaneous reading of words and notes is extremely difficult. Seeing the words distracts children from seeing the notes. Therefore when emphasizing note reading, sing often without words; use nonmelodic chanting and melodic singing or neutral syllables such as "loo" so that attention can be centered on the notation. When preparing to read both words and music at the same time, it is a good idea for the children first to speak the words rhythmically so that they will have a good feeling for the meter and note values.

17. When themes of recorded music are placed on the chalkboard or chart during listening activities, the eye can help the ear, and something about notation may be learned. If the themes are singable, sing them from notation, if possible, before the recording is played.

18. When children observe notation while listening to a recording or to the teacher's singing, find out if they are following the notation by stopping the music and seeing if their fingers are pointing to the last note sounded. Some teachers ask children to "frame" measures with their two index fingers, moving the fingers along as the music progresses.

19. Classroom teachers can use the skills area (see Chapter Three) for group and individual instruction in note reading. Some children are ready for understanding notation while others may not be ready. Some of the failures of the past stem from trying to teach any given aspect of notation to every child in the same way at the same time. This approach is no longer considered good practice in teaching children to read English, and teaching music reading is very similar.

20. Emphasize the instrumental approach to note reading, relating this to singing as described in Chapter Five.

TECHNIQUES AND DEVICES

1. Playing on bells that have been turned on end reveals how ups and downs in pitch look. This can be related to the ups and downs of notes on the staff.

2. A flannel board can be made by stretching and taping outing flannel over heavy cardboard. Lines of the staff can be drawn with

a Flo-master Pen, and notes made of black felt. Children enjoy manipulating the notes, and the appearance of the flannel board notation is superior to that of notation drawn on a chalkboard. Some teachers prefer to use no cardboard but instead fasten the top and bottom of the flannel to slender wooden rods. With this construction the device can be rolled up and stored when not in use.

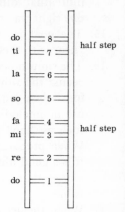

3. The major scale consists of whole-steps with the exception of half-steps between scale tones 3 and 4, and 7 and 8. The keyboard can explain this visually. A time-honored aid to explain the structure of the major scale is the comparison of it to a ladder.

4. The scale can be written vertically on the chalkboard either in numbers, in regular notation, or in syllables. The class sings various scale tones as the teacher points to them.

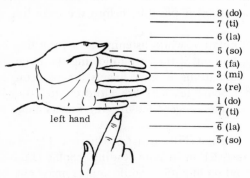

left hand

5. "Singing from the hand" is useful for drill on difficult passages from song material and for intervals. The teacher uses the right hand to point to the scale tones the class sings:

6. The hand is also useful when the fingers are used to represent the staff. Ear-training drills can be done, and some intervals can be practiced when the children sing the "notes" to which the teacher's right index finger points.

7. The "mystery tune" game can be played by placing a few measures of a familiar song on the chalkboard and hiding these by pulling a map down over it. Or this can be written on a chart and its contents concealed by turning its face to the wall. When the children are ready, reveal the notation. The game is to name the tune by studying the notation without humming or playing it.

8. Sing or play from music written on two-by-three tag board as described in Chapter Five, page 153.

9. In the intermediate grades it can be fun as well as challenging to read familiar songs that have been notated in humorously distorted rhythm. Example:

AUNT RHODY

Go   tell Aunt   Rho - dy, etc.   Go   tell Aunt   Rho - dy

Go tell Aunt   Rho - dy   Go   tell Aunt   Rho - dy

10. An ear-training exercise relating physical responses to degrees of the scale can be done while standing.
    Scale tone 1 = arms down at sides
                2 = hands on hips
                3 = fingers on outside of shoulders
                4 = fingers on top of shoulders
                5 = fingers above ears on sides of head
                6 = hands somewhat above head
                7 = arms stretched high above head
                8 = stand on toes with arms stretched high above head
    The teacher may ask the children to close their eyes and respond to scale tones as he plays them on the bells.

11. An interval drill based on the scale can be pictured by drawing an umbrella on the chalkboard as the children sing the intervals. The teacher begins each curved line on *do: do re do mi do fa do sol do la do ti do,* then down the scale: *do ti do la do sol do fa do mi do re do do.* The handle is drawn after the singing is done.

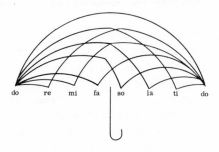

do   re   mi   fa   so   la   ti   do

12. European teachers use hand signs to indicate degrees of the scale, and have children sing the scale tones "from the hand." They plan ear-training drills with this visual method, emphasizing scale and chord pattrns. Hand signs are also used to assist learning difficult parts of songs.

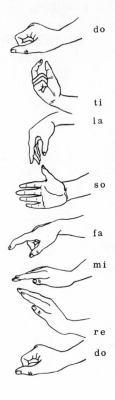

do

ti

la

so

fa

mi

re

do

THINGS TO DO

1. Select a song from a series book and analyze it in terms of possible use for note reading in intermediate grades. Consider the key, the beginning note, note values, scale lines in the melody, chord lines, other note patterns, difficult intervals and rhythms, and measures and phrases that are alike. Present this song to your college class to guide them to help themselves to sight-sing effectively.

2. Study and compare the music-reading programs of the various music series.

3. Demonstrate how music reading can be taught in conjunction with rhythmic reponse, singing, playing, listening, and creating.

4. Demonstrate the use of line notation and numeral notation.

5. Compare the teaching of reading English words and the teaching of reading note patterns and rhythm patterns. Illustrate with melody lines and rhythm patterns found in songs.

6. Explain the functions of Latin syllables, numerals, and letter names in teaching the understanding of notation.

7. Make a flannel board and demonstrate its use to the class.

8. Evaluate from your own experience the playing of keyboard and blowing-type instruments in learning to understand notation and its use.

9. Construct the following audio-visual aid to help children understand the staff. Hang a solidly constructed bell set vertically so that it is over the chalkboard or free wall space. The large bars are downward. Draw a staff on either the chalkboard or light cardboard, the staff having lines that lead horizontally from the appropriate bars of the bells. From bottom to top they will be, E, G, B, D, F. This helps the children visualize the relation between tones sounded on the bells and the notes that represent these pitches on the staff.

10. Construct charts that help teach concepts of notation.

11. Investigate and evaluate the use of primers for introducing notation to young children. Ginn publishes *Singing as We Play, Singing All the Day,* and *Playing as We Sing.* Silver Burdett publishes *I Like the Country* and *I Like the City.*

12. W. Otto Miessner, American music educator and innovator, introduced an original system to use in teaching tonal relationships. Its purpose is to remove the conflict in syllable and numeral systems in which the reader of music must deal with a relative tonal system operating in a fixed pitch staff notation system. Read Mr. Miessner's article, "The Art of Tonal Thinking," *Music Educators Journal* for January, 1962. Explain this system to the college class. Ask the class to sing simple tunes with the Miessner syllables. Ask the class to try to determine whether this system is superior to Latin syllables or numerals.

13. Prepare a short, simple test to measure understanding of tonal relationships and notation to be given in a grade of your choice from three through six.

14. Notate a familiar song in several different meters to produce rhythmically distorted versions that are both fun and challenging to sing.

MUSIC SERIES GUIDE

BIRCHARD MUSIC SERIES (SUMMY-BIRCHARD COMPANY)

BOOK ONE

Charts: high and low tones, 3; songs, 5
Phrasing, 187
Pitch recognition, 187

BOOK TWO

Charts, TM 206
Music theory, TM 20–23

GROWING WITH MUSIC (PRENTICE-HALL, INC.)

The teachers edition for Books 1, 3, 4, 5, and 6 was not available when this Guide was compiled.

MUSIC FOR LIVING (SILVER BURDETT COMPANY)

MUSIC AROUND THE WORLD

Altered scale tones, TM 203
Chords, TM 203
Harmony, TM 204
Intervals, TM 204
Music reading, TM viii–xi, TM 204
Music scores, TM 204
Phrase, TM 204
Scalewise movement, TM 204
Transposition, TM 204

MUSIC FOR YOUNG AMERICANS (AMERICAN BOOK COMPANY)

KINDERGARTEN

Some fundamentals of music for young children, 145–7

BOOK ONE

Some fundamentals of music for young children, 177–9

BOOK TWO

Reading readiness, TM 1
Rhythmic notation, TM 1

BOOK THREE

Music reading, TM 1–2
We learn to read music, 39–58
We sing, play, and read, 86–99

BOOK FOUR

Music reading, TM 1–2
Songs to play, sing, and read, 18–31
More songs to play, sing, and read, 82–97
Reading and rhythm, 147–62

BOOK FIVE

See *Contents:* section organization in terms of key
Music reading, TM 2
Read TM for suggested songs for notation study
Note keyboard illustrations in child's book

BOOK SIX

Music reading, TM 1–2
Note keyboard illustrations in child's book

OUR SINGING WORLD (GINN AND COMPANY) 1951 EDITION

KINDERGARTEN BOOK

Melodic patterns, TM 37–42

FIRST GRADE BOOK

Melodic Patterns, TM 37–42
Music reading, xix

SINGING AS WE PLAY (Primer)

TM 42–45

SINGING ON OUR WAY

Music Reading, TM 95–112

SINGING EVERY DAY (Primer)

TM 45

SINGING AND RHYMING

Music Reading, TM 163–83
We Play and Sing, 4

SINGING EVERY DAY

Music Reading, TM 32–75
We Sing and Play, 4

SINGING TOGETHER

Music Reading, TM 122–94
We Sing and Play, 4

SINGING IN HARMONY

Music Reading, TM 252–300
We Play and Sing, 4

THIS IS MUSIC (ALLYN AND BACON, INC.)

BOOK ONE

Clapping names, 17
Melody instruments, 189
Number notation, 186
Pitch pictures, 186
Word patterns, 17

TOGETHER WE SING (FOLLETT PUBLISHING COMPANY, REVISED)

REFERENCES AND MATERIALS

ARTICLES AND BOOKS

Carabo-Cone, Madeleine, *The Playground as Music Teacher*. New York: Harper & Row, Publishers, 1958.

Flagg, Marion, *Musical Learning*. Evanston, Ill.: Summy-Birchard Publishing Company, 1949. Chapter 10.

Landeck, Beatrice, *Children and Music*. New York: William Sloane Associates, Inc., 1952. Appendix I.

Myers, Louise, *Teaching Children Music in the Elementary School*, 3rd ed. Englewood Cliffs, N.J.: Prentice-Hall, Inc., 1961. Chapter 7.

Nye, Robert E., "If You Don't Use Syllables, What Do You Use?" *Music Educators Journal*, April–May, 1953, pp. 41–2.

Nye, Robert E., Vernice Nye, Neva Aubin, George Kyme, *Singing With Children*. Belmont, California: Wadsworth Publishing Company, 1962. Chapter 5, "Songs for Studying Notation."

Pierce, Anne E., *Teaching Music in the Elementary School*. New York: Holt, Rinehart and Winston, Inc., 1959. Chapter 7.

Rinderer, Leo et al., *Music Education*. Park Ridge, Ill.: Neil A. Kjos, Publisher, 1961.

————, *Sing a Song to Sight Read*. Park Ridge, Ill.: Neil A. Kjos, Publisher, 1961.

SONG BOOKS

Ruff, Edna and Herman Smith, *It's Fun to Sing!* Minneapolis: Schmitt, Hall and McCreary. First steps in sight-singing.

———————— *High Low—Together Go!* Minneapolis: Schmitt, Hall and McCreary. Two-part sight-singing.

Scott, Richard, *Sing at Sight Series*. Milwaukee: Handy Folio Music Company.

Vandre, Carl, *Clap, Tap and Sing Choral Method*, Handy Folio Music Company, 7212 W. Fond du Lac Ave., Milwaukee. For grades 2–5.

———— *Sevenfold Choral Method*. Milwaukee: Handy Folio Music Company. For grades 6–12.

FILMS AND FILMSTRIPS

Johnson Hunt Productions, 6509 De Longpre Ave., Hollywood, Cal.
 Music Reading. 20 minutes. Grades 4–6.

McGraw-Hill Book Company, Inc., 330 W. 42nd St., New York 36, N.Y.
 Young America Sings. Teaching filmstrips. Double-faced 12-inch LP recordings with correlated filmstrips. Rote to note singing. Units for grades 3, 4, 5.

Society for Visual Education, Inc., 1345 Diversey Parkway, Chicago 14, Ill.
 Developing Skills in Music (Group One). All elementary grades. Filmstrips, teacher's guides, and recordings: "Rhythm, the Quarter Note and the Half Note"; "Measures, Whole Notes and Eighth Notes"; "Dotted Notes and Rest"; and "Time Signa-

tures and the Accent." *Developing Skills in Music* (Group Two): "The Staff and Its Notes"; "Major and Minor Scales, Accidentals, and Chromatics"; "Key Signatures"; "Intervals and Phrases."

SPECIAL MATERIALS

Children Should Know Music. Wilkinsburg, Pennsylvania: Hayes School Publishing Company. Master carbons for spirit or liquid duplicators. Book 1: Primary; Book 2: Intermediate; Book 3: Middle and Upper. Notation, Theory, Appreciation, History. $3.50 per book.

Glockenturm (bell tower). Wilhelm Monke, Köln-Ehrenfeld, Gutenburg Strasse 61, Germany. Approximately $15 including postage. A U.S. representative for the German manufacturer is M. Hohner Co., Andrews Rd., Hicksville, N.Y.

Chapter Eleven
MUSIC AND OTHER AREAS

A beautiful song that possesses emotional values and that describes experiences meaningful to children has universal appeal. These aesthetic, emotional, and cultural qualities point toward this song's possible use to add interest, meaning, and enjoyment to other areas of the curriculum. It is also true that the subject matter of other areas can make music activities more interesting, meaningful, and enjoyable. Thus, while the skills in any area are not to be neglected, neither the learning of music nor learning in other areas can in many instances approach completeness without each aiding the other. Music has always been man's most natural artistic medium of expression, and through its use he continually interprets his civilizations, past and present. When music assumes its rightful place throughout the curriculum, marked emphasis is given to it because of its real functions.

RELATING MUSIC AND OTHER AREAS

The following outline consists of some of the more obvious bases for inter-relating music and other areas.

ART

Rhythm is an element common to music, art, and bodily response.
Appropriate recordings stimulate creative art.
Songs can be illustrated by children's drawings.
Song creation can be inspired by pictures.
Pictures can motivate listening to descriptive music.
The making and decorating of simple musical instruments is in the area of arts and crafts.
Some ideas can be expressed in several media: art, music, dance, creative dramatics and writing.
Certain artistic styles are common to both art and music. Examples: impressionism and classicism.

Certain concepts of form are common to both art and music.
Scenery and costumes can be made for musical programs.

PHYSICAL EDUCATION

Singing games and dances are activities considered to be in the areas both of music
and physical education.
Music can be created for a known dance.
Dance can be created for known music.
Basic understanding of note values and meter signatures comes from bodily response.
Rhythm can be expressed in the dance, in music, and in art.
Certain musical forms can be expressed in bodily movement.
Instrumental accompaniments can be created for bodily movement.

SCIENCE

Some music concerns aspects of nature such as clouds, rain, the sea, the seasons, stars.
Aspects of electronics include such things as radio, television, amplifiers, and record-
ing and reproducing sound.
There are many scientists who have music as an enjoyable avocation.
Making and playing musical instruments and experimenting with sound-producing
materials motivate the study of acoustics, the science of sound.
There are songs that help teach health and safety.
Correct posture in singing relates to health.

ARITHMETIC

The study of beats, note values, and meter signatures relates to the understanding of
number concepts.

LANGUAGE ARTS

Poetry and music are closely related; meter, word rhythms and melody rhythms are
often similar or identical.
Appropriate recordings can be employed to stimulate creative writing.
Poetry can be composed; music can be written to make songs based on this poetry;
poetry can be composed for melodies.
Some song interpretations develop creative dramatizations.
There are many books about music, instruments, and musicians.
Music can be composed and recordings can be selected for use with dramatizations,
plays, and puppet shows.
Many songs, operatic and symphonic works are based upon literature and drama.
Aspects of choric reading can relate to the process of learning songs.
Reading of words of songs can be an experience in the process of improving compre-
hension, pronunciation and enunciation.
Music can be selected that relates to children's literature.
Music, dance, and language are communicative arts.
Using symbols of notation is a communicative skill.

SOCIAL STUDIES

(*This can include problems in science, health, safety, language arts, history, geography, citizenship, art, music, and rhythms.*)

Music aids in understanding ideals, religions, and traditions of contemporary and past civilizations, cultures, nations, and times.

Music describes geographical and climatic conditions of various countries.

Music aids in teaching history and patriotism through study of appropriate music and composers.

Music is a unifying factor and morale builder; it aids personality development; it can relieve tensions and alleviate fatigue.

Dances, instrumental compositions, songs, and music plays can be created by children in connection with units of work in social studies.

Children can make musical instruments and costumes to portray the life of peoples of the past and present, and can study these peoples through songs and recorded music.

In some communities, adults from foreign countries may be invited to discuss and illustrate some aspects of their native music and customs.

Music is frequently an important aspect of culminating activities of units of work.

Music reveals mankind's common likenesses and concerns.

It can be seen that there are basic relationships between music and the other areas of the curriculum. However, the area that best lends itself to the combining of subject matter of all types is social studies.

MUSIC IN SOCIAL STUDIES UNITS

The purpose of the social studies program is to help the society it represents provide for the immediate and long-time needs of young people. In some schools specific units are planned by the classroom teacher in terms of a chosen theme for each grade suited to the stage of development of that age group. In developing the theme, subject matter is drawn from several areas. Social studies, science, and language arts make up the core of the program while arithmetic, health, physical education, music, and art are drawn upon to aid in the understanding and in the solution of the problems being studied. However, it should be kept in mind that in most schools having this type of program, additional time is allotted for the development of skills in arithmetic, physical education, music, and art.

The primary concern in the introduction of music into such units is not how much and what specific music can be used in this connection, but how music activities can contribute to a better understanding and solution of the problem under consideration. In such activities, children are free to plan for various types of musical experiences as they relate to the solution of significant problems. The variety of musical experiences possible in a series of such units is almost limitless, and can range from song interpretation and simple dramatization to writing original song plays.

CORRELATION AND INTEGRATION OF MUSIC IN THE CLASSROOM

	CITIZENSHIP	SOCIAL RELATIONSHIPS	LANGUAGE ARTS	SCIENCE
SINGING	Patriotic songs inspire good citizenship, regard for country, emulation of great national figures.	Many songs inspire worldwide regard for other peoples. Songs of our own people broaden appreciation of our own country.	Good singing improves speech and diction. Foreign songs are a practical use of foreign languages.	Vocal techniques depend upon the understanding of some physiology and the physics of sound.
RHYTHMIC ACTIVITIES	Group planning, teamwork and individual expression are training for citizenship.	Folk dances and rhythmic activities are characteristic of many countries. They enhance social studies.	Folk dancing is enhanced greatly when songs are sung and social graces are expressed in their native tongue.	A study of the elements affecting movement, i.e., level, range, focus. Rhythm and mathematics are related.
CREATIVE ACTIVITIES	Teaching children to be creative stimulates critical thinking, problem-solving, and wise use of leisure time.	Creative activities invite the study of other cultures as well as our own.	Creative activities related to music and to the spoken word make for practical application of proper English.	Making instruments (water glasses, etc.) is more a science study than a study of music.
RHYTHM INSTRUMENTS	Working in unity is a lesson in democracy-in-action.	Characteristics of peoples are often revealed in rhythms. The rhythm band is a means of emphasizing this.	An opportunity to study rhythms as they were used in communication—native drums, etc.	A cursive study of sounds and sound effects—a study in physics.
MELODY FLUTES	All group effort requires the co-operation of the class. A lesson in good citizenship.	Flute, pipes have played an important part in the ceremonial life of early culture.	Listening to pitch is an aspect of language arts; symbols of notation constitute a language.	A study of the mathematical ratios of high and low tones produced by pipes is a practical approach to the study of sounds.
LISTENING	Appreciation of things cultural carries over in adult and community life.	The mores and folkways of many periods are reflected in music, thus correlating social studies.	Listening makes use of foreign words. It piques the interest of students for further study of languages.	The principle of tone production on each instrument is a part of appreciation and science of music.

HISTORY	THE ARTS	READING	PHYSICAL EDUCATION	PERSONALITY DEVELOPMENT
Many songs enhance the study of all periods of history. Many songs relate to heroes or great historic events.	Efforts toward artistic expression in music make for appreciation of beauty in all art.	The technique of good singing is carried over to good reading —phrasing, etc.	The action song or singing game has long been a part of physical education.	Expressive singing is emotional experience that broadens personality and dulls undesirable inhibitions.
The evolution of rhythmic expression coincides with the development of civilization.	Develops awareness of the elements of movement in related arts.	A feeling of the rhythmic flow in singing improves reading ability. Choral speaking is a combination of singing and reading.	Rhythmic activities can bring relaxation through a classroom day.	Bodily expression unshackles the spirit and draws personality into view.
Unit studies can include various applications of music, with wide creative opportunities.	Creative work is a medium through which music is correlated with the other arts.	Dramatizing the song helps to give a feeling for the dramatic in reading. This helps in developing the imagination.	Music's creative activities calling for motion are also physical education.	Self-expression is part of personality development. Creativeness is a part of developing self-confidence.
The development of percussion instruments is parallel to the development of civilization.	Rhythm bands emphasize musical form. There is a relationship of musical form to painting, poetry, literature, and the dance.	Using music notation is a form of reading.	Precision marching and walking enter into many instrumental activities, all of which aid in development of coordination.	The group activities of music help to develop poise.
The flute, being one of the older instruments, was a part of tribal ceremonies, and used in courts of kings.	Ensemble playing is an art form better appreciated when an individual has the opportunity to participate.	Using music notation is a form of reading.	Breath control and good posture are developed by music training, both vocal and instrumental.	Musical skills develop confidence and build an extroverted personality.
Great music has been influenced in its creation by historical events, such as the War of 1812, the settling of "America."	Appreciation of fine music is a basis upon which a discriminating taste may be developed for all the arts.	Contributes to the intellectual aspect of literature. Music is often related to great literature and drama.	Active as well as passive bodily activity enter into listening, particularly in the primary grades.	Developing taste for beauty influences the personality characteristics of the individual favorably.

Single copies of this chart, enlarged to 11" x 17", are available free of charge from the American Music Conference, 332 South Michigan Avenue, Chicago, Illinois.

SOME SUGGESTED TOPICS FOR UNITS
IN GRADES ONE THROUGH SIX

How the social studies program should be organized and developed at the various grade levels will depend upon many factors, including the age and maturity of the children, and the problems and conditions of the school and community. This program should be organized in a way that helps children to meet and to solve their own problems of home, school, and community living, in relation to such areas as health, recreation, safety, beautification, conservation, government and citizenship, transportation and communication, economic life, and art and music. Through their attempts to meet and to solve these problems they should develop ability to live and to work democratically with others in individual and group relationships. They should also develop an understanding of being a part of an ever-expanding community. Furthermore, they should be guided in their understanding of the processes of physical and social change, and of man's responsibility for the kinds of change that take place.

Classroom teachers have the task of planning many units. Music consultants have the responsibility of aiding teachers in selecting and planning appropriate music and music activities for the amplification and enrichment of the subject matter involved in these units. In schools that have a music specialist he will find it to his advantage to make music activities more meaningful to boys and girls by relating part of the work in the music period to units of work undertaken by the classroom teacher. In terms of current educational thought, it is also necessary for special music teachers to encourage the concept that music is the property of everyone to be used by all.

Contemporary educational thought places increasing emphasis on the likenesses of all people in the world to encourage the development of international understanding. In the past, the emphasis has been primarily on American problems. While this emphasis is retained, the similar and comparative problems of peoples of the world are now included in social studies units. Some suggested problems to be developed as units are as follows:

Grades One and Two. (The immediate community—home, neighborhood, school.) How can we make our school a safe place in which to live? How can we make our homes safe? How can we make our classroom and school a good place in which to live, work, and play? How can we make a school garden? How can we take care of our toys? Where should we store our food? What animals make good pets and how can we care for pets? How do farmers, firemen, policemen, bakers, and others in the community help us?

Grades Three and Four. (The community and its relationships to other communities.) How can we help make our home, school, and community safe? What are the harmful insects found in our home, school, and community and how can we help destroy them? What types of recreation are found in our community, and how can we select wisely from among these types? How can we make our community a more attractive place in which to live? How can we choose suitable clothing? How do we get our food? How did our community develop? How do the people in our community make a living? In what ways are animals of today similar to and different from animals of long ago? What effect does climate and topography have on the way people live in this and other communities?

Grades Five and Six. (The community, state, and nation and their relationship to other countries.) How can we improve the appearance of the school, home, community, and ourselves? What are the state and nation doing to beautify our country? What are the leading natural resources of our community, state, and nation, and how can we conserve them? What are the sources of electric power in our state and nation? What are some of the improved farming methods used in our state and nation? How do many parts of the nation and of the world help us obtain food? How does the way we keep time today compare with keeping time long ago? How has mail been carried in the United States, from colonial days to the present? How have writing and printing been developed? How have roads and railway systems developed in our state and in the nation? How do other countries influence the price of commodities? How was our country discovered and explored? How did the people live in the early days of our country? How has our country grown to its present size? How can we better understand our neighbors of North and South America and of the world?

Classified indexes of series books lead the teacher to songs listed according to subject matter content. Appropriate songs can be found that relate to the content of almost every social studies unit.

The following outline indicates how music may be used in a unit of work in the primary grades. For the purposes of this book, music in this unit is given more consideration than other activities that would normally receive equal emphasis.

A UNIT IN SOCIAL STUDIES FOR FIRST GRADE

WHAT ANIMALS MAKE GOOD PETS?

I. Introduction

The six-year-old is interested primarily in problems growing out of his home and immediate community. Most children have pets in their homes or know about pets in the homes of their friends. Since children have a natural love for animals and most of them have had association with pets, this unit is based on real-life experience, which vitalizes its content.

II. Purposes

    A. General

      1. To provide opportunity for children to learn to plan, work, and play democratically in a group.

      2. To help children assume more responsibility for the solution of their problems and the problems of others.

      3. To provide for individual differences through the use of a variety of materials and activities.

      4. To make more meaningful and functional the learning of various facts and skills in language arts, science, health, arithmetic, art, music, and physical education.

    B. Specific

      1. To provide the child with materials, experiences, and activities that will foster his understanding of the life of pets and its relation to his own life.

      2. To help the child develop a sense of responsibility through caring for a pet in the classroom.

      3. To help the child understand the environment necessary for the health and safety of pets.

      4. To help the child understand how nature has equipped these pets to protect themselves.

      5. To stimulate children's creative expression through stories, poems, art, music, and rhythms relating to pets.

III. Possible Means of Motivation

    A. Establishing a stimulating environment which may include:

      1. Pictures of pets with names or sentences written beneath.

      2. Sharing experiences about pets.

      3. Pets brought to the classroom.

      4. Songs sung and recordings listened to that are concerned with pets.

      5. Films or slides about pets.

      6. The library center arranged with attractive books about pets.

    B. Excursions to:

      1. A pet shop.

      2. Homes of children having interesting pets.

IV. Content

    A. The different kinds of pets.

    B. The care and training of pets.

    C. The homes of pets.

    D. What pets eat.

    E. How pets protect themselves.

    F. Similarities and differences between pets and children.

    G. Kindness to pets.

V. Suggested Activities

    A. Visit a pet shop and homes to study pets.

    B. Advance planning for excursions.

        1. Discuss responsibilities involved.

        2. List questions for which answers are to be found.

    C. Care for pets in the classroom.

    D. Show motion pictures about pets.

    E. Construct a television roll using stories, songs, poems, and pictures the children have assembled or created.

    F. Draw pictures and paint murals about pets.

    G. Plan and present a pet show.

    H. Look at pictures and read in library books to find information.

    I. Discuss types of pets and their care.

    J. Relate personal experiences in caring for pets.

    K. Read stories and poems.

    L. Write simple group stories, poems, and songs.

    M. Sing songs and play singing games about pets.

    N. Draw pictures to illustrate songs.

    O. Do imitations and dramatizations of pets.

    P. Model pets out of clay or papier-mâché.

    Q. Hatch baby chicks in an incubator and care for them.

    R. Discuss making charts of experience in activities with pets, and then make these experience charts.

    S. Invite a member of the Humane Society to speak on the care and safe handling of pets.

VI. Suggested Activities in Subject-Matter Areas

    A. Language Arts

        1. Read experience charts.

        2. Read labels on pets' cages and on pictures.

        3. Read suggested work lists in caring for pets.

        4. Match names of animals with pictures.

        5. Read pre-primers in basic reading series containing stories on kinds of pets and their care.

6. Make individual and group booklets.
7. Compose original stories, poems, and songs.
8. Provide experiences in choric reading of poems.
9. Write letters such as requests to visit pet shop, invitations to speakers and visitors, and thank-you notes.
10. Dramatize stories, poems, and songs.
11. Discuss experiences in relation to pets.
12. Read stories, legends, and poems to the children.

B. Number Activities
1. Count the number of legs various pets have.
2. Keep a record of how much pets are fed.
3. Weigh the pets to see how much they gain or lose.
4. List the kinds of pets owned by the children and count them.
5. Count the number of children who work in a group.
6. Draw a picture of a pet on each of ten pages; make them into a booklet and number the pages.
7. Use words of comparison in discussions of animals such as big, bigger, biggest; small, smaller, smallest.

C. Health and Science
1. Observe and study body structure of animals and how they are protected by nature.
2. Observe and study animals' eating habits and methods of obtaining food.
3. Compare the basic needs of animals with those of man.
4. Observe and study ways animals keep clean.
5. Learn how climate and seasons affect the lives of animals.

D. Art
1. Illustrate individual and group stories, poems, and songs.
2. Model animals from clay and papier-mâché.
3. Make murals depicting pets.
4. Use charcoal, crayon, and paint to illustrate various activities of the unit.
5. Make posters showing the care of certain pets.
6. Make a television roll and the pictures for it.
7. Study famous pictures of pets.

E. Citizenship
Participating in the planning, executing, and evaluation of various activities:
(a) Excursions.
(b) Care of pets.
(c) Making murals.
(d) Pet show.
(e) Seeing films.

(f) Discussions.
(g) Group writing of stories, poems, and songs.
(h) Dramatization and creative play.
(i) Experience charts.
(j) Hatching chicks.
(k) Writing letters of invitation and thanks.
F. Music and Physical Education

In order for children to act in creative ways in this work unit, they require a relaxed and happy environment. The teacher should understand each child and provide a flexible program with a variety of materials for experimentation. He is fully aware that young children are naturally and normally creative; thus he is alert to the spontaneous creative activity that is usually in evidence. These children enjoy playing with words and creating chants and jingles for all occasions. For example, upon returning from the pet shop there may have been a singing conversation based on the familiar 5 365 3 chant, the teacher singing, "What did you see?" and individual children singing an answer, "I saw a puppy," (or some other animal) in a variety of ways. The teacher may have continued the singing conversation with other questions such as, "What did it say?" and the child answering, "It said 'bow wow.'" Each child could be asked to describe the pet he liked best, telling in his own words the movements and sounds it made. One such description could be, "Soft, soft kitty-cat walked, walked, walked." The children could say these words together to learn them and to feel their rhythm, and eventually the teacher might ask if they thought they could sing it instead of speaking it. From attempts at this, the following melody could result.

KITTY CAT

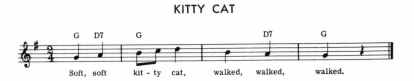

As such a melody is learned, there can be experiences for uncertain singers and in playing on the bells and piano the tones 1 2 345, which accompany the words "Soft, soft kitty-cat," and the tones 3 2 1, which accompany the words "walked, walked, walked." Eventually children can sing such a song as they walk, and pretend they are kittens. Sometimes part of a class may sing while other children imitate kittens. Other words developed in the same way could be the following:

Tone-matching and bells on "quack, quack, quack"; tone-matching on "Little duck":

LITTLE DUCK

LITTLE DUCKY WADDLES

Imitate "waddle" and play on bells and piano:

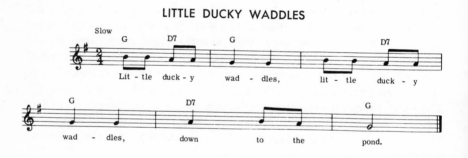

Imitate "run" and play on bells and piano:

RUN, BABY CHICK

Tone-matching, bells, and piano:

ANIMAL TALK

Jump:

LITTLE FROG

After further discussing the eating habits and the homes of the animals they have seen, the children may be interested in developing similar word-phrases and songs about these things.

Bells and piano on scale:

RABBITS EAT LETTUCE

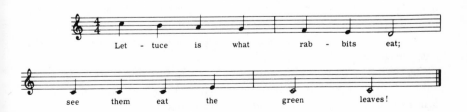

Tone-matching on "singing":

BIRD IN A CAGE

The following song was created by children to inform the children in another first-grade room of an event that took place in the life of one of their pets, a white rat. Notice the change of meter, which adds to the drama of the situation.

A SURPRISE

First Grade
Frances Willard School
Eugene, Oregon

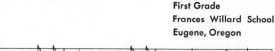

A list can be made of the pets the children saw, and songs about these pets can be found in the music series books for first grade by referring to classified song lists in the indexes. However, it is not enough that these songs be concerned with pets; they must be musically worth while as well, and should conform to the suggestions made concerning the selection of materials in Chapter Three, page 47.

The children may write additional verses for some of these songs and add impersonations, dramatizations, rhythmic movements, percussion instruments, and keyboard instruments when suitable.

After a visit to a farm home, children may be interested in larger pets such as ponies, goats, lambs, pigs, and calves. Experiences involving fundamental movements such as running, trotting, and galloping can result from children's observations. Concepts of high and low in pitch can be made meaningful in terms of imitating the sounds of animals. Concepts of heavy and light can be clarified in terms of dramatizing the movements of animals and be sounded with appropriate percussion instruments. Simple rhythms of animal names can be spoken, played on percussion instruments, and responded to with bodily movements. Examples: horse, horse (walk, walk), chick-en, chick-en (run run run run).

Free rhythmic expression can come from children's responses to selected recordings and piano compositions played by the teacher. A few examples of recordings are: The Decca Album *Animal Pictures in Music,* some of the Phoebe James *Animal Rhythms,* "Hens and Roosters" from *Carnival of the Animals* (Saint-Saëns), "Ballet of the Unhatched Chickens" from *Pictures at an Exhibition* (Mussorgsky), and selections from Victor Rhythm Album I. Examples of piano compositions are found in series books for kindergarten and first grade.

Needless to say, there are infinite possibilities resulting from the use of recordings and from piano compositions. The titles of many of these bear no relation whatever to pets or animals, yet their musical and rhythmic content may be fitting to stimulate creative rhythmic expressions about the pets being studied. Through bodily responses the children can increase their comprehension of such elements as loud, soft, high, low, restful, exciting, light and heavy. They can discover music to which they can walk, run, gallop, and they can learn to identify certain types of music such as the march and the lullaby. They can find by listening that certain parts of the music repeat while other parts are different, that some music tells a story while other music may tell only of a mood, a rhythm, or a melody, and that some musical instruments can be identified. Some children may bring in recordings having to do with pets. However, since six-year-olds are by nature active listeners in a physical sense rather than analytical listeners in an intellectual sense, the creative experience of these children is more valuable to them than their growth in abstract musical knowledge.

A source of other activities is the physical education manual published by most state departments of education, from which appropriate exercises and games can be selected. Examples of exercises may include prancing horses, the cat walk, and the rabbit hop, and examples of games may include those such as bird catcher, ducks fly, and lame fox and chickens. Singing games can be found in music series books.

VII. Anticipated Outcomes

A. Culminating Activities

A culminating activity does not necessarily have to come at the end of a unit; it may take place at the close of any phase of a unit. These activities are usually presented in the classroom for the children themselves, for another class, or for parents. Sometimes they are given in the school auditorium for a larger group of children and parents. Possible types of culminating activities for a unit on pets may include:

1. A pet show.
   (a) A display of experience stories, poems, and songs, with illustrations.
   (b) Announcers.
   (c) A pet parade with rhythm band playing a march for children and their pets. (Some children might be dressed as pets.)
   (d) Singing songs about pets, employing dramatization, and percussion-instrument and bells accompaniments when suitable.
   (e) Displaying pets and telling about their eating habits, how their health and safety may be protected, and the types of homes in which they live.
   (f) Singing games, action songs, and a demonstration of rhythms created to describe various pets.
   (g) Class singing an appropriate concluding song.
   (h) Announcers thanking audience for their attendance and attention.
2. An original play that includes songs, percussion-instrument and bells accompaniments to appropriate songs, rhythms, and singing games both from books and from among those created by the children.
3. An "open house" to show various activities done in connection with pets, displaying creative stories, poems, and songs, television rolls made by the children, pictures, booklets, pets modeled from clay and papier-mâché, and live pets.

VIII. Anticipated Learnings

A. An increased understanding of the child's relation to pets in the basic needs of air, water, food, shelter, and gentle care.
B. An attitude of kindness toward animals.

C. A better understanding of the characteristics of some animals and their habits.
D. A comprehension of how animals are protected by nature.
E. A broader understanding of the importance of cooperation in planning, initiating, and evaluating group activities.
F. Growth in personality adjustment evidenced by:
   1. A greater willingness of the individual child to assume his share of responsibilities.
   2. An appreciation of the work of others.
   3. An improvement in attitudes necessary for efficient working with others.
      (a) A desire to observe work standards agreed upon by the group.
      (b) Consideration of the rights of others.
      (c) Taking turns in group work.
      (d) Caring for materials and sharing them.
      (e) Taking and giving criticism in good spirit.
G. A greater feeling of security in self-expression through art, music, rhythms, and language activities.
H. More curiosity about the surrounding environment and the life in it.
 I. Evidence of increasing skill in:
   1. Helping to make plans, solving problems and completing projects.
   2. Using time and materials wisely.
   3. Listening attentively.
   4. Thinking critically about the solution of problems and experimenting toward that end.
   5. Reading a variety of materials with enjoyment and understanding.
   6. Using a variety of sources of information to find answers to problems: excursions, letter-writing, speakers, films, books, pictures, and observation.
   7. Learning effective oral and written communication.
   8. Using number concepts to solve problems in meaningful situations.
   9. Singing, playing instruments, responding rhythmically to music, listening to music, and creating music.

The next unit is designed for use in grades five or six. As in the preceding unit, the sections other than the one concerning music are not expanded.

A UNIT IN SOCIAL STUDIES FOR FIFTH OR SIXTH GRADE

HOW DO PEOPLE LIVE IN MEXICO?

I. Introduction

As indicated on page 331, the major emphases in the social living area for grades five and six are on problems of the community, state, and nation, and their relationship to equivalent problems in other countries. Therefore the geographical and economic relationships of the United States and Mexico as neighbors aid in the motivation of learning in this unit. The increasing incidence of American travel in Mexico gives added color, interest, and meaning to this popular topic.

II. Purposes

A. To find out how Mexico of today compares with early Mexico.
B. To find out the relationships existing between the United States and Mexico.
C. To develop a growing understanding of the problems of the Mexicans and their similarity to those found in the United States.
D. To develop an appreciation of Mexican art, music, and dance.
E. To develop in the child increased ability in:
  1. Working together by sharing, planning, initiating, and evaluating activities.
  2. Preparing and giving oral reports.
  3. Using effectively a variety of materials and sources of information.
  4. Thinking critically and using facts to solve problems.
  5. Expressing oneself through the media of creative arts—art, writing, music, dance, and dramatics.
F. To develop skills in:
  1. Reading for enjoyment and information: maps, fiction, references.
  2. Participating effectively in discussions.
    (a) Making thoughtful comments.
    (b) Listening courteously.
  3. Expressing ideas effectively through writing.
  4. Music, by means of related activities.
  5. Art, by means of related activities.
  6. Dance, by means of related activities.

III. Suggested Approaches

    A. Arrange an attractive display or exhibit on bulletin board, wall, or table:
        1. Pictures of Mexico.
        2. Books and articles about Mexico.
        3. Mexican dolls, serapes, rebozos, sombreros, leather, pottery, weaving, and silver handicrafts.
    B. Show films.
    C. Invite a speaker to discuss life in Mexico, including music and art.
    D. Discover how much the children know about music in Mexico; have them list what they want to learn about music in Mexico; note misconceptions that should be corrected before the unit is completed.

IV. Suggested Content

    A. History and culture—Indian, Spanish, Mestizo.
    B. Geographical and climatic conditions.
    C. Products, resources, and industry.
    D. Mechanization and transportation.
    E. Living conditions in Mexico.
    F. Education, religion, and customs.
    G. Political, religious, and special holidays and festivals.
    H. The future of Mexico.
    I. Art and handcrafts.
    J. Music and dance in fiestas, religious and political ceremonies and celebrations. One of the most important experiences children have in social studies is learning to plan as a group. In planning the learning that should result in relation to this phase of the unit, the teacher should first discover how much children already know about Mexico, and list on the chalkboard questions they would like to have answered. He will make careful note of the misconceptions the children may have that must be corrected before the completion of the unit.

        Questions children might have that relate to music are as follows: What do the Mexican people do for entertainment? What types of entertainers are there in Mexico, and how might we demonstrate their activities? In what ways can we express work in Mexico? What is a fiesta? What fiestas, political and religious ceremonies and celebrations do they have in Mexico? How can we find out about these? What do people wear to fiestas? Could we dramatize activities of worship such as pilgrimages to shrines and lighting candles? What are some native dances and their origins? Why do some dancers wear masks? Where do they get their ideas for the designs on their costumes? What films and recordings would help us to understand music and dance in Mexico? Can we have a fiesta? Can we collect or make Mexican instruments such as castanets, tambourines, drums, flutes, and maracas? Can we dramatize breaking the piñata and *Las Posadas* (the re-enactment of Mary and Joseph going from house to house seeking shelter)? Who are some famous Mexican musicians, composers, and artists? Is Mexican music different from ours?

Songs from the series books and other sources should be used when they serve to enrich activities of the unit. For example, in the study of the fiesta, appropriate music and dances are essential and integral parts of the study. When the Mexican Christmas is taken up, a piñata can be constructed in arts and crafts, and a song and dance can be created to be used with it. Authentic Mexican folk songs depict the Mexican way of life in the same way that other authentic folk songs depict life in other parts of the world. Songs can be found or created that tell of the Mexican's food, clothing, transportation, holidays, customs, occupations, religion, superstitions, poverty, recreation, feelings and emotions. Mexican dance, music, and art are related in their color, rhythm, and spirited character. Songs and dances have significant meaning when they are a part of the problem-solving activities of the unit.

Songs such as "Carmen Carmela," "The Jarabe," "Cielito Lindo," "La Raspe," "La Cucaracha," and others are commonly found in series books. "La Golondrina" ("The Swallow") is a particular favorite of the Mexican people, and is often used to close meetings. With these songs, the series books suggest activities such as dancing from stated directions or with modified or created steps, making instruments, playing rhythms, part-singing, chording on guitar or autoharp, developing percussion scores, singing descants, creating harmony parts, listening to related recordings, and studying Mexican Christmas and fiesta music and customs. Other activities could include painting colorful pictures to illustrate selected recordings of authentic Mexican music, listening to the music of Carlos Chavez and other Mexican composers, dramatizing a Mexican legend (including authentic or original rhythm patterns, flute playing, and dances), and studying and evaluating the guitar as an important Mexican and Spanish instrument, including listening to recordings of Segovia and other famed concert guitarists.

Characteristic Mexican dances include the following. "Chiapanecas" has as its subject the beauties in nature. Girls' costumes are embroidered with flowers and colorful fruits; boys wear sashes and brilliantly colored neckerchiefs on white suits. "La Cucaracha" has as its leading figure a poor cockroach who cannot walk fast because of his lack of spending money. "Dance of the Little Old Man" ("Los Viejecitos") requires endurance and control of muscles. It is danced by strong young men who wear masks to make them appear old. "La Huapanga" is the most popular dance. It is a major recreational outlet for working people, who plan to dance it every eight days in larger cities. "El Jarabe" has courtship as its subject. The costumes are elaborately Spanish. It is featured in Mexican Independence Day celebrations and all Mexican school children know it. "La Pluma" derives its name from a headdress of feathers worn by the dancers, who reflect the warlike days of the conquistadors and Montezuma.

V. Suggested Activities in Other Areas

    A. Language Arts

        1. Report on visits to Mexico, films seen, and materials read.
        2. Discuss pictures.
        3. Plan a round-table discussion on life in Mexico.
        4. Discuss outstanding Mexicans of the past and present.
        5. Learn new words and how to use them.
        6. Write invitations and thank-you notes to speakers.
        7. Write requests for travel information.
        8. Write and present original plays dealing with aspects of Mexican life.
        9. Write stories and poems.
      10. Give oral and written reports.
      11. Explain the processes used in weaving, pottery making, leather work, and metal work.
      12. Explain how to prepare tamales, frijoles, and tortillas.
      13. Give book reports.
      14. Present oral and written summaries of films seen.
      15. Write letters to pen pals in Mexico.
      16. Organize a story hour, sharing stories about Mexico.

    B. Research and Use of the Community to Solve Problems

        1. Use books, magazines, maps, and bulletins to find answers to questions.
        2. Bring books, maps, and magazines from home to share.
        3. Read graphs and charts.
        4. Invite people from the community to speak to the group about Mexico.

5. Show films, film strips, and slides.
6. Visit a museum.
7. Plan and participate in an interview with people who know about Mexico.
C. Art and Handicrafts
1. Paint pictures of Mexican activities, landscapes, and architecture.
2. Make a mural representing Mexico.
3. Make a class book containing art each child produces.
4. Make dresses and dress dolls in Mexican style.
5. See films on arts and crafts in Mexico.
6. Construct a model of a Mexican village.
7. Weave rugs, serapes, belts.
8. Mold Mexican pottery and paint designs.
9. Construct dioramas and motion-picture and television boxes for rolls containing drawings of Mexico.
10. Draw and make maps of Mexico from papier-mâché, sawdust or salt.
    (a) Political
    (b) Physical
    (c) Climatic
    (d) Products
    (e) Minerals and industry
11. Draw pictorial maps showing distribution of population.
12. Make articles from leather, silver, and other metals, and weave baskets.

VI. Culminating Activities

A. Invite another room or parents to a program, which may include:
1. Mexican music and dances learned from the music series books or created by the children, using percussion instruments and costumes both collected by the children and made by the class.
2. An original play (which may include music and dances).
3. Children dressed in Mexican costumes who serve tea to parents, with Mexican music as background atmosphere along with Mexican art.
4. Exhibition and description of articles from Mexico.
B. Invite another group to hear a planned class discussion about about life in Mexico.

VII. Suggested Outcomes

A. Increased knowledge and understanding of Mexico's problems and Mexico's contributions to the world.
B. Development of an understanding and appreciation of Mexico's place as our neighbor.
C. A greater knowledge and understanding of Mexican music and art.
D. Increased efficiency in the ability to:
   1. Work democratically by sharing, planning, initiating, and evaluating activities.
   2. Prepare and present written and oral reports.
   3. Use effectively a variety of materials and sources of information.
   4. Think critically and use facts skillfully in the solution of problems.
   5. Express ideas through creative media such as art, music, dance, dramatics, and writing.
E. Development of increased skill in:
   1. Reading and organizing research materials.
   2. Participating in discussions.
      (a) Sharing ideas.
      (b) Listening attentively to others.
      (c) Critically evaluating information presented.
      (d) Writing effectively.
F. Generalizations resulting from the music activities of the unit.
   1. All people express the same physical and psychological needs through music.
   2. Man's music is the result of his own basic needs and of the influence of his environment.
   3. The problems man faces in meeting his needs are reflected in a country's culture and its music.
   4. The mingling of cultures affects the music of peoples.
   5. Music affects the daily living of all people.
   6. People who live in isolated places live simply, and this simplicity is reflected in their music. People who live in complex societies live a more complex life, and this is reflected in their music.
   7. Religion is one of the strong forces that have influenced the music of mankind.

In conclusion, music is at the very heart of education and world citizenship. How better can a child see that all of us are more alike than different than through the appeal of music the world over? This is a human approach to social living and one of the vital tools of social studies. It is easy to establish a common ground of understanding through emotional channels. Here is where music applies, because it is truly a force that binds all people together, showing that we have common human problems and desires. These are the things of which music speaks, transcending barriers of geography, language, and color of skin. A glimpse into the geography and climate of Finland is afforded the listener as he hears Jan Sibelius' *Finlandia,* for it speaks of the bold, stark strength and bleakness of the land itself. Its solidarity depicts a people of great vigor in a land of physical features that have demanded much in the adjustment of its people. History, too, is told in a country's music.[1] A glance into the stories of the origins of our country's discovery, exploration, and patriotism, and an account in song of such historical events as the life of the pioneers, the Westward movement, the gold rush to California, the machine age and its work songs, the lives of people in servitude, and the wars and their music are excellent examples. No study of any period of history is complete without an understanding of the art that speaks of the deepest concerns and problems of life in a language that all can understand. The world is a vast stage upon which mankind is endeavoring to form ever increasing harmonious relationships.

THINGS TO DO

1. Find related music and literary works that can be used at the elementary school level. Possible sources include the books by Ruth Tooze and Hazel Kinscella listed under References below.

2. For the elementary education major: Select a unit suitable for the grade level of your choice. Develop it according to the general pattern found in this chapter, selecting suitable music and music activities.

3. For the music education major: Develop a unit for music classes to explore such questions as: "What are the various kinds of waltzes?" "What are the various kinds of marches?" "How does music express weather and seasons?" "How does music express animal life?" In these units, use relationships to science, history, art, the dance, and literature to motivate and enhance the study of music. An excellent reference that illustrates how music specialists and classroom teachers can work cooperatively with units is *Music in the Social Studies, Grade Six,* a 1958 publication of the State Department of Public Instruction, Raleigh, North Carolina. For example, when the social studies unit is concerned with the contributions of primitive people, suggestions and

---

[1] Adapted from *Elementary Music: Grades I–VI.* Austin, Texas: Austin Independent School District, 1961, p. 54.

sources are given for activities in music such as collecting and constructing primitive instruments, developing drum vocabulary for communication, and writing rhythmic patterns of this means of communication.

4. Examine the indexes for the different music series books and report
   their usefulness for the teacher who is using music in other curricular
   areas.

5. Examine the catalogs of educational recordings published by such com-
   panies as the Children's Music Center, 5373 W. Pico Blvd., Los Angeles
   19, California (50¢); Children's Reading Service, 1078 St. John's Place,
   Brooklyn 13, New York; The Greystone Corporation, 100 Sixth Ave.,
   New York 13, New York; Folkways Records, 121 W. 47th St., New York
   36, New York; The Harrison Catalogs, 274 Madison Ave., New York 16,
   New York; RCA-Victor Records, 155 East 24th St., New York 10, New
   York, and evaluate their usefulness.

6. A repetitive rhythm for Chinese songs in 4/4 meter is as follows:
   ♩ ♫ 𝄾 ♪♩ . Select percussion instruments, arranging them from
   low to high in pitch so that each instrument selected plays one beat
   in this rhythm pattern as the pitch ascends. Try this with a Chinese
   song or with an improvised pentatonic tune on the black keys of the
   piano.

7. Tune the strings of a psaltery to the Japanese *Koto* scale: the pitches c,
   d, e-flat, g, and a-flat. Then create your idea of Japanese songs using
   these pitches.

REFERENCES AND MATERIALS

BOOKS

Elliott, Raymond, *Teaching Music Methods and Materials for Elementary Schools.* Columbus, Ohio: Charles E. Merrill Books, Inc. Pages 195–312 relate to social studies in
grades five and six.

Jarolimek, John, *Social Studies in Elementary Education.* New York: The MacMillan
Company, 1959. Pages 347–50.

Kinscella, Hazel, *The Kinscella Readers,* 2nd ed. Lincoln, Nebraska: University Publishing Company, 1949. Books from the second- to eight-grade levels.

Lyons, John H., *Stories of Our American Patriotic Songs.* New York: Vanguard Press,
1942.

Myers, Louise, *Teaching Children Music in the Elementary School,* 3rd ed. Englewood
Cliffs, N.J.: Prentice-Hall, Inc., 1961. Chapter 12, "Music's Role in Understanding
Other Peoples."

Peterson, Frederick A., *Ancient Mexico.* New York: G. P. Putnam's Sons, 1959. Chapter 9, "Song and Dance." Describes ancient musical instruments.

Stevenson, Robert M., *Music in Mexico.* New York: Thomas Y. Crowell Co., 1953.

Sur, William R., et al., *This Is Music,* Book Five. Boston: Allyn and Bacon, Inc., 1962.
Pages 18–161 reflect the history of the United States in song.

Tooze, Ruth and Beatrice Krone, *Literature and Music as Resources for Social Studies.*
Englewood Cliffs, N.J.: Prentice-Hall, Inc., 1955.

Suggested
Grade Level

Bowmar Educational Records, 10515 Burbank Blvd.,
North Hollywood, California
Albums
    Songs of Home, Neighborhood and Community   1-3
    Holidays and Seasons
    Folk Songs of the U.S.A., Folk Songs of Many People, Latin American   4-8
    Folks Songs, Folk Songs of Canada, Folk Songs of Our Pacific Neighbors,
    Folk Songs of California and the Old West, North American Indian
    Songs, Children's Songs of Mexico
Dance Albums
    Mexican Folk Dances, Canadian Folk Dances, Album 4 *(Around the*   4-8
    World), Album 5 *(American),* Album 6 *(Latin American)*
Foreign Language Study
    Songs for the Spanish Class, Songs for the French Class, Sing and   3-6
    Speak Spanish (5 albums)

Children's Music Center, Inc., 5373 W. Pico Blvd., Los Angeles 19, California

The catalog of this company lists recordings, books, and filmstrips that relate to astronomy and space, science of sound, weather, geography, climate, animals, foreign language study and other categories.

Children's Record Guild and Young People's
Records, The Greystone Corporation,   *Suggested*
100 Sixth Ave., New York 13, New York   *Grade Level*

Individual disks
    "Fog Boat Story" (transport)   1-3
    "Jump Back, Little Toad" (safety)   K-3
    "Ship Ahoy" (transport) (dramatization)   2-5
    "Build Me a House" (social studies)   1-3
    "Creepy Crawly Caterpillar (nature)   K-3
    "Little Pedro in Brazil" (social studies)   4-6
    "Pedro in Argentina" (social studies)   4-6
    "Going West" (westward movement)   3-6
    "Folk Songs for Orchestra" (social studies) (Russia)   3-6
    "Chisholm Trail" (westward movement)   2-6
    "Daniel Boone" (westward movement)   2-6
    "Working on the Railroad" (transport)   2-5
    "By Rocket to the Moon" (astronomy)   2-6
    "Timber-r-r" (occupations)   3-6
    "Pony Express" (westward movement)   3-6
    "Christopher Columbus" (exploration)   1-6
    "Around the World" (modes of travel)   N-1
    "Yankee Doodle" (westward movement)   2-6
    "Let's Be Policemen" (occupations)   K-2
    "Peter the Pusher" (manners)   N-1
    "The Singing Water" (nature and science)   1-4
    "Let's Play Together" (co-operation)   N-2
Albums
    Children's Almanac (12 disks on seasons)   1-8

America the Beautiful (history and legend)	2–6
Places and Things (science and social studies)	K–4
Cowboys and Indians	1–4
Trains, Planes and Ships (transportation)	K–3
Animals (The World Around Us)	K–3

Columbia Recording Corporation,	*Suggested*
1473 Branum Ave., Bridgeport, Connecticut	*Grade Level*

Columbia World Library of Folk and Primitive Music
Individual 12″ disks   5–12
Irish Folk Songs,
African Music from the French Colonies,
English Folk Songs,
French Folk Songs,
Australian Aboriginal Songs and Songs from the Eastern New Guinea,
Folk Songs from Scotland,
Indonesian Music,
Canadian Folk Music,
Venezuelan Folk and Aboriginal Music,
Bantu Music from British East Africa,
Folk Music from Japan,
Indian Folk Music,
Spanish Folk Music,
Yugoslav Folk Music

Decca Records, Inc., 50 West 57th St.,
New York 19, New York

Albums
Songs of Safety (safety)   1–3

Enrichment Records, 246 Fifth Ave.,
New York 1, New York

Albums
Pocahontas and Captain John Smith,   4–6
Daniel Boone: The Opening of the Wilderness,
The Winter at Valley Forge,
Sam Houston: The Tallest Texan,
Voyages of Christopher Columbus,
Landing of the Pilgrims,
California Gold Rush,
Riding the Pony Express,
Paul Revere and the Minute Men,
Our Independence and the Constitution,
Building the First Transcontinental Railroad,
Wright Brothers: Pioneers of American Aviation,
Explorations of Père Marquette,
Lewis and Clark Expedition,
Monitor and the Merrimac,
Lee and Grant at Appomattox

Folkways Records, 121 W. 47th St., New York 36, New York

The catalog *Folkways Records in Music Education* lists authentic folk   K–8
music, ethnic music, music appreciation, and music history, with descriptive information on each album.

Neil A. Kjos Music Company, 525 Busse Highway,
Park Ridge, Illinois

Albums (in French and German)
Chantons en français! (two albums)
Singen wir auf Deutsch! (two albums)

Oak Publications, 121 W. 47th St., New York 36, New York

Publishers of folk songs of America and of the world, including those of the present
day, and of a folk song magazine, *Sing Out!*

Peripole, Inc., 51–17 Rockaway Beach Blvd.,
Far Rockaway 91, Long Island, New York

Supplier of *Sound Kits* and *Musikits* for units concerned with the science of sound.

FILMS

Shelter, Donald J., *Film Guide for Music Educators*.
Washington 6, D.C., Music Educators National Conference,
1201 16th St. N.W., 1961

Indexes of 16 mm. films: *Ballet and Folk Dance, American Music, Music of Other
Lands, Holiday Music,* and *Visual Interpretation of Music.* See pp. 68, 72. This
valuable reference describes and rates each film, and recommends its use in specific
subject areas at specific age levels.

MUSIC AND DANCE BOOKS

Boni, Margaret Bradford, *Fireside Book of Folk Songs.* New York: Simon and Schuster,
Inc., 1947.
Botsford, Florence Hudson, *The Universal Songster.* New York: G. Schirmer, Inc., 1937.
Duggan, Anne, Jeanette Schlottmann, and Abbie Rutledge, *Folk Dances of the British
Isles; Folk Dances of European Countries; Folk Dances of Scandanavia; Folk Dances
of the United States and Mexico; The Teaching of Folk Dances.* New York: A. S.
Barnes and Co., 1948.
Grant, Louise, *A Child's World,* Books 1 and 2; *Your Book of Poems and Art Songs,*
Books 1 and 2. Rockville Centre, New York: Belwin, Inc. For primary grades, with
implications for religious-ethical education and social studies.
Karpeles, Maud, ed., *Folk Songs of Europe.* London: Novello, 1956. Authentic folk
songs edited for the International Folk Music Council.
Krone, Beatrice Perham, *Janet and Jerry on the Farm; Come, Let Us Make a Garden;
Songs of Travel and Transport.* Park Ridge, Ill.: Neil A. Kjos Music Company.

Krone, Beatrice and Max, *Songs from the Four Corners; Songs of Norway and Denmark; Songs of Sweden and Finland; Spanish and Latin American Songs; Inter-Americana; Songs of Many Lands; Folksongs of Brazil; Mexican Folk Songs; Songs and Stories of Our American Indians.* Park Ridge, Illinois: Neil A. Kjos Music Company, 1941–1959.

Krugman, Lillian and Alice Ludwig, *Little Calypsos.* Far Rockaway, New York: Peripole, Inc., distributors, 1955. Songs and stories about the West Indies, with instructions for writing calypsos.

Landeck, Beatrice, *Echoes of Africa in Folk Songs of the Americas.* New York: David McKay, Inc., 1962.

Luther, Frank, *Americans and Their Songs.* New York: Harper & Row, Publishers, 1942.

Niles, John Jacob and Helen Louise Smith, *Folk Ballads for Young Actors.* New York: Holt, Rinehart & Winston, Inc., 1962.

Rhorbough, Lynn, ed., *Songs of Many Nations,* and many other song books, some of them dealing with specific nations and peoples such as *Folk Songs of Austria,* and similar booklets concerned with Africa, Asia and the Pacific, Latin America and the Caribbean; *Play Party Games of Pioneer Times; Treasures from Abroad* (folk dances); *The Folk Dance Set.* Delaware, Ohio: Co-operative Recreation Service, Inc.

Seeger, Ruth Crawford, *American Folk Songs for Children; Animal Folk Songs for Children.* New York: Doubleday & Co., Inc., 1948, 1950.

Chapter Twelve
PERFORMING FOR AUDIENCES

Many programs presented by elementary school children are comprised of related or integrated activities that include or stress music as an important aspect. To make music for others is one of mankind's oldest interests and is a prime motivator for learning. The term "program" is used to denote many types of presentations from a unit-culminating activity done by boys and girls for themselves in their own classroom to a festival-type affair encompassing the entire school or groups of schools and presented before large public audiences. Other programs are school assemblies, concerts, special day programs, song plays (original or published), radio and television presentations, simple programs in which one class invites another to share its interests and accomplishments, and instrumental recitals.

Programs should be organized for specific educational purposes and therefore should have high educational value. They should be logical culminations of interesting daily activities, not something unrelated to normal experience. Children should enter into the planning along with teachers and administrators. Good programs inform parents of the purposes of the music program and the activities through which purposes are achieved. They should reveal the children's musical growth and development. For example, one program presented to parents by a first-grade class was in five parts. The titles of the five sections were:

1. We *hear* and *sing* sounds and give them names and numbers.
2. We find sounds on a *staff*.
3. We do things with *rhythm*.
4. We find sounds on the *keyboard*.
5. We sing and *interpret*.

A second-grade class organized its program this way:

1. We *hear* and *sing* sounds.
2. We find sounds on a *keyboard*.

3. We *listen* to appreciate.
4. We *read* sounds on the staff.
5. We learn to *read* a new song.
6. We sing and *interpret*.

Under each of the headings were songs and activities selected from daily classroom experience through which the children could share their musical progress with their parents.[1]

It is entirely possible that pressures from school and community can result in programs that are contrary to good educational practice. Should this occur, the teacher should strive to orient parents and others in the types of program that are, and are not, justifiable from the standpoint of education. Neither children nor teachers should be exploited. Children's interests and development should come first; they should not be sacrificed for dubious entertainment or public relations values.

Since an important reason for the existence of programs is the value they have in building feelings of confidence, security, and belonging, all children should appear in them whenever possible. When it is impossible for every child to take part, perhaps scheduling two performances with alternate casts might remedy the difficulty. When there is no solution to this problem, the class should choose those of their number whom they wish to represent them.

To find songs relating to specific types of programs the teacher should refer to classified indexes of series books, and specialized song books dealing with Christmas, folk songs, singing games and dances, songs of specific nations and peoples, and types of part-singing. Such books are often exhibited at professional conventions and can be purchased at music stores and educational supply houses. Public libraries are another source.

Costumes should be kept simple and inexpensive. Whenever possible, they should be made by the children in school. When parents are assigned this responsibility, unhappiness can result from some children being underdressed or overdressed by comparison with others. When the children are dressed simply and identically (as much as the performance permits), this problem is minimized.

Large-scale programs are apt to interrupt the normal school day. When such programs are contemplated, teachers and administrators should decide whether their educational values are great enough to offset the losses due to interruption of normal class activities.

Although good performance is a worthy goal, too much emphasis on drill and "perfection" can destroy spontaneity and joy. Such programs are not worth the placing of children and teachers in an atmosphere of tension and emotional disturbance. A happier situation comes from an

---

[1] St. Frances Cabrini School, Tacoma, Washington.

atmosphere of calm encouragement and relaxed enjoyment, stemming from well-laid plans organized by the children and teachers. After all, the major consideration should be what is happening to the boys and girls. This is often overlooked when adult standards of performance are mistakenly sought.

Programs presented for and by children in primary grades should be brief, with 30 minutes as a maximum length. Those presented for and by children in intermediate grades are ordinarily limited to not more than one hour. A trend has been in evidence toward shorter programs than were once presented in elementary schools, and it can be added that many parents are averse to lengthy presentations. Perhaps the competition of television has spurred the trend toward brief and fast-moving programs for adults as well as for children. The most common faults of school presentations are (1) they are too lengthy, (2) the action is too slow-moving, (3) the children's speaking voices cannot be heard by the audience.

Although the emphasis today is to place educational values uppermost in school programs, entertainment values need not be shunned, for the one does not eliminate the other. The best programs are probably those in which educational and entertainment values are so well combined that they are inseparable.

Programs that include a number of classrooms require joint faculty planning and co-operation. One teacher explains,

> In our school the fifth-grade teacher, the art teacher and the music teacher plan a tentative program which is submitted at the next teachers' meeting for discussion. After changes have been made and it is acceptable to all concerned, each teacher selects a project or part of the program to work out with her class. The music teacher is the co-ordinator, the fifth grade teacher handles the speaking parts, and the art teacher takes care of props and stage. Classroom teachers are responsible for their own class's part in the whole program. We try to let every child "in on the act" whether it be in the chorus, participating in pantomimes, stagework, props, lighting, costumes, speaking parts, ushers, and publicity so that everyone feels that he has had a part. Parent help also aids in developing a closer tie with the home, and it can improve public relations.

PROGRAMS RESULTING FROM CULMINATION ACTIVITIES

This type of program has been discussed in Chapter Eleven. It represents a contemporary trend toward programs that grow directly out of normal classroom activities and that convey to parents the learning that has taken place, revealing growth not only in subject-matter skills but in all areas—especially in democratic processes and emotional security. The following song was written by children for such a program, the culmination of a unit on clothing.

MY RAYON COAT

Fourth Grade
Kilby Training School
State Teachers College
Florence, Alabama

I have a ray-on coat,— as cute as cute can be, but to wear it in a boat would be sil-ly as you see,— so just to make it right,— I'll leave it home to-night and— wear in-stead my bright lace and ny-lon be-ret.—

PROGRAMS FOR SPECIAL DAYS

Special-day programs include Thanksgiving, Christmas, Lincoln's Birthday, Valentine's Day, Washington's Birthday, Easter, and others. Con-

HALLOWE'EN FUN

Ravinia Fifth Grade
Highland Park, Illinois

On the ee-rie night of Hal-lo-we'en, we are sure to meet a scar-y scene, the trees are sway-ing to and fro, the witch-es lan-terns are a-glow, it's beg-gar's night, you're sure to know!   BOO!

tributing to such programs are appropriate songs and dances from the music series books and from supplementary sources including those from among the songs and dances created by children. Original scripts and plays can be much more meaningful than set plans found in books and magazines, yet much good can come from the creative adapting of such material by children and teachers to better fill their own needs. The song on page 357 was written by a fifth-grade class for its Hallowe'en program.

The most important special-day programs are ordinarily those at Christmas time. They have two general aspects, the sacred and the secular, the latter having to do with the fun and gaiety of holiday good fellowship, Santa Claus, and the exchange or the giving of presents. The most common type of program is probably the one that relates the singing of Christmas songs to a script read by one or more readers. This has the advantage of being one of the easier types to prepare, but the disadvantage of being without action. It usually offers fewer opportunities for creative effort than some of the other types of programs. An examination of the titles of Christmas programs presented over a period of years in a large city system yielded the following kinds of programs and titles of plays:

Those presented and attended by entire schools, by intermediate grades, by primary grades, or by individual rooms
Customs and carols of many lands
Original play with carols and dances
Tableau with choric reading, carols, and choral music (possible themes: the Nativity, Christmas around the world, Christmas cards)
Dramatized carols
Contrasting holy day and holiday
Carols and dances
Carols and shadow plays
Hanukkah and Christmas
Combined singing, instrumental music, and drama
The Nutcracker Suite with dances, singing, and orchestra
Christmas cantata
Operetta, "Santa Claus Is Coming to Town"
Band and choral music with tableau
A carol sing
Creative rhythms, songs, and dances
Favorite songs of the holiday season

Plays:
  Why the Chimes Rang
  Dickens' Christmas Carol
  Birds' Christmas Carol
  Night before Christmas
  Spirit of Christmas
  No Room at the Inn
  Christmas Blessing

Magi's Gift
Littlest Angel
Melody of Christmas
Man Who Found the King

FESTIVALS

Elementary school music festivals are held most frequently in the spring, and thus are often considered a culminating project that is a logical outgrowth of the school year's work in music. A festival implies a large number of participants. Advantages of the festival include the thrill of participating in large groups, the uniting of many teachers and students in one project, and the opportunity to display progress in music to the school and community. Disadvantages include children tiring of the music in repeated rehearsals, the near absence (in many situations) of creative elements, and the lack of democratic elements due to dictatorial direction impossible to avoid in most large festivals. The selecting of songs is ordinarily done by the classroom teachers. For example, the third-grade teachers and their pupils agree upon the songs they want to sing, thus making a higher standard of co-operation likely than when a music director dictates the list of songs. However, no list of songs can suit every third-grade group and, while the majority of the children may be well served by the selection, there will always be those who find the songs too difficult or too easy. As in the case of other large-scale programs which sometimes disrupt the normal school day, teachers, children, and administrators should evaluate each festival carefully to determine whether the results are worth the effort involved. It is likely that the music festival's educational value for children is greater in small school systems than in large systems. For example, a four-room rural school or one city elementary school can conceivably produce a festival with many original and creative aspects, while a large city or county festival may become a routinized end within itself rather than an avenue that opens the door to further musical growth.

Many festivals bear no title except general ones such as "All City Music Festival" on "Spring Music Festival." Others have titles or even slogans or themes such as "This is Music!" "Make Your Life More Musical," "Music Enriches Life," "A Montana Ranch Corral," "Pioneer Times," "Music, a Universal Language," "Music for Every Child, Every Child for Music," "The Old South," "Music Through History," and "Music of the Americas." In some localities, games are included with music to make the spring festival a "play day" for children.

Operettas. The elementary school operetta has the advantage of any activity that requires the working together of many teachers and children, such as developing a spirit of unity in the school, furthering the ability of children to work together in groups, and developing individual personalities—but the disadvantages have outweighed these if the frequency of programs of this type is a reliable criterion. Teachers have found a shortage of suitable material; few children's voices are capable of singing leading roles; there is often little opportunity found for creative aspects; the rehearsing of the leading parts can result in the neglect of the other children; and too much time may be required to prepare the operetta properly for public performance. Tiny original "operettas" are found today in some unit-culmination programs, thus illustrating the fact that it is possible for children to write their own small-form operettas.

When a teacher presents a program he must consider such aspects as the space necessary in which to present it; the space necessary for seating the expected audience; the time it will require to rehearse the program; the means of publicity; whether or not admission is to be charged, and if admission is charged, how the tickets are to be distributed and sold; whether there will be an announcer or a printed or mimeographed program; and if risers and other special equipment are necessary. The piano should be placed so that the accompanist and director can see each other and so the performers can hear it distinctly. After the program the teacher should evaluate it with the children.

THINGS TO DO

1. Select a type of public program, develop it, and list the administrative details involved in its presentation. How will you involve the children in its planning and execution? What is the learning you would expect to result from this program?

2. Attend elementary school music programs and evaluate them.

3. Plan a song-play with a music or social studies subject. Sketch the action and spoken lines; select and create the music.

4. Plan a special-day program to be presented by the children for themselves in their classroom. Then plan how it might be expanded to include parents as both audience and participants.

5. Listen to and evaluate children's concerts on radio and television.

6. Attend a children's concert given by a symphony orchestra or other adult professional group. Evaluate its effectiveness in terms of educational and social values.

REFERENCES AND MATERIALS

Murray, Josephine and Effie Bathurst, *Creative Ways for Children's Programs*. Morristown, N.J.: Silver Burdett Company, 1938.

Mursell, James L., *Music in American Schools*. Morristown, N.J.: Silver Burdett Company, 1953. Chapter 11, "Public Performance."

Pierce, Anne E., *Teaching Music in the Elementary School.* New York: Holt, Rinehart & Winston, Inc., 1959. Chapter 12, "Special School Programs."

MUSIC FOR CHRISTMAS PROGRAMS

Coleman, Satis N. and Elin Jorgensen, *Christmas Carols from Many Countries.* New York: G. Schirmer, Inc., 1934.

Dearmer, Percy, Ralph Vaughan-Williams and Martin Shaw, *Oxford Book of Carols.* New York: Oxford University Press, 1928.

Gearhart, Livingston, *A Christmas Singing Bee.* Delaware Water Gap, Pennsylvania: Shawnee Press.

Grime, William, *New Songs and Carols for Children.* New York: Carl Fischer, 1955.

Heller, Ruth, *Christmas, Its Carols, Customs and Legends.* Minneapolis: Schmitt, Hall & McCreary Company, 1948.

———— *Christmas 'Round the World,* Books I and II. Evanston, Ill.: Summy-Birchard Company, 1962.

Krone, Beatrice and Max, *Descants for Christmas.* Park Ridge, Ill.: Neil A. Kjos Music Company, 1949.

Kvamme, Torstein O., *The Christmas Carolers' Book in Song and Story.* Minneapolis: Schmitt, Hall & McCreary Company, 1935.

Nye, Virginia and Lois Gurske, *Julenissen: The Christmas Elf,* and other authentic folk tales, customs, songs and dances from Norway, Holland, England and Austria. Middleton, Wis.: Modern Productions, Inc., 1962.

Perham, Beatrice, *Christmas, Its Origins, Music & Traditions.* Park Ridge, Ill.: Neil A. Kjos Music Company, 1937.

Seeger, Ruth Crawford, *American Folk Songs for Christmas.* New York: Doubleday & Company, Inc., 1953.

Simon, Henry W., *A Treasury of Christmas Songs and Carols.* Boston: Houghton Mifflin Company, 1955.

Vernon, Mary Strawn, et al.: *Descants on Christmas Carols.* Minneapolis: Schmitt, Hall & McCreary Company, 1952.

FILMSTRIPS

Christmas Celebrated in Song. 1345 Diversey Parkway, Chicago 14, Ill.: Society for Visual Education, Inc. Two filmstrips, recording, and teacher's manual. Useful for group singing.

Story of the Nutcracker. Same source. Filmstrip, recording, and guide. 32 minutes. Tchaikovsky's *Nutcracker* Suite.

Chapter Thirteen
EVALUATING ELEMENTARY SCHOOL MUSIC

When the major goal of music teaching became to instill in children a lifelong love and appreciation of music rather than to implant an exact knowledge of symbols and terms of music notation, objective grading of pupil achievement became practically impossible. Subjectively, by observation, teachers can state whether or not a particular child has such characteristics as a growing confidence in use of the singing voice and musical instruments, a consistent desire to take part in various musical activities, a growing skill in using and interpreting notation, an enthusiasm for music, the ability to take part in activities appropriate for his individual maturity, and an expanding knowledge of music and musicians. Sometimes grades are estimated by considering these factors. Some music educators suggest that keeping an anecdotal record of each child's reactions is as good a method as any on which to base grades subjectively. Dykema and Cundiff[1] write of a method of grading whereby each child is rated according to his musical potentialities and his musical attainment in seven categories (five areas of music activities, also music notation, and "home and social arts") on a scale of 1 to 5, with 5 excellent, 4 above average, 3 average, 2 below average, and 1 poor. This results in two columns of seven numbers. The total of the potentialities column is divided by the total of the attainments column to find the grade.

Since the majority of teachers realize that grades can be a serious

_____

[1] Peter W. Dykema and Hannah M. Cundiff, *School Music Handbook,* new ed. (Evanston, Ill.: Summy-Birchard Publishing Co., 1955), p. 298.

psychological barrier between the child and his love of music, they usually try to avoid giving them. When they are compelled to do so by traditional grading systems, they tend to give high grades. When grades must be given, it is recommended that teachers do their best to collect evidence of pupil progress (such as the ancedotal record suggested above) or devise some system as Dykema and Cundiff suggest in order to attempt to explain to children and parents as exactly as possible how grades are determined.

Since there has existed for some time a trend toward abolishing traditional grading, it is hoped that it will not be long before all teachers will be relieved of grading children by letters or numerals. Music is a particularly revealing area in which to illustrate the futility of trying to make accurate evaluations of children's achievement because the aim of music education is something that cannot be measured in any precise way. It is to instill in children a love of music with the long-term result that the growing individual becomes developed aesthetically and emotionally, more refined morally, uplifted spiritually; his life is otherwise enriched by having music as a life-long interest and source of relaxation and inspiration. How progress in this kind of development can be represented by numbers or letters on report cards is likely to remain an unanswered question.

There is another kind of evaluation, not for individuals, but indicative of the progress of a class as a group. In some intermediate grades a committee of children may keep notes on all music activities during each day. These notes are compiled weekly and kept in a notebook or wall chart. This is so organized that it can be useful for review purposes, useful also as a summary of the types and amount of music activities during the year, and constitutes something that can be given to next year's teacher along with other cumulative records for the purpose of providing continuity in the music program.

It should be kept in mind that evaluation should be an integral part of all musical activities. It may be an important part of the motivation, the procedure, and the conclusion of a daily lesson, a year's music program, or of an entire school's music program, grades 1–6. Evaluation is based upon or related to the degree of realization of the stated purposes of the lesson or program, and thus is a continuous process. It implies planned, sequential development of all aspects of a balanced music program and therefore its results become a basis for improving the quality of musical learning.

EVALUATIVE CRITERIA

It is a popular procedure in education today to draw up check-lists of criteria by which to attempt to measure the degree of effectiveness of any given area of instruction. It is agreed that effective instructional programs are possible only when school personnel intelligently evaluate both the purposes of programs and the means by which these purposes are to be realized. In American education this evaluation may involve teachers, principals, supervisors, children, and parents. Many of the criteria suggested below are general, thus some will refer to all grade levels while others will refer to some and not to others. Each criterion is to be followed by an evaluation of either *yes*, *no*, or *to some degree*, and these choices are to be followed by specific *plans for improvement*.

Activities and procedures in the classroom: *yes*   *no*   *to some degree*   *plans for improvement*

are selected in terms of the developmental levels of the children.

are presented in a manner through which the children understand clearly the purposes of the activity.

are developed in ways that actively involve the children.

provide opportunities for children to "learn by doing."

are sequentially planned so that children achieve the satisfaction of definite degrees of mastery of skills.

foster enjoyment, understanding, and skills.

provide for individual differences.

are based upon knowledge of human growth and development.

relate to present-day life in the home, community, and world.

provide for aesthetic, emotional, and intellectual development.

sometimes have their origins in related areas of instruction, and sometimes stimulate interest in related areas.

assist in developing good personalities.

assist in understanding all mankind.

The child's musical growth is measured by:

his favorable attitude toward music.

his musical discrimination and taste.

his appreciation of aural beauty.

his use of music out of school.

his progress in singing.

his progress in playing.

his progress in rhythmic response.

his progress in listening skills.

his acquisition of a musical repertoire of value that is appropriate to his developmental level.

the maximum development of his musical talents at a given time.

his ability to analyze how music produces moods, emotions, descriptions, beauty, and intellectual concepts and forms.

his ability to solve musical problems through understanding and using the components of music.

his ability to use notation.

his ability to evaluate his performance heard on a tape recorder.

his ability to participate satisfactorily in group activities requiring co-operation and self-discipline.

his ability to understand and use music vocabulary.

his ability to sing his part in two, or three-part songs.

his knowledge of instruments of the orchestra, their special characteristics and uses.

his interest in outstanding performers, composers, and conductors.

his knowledge of the larger musical forms.

his ability to perform musically both individually and in small and large groups.

The teacher of music:

is well prepared to teach the subject.

knows the purposes of music instruction.

understands and enjoys music, and is enthusiastic about it.

recognizes that children have varying interests and talents which are furthered through emotional, social, and intellectual contacts with music.

participates professionally in efforts to improve both his teaching skills and the music program of the school.

participates in community efforts to raise musical standards and to provide musical opportunities.

knows the materials of instruction.

knows the various activities appropriate for the children he teaches.

has adequate facility on the piano.

understands music as an important part of man's cultural heritage.

can follow a logical sequential program of music instruction.

can teach a balanced music program with its varied activities.

continually evaluates the results of his teaching.

The elementary school music program:

is accepted as an integral part of general education for every child.

is a balanced program, with a variety of activities.

is a well-planned and sequentially organized program.

has a well-qualified staff.

is supported by adequate materials of instruction.

is recognized as basic to the secondary school music program.

is being continuously evaluated in its scope, sequence, and balance by teachers, principals, supervisors, parents, and children.

is a co-operative endeavor of classroom teachers, music specialists, principals, and parents who are working together to improve the musical education of children.

has general and specific purposes that have been co-operatively established.

utilizes community resources such as adult performers, concerts, television and radio.

The elementary principal makes sure that:

the teaching staff is well-qualified to teach music.

the teaching staff is interested and enthusiastic in its music teaching.

the teaching staff has a good knowledge of the materials, equipment, and activities involved in teaching music.

the teaching staff has adequate piano facility.

the teaching staff is constantly evaluating and improving its music teaching competency.

the teaching staff co-operatively plans a music program that is organized logically, consistently, and sequentially.

the music specialist is professionally oriented, is a member of the Music Educators National Conference, and attends its professional meetings.

there are two or more sets of music series books available in each classroom.

the record players are of a quality that reproduces music of maximum aesthetic appeal.

an ample number of autoharps, bell sets, pianos, percussion instruments and other items of equipment are supplied.

each child has the opportunity to develop musically to his maximum capacity.

the children demonstrate aesthetic quality in their musical performance.

the children show evidence of discovery, creativity, and sensitivity in their approach to music.

the children reveal evidence of using knowledge of the components of music to solve musical problems.

the children learn to use musical terms and the symbols of notation.

the children reveal ability to perform music individually, in small groups, and in large groups.

the music room is acoustically adequate, has necessary storage space, is properly lighted, heated, ventilated, and has sufficient office facilities.

adequate time is provided for music in the schedule.

the music program reflects the enjoyment and enthusiasm of children, teachers, and parents.

the music program reflects pride, dignity, and respect.

the music program is doing its full share in fulfilling the educational purposes of the school.

there is evidence that the program relates to music in the home and community, and that it is a positive force in raising the cultural level of the community.

public musical performances are planned for educational purposes and values, not for exploiting children in the name of public relations.

THINGS TO DO

1. Examine courses of study in music published by city, county, and state educational agencies to learn what provisions are suggested for evaluation and to what extent evaluations are made in terms of purposes.

2. Invite a guest speaker who is a director of music, a music supervisor, or an elementary principal to discuss how his music curriculum is evaluated and how improvements are made as a result of evaluations.

3. Arrange to observe a teacher teach a class in music, and discuss with him his evaluative techniques for improving his teaching effectiveness.

REFERENCES AND MATERIALS

Andrews, Francis M. and Clara E. Cockerille, *Your School Music* Program. Englewood Cliffs, N.J.: Prentice-Hall, Inc., 1958. Chapter 19.

Jones, Archie N., *Music Education in Action*. Boston: Allyn and Bacon, Inc., 1960, pp. 345–54. Measurement in music education; Grades and grading

Pierce, Anne E., *Teaching Music in he Elementary School*. New York: Holt, Rinehart & Winston, Inc., 1959, pp. 32–36, 196–7.

Shane, Harold G. and E. T. McSwain, *Evaluation and the Elementary Curriculum*, rev. ed. New York: Holt, Rinehart & Winston, Inc., 1958. Chapter 13.

Wiles, Kimball, *Teaching for Better Schools*. Englewood Cliffs, N.J.: Prentice-Hall, Inc., 1952. Chapter 14.

Chapter Fourteen

THE TEACHER'S ROLE IN THE PROFESSION AND IN THE COMMUNITY

DUTIES OF THE MUSIC SPECIALISTS

The music specialist in city and county school systems works with teachers and children in planning music activities for the classroom and school programs. He helps teachers select suitable music for units of work in which music has a part. He may do demonstration teaching; introduce new activities, materials, and equipment; and teach any phase of the program that needs his assistance; and he may teach regularly in a classroom from two to five days a week. Sometimes he acts as a resource person who locates special materials needed by teachers. He may prepare lists of source materials to help teachers find appropriate music and recordings quickly and easily. He frequently acts as an agent for the teacher in arranging for people to come to the class room or the school auditorium for special musical demonstrations or performances. He offers expert aid to the uncertain singer and helps provide special opportunities for the gifted child. He suggests activities that the retarded child can do with satisfaction. He is sometimes a special music teacher who is helping prepare a classroom teacher to take eventual responsibility for music teaching.

Although music consultants comprise a small minority of specialists, the consultant is an important concept in supervision. The consultant plans with the teacher who requests his assistance, then presents a demonstration lesson to help meet his needs. He gives individual instruction to teachers who desire such aid. When he is asked to observe a classroom teacher teach music, he does not take notes because this is poor psychology from the standpoint of both children and teacher. Instead, he has an early conference with this teacher before important items are forgotten. He usually watches the children, not the teacher, to find out how effective the teaching is. He helps teachers and children evaluate their progress in music.

When he works with teachers who have not taught music before, he finds one thing they can do well, and advances from there. He finds subtle ways to feature the excellent teacher of music to show others that "it can be done," and he encourages intervisitation as an important type of in-service training. He never forgets that genuine interest and friendship, not coercion, form the foundations for modern supervision. He knows that each classroom teacher is *an individual* with talents, interests, and problems that make him, to some extent, different from any other teacher. Therefore, his aid is planned on an individual basis much of the time. To do this effectively he should know each teacher well, and he should not be assigned too large a number of teachers to assist. Although there has been established no exact number of teachers for which a music consultant should be responsible, it has been stated that he should be expected to aid *no more than* 75 in a full-time position. He should frequent the classroom and know the children.

The consultant plans teachers' meetings with great care. Immediately after school in the afternoon is the most common time for such gatherings, and the drinking of coffee may help to restore some energy to tired teachers who are psychologically at the close of their work day. The content of the meeting should be co-operatively planned and the consultant should strive to cover only a comparatively small amount of material—but to cover it thoroughly. A common fault is attempting to treat too many things in a given time. There are many possible purposes for such teachers' meetings. Some of them are the planning of public programs and school-wide programs, helping the teachers of a specific grade level with common problems, helping a group of teachers who express special interest in learning a specific activity or skill, solving scheduling problems, demonstrating new materials and equipment, selecting new materials such as music series books and supplementary books, and orienting teachers new to the school.

Another duty of the consultant is aiding teachers in the use of audio-visual materials. This may include guidance in locating illustrative materials for bulletin boards, use of bells as an audio-visual aid, use of the record machine and recordings, use of the tape recorder in music teaching, use of various film and slide projectors, and use of radio programs and the planning of live ones. The consultant evaluates commercial radio, television, and films for school use, and evaluates the new educational and children's recordings which are constantly being placed on the market. He may prepare special bulletins on audio-visual aids. These may contain help in the teachers' preparation for class listening to radio programs and viewing of television programs and films.

An additional responsibility is to recommend materials for the school library as well as for the teachers' resource library.

The music specialist works closely with administrators, for he knows that if school principals do not understand and support the music program and help him and other teachers plan it, there will seldom be united faculty opinion or action for music. Consequently there must be planning with administrators and conferences with them throughout the school year so that they are fully informed and have a positive, favorable attitude toward the music program. Working with the administration in preparation of the music budget, inventory, and scheduling is another important phase of the specialist's duties unless a supervisor or a director of music has these responsibilities.

He seeks ways to guide teachers into college courses and workshops that will aid their musical growth. He often plans with college staffs to help make possible such courses and summer session classes. He may provide workshops in which he directs the activities for teachers at the beginning of the school year. He may also arrange for helpful visitations by the music education consultants employed by publishers of music series. He provides leadership for music education.

When a music teacher is assigned to teach music as a special subject and thus has no official responsibility to help classroom teachers, he finds that he is unable to do his best for music without taking upon himself many of the duties of the consultant. Although his time is limited, he will offer friendly aid to classroom teachers and he will be actively interested in expanding the use of music by all of the teachers. It will be to his advantage to be able to relate some of the music he uses to the units of work being carried on in the various classrooms. The closer the relationship he establishes between himself and the classroom teachers, the more help he will be able to receive from them with regard to knowledge about the children under his instruction. He needs such help because he may teach several hundred children and thus might know them only superficially while each classroom teacher may have no more than 30 and thus should know them well. Since each needs the assistance of the other, there should always be close co-operation between them in order to provide the best education in music for the children.

DUTIES OF THE CLASSROOM TEACHER

One of the most quoted statements concerning the competence necessary for classroom teachers to teach music was made by Burmeister[1]: a

---

[1] C. A. Burmeister, *Basic Concepts in Music Education,* 57th Yearbook, National Society for the Study of Education, ed. Nelson B. Henry. (Chicago: University of Chicago Press, 1958), p. 226.

positive attitude toward teaching music; ability to use the singing voice accurately and with reasonably pleasant quality; functional piano facility; ability to teach rote songs; knowledge of the elements of notation; basic knowledge about voices and instruments; a repertoire of good songs suitable for the level taught; and a knowledge of fine music literature to draw on for resource material. Others have stated that the classroom teacher is essential to any music program, and that he has natural advantages in such respects as the use of music for informal situations—rest, relaxation, and recreation; in units of work in other areas of the curriculum; in the teaching of rhythmic and dance activities; and in social education and personality development. The implication of the preceding statement is that the music program might be one in which a form of team teaching is utilized. The classroom teacher would be responsible for the parts of the music program that he is adequately prepared to teach, and the music specialist would teach the parts of the program beyond the classroom teacher's scope.

As has been indicated earlier, the responsibility of the classroom teacher in teaching music ranges in different school systems from responsibility to no assigned responsibility. While the exact proportion of children who obtain all their instruction in music from classroom teachers is not known, it has been estimated at a number as high as 70 per cent in some states. In any case the dedicated classroom teacher is not content to teach without music. Even though a school district may consider music a special subject to be taught by a special music teacher, the classroom teacher continues to accept certain responsibilities. He participates with his children when the specialist comes, aids him and learns from him. Since this classroom teacher draws upon music at any time it is needed during the school day, he is in effect a music teacher even though official responsibility in this instance happens to rest with the music specialist.

The classroom teacher who is completely responsible for teaching music has all the responsibilities discussed in this book. They are similar in many ways to those of the music specialist. In some schools this teacher can obtain assistance from specialists when he needs and asks for it, something it is his professional duty to do. Since he is the music teacher, it is also his duty to achieve musical competence in teaching the subject to children. Therefore he helps plan teachers' meetings called for the purpose of improving music instruction, and he attends these meetings; he works closely with the available music specialist; he works with committees to evaluate and improve instruction; he helps represent music in the community; he works with administrators and parents for the improvement of the program; he attends appropriate college courses; and he may take private lessons.

PROFESSIONAL ORGANIZATIONS

The professional music specialist is a member of the Music Educators National Conference.   The Conference is the largest subject matter division of the National Education Association.   Since its organization meeting in 1907 it has grown to a membership of approximately 40,000 music education teachers and student members in colleges and universities.   It heads a number of subsidiary organizations, commissions, and special committees.   The MENC publishes the *Music Educators Journal,* the *Journal of Research in Music Education,* and a large number of books and pamphlets.   It has biennial conventions, alternating years with the conventions of its six regional divisions.   The Music Teachers National Association, formed in 1876, is an important association of private music teachers.   However, many college music teachers and music educators are members.

Teachers become members of such professional organizations in order to contribute their ideas and efforts to improving the profession, the quality of music programs, and the competence of the individual music teacher.   Such organizations serve to assist in the improvement of every aspect of the music program for children.

THE PLACE OF PARENTS IN THE MUSIC PROGRAM

Since the pre-school years of children have been found to be exceedingly important to their later musical growth, and since teachers have become aware of the great importance of the home environment of children throughout their school years, parents and teachers have become increasingly concerned with working together to arrange the best learning environment for children.   Even though few parents are reluctant to visit the school, it is often necessary for teachers to take the first steps in building a relationship in which home and school can co-operate for the good of the children.   This is done in various ways including parent-teacher conferences; parent-teacher-pupil conferences; report card comments; informal reports; musical programs for parents; explanations of the music program at PTA and Room Mother meetings that include information on how parents can help children at home; and including talented parents as demonstrators of aspects of music in the classroom.   The good teacher realizes that he does not know the child fully until he knows the parents and the home environment also.

When parents understand the purposes and activities of the music program and the values of music for their children they usually become strong allies of music education.   Since the musical environment of American children begins at birth, not in the kindergarten, it is important that mothers and fathers know the significance of singing to babies, be advised on how they can assist children to learn to sing in tune, and be informed about recordings, instruments, books, and music recommended for home use. For example, a book such as *Singing With Children* (Wadsworth Publishing Company, 1962) might be the basis for a lecture-demonstration or even a series of demonstrations in which the teacher takes the part of the parents and the parents take the part of children as the purposes and uses of songs are discussed. Subjects such as how to help the uncertain singer, the importance of rhythmic responses and how to assist rhythmic development, listening to and discussing recordings for children, and a discussion of radio and television programs of musical value to children are of great interest to parents. One of the most frequently asked questions of parents is, "How can I help at home?" They want to know what their children are learning in music and appreciate demonstrations with the children that clarify this.

Private teachers of piano form an important part of music in the community. When parents ask teachers to recommend a piano teacher for their children, it is not professionally advisable openly to recommend one above the others. To avoid singling out one, the teacher may suggest that the parent investigate by talking with other parents whose children take lessons from certain teachers. Another way of answering is to list several teachers, mentioning the preferred teacher first—without stating this preference. Still another is to recommend a method of piano instruction without mentioning names of teachers who use the method. Piano teaching has improved rapidly, and the private teacher often starts younger children in social groups that engage in many of the same activities they encounter in the schoolroom. Effective teachers of piano give increased attention to the child's learning to play music which is interesting, challenging, meaningful and purposeful to him, and he is given frequent opportunities to share his progress with others. Thus, this private piano teacher, the parents, and the school music teacher have much in common. They should recognize this and work together to enhance the musical learning of children.

THE COMMUNITY

The quality of the music program in American schools is the business of the entire community, and it is a continual part of the work of the teacher of music to provide the community with constructive reminders of this. It has been mentioned earlier that in the United States parents assist in the teaching of children at home, and the citizen in general assists in evaluating educational programs and helping to establish policies. This is true not only because it is part of our democratic heritage to include everyone in community projects but because in this country education is the province of the state governments, not the federal government. This has resulted in the delegation of much power by the state to the local communities, i.e., boards of education. This local authority is unique in a world in which education is the province of national governments, and in which communities have little or no control over the schools their children attend. Thus, American education is subject to many pressures of immediate public opinion not felt by the educational systems of other nations. To maintain stability it is therefore essential that members of boards of education be persons of high educational stature, and even more essential that teachers and administrators work closely with the community so that the citizenry has a part in establishing school policies, so that it is kept fully informed about educational values and problems, and so that it supports sound educational policy. If this is not the case, then music or any other area of the curriculum is in constant danger of being suppressed, neglected, or eliminated. It is also true that a curricular area can be overemphasized by unwise popular demand. Thus every school teacher must of necessity be an active member of the community, and must continually explain educational purposes and values and how these are implemented in order for them to be realized for the children. Besides teaching the children he must keep the community informed and co-operative so that a balanced educational program of quality can exist. *Quality teaching* is paramount, for the best public relations medium is the child who is a happy, satisfied learner of music and who reveals this unmistakably to his parents and to the community. Second, there must be a constant flow of information into the community about the music program, its educational values, and its place in a balanced curriculum. American communities will support quality education for their children; they will not continue to support substandard programs; they want either improvement or eventual elimination of them. Because music has sometimes been mistakenly called a peripheral area, it may have more need for this type of community work than some of the other subjects, and music teachers must give much time, thought, and effort to this. An agency that can be of assistance in establishing community music councils and in widening the use of music generally in the community is the American Music Conference, 332 South Michigan Avenue, Chicago 4, Illinois. This concern is sponsored by the music industry and provides printed materials, films, advice, and a professional field staff at no charge to assist personally in school, industrial, and community music efforts.

Community music resources should never be neglected. There are adults who can perform for children, helping to create greater interest in music in school and community. It is especially fine when a family group can perform, with parents and their children showing others how they make music together in their home. Some adults specialize in folk music of various countries and may appear in costume and with native instruments. Through such performances children can learn of the music of other cultures and more about world understanding. Teachers should compile a file of such resource persons in the community.

Teachers and parents should provide the leadership needed to improve the musical environment of the community by working together with the program directors of radio and television stations to establish higher musical standards in these mass media. In the United States many of the radio stations currently rated highest in listener appeal are those that operate an automated 24-hour playing of the "top 40 tunes" over and over again. Since these 40 tunes are largely of the "rock and roll" type, these radio stations are at virtually the lowest musical level in the community. The problem is a serious one, involving the question of which radio stations should be supported by listening audiences in the home. While rock and roll has its place, it is a small place indeed in our musical culture. Our children deserve far better music than the repeated belaborings of three chords, and they are far too intelligent to accept such music if parents and teachers will make it possible for them to come in contact with music of more interest, appeal, and value. Children's musical tastes are not innate; they must be cultivated. Therefore teachers and parents must strive to surround them with music of a significantly high cultural level by planning a variety of worth-while music activities with children that include listening to recordings, radio, television, and live concerts of quality.

THE FUTURE OF ELEMENTARY MUSIC EDUCATION

The future of music in the elementary school depends upon the recognition of the values of music in general education and upon the competence of those assigned to teach it. No beginning teacher is *fully* prepared to teach any subject. Most experienced teachers say that they feel they learned more in their first year of teaching than they did in their four years of college preparation. Therefore, let us grant that the art of teaching is continually a learning situation for the teacher, and that the good teacher is continually striving to be a better teacher each successive year that he teaches. It is fair to state that the musical preparation of the classroom teacher in teacher-training institutions is generally limited, and that most classroom teachers require the friendly aid and encouragement of music supervisors if they are to become successful teachers of music. Consequently, there is a pressing need for in-service training in music for elementary classroom teachers.

There is no doubt that many school systems have provided insufficient numbers of music specialists to help classroom teachers improve their teaching. Inadequacy of college preparation combined with inadequate in-service aid has resulted in failures. This has caused some persons to doubt the wisdom of permitting classroom teachers to teach music, and voices have been raised that call for a return to music as a special subject taught exclusively by specialists. It is the opinion of the writers of this book that college courses in music education have improved in content, manner of approach, and effectiveness and that many school administrators have seen the necessity for additional music specialists to assist classroom teachers. They also realize that the present quality of elementary school music teaching needs great improvement. It is hoped that every classroom teacher who reads these words is dedicated enough to be anxious to do his part to justify the confidence placed in his ability, for he is the person best able to teach music effectively if he is prepared to do it.

It has been found that only a minority of classroom teachers of elementary school music have accomplished their task successfully.[2] The primary cause of the majority's failure is asserted to be the lack of good music programs in the elementary schools these teachers attended when they were children. College teachers seeking to remedy this deficiency have been greatly handicapped by the fact that musical proficiency requires sequential development over a span of years.

The shortage of elementary school teachers in the 1940's and 1950's resulted in the employment of teachers who lacked musical competence for self-contained classroom positions. A general collapse of effective music supervision aggravated the deterioration of many music programs, along with the failure of some school systems to remedy this by employing specialists to teach children music in cases where the classroom teacher could not. Thus, inadequate music programs have continued to produce prospective classroom teachers who fear teaching music and may never be able to attain the quality of music teaching necessary to impart its values to children. There is little doubt that the best person to teach music is the classroom teacher who is musically competent. However, the application of this concept in situations where teachers lack musical competence has resulted in what is probably the most obvious failure of the self-contained classroom organization plan, and in the resurgence of music as a special subject taught by music specialists in an effort to rebuild elementary music programs that have fallen into decay.

The most effective elementary school music program will be taught co-operatively by music specialists and classroom teachers, *all* of whom are musically competent, prepared to teach music, understand and enjoy children, and are provided with a large variety and amount of quality

---

2 Nye, Robert E., *Music for Elementary School Children.* Washington, D.C.: Center for Applied Research in Education, Inc., 1963.

materials of instruction. Every teacher, parent, and citizen should help in the effort to gain for America's children a high-quality balanced program of education that assures the aesthetic, creative, emotional, social, and intellectual development of children, who are our future.

THINGS TO DO

1. Write to the American Music Conference, 332 South Michigan Avenue, Chicago 4, Illinois, for information concerning the organization of community music councils, and the stimulation of community interest in and support of music.

2. Write to the Music Educators National Conference, 1201 Sixteenth Street N.W., Washington 6, D.C., for information about student membership, professional membership, the services of the organization, and it many publications.

3. Evaluate the daily program of a typical radio or television station from the point of view of our musical culture.

4. Organize a panel discussion or symposium on the subject, "Criteria for Programing Radio and Television Music." The speakers might include students, parents, radio and television program directors, and citizens-at-large.

5. Form a committee to discuss the quality of music coming from a selected radio station and agree on definite opinions and recommendations. Then call on the manager of the station and discuss these with him. Remember that some stations deserve compliments, and that these should be given when due. Write letters of commendation as well as letters that suggest needed improvements, and send them to radio and television stations.

6. Formulate a questionnaire to be sent to children's homes to inform you of the musical activities and materials that exist in the home so that you can have a basis on which to build a music program for the children.

REFERENCES AND MATERIALS

Benn, Oleta A., "Excellence in Elementary Music Programs," *Music Educators Journal*, November–December, 1962, pp. 34–8, 59.

Davis, Ennis, *More Than a Pitchpipe.* Evanston, Ill.: Summy-Birchard Publishing Co., 1941. A book for the music major.

Graham, Floyd F., *Public Relations in Music Education.* New York: Exposition Press, 1954.

Morgan, Russell V., *Music, a Living Power in Education.* Morristown, N.J.: Silver Burdett Company, 1953. Chapter 11, "Community Activities and Relationships."

Nye, Robert E., *Music for Elementary School Children.* Washington, D.C.: Center for Applied Research in Education, Inc., 1963. Chapter 8, "Selected Issues and Related Research."

CODE OF ETHICS FOR THE TEACHING PROFESSION[1]

WE, THE MEMBERS of the National Education Association of the United States, hold these truths to be self-evident—

—that the primary purpose of education in the United States is to develop citizens who will safeguard, strengthen, and improve the democracy obtained thru a representative government;

—that the achievement of effective democracy in all aspects of American life and the maintenance of our national ideals depend upon making acceptable educational opportunities available to all;

—that the quality of education reflects the ideals, motives, preparation, and conduct of the members of the teaching profession;

—that whoever chooses teaching as a career assumes the obligation to conduct himself in accordance with the ideals of the profession.

As a guide for the teaching profession, the members of the National Education Association have adopted this code of professional ethics. Since all teachers should be members of a united profession, the basic principles herein enumerated apply to all persons engaged in the professional aspects of education—elementary, secondary, and collegiate.

First Principle: The primary obligation of the teaching profession is to guide children, youth, and adults in the pursuit of knowledge and skills, to prepare them in the ways of democracy, and to help them to become happy, useful, self-supporting citizens. The ultimate strength of the nation lies in the social responsibility economic competence, and moral strength of the individual American.

In fulfilling the obligations of this first principle the teacher will—

(1) Deal justly and impartially with students regardless of their physical, mental, and emotional, political, economic, social, racial, or religious characteristics.

(2) Recognize the differences among students and seek to meet their individual needs.

(3) Encourage students to formulate and work for high individual goals in the development of their physical, intellectual, creative, and spiritual endowments.

---

[1] *NEA Handbook for Local, State, and National Associations* (Washington: National Education Association of the United States, 1954), pp. 361–3.

(4) Aid students to develop an understanding and appreciation not only of the opportunities and benefits of American democracy but also of their obligations to it.

(5) Respect the right of every student to have confidential information about himself withheld except when its release is to authorized agencies or is required by law.

(6) Accept no remuneration for tutoring except in accordance with approved policies of the governing board.

Second Principle: The members of the teaching profession share with parents the task of shaping each student's purposes and acts toward socially acceptable ends. The effectiveness of many methods of teaching is dependent upon co-operative relationships with the home.

In fulfilling the obligations of this second principle the teacher will—

(1) Respect the basic responsibility of parents for their children.

(2) Seek to establish friendly and cooperative relationships with the home.

(3) Help to increase the student's confidence in his own home and avoid disparaging remarks which might undermine that confidence.

(4) Provide parents with information that will serve the best interests of their children, and be discreet with information received from parents.

(5) Keep parents informed about the progress of their children as interpreted in terms of the purposes of the school.

Third Principle: The teaching profession occupies a position of public trust involving not only the individual teacher's personal conduct, but also the interaction of the school and the community. Education is most effective when these many relationships operate in a friendly, cooperative, and constructive manner.

In fulfilling the obligations of this third principle the teacher will—

(1) Adhere to any reasonable pattern of behavior accepted by the community for professional persons.

(2) Perform the duties of citizenship, and participate in community activities with due consideration for his obligations to his students, his family, and himself.

(3) Discuss controversial issues from an objective point of view, thereby keeping his class free from partisan opinions.

(4) Recognize that the public schools belong to the people of the community, encourage lay participation in shaping the purposes of the school, and strive to keep the public informed of the educational program which is being provided.

(5) Respect the community in which he is employed and be loyal to the school system, community, state, and nation.

(6) Work to improve education in the community and to strengthen the community's moral, spiritual, and intellectual life.

Fourth Principle: The members of the teaching profession have inescapable obligations with respect to employment. These obligations are nearly always shared employer-employee responsibilities based upon mutual respect and good faith.

In fulfilling the obligations of this fourth principle the teacher will—

(1) Conduct professional business thru the proper channels.

(2) Refrain from discussing confidential and official information with unathorized persons.

(3) Apply for employment on the basis of competence only, and avoid asking for a specific position known to be filled by another teacher.

(4) Seek employment in a professional manner, avoiding such practices as the indiscriminate distribution of applications.

(5) Refuse to accept a position when the vacancy has been created thru unprofessional activity or pending controversy over professional policy or the application of unjust personal practices and procedures.

(6) Adhere to the conditions of a contract until service thereunder has been performed, the contract has been terminated by mutual consent, or the contract has otherwise been legally terminated.

(7) Give and expect due notice before a change of position is to be made.

(8) Be fair in all recommendations that are given concerning the work of other teachers.

(9) Accept no compensation from producers of instructional supplies when one's recommendations affect the local purchase or use of such teaching aids.

(10) Engage in no gainful employment, outside of his contract, where the employment affects adversely his professional status or impairs his standing with students, associates, and the community.

(11) Cooperate in the development of school policies and assume one's professional obligations thereby incurred.

(12) Accept one's obligation to the employing board for maintaining a professional level of service.

Fifth Principle: The teaching profession is distinguished from many other occupations by the uniqueness and quality of the professional relationships among all teachers. Community support and respect are influenced by the standards of teachers and their attitudes toward teaching and other teachers.

In fulfilling the obligations of this fifth principle the teacher will—

(1) Deal with other members of the profession in the same manner as he himself wishes to be treated.

(2) Stand by other teachers who have acted on his behalf and at his request.

(3) Speak constructively of other teachers, but report honestly to responsible persons in matters involving the welfare of students, the school system, and the profession.

(4) Maintain active membership in professional organizations and, thru participation, strive to attain the objectives that justify such organized groups.

(5) Seek to make professional growth continuous by such procedures as study, research, travel, conferences, and attendance at professional meetings.

(6) Make the teaching profession so attractive in ideals and practices that sincere and able young people will want to enter it.

CLASSIFIED LIST OF SONGS FOR COMMUNITY SINGING

OPENING SONGS

Hail, Hail, the Gang's All Here (using appropriate words)
S-M-I-L-E
He's a Jolly Good Fellow
Pack Up Your Troubles
Vive l'Amour
Hello Song (*Singing in Harmony*, p. 22)

SENTIMENTAL SONGS

Let Me Call You Sweetheart
When Your Hair Has Turned to Silver
Moonlight and Roses
When Irish Eyes Are Smiling
When I Grow Too Old to Dream
My Wild Irish Rose
There's a Long, Long Trail
Keep the Home Fires Burning
Till We Meet Again
Let the Rest of the World Go By
The Bells of St. Mary's
I Want a Girl Just Like the Girl that Married Dear Old Dad
Shine On, Harvest Moon

GAY NINETIES SONGS

A Bicycle Built for Two
Sidewalks of New York (East Side, West Side)
When You and I Were Young, Maggie
In the Shade of the Old Apple Tree
That Old Gang of Mine
After the Ball Is Over
School Days
In the Good Old Summertime
The Band Played On

FUN SONGS

Polly Wolly Doodle
Old MacDonald
The Camptown Races
The Horses Run Around (Go Get the Axe)
I've Been Workin' on the Railroad
She'll Be Comin' Round the Mountain
Little Tom Tinker (action song: stand and sit when singing "Ma-a")
John Brown's Baby (action song. Tune: Battle Hymn of the Republic)
Oh! Susanna
Cindy

FOLK SONGS OF OTHER LANDS

Marianina (Italian)
Weggis Walking Song (Swiss)
Came a Riding (Czech)

The Little Ole (Norwegian)
Over the Meadows (Czech)
Marching to Pretoria (Dutch South African)
All Through the Night (English)
Vrenily (Swiss)
Stellenbosche Boys (Dutch South African)
Alpine Morning (Swiss)
Cielito Lindo (Mexican)
Waltzing Matilda (Australian)
Santa Lucia (Italian)
Drink to Me Only with Thine Eyes (English)
John Peel (English)

ROUNDS

White Coral Bells
Kookaburra
Are You Sleeping?
Row, Row, Row Your Boat
Lovely Evening
Three Blind Mice
Puffer Billies (Down By the Station)

OLD FAVORITES

Aunt Dinah's Quilting Party (Seeing Nellie Home)
Juanita
Long, Long Ago
Old Black Joe
My Old Kentucky Home
Carry Me Back to Old Virginny
Love's Old Sweet Song
Listen to the Mocking Bird
Silver Threads Among the Gold
Coming through the Rye
Tenting Tonight
Stars of the Summer Night
Darling Nellie Gray
Keep the Home Fires Burning
Home, Sweet Home
Old Folks at Home

AMERICAN FOLK SONGS

Billy Boy
Red River Valley
Nellie Bly
Cape Cod Chantey
Short'nin' Bread
Down in the Valley
Clementine
Yellow Rose of Texas
Erie Canal
Home on the Range
Dear Evelina
The Old Gray Goose

SERVICE SONGS

The Marine's Hymn
The Caisson Song
I've Got Sixpence
Anchors Aweigh
The Army Air Corps

SPIRITUALS

I Ain't Gonna Grieve No More
Dry Bones
Oh, Won't You Sit Down?
Were You There When They Crucified My Lord?
Standin' in the Need of Prayer
I Want to be Ready
Every Time I Feel the Spirit
I've Got Shoes
O, Dem Golden Slippers
The Old Ark's a'Moverin'
Swing Low, Sweet Chariot
Little David
Joshua Fit de Battle of Jericho

NATIONAL AND STATE SONGS

America
The Star-Spangled Banner
America the Beautiful
Battle Hymn of the Republic
Columbia, the Gem of the Ocean
Dixie
Yankee Doodle
(appropriate state songs)

SONGS FOR GRACE

For Health and Strength (p. 188)
The Doxology
O, Give Thanks (round)

SACRED SONGS

Onward Christian Soldiers
Song of Peace (Tune: Finlandia)
God of Our Fathers
Faith of Our Fathers
The Netherlands Hymn
A Mighty Fortress Is Our God

CLOSING SONGS

Han Skal Leve (Danish)
God Be With You
Auld Lang Syne
A Perfect Day
Aloha Oe

Goodnight Ladies
Lullaby (Brahms)
Now the Day Is Over
Taps
In the Evening by the Moonlight (ending with Hear Them Bells)

SUGGESTIONS FOR SELF-HELP IN EAR-TRAINING

Most classroom teachers would like to write easily in music notation the songs the children create. This skill usually is attained only after long study and drill. However, if the teacher will learn to be more and more conscious of the relationships of scale tones, intervals, and chord tones, he will grow in his ability to *see* in notation what he hears sung in the classroom.

THE SCALE

When the steps of the scale are superimposed on the 1–3–5 chord (I chord), scale tones, 1, 3, 5, and 8 are stable and the listener does not feel compelled to move from them to another tone. Because they are the home tones, 1 and 8 are highly stable; 3 will sometimes desire to move down to 1, and 5 will sometimes desire to move to 8 or 1. Scale tones 2, 4, 6, and 7 are definitely restless and wish to move to tones of the 1–3–5 chord. Tone 7 leads strongly to 8, and 4 leads strongly to 3. Tone 6 finds satisfaction in leading to 5, and 2 leads to 1 (and, less strongly, to 3). The illustration represents the usual movement of tones in melody lines or parts of melodies that are accompanied by the I chord. Although one will find many exceptions to this, a valuable exercise for the learner of ear-training is to write on staff paper his own melody lines in which the pitches are kept moving in accordance with those of the drawing. Then he should sing what he has written, using the piano or bells as a temporary guide if necessary.

8
↑
7

6
↓

5

4
↕
3
↑
2
↓
1

INTERVALS

Another suggestion is to sing interval drills, learning first to identify intervals based on the scale, then later independent of the scale, and in connection with songs. Relating the different intervals to the scale and to particular aids in learning to identify them, i.e., "see" them in notation. Playing intervals on piano or bells will aid at first. Learn to sing them independently of such help.

| major second | major third | perfect fourth | perfect fifth | major sixth | major seventh | perfect octave |

All of the above intervals are major intervals except the fourth, fifth, and octave, which are called "perfect." Minor intervals are one half-step smaller than major intervals. They can be represented by a minus sign.

	-2	-3	4	5	-6	-7	octave
	minor second	minor third	perfect fourth	perfect fifth	minor sixth	minor seventh	octave

Two people working together on a study of intervals can take turns at the piano or bells, one playing intervals which the other is asked to identify, thus making something of a game of this drill. (When a minor interval or a perfect interval is made a half-step smaller, it is called a *diminished* interval. When a major interval or a perfect interval is made a half-step larger, it is called an *augmented* interval.)

CHORD TONES

The practice of piano chording is of great help in ear-training because the player can both see and hear what he does. When the learner is well grounded in piano chording, melodies written in notation become much more understandable. A simple example of this is the song "Bow Belinda." The person who knows piano chording sees almost instantly that the melody is based on I and V chords in root (1 3 5) position, and that it ends with a scale line.

BOW BELINDA

Bow, bow, bow, Be - lin - da, bow, bow, bow, Be - lin - da,

Bow, bow, bow, Be - lin - da, Won't you be my dar - ling?

The student of ear-training should analyze melodies in terms of chords, scales, and intervals. He should write melodies to sing and to play that are based on his piano chording and on his awareness of scale lines of notes. Singing chord progressions is another important way to increase one's skill in ear training.

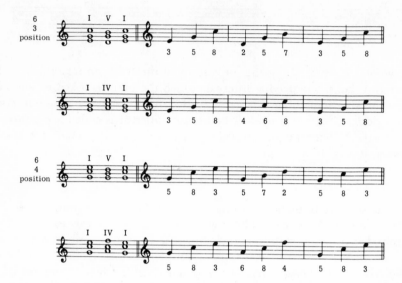

With this introduction, the learner can write his own chord progressions in the three positions in various keys and practice singing them. Progressions employing minor chords or both major and minor chords can be written and sung after the major chords are well learned. Tone 7 of the V_7 chord can also be added when desired.

Thoughtful drill on the above suggestions and application of the concepts involved should help make the melody lines of the songs children create become more readily identifiable.

ADDRESSES OF MUSIC TEXTBOOK PUBLISHERS

Allyn & Bacon, Inc., 150 Tremont St., Boston 11, Mass.

American Book Co., 55 5th Ave., New York 3, N.Y.

Follett Publishing Co., 1010 West Washington Blvd., Chicago 7, Ill.

Ginn & Co., Statler Bldg., Boston 17, Mass.

Prentice-Hall, Inc., Englewood Cliffs, N.J.

Silver Burdett Co., Park Ave. & Columbia Road, Morristown, N.J.

Summy-Birchard Company, 1834 Ridge Ave., Evanston, Ill.

CODE FOR THE NATIONAL ANTHEM[2]

"The Star-Spangled Banner" should be sung or played only on programs and in ceremonies and other situations where its message can be projected effectively.

Since the message of the Anthem is carried largely in the text, it is essential that emphasis be placed upon the *singing* of "The Star-Spangled Banner."

The leader should address himself to those assembled and invite their participation. If an announcement is necessary, it might be stated as follows: "We shall now sing our National Anthem," or "So-and-So will lead you in singing our National Anthem."

On all occasions the group singing the National Anthem should stand facing the flag or the leader, in an attitude of respectful attention. Outdoors, men should remove their hats.

It is suggested that, when it is not physically inconvenient to do so, the members of a band or orchestra stand while playing the National Anthem.

If only a single stanza of the National Anthem is sung, the first should be used.

Our National Anthem is customarily sung at the opening of a meeting or program, but special circumstances may warrant the placing of it elsewhere.

In publishing the National Anthem for general singing, the melody, harmony, and syllable divisions of the Service Version of 1918 should be used. In publishing for vocal groups, the voice parts of the Service Version should be adhered to. For purposes of quick identification, the words "Service Version" should be printed under the title.

It is not good taste to make or use sophisticated concert versions of the National Anthem, as such. (This does not refer to incorporating the Anthem, or portions of it, in extended works for band, orchestra, or chorus.)

For general mass singing by adults, and for band, orchestra, or other instrumental performances, the key of A♭ is preferable. For treble voices, the key of B♭ may be used.

If an instrumental introduction is desired, it is suggested that the last two measures be used.

When the National Anthem is sung unaccompanied, care should be taken to establish the correct pitch.

The National Anthem should be sung at a moderate tempo. (The metronome indications in the Service Version are quarter note = 104 for the verse and quarter note = 96 for the chorus.)

The slighting of note values in the playing or singing of the National Anthem seriously impairs the beauty and effectiveness of both music and lyric. Conductors should rehearse painstakingly both instrumental and vocal groups in the meticulous observance of correct note values.

This Code for the National Anthem is intended to apply to every mode of civilian performance and to the publication of the music for such performance.

---

[2] Reprinted with permission of the Music Educators National Conference.

CODE FOR RELATIONS WITH
THE PRIVATE MUSIC TEACHERS[3]

To promote co-operation in and understanding of the interrelating fields of music teaching the Ohio Music Teachers Association and the Ohio Music Education Association adopt the following statement of policy:

I. MUSIC EDUCATION

The school music teacher is a public employee and is obligated to serve the interests of the whole community. It shall be his privilege and responsibility to advise parents on questions pertaining to the private instruction of pupils under his jurisdiction. At all times the best interest of the pupil is of first importance. It shall be the obligation of the public-school music teacher to give to parents, upon request, the names of private teachers who are competent. In so doing, the school music teacher shall avoid recommending a single private teacher above all others, but shall suggest two or more, the final choice to be made by the parents. In communities where the choice is limited, it shall be incumbent upon the school music teacher to serve the interests of the student within the limitations of the resources available in the community.

II. MUSIC STUDIO INSTRUCTION

Music studio instruction is defined as lessons given for a consideration by individual music teachers or groups of teachers who are not employed by, or under the jurisdiction of, a public school or institution supported by public taxation.

As a citizen, the studio teacher shall co-operate in the support of public education, including music instruction at elementary music levels in the schools for the general good of the community.

III. AGREEMENT

It is mutually agreed, between the aforesaid organizations that it is unethical for any music teacher, whether teaching in school or in a private studio:

(a) To discuss with parents or pupils the work of another teacher in such manner as will injure the professional reputation of any teacher;

(b) To claim sole credit for the achievement of pupils under separate or co-operative instruction, when such claim shall reflect or imply discredit upon a preceding or co-operating teacher.

It is the common purpose of music teachers to co-operate:

(a) In raising standards of music instruction;

(b) In promoting interest in active participation in music performance;

(c) In developing wider appreciation of music;

(d) In establishing opportunities for elementary music instruction under the auspices of the school for exploratory purposes;

(e) In encouraging study with private teachers at the end of the period of exploratory instruction;

(f) In extending opportunities for music study to the underprivileged

---

[3] Reprinted with permission of the Ohio Music Education Association.

child through scholarships or extension of school instruction in individual instances;

(g) In encouraging regularity of attendance at both school and private lessons, rehearsals, recitals, and performances;

(h) In operating an organized plan for giving credit toward graduation study with recognized studio teachers;

(i) In alleviating the influence and practice of unethical methods of music instruction.

It is further agreed that each organization will maintain a permanent Code of Ethics Committee.

A COPYRIGHT LAW GUIDE
FOR MUSIC EDUCATORS

A. Even though music is protected by copyright under the United States Copyright Law there are various things which you can do without securing permission of any type and without fear of infringing.

You may purchase a copyrighted musical composition, orchestration or other form of published music and do the following with it:

(1) You may sell it or give it away.

(2) You may perform it in private, or in public for non-profit.

(3) You may use it for teaching in a classroom, at home or in a pupil's home. Solely for teaching purposes you may write symbols and indicate instructions upon it.

(4) Provided the composition has already been recorded by others, under the authorization of the copyright owner, for the manufacture of phonograph records serving to reproduce the same mechanically, and provided further that you notify the copyright owner by registered mail of your intention to make such use (with a duplicate of such notice to the Copyright Office, Washington 25, D.C.), you may make similar use thereof upon making monthly payments of the statutory royalty, to the copyright owner.

B. If you wish to make some other type of use which is not described above, you should write to the copyright owner for specific permission in each instance. The following are some of the things you may not do without specific permission:

(1) Reprinting or copying the work or any part of it by any method or means whatsoever.

(2) Arranging, adapting, orchestrating, translating or making any versions of the work or any part of it.

(3) Photographing or reproducing the work or any part of it by any method or means, including on film or slides or by opaque projector.

(4) Performing the work in public for profit.

(5) Recording the work by any method or means or for any use or purpose, other than as provided in "A. 4" above, including in synchronization with motion pictures or for television, and whether on records, film or tape.

(6) Writing of parodies upon lyrics.

To avoid infringement, the right to do each or any of these acts must be cleared, and the clearance of one particular right does not clear any of the other rights. All rights are separate, distinct and independent. For instance, the clearance for broadcast does not carry with it the right to copy, or to arrange, or to record; clearance of the right to record does not carry with it the right to perform. The obligation is upon you to make certain that the right involved in the act you intend to do, has been cleared.

C. If you have occasion to perform the composition publicly for profit, guide yourself as follows:

If the performance is to be in a theatre or over a radio or television station, in all likelihood the theatre, radio or television station will have a license for you to perform the musical composition publicly for profit. However, it is your obligation to make certain of this and to secure a license if there is none.

If the performance is to take place elsewhere, there is less likelihood that the establishment has a license for you to perform publicly for profit and in such event a license must be secured. There are three important performing rights societies which license the great majority of copyrighted works: American Society of Composers, Authors and Publishers (usually referred to as "ASCAP"), 575 Madison Avenue, New York 22, New York; Broadcast Music, Inc. (usually referred to as "BMI"), 589 Fifth Avenue, New York 17, New York, and SESAC, INC., 10 Columbus Circle, New York 19, New York.

If you have occasion to present a musical play or other dramatic work on the stage at your school or elsewhere, whether for profit or non-profit, you must secure a license from the owner of the work or his agent.

D. When you see the word "Copyright" or the distinctive © printed on a piece of music, it is the notice that protects the copyright owner of of the work and authorizes him to exclusively exercise and enforce all rights secured to him under the United States Copyright Law, and at the same time it is the notice that informs *you* that the exercising by you of any such acts, including those described in B and C above, *unless authorized*, will subject you to liability under such law.

A printed copy of a musical composition published in the United States, bearing no copyright notice, indicates that the composition is in the public domain in the United States and may be used freely. However, if an arrangement, adaption or other version of such a work has been copyrighted, utmost caution must be exercised in treating the same as you would any other copyrighted work. But nothwithstanding such copyrighted arrangement, adaption or other version, of a work in the public domain, you are still free to treat the basic composition as being in the public domain. A work in the public domain reprinted in a compilation is not protected, even though the compilation itself is copyrighted, unless the reprint is a copyrightable or copyrighted arrangement, adaptation or other version thereof.

INDEX OF SONGS

INDEX

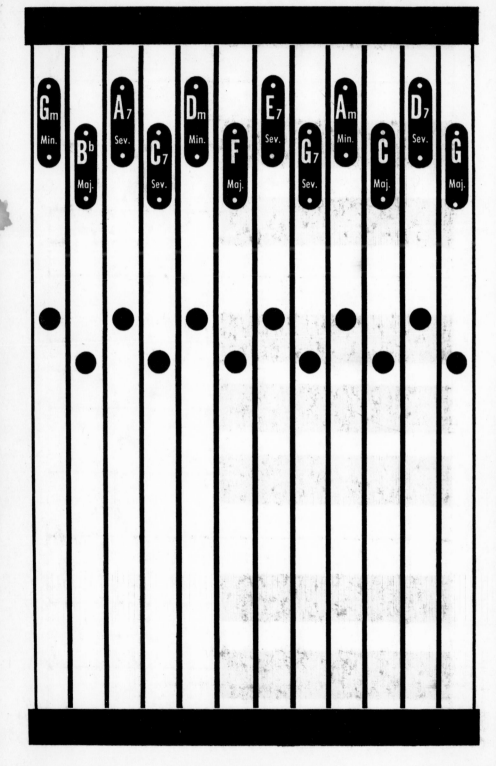